HISTORY OF ICELAND

THE MACMILLAN COMPANY
NEW YORK · BOSTON · CHICAGO · DALLAS
ATLANTA · SAN FRANCISCO

MACMILLAN & CO., Limited
LONDON · BOMBAY · CALCUTTA
MELBOURNE

THE MACMILLAN CO. OF CANADA, Ltd.
TORONTO

HISTORY *of* ICELAND

BY

KNUT GJERSET, Ph.D.

New York

THE MACMILLAN COMPANY

1925

PREFACE

ICELAND, the saga island, lying on the very borders of the unknown, has attracted much attention ever since the time when the enigmatic name Thule was the only knowledge possessed of a land in this distant region of the earth. After the discovery and colonization of the island by the Norsemen, voyagers and traders were gradually attracted to it by rich codfisheries, sulphur deposits and other products of value to European trade. But it was especially as a center of literary activity, as the home of scaldic song and saga literature that Iceland won its widest fame among European nations. In modern times commercial intercourse with Iceland has grown rapidly, and numerous travelers are visiting the island because of its literary fame, its picturesque scenery, and the charming hospitality and simple rural life of the people. To these and other attractive features a new one was added when Iceland became a sovereign state acquiring interest as a member of the world's brotherhood of nations. The Icelanders have an old history, and have contributed so much to the world's intellectual life and culture that they will be welcomed in the circle of nations into which they have lately entered, not as a new arrival, but as one of Europe's oldest cultural peoples which has finally come into its own. Numerous books have been written about Iceland by able writers of many lands. Most of these have been written from the tourist's point of view, picturing the country as a land of great interest to the sightseeing traveler. But now that Iceland is an independent sovereign state, if for no other reason, the world may want to know something of the history of this island nation living apart within the lonely shadows of the arctic circle. It is for this purpose that the present volume is offered. Scarcely anything which could

be written about Iceland could be of more real interest than
the people's own saga, the story of their national development, their unique political institutions, their social life,
their literary achievements, their economic struggles, their
patient sufferings, their hard won victories in their distant
and inhospitable island kingdom which they have loved so
dearly and built so well. Only when possessing this knowledge will the visiting traveler be able to interpret what he
sees. Iceland will no longer be a charming wilderness of
smoking geysers and flaming volcanoes, but the home of
one of the most intelligent and remarkable nations on the
earth.

To Prof. Halldor Hermannsson of Cornell University I
am under special obligations for most valuable assistance
rendered me in many ways in the writing of this volume.
Professor Runolfur Marteinsson of Winnipeg, Canada, has
also aided me with valuable information. Rev. H. B.
Thorgrimsen of Grand Forks, N. Dak., and Prof. B. K.
Savre of Glenwood, Minn., have kindly read the manuscript
and offered valuable suggestions.

KNUT GJERSET,

LUTHER COLLEGE, DECORAH, IOWA,
    December 11, 1922.

CONTENTS

HISTORY OF ICELAND

HISTORY OF ICELAND

1. Early Explorations and Discoveries in the Far North

The first people who acquired any knowledge of the remoter regions of northern Europe were the Phœnicians, who surpassed all other nations of antiquity as enterprising traders and daring voyagers. In very early ages their navigators became familiar with all parts of the Mediterranean Sea, and colonies were founded on the north coast of Africa, in Sicily, Sardinia, southern Gaul, and also in Spain, where the city of Gadir (Cadiz) became a chief seaport and leading commercial center. Not only did they venture beyond the Pillars of Hercules into the broad Atlantic, but in the reign of Necho of Egypt, 610-595 b.c., their sailors in the employ of that king circumnavigated Africa by sailing from Arabia southward and returning by the way of Gibraltar.[1] On their seacoast voyages they discovered Madeira and the Canary Islands, and in 460 b.c. Hanno of Carthage attempted to plant a colony on the west coast of Africa.[2] The development of trade drew them northward as well as southward along the Atlantic seaboard; but little is known of their operations in these

---

[1] "When Necho discontinued the work on the canal which was to connect the Nile with the Arabian Sea, he sent Phœnician sailors with ships and commanded them to return by the way of the Pillars of Hercules. The Phœnicians sailed from the Red Sea into the southern ocean. And when fall came, they landed and sowed fields wherever they happened to be in Labya (Africa). They waited for the harvest, and when they had harvested the grain they went on board their ships, so that after two years had passed they returned through the Pillars of Hercules and came back to Egypt. And they hold (I can, indeed, not believe it, but perhaps others can) that when they rounded Labya they had the sun on their right hand." Herodotus, lib. iv, 42.

[2] Plinius the Elder, Historia Naturalis, ii, 67, 165.

1

HISTORY OF ICELAND

1. EARLY EXPLORATIONS AND DISCOVERIES IN THE FAR NORTH

THE first people who acquired any knowledge of the remoter regions of northern Europe were the Phenicians, who surpassed all other nations of antiquity as enterprising traders and daring voyagers. In very early ages their navigators became familiar with all parts of the Mediterranean Sea, and colonies were founded on the north coast of Africa, in Sicily, Sardinia, southern Gaul, and also in Spain, where the city of Gadir (Cadiz) became a chief seaport and leading commercial center. Not only did they venture beyond the Pillars of Hercules into the broad Atlantic, but in the reign of Necho of Egypt, 610-595 B.C., their sailors in the employ of that king circumnavigated Africa by sailing from Arabia southward and returning by the way of Gibraltar.[1] On their seacoast voyages they discovered Madeira and the Canary Islands, and in 460 B.C. Hanno of Carthage attempted to plant a colony on the west coast of Africa.[2] The development of trade drew them northward as well as southward along the Atlantic seaboard; but little is known of their operations in these

[1] "When Necho discontinued the work on the canal which was to connect the Nile with the Arabian Sea, he sent Phenician sailors with ships and commanded them to return by the way of the Pillars of Hercules. The Phenicians sailed from the Red Sea into the southern ocean. And when fall came, they landed and sowed fields wherever they happened to be in Libya (Africa). They waited for the harvest, and when they had harvested the grain they went on board their ships, so that after two years had passed they returned through the Pillars of Hercules and came back to Egypt. And they hold (I can, indeed, not believe it, but perhaps others can) that when they rounded Libya they had the sun on their right hand." Herodotus, lib. lv, 42.
[2] Plinius the Elder, *Historia Naturalis,* ii, 67, 169.

1

waters, as they kept their trade routes secret in order to
maintain commercial supremacy over Greek and Roman
competitors. The only expedition northward of which we
have any information is that of Himilco, mentioned by
Plinius the Elder who says that Himilco made an expedition
to explore the farthest coast of Europe at the time when
Hanno sailed to the west coast of Africa.[3] It is quite
certain, however, that the Phenicians brought the much
sought amber from northern Europe, possibly from the
coasts of Germany and the Danish peninsula bordering on
the North Sea,[4] and that from Britain as well as from
Spain they imported tin, a metal essential to the production
of bronze from which weapons and edged tools were manu-
factured. Britain must also have been known to the Greeks,
who pressed hard in the wake of the Phenician voyagers.
The *Cassiterides* or Tin Islands are mentioned both by
Homer and Herodotus. Of their location nothing is known,
but the name was probably applied to the British Isles
where this metal was found.[5]

A desire to explore the unknown northern regions, chiefly,
perhaps, for commercial reasons, but possibly also in order
to gain more accurate astronomical and geographical knowledge, led Pytheas, a Greek scholar and navigator, to undertake a voyage to Britain and the far north about 330 B.C.
He lived in the Greek city of Massilia (Marseilles) in
southern Gaul, and seems to have possessed great ability
both as astronomer and sea-captain. Our knowledge of
him is limited, as his work written about his expedition is
lost.[6] But from the fragments of his writings which have

[3] C. Fisher, *De Carthageniensis Periplo,* Leipzig, 1893.
[4] Fridtjof Nansen, *Nord i Taakeheimen (In Northern Mists),* p. 18-25.
D. Gustav Moritz Redslob, *Thule. Die phönicischen Handelswege nach
dem Norden.*
[5] Herodotus, lib. iii, ch. 115. The Cassiterides may have been the Scilly
Islands, as H. C. Hamilton and W. Falconer, the translators of Strabo, hold.
But it seems more probable that the name conveyed to the Greeks only a
very vague geographical idea. Herodotus says that he has been unable to
gain any information regarding the ocean in that part of Europe, and he
knows nothing about the location of the Cassiterides.
[6] W. Bessel, *Ueber Pytheas von Massilien.* D. Gustav Moritz Redslob,
Thule. Die phönicischen Handelswege nach dem Norden. M. Fuhr, *Pytheas*

been preserved it is evident that he was one of the foremost scholars of his age. He showed for the first time that the ocean tides are due to the influence of the moon. He established quite correctly the latitude of his home city, Massilia, and located the north pole of the heavens with remarkable accuracy outside of the pole-star. Since Pytheas, according to Polybios, was a private person in narrow circumstances, it is likely that his expedition to the North was organized either by the state or by interested private individuals.

On his voyage Pytheas reached Britain, which he seems to have circumnavigated, as he describes the shape and size of the island. The longest day there he found to be eighteen hours, and in an inhabited country north of Britain the longest day was observed to be nineteen hours, which is the length, respectively, of the longest day in northern Scotland and the Shetland Islands. He penetrated still farther and came to a land called Thule, "where the summer tropic becomes one with the arctic circle." [7] This would correspond to 66° 15', the latitude of northern Iceland. An old Greek astronomer, Geminos from Rhodos, says about these regions where the days grow perceptibly longer as we go northward:

"This region Pytheas of Massilia must also have reached. He states at least in a treatise which he has written about the great ocean: 'The barbarians showed us where the sun sets. For it happens that in these places the night is very short, in some places two and in others three hours, so that the sun rises again a short time after it has set.' " [8]

That he came to a region so far north that the day was twenty-two hours long is quite noteworthy. "The people of Thule," says Pytheas, "live on hirse and herbs as well as on fruit and roots. Those who have grain and honey make also a drink from these. When they have cut the

von Massilien, Historisch kritische Abhandlung, Darmstadt, 1842. Strabo, 60 B.C. to 20 A.D., noted Greek historian and geographer.

[7] Strabo, Geography, translated by H. C. Hamilton and W. Falconer, vol. 1, p. 173 and footnote. Nansen, Nord i Taakeheimen (In Northern Mists), p. 41 f.

[8] Fridtjof Nansen, Nord i Taakeheimen, p. 41.

grain, they bring it into large houses and thrash it there, because they have no bright sunshine, and thrashing floors in the open would be useless because of excessive rains." [9]

Many have thought that Thule mentioned by Pytheas must be Iceland,[10] but this view has been generally abandoned, since his description of Thule in no way corresponds to conditions in Iceland. Claudius Ptolemy of Alexandria, who lived in the second century A.D., also speaks of Thule saying that it lies north of the Orcades (Orkney Islands), that its northern extremity lies in latitude 63° 15',[11] its middle part in latitude 63°, and its southern part in latitude 62° 40'. This statement of the great geographer has led many scholars to believe that Thule must be the Shetland Islands.[12] But Pytheas' description is no more applicable to the barren Shetland Islands than to Iceland, and if Ptolemy's Thule is identical with the Shetland group he must have applied the name to a region very different from the one Pytheas had in mind. That Thule was neither Iceland nor the Shetland Islands seems further verified by Procopius, who describes it in such a way that it can only mean Scandinavia. He had talked with people from Thule, and had reliable first-hand information.[13] The question can not be settled with certainty from the meager existing

[9] Strabo, lib. iv, ch. v, 5.

[10] W. Bessel, *Ueber Pytheas von Massilien*, Göttingen, 1858; and Richard F. Burton, *Ultima Thule or a Summer in Iceland*, hold this view. Adam v. Bremen says: "This Thule is now called Iceland because of the ice which fetters the ocean." *Gesta Hammaburgensis Ecclesia Pontificum*, iv, 35. The Icelandic scholar Arngrímur Jónsson in his work *Crymogœa* for the first time pointed out that Thule could not be Iceland. But his views were opposed by the Danish historical writer Pontanus, and also by Thordr Thorlaksson, later Bishop of Skálholt in Iceland. See Thorvald Thoroddsen, *Landfrœdissaga Islands*, p. 11 f.

[11] *Geographia*, lib. ii, ch. iii.

[12] K. Müllenhoff, *Deutsche Alterthumskunde*, vol. 1. J. Ziegler, *Reise des Pytheas*, Dresden, 1861.

[13] Procopius, *De Bello Gothico*, ii, 15. Procopius had spoken with people from the North who had journeyed to southern Europe at the time of the Migrations. He represents Thule as very large, ten times the size of Britain, and says that thirteen peoples, each with their own king, live in the inhabited part. The largest tribe are the Gautai (Götar), well known in all history as the inhabitants of southern Sweden. He states that the mouth of the Rhine lies midway between Thule and Britain.

data, but Pytheas' account indicates that he reached the
west coast of Norway, and that he called this region Thule.

Pytheas' work, or rather the small fragments which were
preserved of it, was the chief source of information regarding
Britain and the far North possessed by the Greeks.   The
Romans gained more definite knowledge of northern Europe
through their conquests in Gaul and Britain, but about
Scandinavia and Iceland they had no reliable information.
Many of their writers mention Thule and Scandinavia, but
these brief and vague notices only reveal how little they
knew about these northern lands.   Thule is mentioned by
Plinius the Elder in his "Historia Naturalis," by Tacitus
in his "De Vita et Moribus Agricolæ," and also by Solinus,
a Roman historical writer of the third century A.D. who was
much read in the Middle Ages.   In poetry as well as in prose
the name of Thule or Thyle was used by Roman writers.[14]
But for want of definite knowledge of the North it gradually lost all real geographical significance and was used in
a general way to designate an island supposed to lie some-
where in the remote northern regions of the earth.   The
countries and peoples of the North still remained in the
dark unknown.   Only after the Migrations had brought
them into direct contact with the Roman world, could
writers like Procopius and Jordanes write accounts of
Scandinavia which reflect a more direct knowledge.[15]

The only positive knowledge of Iceland prior to its discovery by the Norsemen seems to have been possessed by
Celtic monks, who have left us the first definite information
regarding the island.   For religious reasons Irish hermits
sought seclusion from the world in the uninhabited islands
north of Britain, and, so far as we know, these hermits were
the first inhabitants of Iceland and the Faroe Islands.
Adamnan, Abbot of Iona from 679 to 704, mentions in his
"Vita S. Columbæ" a prophecy of the saint regarding a man
named Kormak who in Columba's days (521-597) made
three voyages from Ireland in search for the *Desert in the*

[14] Virgil, *Georgicon*, i, 30: "Tibi serviat ultima Thule."   Statius, v, i, 91 f:
"Et refluo circumsona gurgite Thule."
[15] Jordanes, *De Origine Actibusque Getarum*.

Ocean (eremeum in Oceano). This term, so descriptive of
Iceland, seems to render safe the assumption that this island
is actually meant, especially since later sources show that
Iceland was known to the Irish long before the coming of
the Norsemen. The Venerable Bede (674-735) also speaks
of people of his own time who, coming from the island of
Thule, declared that in summer the sun could be seen at
midnight for a few days.[16]   In 825 A.D. the Irish monk Dicuil
wrote a work, "Liber de Mensura Orbis Terræ," in which he
describes the islands in the northern ocean which he says
he has not yet found mentioned by other writers. What he
knows of geography in general he has gathered from Greek
and Roman writers, but of Iceland, which he calls Thule,
he has very definite knowledge, which he says he has
obtained from Irish hermits who have visited the land:

"It is now thirty years since some priests (*clerici*) who had
stayed in that island from February 1st till August 1st told me
that not only at the summer solstice, but also in the days there-
about, the setting sun hides itself at the evening hour as it were
behind a little hill, in such a way that no darkness occurs even
for the shortest time, . . . and if they had been on the high
mountains of the island, the sun would probably never have
been hidden."

About the Faroe Islands he says:

"There are still other islands in the ocean north of Britain
which can be reached from the northern British Isles in two days'
and two nights' straight sail with full sails and a steady favorable
wind. . . . These islands are generally small; nearly all are
separated from one another by narrow sounds. On these islands
hermits which sailed from our Scotia (Ireland) have lived about
a hundred years. But as they have always been uninhabited
since the beginning of the world, so they are now, because of
Northern robbers, empty of hermits, but full of numberless sheep
and a great many kinds of aquatic birds." [17]

It is quite evident from these statements that long before
Dicuil wrote his book the Irish were familiar with Iceland

[16] Beda, *De Ratione Temporum. Comment on 2 Kings,* xx, 9.
[17] *Liber de Mensura Orbis Terræ,* ed. Wolkenaer, Paris, 1807, p. 29.

and the Faroe Islands, and that hermits, and undoubtedly also other settlers, had established permanent habitations there.[18] Two islands in the Faroe group, *Stóra Dímon* and *Litla Dímon*, still bear their original Irish names, *Dímon* being an Irish word meaning *Twomountain*. Other Irish place names as *Dungansvik* and *Dungansnes* are also found. The etymology of *Thule* is still unsettled; but since the name was applied to Iceland by Dicuil after he had spoken with Irish monks who had been there, it is not unlikely that it was the old Irish name of the island which Pytheas had learned from the Britons, and that Iceland was known to them when he made his expedition to the North in 330 B.C.

When the Norsemen first appeared as Vikings on the coasts of Britain and the neighboring islands is not known, but they must have taken possession of the smaller and more distant island groups like the Shetland and Faroe Islands not later than 700 A.D. The Viking voyagers soon gained full control of these islands, and Dicuil says that the Christian Celts fled because of Northern robbers. This statement, which no doubt is true in a general way, must not be taken too literally. No sudden emigration even under those circumstances was possible, as the Celts at that time had no ships, but only frail boats made of skin, with which the voyage from the islands to Scotland or Ireland could be made only with great difficulty. The greater number of the original inhabitants must have remained in the islands and amalgamated with the Norse settlers, which can be seen also from Celtic loan-words incorporated in the Norse language of the islands,[19] and from elements of culture traceable to Celtic influence. From the Celtic inhabitants the Norsemen learned to know Christianity and

---

[18] Alexander Bugge, *Vesterlandenes Indflydelse paa Nordboerne i Vikingetiden*, p. 355. Fridtjof Nansen, *Nord i Taakeheimen (In Northern Mists)*, p. 45.

[19] J. Jakobsen, who has made a special study of the nomenclature and other remnants of Norse language in the Shetland Islands, finds that many names show word-formations which had gone out of use at the time Iceland was colonized. *Shetlandsøernes Stedsnavne, Aarbøger for nordisk Oldkyndighed*, 1901.

higher ideals of life.[20] From them, too, they must have
heard of Iceland, which was so well known to the Celts, a
new region beckoning the Norse voyagers with all the
romantic charm of the unknown. The islands became step-
pingstones leading to the discovery of Iceland by the Norsemen, and many noble traits of the early settlers are traceable to the influence which the Christian Celts are known
to have exerted on life and customs in these early Norse
colonies.

When Iceland was first discovered by the Norsemen, and
by whom the discovery was made, is not definitely known.
Traditions which have been preserved by old Icelandic
writers credit the Norseman Naddod and the Swede
Gardar with the discovery, but the accounts do not agree,
and can not well be regarded as anything but reminiscences
of early voyages to the island. Sturla Thordsson's version
of the "Landnámabók" ("Sturlubók") has the following
account:

"It is said that some men were to sail from Norway to the
Faroe Islands; some say that it was Naddod the Viking. But
they were driven westward into the ocean, and found there a big
land. In the Eastfjords they ascended a high mountain, and
looked about if they could see smoke or any evidence that the
land was inhabited, but they saw none. They returned in the fall
to the Faroe Islands, and as they sailed away, heavy snow fell
in the mountains, and they called the land *Sneland* (Snowland).

"There was a man by the name of Gardar, a Swede by birth.
He went to seek Sneland with the advice of his mother who
was clairvoyant. He came to land east of the Eastern Cape
Horn where there was a haven. Gardar sailed around the land
and showed that it was an island. He spent the winter in
Husavik in Skjálfanda, where he built a house. In the spring
when he was ready to set sail there drifted away from him in a
boat a man by the name of Náttfari, a slave and a servant girl.
He built later at this place called Náttfaravik. Gardar returned
to Norway and praised the land much. The land was thereafter
called *Gardarsholm*, and there were at that time woods between
the mountains and the sea." [21]

[20] Alexander Bugge, *Vesterlandenes Indflydelse*, 338 ff.
[21] *Landnámabók*, i.

According to this account Naddod appears as the first discoverer of Iceland. But in Hauk Erlendsson's version of the "Landnámabók" ("Hauksbók") the story is told in a somewhat different way, and Gardar Svavarsson is represented as the one who first visited Iceland. Hauk Erlendsson used Sturla's version of the "Landnámabók" ("Sturlubók") as his source, but in this instance he departs from it.[22] His account here agrees with two old works about Norway written in Latin, "Historia de Antiquitate Regum Norwagiensium" [23] and "Historia Norwegiæ," which may have served as sources for this part of his narrative. Also the "Njálssaga" mentions Gardar as the discoverer of Iceland.[24] Writers like Finnur Magnusson and Konrad Maurer think that he must be credited with the discovery of the island, but it can not be regarded as certain.[25]

A third Viking voyager who, according to the "Landnámabók," visited Iceland was Floki Vilgerdsson from Rogaland in western Norway. Sailing by way of Shetland and the Faroe Islands Floki and his companions reached the east coast of Iceland.

"They sailed then to the south of the land," says the author. "But when they sailed west of Reykjanes, and the fjord opened

[22] *Hauksbók*, iv, ch. iv.

[23] The *Historia de Antiquitate Regum Norwagiensium* is a history of Norway in Latin, covering the period 858-1130, written by a Norwegian monk, Theodricus Monachus (Thjóðrek Munk). The date of the work is probably 1177-1180. The *Historia Norwegiæ* is a similar work from the thirteenth century by an unknown author. It says about the discovery of Iceland: "Thereafter towards the west is a large island which the Italians call Ultima Thule, now inhabited by quite a number, but formerly an uninhabited land and unknown to men till in the time of King Harald Haarfagre. Then some Norsemen, Ingolf and Hjörleif, fled from their own country with their wives and children because of homicides which they had committed, and sought the island which was first discovered by Gardar and later by another. And they found it at last as they sounded the billows with a plumbline." G. Storm, *Monumenta Historia Norwegiæ*. The account of the discovery in the *Historia de Antiquitate Regum Norwagiensium* resembles still more closely that of the *Hauksbók,* and Gardar is mentioned as the first discoverer.

[24] *Njálssaga*, ch. 19, 47. *Saga Ólafs Konungs Tryggvasonar, Fornmannasögur*, vol. i, 113 ff.

[25] *Grønlands historiske Mindesmerker*, i, p. 89 ff. K. Maurer, *Upphaf Alsherjarrikis á Íslandi*, p. 29. *Saga Ólafs Konungs Tryggvasonar, Fornmannasögur*, vol. i, 113 f.

so that they saw Snefellsnes, Faxi said: 'It must be a big land which we have found; here are large rivers.' That is since called Faxáos. Floki and his men sailed westward over Breidafjord. The fjord was full of fish, and because of the fishing they neglected to provide themselves with hay, and their cattle all died in the winter. The spring was rather cold. Floki went north on the mountain, and saw a fjord full of ice; and they called the land *Iceland,* as it has since been called. In the summer they returned to Norway." [26]

The voyages of Naddod, Gardar and Floki are supposed to have been made about 860-870. But the oldest and most reliable work on the early history of Iceland, the "Islendingabók," by Ari Frodi (1120-1130), mentions neither of these three. In a very terse style this author records only such facts concerning the discovery as he considers based on the best authority, allowing no room for peradventure or literary embellishment.

"Iceland," he says, "was first settled from Norway in the days of King Harald Haarfagre, the son of Halvdan Svarte, according to Teit, Bishop Isleif's son, my foster-father, the wisest man I have known; Thorkell Gellison, my uncle, who had good memory of past events, and Thorid, the daughter of Snorri Godi, who was both wise and truthful. It happened at the time when Ivar Lodbroksson killed St. Edmund, the king of the Angles. But that was 870 years after the birth of Christ, as it is written in his saga. Ingolf was the name of the Norseman about whom it has been truthfully said that he went first from there (Norway) to Iceland when Harald Haarfagre was sixteen years old, and the second time a few years later. He settled south in Reykjavik, which is called Ingolfshofdi, east of Minthakseyr, where he first landed. But later he took possession of Ingolfsfell, west of Ölfusá." [27]

In the "Landnámabók" the account of Ingolf's voyage is wrought into a more complete historical narrative. According to this account the two foster-brothers Ingolf Arnarson and Leif Hrodmarsson from Dalsfjord in western Norway went on a Viking expedition together with Atli Jarl's

[26] *Landnámabók*, i, 2.
[27] *Íslendingabók*, 1.

sons Hallstein, Herstein and Holmstein. So cordial were their relations that in the winter after their return Ingolf and Leif prepared a feast for the sons of the jarl. At this feast Holmstein made the vow that he would marry Helga, Ingolf's sister, and Leif, who was in love with Helga, was greatly offended. The enmity between the two grew so bitter that in the spring the foster-brothers prepared an expedition against the sons of the jarl, and Holmstein fell in battle at Hisargafl. The following winter Herstein also lost his life in a new encounter, but the feud finally ended through the mediation of friends. Leif married Helga, and the two foster-brothers fitted out a ship and set out to find Iceland. They made landfall in a fjord on the east coast, where they spent the winter. In the spring they returned to Norway, but the new land pleased them so well that they resolved to settle there. As Leif had lost his property in his feud with the sons of Atli Jarl, he made a Viking expedition to Ireland in order to replenish his stores. On his return he brought back ten Irish slaves and also a sword which he had won in a duel, a valued trophy from which he got the name Hjörleif, from *hjör,* a swordblade. Ingolf had in the meantime sold his possessions in Norway. In 874 the foster-brothers fitted out two ships and emigrated to Iceland. They brought with them the most necessary implements, household goods and other supplies, together with a number of slaves and a few freemen who went out as settlers. Ingolf sacrificed to the gods before his departure to secure good luck, but Hjörleif would not sacrifice, possibly because he had been influenced by Christianity, which he may have learned to know on his expeditions to the British Isles. The two sailed together until they sighted Iceland, when they parted. Ingolf then threw the pillars of his high-seat into the sea, and said that he would make his home where they came to shore, but temporarily he settled at Ingolfshofdi on the southern coast. Hjörleif landed farther west on the same coast at a place since called Hjörleifshofdi, where he erected two large houses, one eighteen and the other nineteen fathoms in length.[28]

[28] *Landnámabók,* ch. 3 ff.

In the spring, when he was going to sow, he let his Irish slaves pull the plow, as he had only one ox. This treatment the slaves resented, and one of them by the name of Dufthak formed the plot that they should kill the ox and say that the bear had taken it. Later they were to attack Hjörleif and his men if they went hunting for the bear. The bear hunt was begun. The men scattered in the woods, and the slaves attacked them and killed them all. They then fled with the women and the property in a boat to some islands which they saw to the south in the ocean, and dwelt there. When Vifill and Karli, Ingolf's slaves, who had been sent westward to look for the pillars of his high-seat, came to Hjörleifshofdi, they found Hjörleif and his men dead, and they hastened back to tell Ingolf the news. He went to Hjörleifshofdi, and when he saw his friend's corpse he said: "An evil fate has befallen a good man that he should be killed by his slaves, but a like fate will befall all those who will not sacrifice to the gods." Ingolf buried Hjörleif and his men, and took care of his ship and other belongings. On the islands in the ocean he found the slaves and put them all to death. These islands were since called *Vestmannaeyjar* because the slaves were Vestmen (Celts) Ingolf took with him the women who had been carried away, and returned to Hjörleifshofdi, where he remained that winter. The following summer he sailed westward along the coast spending the third winter near a mountain called Ingolfsfell, west of Ölfusá. In the spring he went farther to the westward, and settled at Reykjavik, where the pillars of his high-seat had come to shore.

2. The Colonization of Iceland

Ingolf Arnarson and Hjörleif Hrodmarsson were the first *landnámsmenn* or permanent settlers in Iceland. But political and social conditions in Norway so stimulated emigration that before many decades had passed Iceland was one of the most populous of Norse overseas colonies. According to Snorri Sturlason the cause of this emigration was the tyrannical rule of King Harald Haarfagre, who had united all Norway under his sway after crushing the chieftain class in the battle of Hafrsfjord in 872. The king is said to have robbed the people of their *odel*.[1] Those who refused to swear him allegiance and pay the required taxes had to flee, and their estates were forfeited to the crown. The demand of submission to a royal overlord was regarded as tyranny; taxes, not before levied, were looked upon as tribute imposed on a free people, and many of the chieftains chose to emigrate rather than submit to the king's oppressive rule. Recent investigation has shown that this explanation can be accepted only with great modifications.[2] The colonization of Iceland was a part of a general movement of emigration and the founding of colonies in the western islands begun long before the Hafrsfjord battle was fought. A general political and social unrest prevailed in Norway in the ninth century, the reason for which is not known, but it seems that unfavorable economic conditions were largely responsible for the exodus to the islands of the West at this time. Few are known to have left Norway because of their opposition to the king, though his victory over the chieftains naturally tended to increase emigration to the West.

Ulf or Kveldulf Bjálfason and his sons Thorolf and Skallagrim were powerful men in Firdafylke in southwestern Norway. Thorolf entered King Harald's service and fought valiantly in the battle of Hafrsfjord. Through royal favor he became a very rich and influential man, but envious persons aroused the king's suspicion, and he was slain. Kveldulf and Skallagrim had refused to support the royal cause, and Thorolf's death at the hands of the king's own men turned their sullen ill-will into open hostility. As resistance

---

[1] According to the law of *odel* the ownership of land rested jointly in the family, but the home estate should remain in possession of the oldest son, and he should purchase the shares of the younger brothers at such a price as they might agree upon. This law maintained the estates undivided and indivisible, but it reduced the chances for the younger members of the family to become owners of land.

[2] Halvdan Koht, *Innhogg og Utsyn*, 98 ff. Finnur Jónsson, *Norsk-islandske Kultur-og Sprogforhold i 9 og 10 Aarh.* (Copenhagen 1921) p. 19 ff. Yngvar Nielsen, *Norsk Historisk Tidsskrift*, 4 R, iv, p. 20 ff.

to the new rule was no longer possible, they decided to emigrate. Two ships were fitted out for the voyage to Iceland, each carrying, besides the two chieftains and their families, a crew of thirty men, together with servants, slaves, household goods and such domestic animals as could be brought along. Kveldulf died on the voyage, but Skallagrim reached Iceland, and settled at Borg in Borgarfjord, where he became a great chieftain and the founder of a powerful family.[3] His son was the great scald Egill Skallagrimsson, the hero of the "Egilssaga." The story of Egill's granddaughter, Helga the Fair, is told in the "Gunnlaugssaga Ormstungu."

Especially prominent among the early settlers was the family of Ketill Flatnef, a chieftain in Sogn in western Norway, who was sent by the king to rule the Hebrides. Ketill became a very powerful man in the western colonies; but he paid no taxes to the crown, and he soon rebelled and seized the islands which he was sent to govern. As punishment for this breach of faith King Harald drove away his son Björn the Easterner, seizing his possessions in Norway. Björn fled to his friend Thorolf Mostrarskegg, chieftain and temple priest on the island of Moster. But King Harald banished Thorolf because he harbored the king's enemy, and both had to flee from Norway. Björn the Easterner went to the Hebrides, where his brother Helgi Bjola and his sister Aud the Deepminded also dwelt, but Thorolf sailed to Iceland settling at Hofstadir in Breidafjord on the west coast. On his departure from Norway he razed the temple at Moster, and brought with him the timber to his new home, where he again reared the old sanctuary to the god Thor. Björn the Easterner and his brother Helgi Bjola, who came to Iceland from the Hebrides, settled in the western districts. From these chieftains some of the leading Icelandic families descended, as is shown especially by the "Eyrbyggjasaga" in which their family history is narrated. Thorolf's son Thorstein Thorskabit became so powerful a man that he always had thirty freemen about him. He was an ardent worshipper of the

[3] *Egilssaga*, ch. i.

god Thor. He resided at Helgafell, which became the greatest sanctuary in Iceland in early times.[4]

Geirmund Heljarskin, son of the king of Hordaland in Norway, had long been on Viking expeditions, and had become a great sea-king. He had aided the chieftains in their struggle against King Harald, but when he saw that further resistance was useless, he went to Ireland accompanied by his friends and companions in arms Ulf Skjálgi and Steinulf Lági. They settled on the west coast, where so many colonists had already established their homes. But later Geirmund moved to northwestern Iceland, where he took possession of a large district. He was the wealthiest and most powerful of all the early settlers in Iceland. "Geirmund was a powerful man," says the "Sturlungasaga," "and never kept less than eighty armed men about him at Geirmundsstad."[5] Ulf Skjálgi was accompanied to Iceland by his friend Hall, a man of wealth and influence who, according to the "Thorskfirðingasaga," settled at Hofstadir in Thorskafjord, where he built a temple. Önund Treefoot, who had lost a leg in the battle of Hafrsfjord fighting against King Harald, also settled in the western part of Iceland. From him descended Grettir Ásmundsson about whom the "Grettissaga" is written.

Few if any of the early settlers in Iceland was more influential than Aud the Deepminded, Ketill Flatnef's gifted daughter. She was the widow of King Olaf the White of Dublin, and when her father and her husband Thorstein died, she seems to have become the recognized head of the family. Because of her lonely state she decided to emigrate to Iceland to join her brothers Björn and Helgi. Besides her grandchildren, slaves and servants she also brought a

---

[4] Helgafell is a small isolated mountain at Thorsnes. The *Eyrbyggjasaga* relates that Thorolf Mostrarskegg regarded it as so sacred that no one was allowed to look at it with unwashed face. No living being on that mountain should be harmed except it left the place of its own accord. Thorolf thought that after death he and his friends would be taken into the mountain and live there. After the introduction of Christianity Helgafell retained its sacred character. A church was built, and hermits took up their abode there. The Helgafell monastery was erected in the twelfth century.

[5] *Sturlungasaga*, vol. 1, p. 3. *Landnámabók*, ch. 19.

number of colonists, among whom are mentioned Koll, Erp and Hörd, as well as her grandson Olaf Feilan, who became a prominent man in Iceland. She spent the first winter with her brother Björn the Easterner, but settled later at Hvam in Hvamsfjord, where she gave land to her liberated slaves as well as to the settlers who accompanied her. Her granddaughter Thorgerd was married to Koll or Dalakoll, a trusted assistant and adviser, who accompanied her to Iceland. Their son was Hoskuld Dalakollsson, the father of Olaf Pá of Hjardarholt, and grandfather of Kjartan Olafsson, who are numbered among the foremost men in early Icelandic history. The story of Aud and her most prominent descendants is told in the "Laxdælasaga."

Helgi Magri, the son of Eyvind the Eastman and the Irish princess Rafarta, was born in Ireland, but emigrated to Iceland with his sons Ingjald and Hrolf, and his son-in-law Hámund Heljarskin, a brother of Geirmund. He settled at Eyjafjord in northern Iceland, where he took possession of a large district, and built a residence which he called *Kristnes* in honor of Christ in whom he believed. Both Hámund Heljarskin and Helgi's sons settled in the same district. Ingjald lived at Tverá, where he built a temple. From him descended the scald Vigaglum, the hero of the "Vígaglúmssaga." Many colonists came at Helgi's request and settled in the district of which he had taken possession. One of these colonists was Thorstein Svörfud from Namdalen in Norway, who settled on the west side of the Eyjafjord towards the sea, a district which from him received the name of Svarfdal. His story is told in the "Svarfdælasaga." The "Valaljótssaga" continues the narrative about him and his descendants.

In Romsdal in Norway lived the great chieftain Ingimund the Old about whom the "Vatsdælasaga" is written. He was the grandson of the *hersir* Ketill Raum, and had been on many Viking expeditions together with his foster-brothers Grim Ingjaldsson and Sæmund from Sogn. Ingimund joined the king's forces in the battle of Hafrsfjord, but Sæmund did not. After the battle he followed Ingimund's advice and went to Iceland. He took possession of a large district at Skagafjord in the northern part, where much of the land was still unsettled. Those who accompanied him also settled in this district, and he became a man of great influence. Ingimund came over later settling at Vatsdal, which extends southward from Hunafjord. Here he built a residence called *Hof* from timber which he brought with him from Norway. Many people settled around him, says the saga, and law and justice were established. When he became old, he was mortally wounded by the violent and selfish Hrolleif, who had once belonged to Ingimund's household, and had been befriended in many ways. Ingimund rode home, called a servant boy and said to him: "Go at once to Hrolleif and tell him that I believe my sons will seek to avenge their father before the next day dawns. It is best for him that he flees before daylight. I regard his death as no revenge, and it is proper that I should protect, as long as I can, him who has once belonged to my household, whatever may since come to pass."[6] The sons, however, who were less forgiving than the father, slew Hrolleif shortly afterward in spite of the warning given him.

The northwestern part of Iceland, as well as the districts along the east coast, were sparsely settled during the period of colonization. The more noteworthy settlers in those districts were Thorstein the White Graut-Atli and his brother Ketill, Brynjolf the Old, Hrafnkell Godi, about whom the "Hrafnkelssaga Freysgoða" is written, Hrollaug, the son of Ragnvald Jarl, and Bárd, son of Heyangr-Björn of Sogn. Bárd settled at Skjálfandafljot, but when he found that the wind from the land was more agreeable than from the sea, he resolved to move. He crossed Iceland from north to south, and settled in Skaptafellssysla, where he took possession of the whole of Fljotswharf.

The first settlers in Iceland, Ingolf Arnarson and Hjörleif Hrodmarsson, built their homes on the south coast, as already mentioned. When Hjörleif was killed, Ingolf moved to Reykjavik, and the southern districts were not settled till quite late because the approach to the island from this side is rendered difficult by prevailing fogs and the absence

[6] *Vatsdœlasaga,* xxii.

of good harbors. Gradually, however, many families of
note came to live in the southern seacoast districts, which
have given not a few illustrious names to the narratives
of saga literature. Ofeig and his wife Asgerd from Romsdal
in Norway resolved to emigrate, as they could not agree
with King Harald Haarfagre. But before they could leave,
Ofeig was slain by King Harald's men. His widow with her
children and her brother Thorolf went to Iceland, where
they took possession of a tract of land between Seljelands-
mula and Markarfljot. Her son Thorgeir Golner was the
father of Njáll of Bergthorshváll, one of the noblest char-
acters in all saga literature, whose tragic story is told in the
"Njálssaga." Ketill Hœing, a chieftain from Namdalen in
Norway, came to Iceland and settled in the district between
Thorsá and Markarfljot, after he had avenged the murder
of his friend Thorolf Kveldulfsson. His son Hrafn was the
first *lögsögumaðr* in Iceland. From another son, Storolf,
descended Gunnar of Hlidarendi, the "Njálssaga" hero.
Sighvat from Haalogaland in Norway settled at Bolstad
west of Markarfljot. Jörund Godi settled at Svertingsstad,
where he built a temple. From him the Sturlung and
Oddverjar families descended. Among the chieftains who
settled in the southern districts were also Ketillbjörn, a
grandson of Jarl Haakon Grjotgardsson of northern Norway. He came to Iceland with his ship "Eliði," spending
the first winter with his father-in-law Thord Skeggi. In the
spring he set out with his men to find a suitable homestead.
They came to a river which they called Öxará, where the
Althing was since held. Here he took possession of a large
tract and built a residence called Mosfell. From him descended many people distinguished in saga literature.

How many *landnámsmenn* or emigrating chieftains came
to Iceland during the period of colonization is not definitely
known. The "Landnámabók," which gives the most detailed account, mentions 400, but even this careful survey
does not include all. Some names can be supplied from
other sources, but no complete enumeration can be given.
Still more purely conjectural must be the attempt to determine the total number of colonists who came to Iceland

during the early period of settlement. As the *landnáms-menn* were persons of rank and influence in their home districts, they were accompanied, not only by their families, but by a number of friends, relatives, freedmen, servants and slaves, so that the number of persons constituting the household and immediate surroundings of each chieftain formed in the aggregate a considerable colony. Of Geir-mund Heljarskin it is said that he had fourteen slaves, that when he rode about from one estate to another he was accompanied by eighty men. Aud the Deepminded came to Iceland with twenty freemen; and as many of these had families and established homes of their own, it is evident that the total number of emigrants must have been quite large. Some scholars have estimated that at the close of the period of colonization (874-930) Iceland must have had a population of about 25,000.[7] Some place the number even higher,[8] though there seems to be no good reason for going beyond this more conservative estimate. The first *landnámsmenn* took possession of extensive tracts in the inhabitable seacoast districts, where they built their own homes, and parcelled out lands to their followers and also to later emigrants who might be invited to settle within their possessions. The tracts thus taken were often very large. The "Landnámabók" states that when Einar Laug-arbrekku freed his slave Hreidar, he gave him as much land as he could carry fire around in three days. In this way a few powerful chieftains might soon divide all the land between them, so that later immigrants would find no place to settle. An appeal was made to King Harald Haar-fagre. Through his mediation it was decided that no one who arrived in command of a ship should take more land than he and his crew could carry fire around in one day. This appeal would seem to indicate that a reconciliation had

[7] P. A. Munch, *Det norske Folks Historie*, vol. 1, 555 f. J. E. Sars, *Udsigt over den norske Historie*, vol. 1, p. 213.

[8] Prof. Paul Hermann, *Island, das Land und das Volk*, Leipzig und Berlin, 1914. Prof. Hermann thinks that Iceland had a population of 60,000 in 965. James Bryce, *Studies in History and Jurisprudence*, p. 266, estimates the population of Iceland at the close of the period of settlement to have been about 50,000.

been brought about between King Harald and the colonists. According to Ari Frodi, so many people continued to go to Iceland that the king finally forbade further emigration for fear that his realm should be depopulated. Through a timely compromise, however, this arbitrary order was so modified that people were allowed to emigrate on the condition that each person leaving the country should pay a tax of five *aurar* to the king.[9] This was the beginning of the *landaurar* tax,[10] which for many centuries was levied on all ships leaving Norwegian harbors. The king seems to have recognized the right of the Icelanders to govern themselves. They should pay a small tax to the crown, but in return they retained their Norwegian citizenship to such an extent that when they returned to Norway they had *hölds-rétt,* or the right of chieftains to own and inherit property, and to belong to the king's *hirð* or court. The reconciliation between the king and the Icelandic chieftains seems to have been effected towards the end of the period of colonization. The Icelandic settlers continued to regard themselves as citizens of Norway. Their national traditions remained unbroken, and the most intimate relations were established between the colony and the mother country.

At the time of the colonization of Iceland Christianity had not yet been introduced in Norway. Many of the more prominent colonists had been priests in the heathen temples at home, and on their arrival in Iceland they built temples and established the old worship. Thorolf Mostrarskegg, who is said to have brought with him the timber of the temple of Moster, rebuilt the old sanctuary near his residence at Hofstadir. Thorhad the Old, a temple priest at Mæren in Trøndelagen, Norway, who settled in Stodvarfjord

---

[9] *Eyrir,* plural *aurar* (Norwegian *øre*). From early times till the 11th century various products, but especially linen and woolen cloth, were used as measures of value. Cloth was counted in *öln* (plu. *alnir*) or hundred *alnir* (i.e. 120). From the Older Iron Age gold and silver were used as money, divided according to weight into *mörk, eyrir* and *örtog.* The *mörk* = 8 *aurar* = 24 *örtogar,* in weight 215.8 grams. Gold was the standard of value in the Older Iron Age, silver in the Viking Age. Absalon Taranger, *Udsigt over den norske Rets Historie,* p. 127 ff. Hægstad og Torp, *Gamalnorsk Ordbok.*

[10] *Íslendingabók,* 1.

on the east coast, dedicated the whole valley to the Mæren
sanctuary so that nothing living could be killed there except
cattle and other domestic animals.[11]　Ingjald and Hrolf, the
sons of Helgi Magri, erected temples to the heathen gods;
so did also Jörund Godi, Hall the friend of Ulf Skjálgi, and
many other leading *landnámsmenn*.　Among the early settlers fetish worship still prevailed to some degree.　Thor
Snepil sacrificed to a clump of trees, Thorstein Raudnef
to a waterfall, and Eyvind Lodinsson in Flateyjardal wor-
shipped two large boulders.　Some had lost faith in the old
gods, and believed in nothing but their own strength and
prowess, while others, who seem to have been touched by
Christian influence, prayed to the god who created the sun.
But in spite of the prevailing heathen religion early Icelandic society was neither so wholly pagan or so complete a
reproduction of that of the mother country as might have
been expected.　From the British Isles Christianity had
thrown its first faint rays upon the shores of Iceland even
before the arrival of the Norsemen, and many of the early
colonists had experienced its ennobling influence on their so-
journs in the western islands.　From Dicuil's account we
have seen that Iceland was known to the peoples of Britain
and Ireland, and that Irish monks lived on the island long
before the Norse discovery.　In speaking of the early Norse
colonization the old Icelandic historian Ari Frodi says:

"Iceland was first settled from Norway in the days of King
Harald Haarfagre . . . but that was 870 years after the birth of
Christ.　Then there lived Christian men there, whom the Norsemen called *Papar*, but later they went away because they would
not live together with heathens.　They left behind books, bells
and croziers, from which it could be seen that they were Irish."[12]

That the Irish hermits left Iceland after the arrival of
the Norsemen because they did not wish to live together
with heathen people, as Ari states, must be true.　But they
seem to have stayed for some time after the new colonization began, and it is not unlikely that they exercised some

[11] *Landnámabók,* 6.
[12] *Islendingabók,* 1.

influence upon their new pagan neighbors. The Norsemen called them *Papar*, an Irish name meaning priest or monk. The croziers they called *baglar*, from the Old Irish *bachall*, derived from Latin *baculus*, a cane.[13] These are loan-words which the Norse settlers could have learned from the Irish hermits only after having known them for some time. The hermits seem to have dwelt especially in southeastern Iceland, where place-names like *Papey, Papos, Papafjord,* and *Papyli* still preserve their memory. Similar reminiscences of early Irish occupation are found also in other parts of Iceland, as in the southern districts where the hermits seem to have had a church in a place which is still called *Kirkjubær*, while names like *Iragerði, Irska leið,* and *Írsku búðir,* according to tradition a seat of Irish trade, seem to be of later origin.[14] The "Landnámabók" tells of Ásolf Alskik, missionary and hermit, that his mother was Irish, and that he came from Ireland to Osar in the Eastfjords. As he was a Christian, he would have nothing to do with heathen men, and would not even receive food from them. They were twelve together; evidently twelve Irish Culdees, as it was customary among them to travel about twelve together like the apostles of Christ. They went westward to Thorgeir Hördska at Holt near Eyjafjollum, where they raised their tent, but Asolf's companions were then sick, and they died there. The priest Jon Thorgrimsson later found their bones and buried them by the church. After the death of his companions Asolf built himself a house called *Asolfsskála,* but later he moved west to Irá (Irish River), so called because the men were Irish, and he lived there as a settler. In his old age he became a hermit, building himself an hermitage where the church now stands. He dwelt there till his death, and was buried at Holm, where a church was erected over his grave and dedicated to St. Columba. Asolf was later venerated as a saint. His remains were enshrined and placed on the church altar.

[13] Alexander Bugge, *Vesterlandenes Indflydelse,* p. 366 f. K. Maurer, *Die Bekehrung des norwegischen Stammes zum Christenthume,* 1. 9.
[14] Finnur Jónsson, *Norsk-islandske Kultur- og Sprogforhold i 9 og 10 Aarhundrede,* p. 48.

There can be little doubt that he and his companions were Irish Culdees who undertook missionary work among the Norse colonists in Iceland, the first known attempt to bring Christianity to the Norwegian people. Many Irish names, both personal and place names, are found in early Icelandic literature. These must have come into use at the time of the colonization or later. But Irish influence in Iceland, of which these names furnish evidence, was due, not so much to the presence of the Irish hermits who lived in the island at the time, but rather to the fact that many of the early settlers had stayed in Ireland, Scotland or the western islands for longer or shorter periods before they settled in Iceland.[15] The Faroe Islands, Shetland, the Orkneys, Hebrides, Man, and large parts of Ireland and Scotland had long been well populated Norse colonies. During King Harald Haarfagre's reign his enemies flocked to these settlements and continued to ravage the coasts of Norway until the king made an expedition to the West and drove them out. The only remaining retreat where they could escape the wrath of the angry king was Iceland, where large numbers of settlers arrived, not only from Norway, but from all the western Norse colonies.

How many of the *landnámsmenn* in Iceland came from the western islands is not definitely known. The Norwegian historians P. A. Munch and J. E. Sars, as well as the Icelandic scholar Gudbrand Vigfusson,[16] think that a large number of the early settlers came from the Norse colonies. Munch says about the "Landnámabók": that if we examine this remarkable work closely, we will find that of the four hundred leading colonists who divided the island among them, the most powerful and influential, those who brought the largest families with them, did not come directly from Norway, but from the Scottish isles, whither they had emigrated from Norway. "For the Icelanders," he continues, "the islands west of Scotland are the cradle of their race in a much higher sense than even their motherland

[15] Alexander Buggè, *Vesterlandenes Indflydelse*, p. 367 f. Kålund, *Beskrivelse af Island*, ii, p. 266.
[16] Gudbrand Vigfusson, *Safn til Sögu Íslands*, vol. i, p. 186.

Norway." [17]   J. E. Sars says: "The Landnámabók mentions in all four hundred *landnámsmenn*. All these colonists were Norsemen or of Norse family, except very few Scotch and Irish and a couple of Swedish settlers. But one-half their number, or even more, did not come directly from Norway, but from the Norse colonies, where long before they had settled and held possession." [18]   The Icelandic scholar Finnur Jónsson holds a different opinion. He says that only thirty-six *landnámsmenn*, or about one-ninth of their whole number, are known to have come from the Hebrides, Ireland, Caithness and England, and some of these were Vikings who happened to sojourn there. Later he has modified this view, holding the number to be fifty. But he thinks that Celtic influence in Iceland has been very small.[19]   The Icelandic historian Bogi Melsted holds that seventy-five of the *landnámsmenn* came from the western colonies. Alexander Bugge has found that of the four hundred or more *landnámsmenn* whose names are mentioned, one hundred and fifteen came from the Norse colonies. The greater number of these, however, must have stayed there only for brief periods while engaged in Viking expeditions, or because they had fled from Norway to the western settlements prior to their emigration to Iceland. But in speaking of the influence of these settlers from the colonies on early Icelandic society we must bear in mind, as P. A. Munch has pointed out, that many of the most influential *landnámsmenn*, those who brought the largest families with them, came from the western colonies. From these settlements came Geirmund Heljarskin and his brother Hámund, sons of the king of Hordaland; Helgi Magri, son of Eyvind the Eastman and the Irish princess Rafarta; Aud the Deepminded, widow of King Olaf the White of Dublin; Björn the Easterner and Helgi Bjola, the sons of Ketill Flatnef, and many other prominent chieftains. These leaders brought with them a large number of settlers,

---

[17] P. A. Munch, *Chronica Regum Manniæ et Insularum*, introduction.

[18] J. E. Sars, *Udsigt over den norske Historie*, vol. i, 179.

[19] Finnur Jónsson, *Den oldnorske og oldislandske Literaturs Historie*, vol. ii, 188. See also Finnur Jónsson, *Norsk-islandske Kultur- og Sprogforhold i 9 og 10 Aarhundrede*.

servants and slaves, many of whom must have been of
Celtic birth. Among the freed slaves in Aud's company
are mentioned Hörd, Vifill, Hundi, Erp and Sokkolf, who
received land from her. Hundi was of Scotch family, says
the "Landnámabók." We have seen that Geirmund Heljarskin had fourteen slaves, and that he rode about with an
escort of eighty men; that Hjörleif Hrodmarsson, one of the
first *landnámsmenn*, was slain by his Irish slaves. About
Ketill Örlygsson the "Landnámabók" states that he came
to Iceland late in the period of colonization, and that he
brought with him Irish slaves which he had taken on his
Viking expeditions in the West. The number of Irish
personal names found in the "Landnámabók" and elsewhere
in the sagas shows that slaves and also other persons of
Celtic origin must have been quite numerous in Iceland.[20]
Not a few of the *landnámsmenn* who came to Iceland from
the Norse colonies were born in the western islands. Some
of them had Irish mothers, as concubinage and intermarriage
with Irish women was quite common in the Norse settlements in the West. Only a few noteworthy instances of
this relation need here be mentioned.

Aud the Deepminded had a freedman by the name of
Erp, who was the son of Meldun Jarl of Scotland and the
Irish princess Myrgjol, who had been carried away from
her home, and had become servant to the jarl's wife. Aud
bought Myrgjol and her boy, and both received their freedom. Erp received Saudafell from Aud. From him the
Erpling family descended.[21] Höskuld Dalakollsson, who
married Aud's granddaughter, bought a girl at a slave
market. He learned later that she was an Irish princess
by the name of Melkorka (Mael-Curcaigh), daughter of
the Irish king Muircertach.[22] She became the mother of
Olaf Pá of Hjardarholt, one of the foremost of Icelandic
chieftains. The mother of Helgi Magri, who settled in the
north of Iceland, was Rafarta, daughter of King Cearbhall

[20] Of Irish personal names in Iceland may be mentioned *Kjallakr* from
Ceallah, Kylan<Ceolán, Bekan<Beccán, Dufþakr<Dubhthak.
[21] *Landnámabók*.
[22] *Laxdœlasaga*.

of Ireland, as already mentioned. Helgi was born in Ireland and reared in the Hebrides.[23] Two other daughters of the same king, Fridgerd and Kormlöd (Gormflaith),[24] married the *landnámsmenn* Thor and Grimolf. The princess Nidbjörg, daughter of the Irish king Bjolan (Beolan), married Helgi Ottarsson, a grandson of Björn the Easterner. Myruna, daughter of King Maddad (Maddadh), married the *landnámsaðr* Audun Stoti.[25]

The influence exerted on the colonists through their relations with the peoples of the West comes to view also in the traces of Celtic culture in early Icelandic sociecy. Especially noticeable is the tinge of Christian faith in the still pagan religion of the settlers. The *landnámsmenn* who came from the western islands usually brought with them a number of dependents, both freedmen and slaves, whom they had secured either as prisoners of war, or as slaves bought in the numerous slave ma kets. Many of these were Christian Celts, who would not abandon their faith even in their new surroundings. Not a few of the *landnámsmenn* who came from the colonies in the West had accepted the Christian faith in some form, and some of them were baptized. The "Landnamabók" says:

"Wise men say that some of the *landnámsmenn* who settled in Iceland were baptized, for the most part those who came from the West over the sea. Thus are mentioned Helgi Magri, Örlyg the Old, Helgi Bjola, Jörund the Christian, Aud the Deepminded, Ketill Fiflski, and still other men who came from the West over the sea. Some kept their Christian faith till their death day. But it did not last long in their families; for some of their sons sacrificed to the heathen gods, and the land was altogether heathen for about a hundred years." [26]

Örlyg was reared by Bishop Patrick of the Hebrides. He brought with him to Iceland timber for a church, a church bell, a plenarium and some consecrated Christian soil. He built a church near his residence and dedicated it to St.

[23] *Landnámabók*, iii, 11.
[24] *Ibidem*, v, 13.
[25] *Ibidem*, ii, 10.
[26] *Ibidem*, v, 15.

Columba, whom he worshiped as a deity.[27]   It appears
also that his son Valthjof (A. S. Wealhþeow) because of
his English name must have been a baptized Christian, as
were probably also the *landnámsmenn* Koll, Thorolf Spör
and others who accompanied him from the western colonies.   Many of the settlers who came to Iceland with Aud
the Deepminded must also have confessed the Christian
faith.   Aud, who was baptized, performed her worship before some crosses which she erected at a place called *Kross-
holar,* which her friends and descendants regarded as a
sanctuary, and where they built a *hörg* or altar to the gods
when the Christian faith finally became extinct in her
family.   The memory of Aud as a Christian lady has been
preserved in Icelandic folk-tales, where her contest with the
sorceress Gullbrá symbolizes the struggle between paganism
and Christianity.[28]   Thormod the Old and Ketill Bresason,
who, according to the "Landnámobók," came from Ireland
and took possession of Akranes between Örridará and
Kalmansá, must also have been Christians; likewise also
Kalman, who came with him from the Hebrides, where he
seems to have been born.   Jörund the Christian, the son of
Ketill Bresason, lived at Jörundarholt, which was later
called Gardar.   The saga says that he kept well his Christian
faith, and became a hermit in his old age.   His sister Edna
was the mother of the missionary Ásolf Alskik, who died as
hermit in Iceland.   Kalman returned to the old faith, and
was mound-buried according to heathen custom.   His son
Sturla built a temple and sacrificed to the gods, but
Christianity was not altogether extinct in their family.   It
is said that Sturla's son Bjarni quarrelled with a neighbor
about a piece of land.   He made the vow that if he won he
would accept Christianity.   It happened that the river
Hvitá was turned out of its channel so that the land in
dispute became connected with Bjarni's property, and he
then received baptism and built a church near his home.
Ketill Fiflski had received the sobriquet of *fiflski* (foolish)

---

[27] *Landnámabók,* i, 12.
[28] *Ibidem,* ii, 16.   Jon Arnason, *Íslenzkar þjóðsögur og æfintyri,* i, p. 146 ff.

because he was a Christian, and Kirkjubær, where he lived,
was regarded as a sanctuary where no heathens were allowed to dwell.[29]   A monastry for Benedictine monks was
erected there in 1186.[30]

Not many of the colonists in Iceland who had learned
to know Christianity had accepted it as a distinct worship.
Usually they were so little informed as to the Christian
doctrine that they regarded Christ only as a god among
other gods, as did Helgi Magri, of whom it is said that he
was much mixed in his faith. He named his home Kristnes
in honor of Christ, but though he was nominally a baptized
Christian, he prayed to Thor when he was in distress or in
danger on the sea.[31] His sons Ingjald and Hrolf seem to
have been wholly pagan, as they built temples and sacrificed
to the heathen gods. Even those who called themselves
Christians could not read; they had no priests to instruct
them or to preach the gospel to them. In the midst of
heathen surroundings they were able only to cling as well
as they could to the outward symbols of Christianity.
When they built a church they placed a simple cross on the
altar, possibly also a few candles, as the structure, undoubtedly, was windowless and dark. Before this altar they
knelt to do reverence to the cross, as they had seen Christians do in Ireland and elsewhere, and they would repeat
the name of Christ or some favorite saint, which must have
been in the main their church service. It was a dim light
this Christianity which they knew, but it was the light of
the world, which brought with it new moral and social
ideals. They knew that Christianity taught charity, for-
giveness, purity of life, principles wholly wanting in the
old faith, and the new ideals attracted them and touched
their hearts. That some even sought to practice them we
see in Ingimund's willingness to forgive Hrolleif, in Aud the
Deepminded's kindness to her liberated slaves, in Svartkell's
simple prayer which he is said to have been in the habit of
repeating before the cross: "May good befall the old men

[29] *Landnámabók*, iv, 11.
[30] Kålund, *Beskrivelse af Island*, vol. i, 315.
[31] *Landnámabók*, iii, 12.

and may good befall the young." For want of aid and
encouragement the early Christians in Iceland gradually
lapsed into the paganism which surrounded them, but the
influence of their faith helped to pave the way for the
missionaries who came to preach Christianity a hundred
years later.

During the period of settlement the traces of western
influence is clearly visible in colonial life in Iceland. Many
attractive features in the early development of the colony
were due to this new cultural force which here and there
throws a pleasing light against the somber background of old
Norse paganism. But this influence was of little permanent
importance, as it was not strong enough to effect any lasting
change in the people's life and thought. At the close of the
period of colonization the settlements in Iceland were as
fully pagan as they were fully Norse. The national traits
only reasserted themselves with increased force in the new
colonial environment.

3. ORGANIZATION OF THE ICELANDIC STATE AND GOVERNMENT

THE leading *landnámsmenn* in Iceland belonged to the
old Norwegian aristocracy. Some were sons of kings and
jarls, others were *hersar* or local chieftains, who also acted as
priests in conducting the public worship. In religious matters as well as in political and military affairs they were
the leaders of the people, an upper class with extensive
time-honored privileges. In defense of their aristocratic
social organization many of them had waged war against
the king, who sought to create a united Norway under the
rule of a monarch exercising sovereign authority in all
administrative affairs. Some had dwelt for longer or shorter
periods in the loosely governed Norse colonies in the western
islands. In Iceland they naturally sought to reproduce as
far as possible the old Norwegian social organization, but
the creation of a new state nevertheless brought about
important changes. The institution of kingship, or central

authority vested in a ruler, which had existed in Norway in some form long before the time of Harald Haarfagre, disappeared in Iceland. As no one in these new settlements could claim any rank of superiority, the chieftains remained wholly independent and continued to rule their adherents and subordinates according to the most ancient local custom. The new colony was at first not a state, but a group of chieftaincies without any tie of union under a central government.

The *landnámsmenn* built their homes in some well selected location within their possessions, and in close proximity usually also a temple, which became the place of worship for the settlers within the district. The function of priest was exercised by the chieftains themselves, who assumed the rank and title of *goði*,[1] an office which combined with the dignity of priesthood also administrative and judicial functions, corresponding in a general way to that of *hersir* in Norway. How many temples were erected by the first settlers is not known, but some chieftains are mentioned in the "Landnámabók" and elsewhere in the sagas as builders of temples, as Thorolf Mostrarskegg, Ingimund the Old, Jörund Godi, Bödvar the White, the sons of Helgi Magri, Audun the Red and others. The frequent use of the word *hof* (temple) in place-names as *Hof, Hofstadir, Hofsvág, Hofsland, Hofsteig* indicates that quite a number were built.

[1] The title of *goði* was used more frequently in Iceland than elsewhere, but it was also known in Norway and Denmark and seems to be of old Germanic origin. The *Landnámabók* says of Thorhad the Old that he was *hofgoði* in Mæren, Norway, before he came to Iceland. Snorri says in the *Heimskringla:* "It was a custom there that twelve *hofgoðir* were the leaders. They had charge of the sacrifices and of the decisions rendered between men." Saxo Grammaticus in his *Historia Danica*, viii, 381, mentions a *Lyuthguthi*, and on some Danish rune-stones are found the names *Nuragupi* and *Sauluagupi*. The Gothic form is *gudja*. See K. Maurer, *Island von seiner ersten Entdeckung bis zum Untergange des Freistaats*, p. 45.

Priestesses (*gyðja*) might have charge of the temples and conduct the sacrifices. *Thorlaug gyðja* is mentioned in the *Landnámabók*, i, 21; *Thurid gyðja*, *Landnámabók*, iii, 4, and *Vatsdælasaga*, 27. Priestesses are frequently mentioned in the sagas; in *Vápnfirðingasaga*, ch. 10, the *Ynglingasaga* of the *Heimskringla*, the *Kristnisaga*, also in the *Hyndluljóð* in the *Elder Edda* and elsewhere. The priestesses seem to have been regarded as especially holy. Tacitus says: "The Germans think that women possess a certain sacredness and prophetic gift." *Germania*, 8.

As a rule they must have been structures of considerable size, as excavations of old Icelandic temple ruins made in recent years show the length of some to have been a hundred feet. The "Eyrbyggjasaga" says of Thorolf Most-rarskegg and the temple which he built at Hofstadir:

"He erected a great dwelling at Hofsvág and called it Hof-stadir. There he also built a temple, and it was a large structure. There were doors on the side walls toward the ends. Inside stood the pillars of the high-seat in which were bolts called *reginnaglar* (sacred bolts). In the interior was a sanctuary. Farther in the temple was a room resembling the choir of a church, with the *stallr* like an altar, on which lay a jointless ring weighing twenty *aurar*. On this ring all oaths had to be sworn, and the temple priest should have it on his arm on all public occasions. On the *stallr* should also stand the *hleytbolli* with the *hleytteinn* to sprinkle with. With it the blood, which was called *hlaut*, was to be sprinkled; this was the blood from the animals which were sacrificed. Around the *stallr* the images of the gods were placed within this room. All men had to pay taxes to the temple. It should also be their duty to accompany the priest on all his journeys, as the *thingmenn* now accompany the chieftains. But the *goði* should maintain the temple at his own expense, so that it should not fall to ruin, and he should conduct the sacrifices there." [2]

The smallest local unit in the Icelandic state organization was the *hreppr* (plu. *hreppar*), at the head of which stood the *hreppstjóri*, but these districts of about twenty families were chiefly concerned with matters pertaining to public charity. The districts over which the *goði* exercised reli-

[2] *Eyrbyggjasaga*, 4. *Landnámabók*, iv, 7. *Melabók*. In the north remnants of old heathen temples have been found only in Iceland. In the Scandinavian countries, where the buildings were erected of timber, they have entirely disappeared. In Iceland, where building timber had to be imported, the walls of all buildings were usually constructed of sod and rock, and remnants of such walls have been discovered in many places. The best known of these temple ruins is that of Hofstadir near lake Myvatn, in northern Iceland, excavated by Prof. Finnur Jónsson and Daniel Bruun in 1908. *Aarbøger for nordisk Oldkyndighed og Historie*, vol. 24, p. 245 ff. Kålund, *Islands Beskrivelse*, ii, 167. Daniel Brunn, *Fortidsminder og Nutidshjem*, 174 f. *Foreningen til norske Fortidsmindes-merkers Bevaring, Aarsberetning*, 1906, 1907, 1908. Daniel Bruun, *Udgravninger paa Island, Geografisk Tidsskrift*, xvii, 21 ff.

gious and civil authority constituted a *goðorð*, which formed
the basis of Iceland's hierarchic aristocratic social organization. Each *goðorð* had a temple, and near it was a meeting
place of the *thing*, or popular assembly, where the freemen
of the district, the *thingmenn*, met to settle their disputes.
The *goði* presided over the *thing* and appointed the judges
who were to decide the cases brought before it. On all such
occasions, as well as when he acted as priest, he wore on his
arm the temple ring as a sign of his high office.[3] It was his
duty to administer the law, to keep order within his *goðorð*,
and to aid his *thingmenn* in obtaining justice and settling
their disputes, As the temple was a part of his estate, the
office and rank of *goði* was regarded as the chieftain's personal possession, usually transmitted as an inheritance from
father to son,[4] but it might also be sold or given away like
other property. The *thingmenn* had no voice in the disposal of the *goðorð*, but they could transfer their allegiance
from one *goði* to another according to their own free will.
As they could attach themselves to any *goði*, even to one
living at a great distance, the *goðorð* could not be said to
have any fixed boundaries. Its religious character was so
predominant that it resembled more closely a modern free-
church congregation than a definitely established administrative district.[5]

At first no connection existed between the different
goðorðs and local *things*. But even in the early years of the
colonial period the need was felt of some higher tribunal
which could try cases arising between members of different
goðorðs. Shortly after he had settled in Iceland, Thorolf
Mostrarskegg established the Thorsnesthing, which should
be a *heraðsthing*, as it was established with the consent of
all the people within that district, but it seems to have been
only a local *thing* connected with the Thorsnes *goðorð*.[6]
Thorstein, the son of Ingolf Arnarson, organized the
Kjalarnesthing, which seems to have exercised more general

[3] Pétur Pétursson, *Commentatio de Jure Ecclesia in Islandia*, p. 9 ff.
[4] *Eyrbyggjasaga*, 9-15. R. Keyser, *Nordmœndenes Religionsforfatning i Hedendommen*, p. 57 ff.
[5] *Grágás*, ch. 81.
[6] *Eyrbyggjasaga*, 4. *Landnámabók*, ch. 12.

jurisdiction, since several chieftains were united in it.[7] But even this step could not meet the growing needs of the new state. No general system of laws had yet been adopted, and no popular assembly existed which could deal with problems pertaining to the public welfare. The need of some form of general government, so keenly felt also in the new environment, must have been frequently discussed by the chieftains, who finally decided to create a new political organization for the whole island. A man by the name of Ulfljot from Hordaland in Norway, who had settled in the southern districts, was chosen in 927 to prepare a code of laws. He went to Norway, where he spent three years studying the "Gulathingslög," the code of the southwestern districts of the kingdom. With the aid of his uncle, Thorleif Spaki, he prepared, on the basis of this code, a body of laws known as "Ulfljot's Law," which, according to Ari Frodi, was adopted as the law of Iceland in 930.[8] While Ulfljot was in Norway, his foster-brother, Grim Geitsko, was delegated to select a suitable meeting place for the new national assembly which was to be created. The "Íslendingabók" states that a tax of one *peningr* was collected from each man in order to pay Grim, but that he gave the money to the temple. The place selected was Thingvellir on the banks of the river Öxará, north of lake Thingvalla, a convenient and most impressive location. About "Ulfljot's Law" very scant information has been preserved. It contained many ritualistic provisions governing public worship; how the favor of the protecting spirits should be secured; how the temple ring should be preserved, and what should be the form of the oath administered by the *goði*. But more important than these minor regulations were the provisions made for a central government and the organization of a general assembly, the Althing. This assembly was to remain in session for two weeks every summer at Thingvellir, where all the settlers in Iceland could meet.[9] Through this fundamental law the separate communities

---

[7] *Íslendingabók,* ch. 3. *Landnámabók,* i, 9.
[8] *Íslendingabók,* ch. 2. *Melabók.*
[9] *Íslendingabók,* ch. 2, 3, 7.

were merged in a new state organization, a sort of aristocratic republic with a national assembly as the highest central authority. The Althing was undoubtedly patterned on
the Norwegian *lagthings*, but these were four in number
and were local rather than national in character. The
Althing was a distinctly organized national assembly, and is
of special interest as one of the first bodies of this kind in
history. Regarding its early functions, and how it was at
first constituted, no satisfactory information is given in the
old writers. But it is quite clear that it possessed both legislative and judicial powers, and that these functions were
separated even from the beginning through the establishing
within the assembly of an *alþingisdómr*, or high court of justice, consisting of thirty-six judges, a tribunal which exercised the highest legal jurisdiction for the whole land. The
law-making power was given to another select body within
the assembly, the *lögrétta*. These two bodies exercised so
complete powers, each in its own sphere, that the decisions
rendered and the new laws which were adopted were not
even sanctioned by a general vote of the assembly, as in
Norway, but were only formally proclaimed to the assembled *thing*. The highest official in the new general government was the *lögsögumaðr*, who presided over the
Althing, proclaimed the new laws and decisions from the
Mount of Laws, and recited certain portions of the laws
each year before the assembly. He was elected for the term
of three years,[10] but by repeated reëlections was kept in
office for so long a period that his tenure was often equivalent to a life incumbency.[11] Such an extended tenure of

[10] "All laws shall be recited in the period of three years, and the *lögsögumaðr* shall then resign his office." *Grágás,* ch. 19.

[11] Ulfljot himself must have served as *lögsögumaðr* till his death in 930.
Hrafn, the son of Ketill Hæng, was then elevated to the office, and served
for twenty years, 930-949. He was succeeded by Thorarin Olafsson, who
also served for twenty years, 950-970. Thorkell Máni, who followed him in
office, served till his death in 985. Thorgeir Thorkelsson served seventeen
years. Gellir of Mosfell served two years, when he resigned because his
voice failed him. He was succeeded by his nephew, Skapti Thorodsson,
who was chosen at his request, and remained in office twenty-seven
years. *Islendingabók,* ch. 3 ff. Jon Sigurdsson, *Lögsögumanna tal og
lögmanna á Íslandi, Safn til Sögu Íslands,* vol. ii, p. 1 ff.

office must have been necessary, as few persons possessed sufficient knowledge of the laws to hold so important an office.

The Althing was of great importance not only as a legislative body and a high court of justice, but also as a center of national life where the leading men from all Iceland could meet every year and exchange views on all important public questions. It formed a bond of union between the local districts, and did much to foster a national spirit. But the almost total absence of administrative authority left the new national government weak and inefficient. The Althing could raise no military forces nor could it exercise any police authority, as these very essential powers of government were still retained by the *goðorðs*. So jealously did the chieftains watch over their own powers that they failed to vest the *lögsögumaðr* or any other functionary with executive authority. The decisions rendered in judicial matters could, indeed, be enforced in a general way by the public at large. If a person was fined, outlawed or banished, the people would know how to make the decree effective. But if the guilty person was a powerful chieftain, he might defy both the law and the court, and blood-feud would be resorted to as a final settlement of the dispute. Even the Althing itself, though hedged about with all the inviolability of a sanctuary, became at times the scene of bloody conflicts between angry litigants and their adherents, as no armed force existed which could maintain order and prevent violent outbreaks. Cases of bloodshed and disorder at the *thing* were, indeed exceptional, but several instances recorded in the sagas show the utter helplessness of the assembly, if the chieftain chose to ignore its decrees and disregard its sanctity. The "Hoensathórissaga" tells about Thord Gellir and Tungu-Odd that they were involved in a controversy and finally brought their case before the Althing. When Odd arrived at the *thing* with 300 armed followers and sought to prevent Thord from gaining access to the sacred thingstead, an armed conflict followed which was stopped only after six of Odd's men had fallen. Still more serious was an armed clash which took place at the

Althing in 1012. According to the "Njálssaga" Mord Valgardsson brought suit in the *fjorðungsdómr* (quarter court)
against Flosi Thordsson, the leader of the band who had
burned Njáll of Bergthorshváll and his family. No doubt
could exist regarding the guilt of Flosi and his men, but
through skilful manipulation of the technicalities of court
procedure Mord and the friends of Njáll failed to obtain a
favorable verdict. This so exasperated them that they
attacked Flosi and his adherents, and a general battle resulted in which a great number lost their lives before better
counsel prevailed. When order was restored, the leaders
deplored the unfortunate occurrence, and the case was finally
settled according to the acknowledged principles of law and
justice.

The absence of effective central control not only tended
to impair all good features of the established government,
but it also encouraged the development of a spirit of feud
and violence which proved very baneful to the social well-
being and national progress of the people. The inefficiency
and incompleteness of the new national organization became more clearly apparent as the need of a better regulated
social life made itself felt in the new state. The local
things had been established by the chieftains without any
general plan. Since no boundaries existed between the different districts, their jurisdiction was uncertain, and their
ability to grant impartial justice was often very small. The
defects in the judicial system had been so clearly demon-
strated by the case between Thord Gellir and Tungu-Odd,
that a reorganization was finally made in 965. All Iceland
was now divided into four quarters, each of which should
contain three *thing* districts, except the northern quarter
which should have four districts, as the people of that quarter would agree to no other arrangement. Each of these
thirteen *thing* districts should comprise three of the thirty-
nine principal *goðorðs,* and should have its own local court,
the *várthing,*[12] which should be in session from four days to
a week in the spring of each year. Each of the three *goðar*

---

[12] *Hœnsathorissaga. Grágás,* ch. 56 f.

in the district should appoint twelve of the thirty-six judges constituting the *thing*. Another session of two days (*leið*) was held two weeks after the close of the Althing in order that the decisions of that tribunal might be brought to the knowledge of those who had not been able to attend the session at Thingvellir. Other matters might also be brought before the court at this session. It is clear that the new organization of the *várthings* made them more efficient judicial tribunals than they had been hitherto. They had now received 3×12 judges according to the old universal practice in the North, and as the three *goðar* were associated in each court, and presided in turn over its sessions, there was no longer the danger of unfairness and partiality which always existed so long as only one *goði* conducted the *thing*. The number of principal *goðorðs* was also fixed by this system of organization at thirty-nine, and their position as units in the framework of government was clearly defined. New *goðorðs* might, indeed, be established, but they could not be classed with the principal *goðorðs*, nor could they gain recognition as a part of the system of state organization.

It seems to have been the plan to organize a superior court for each of the four quarters. The "Eyrbyggjasaga" and the "Landnámabók" state that Thord Gellir organized a quarter court for the Vestfjord quarter at Thorsnes about 930 with the advice of all the men of the quarter [13]; and the "Íslendingabók" says that after the land was divided into quarters, quarter courts were established.[14] But as these courts do not seem to have been regularly assembled, they soon disappeared. So many cases were brought directly to the Althing that it was found necessary to make important changes in its organization. Four superior courts, *fjorðungsdómr*, one for each quarter, were attached to it to take charge of all judicial matters which would regularly come under the quarter courts. These courts had thirty-six judges, the nine *goðar* of the quarter each choosing four judges, except in the northern quarter, where each of the

[13] *Eyrbyggjasaga*, ch. 10. *Landnámabók*, ii, ch. 12.
[14] *Íslendingabók*, ch. 3.

twelve *goðar* chose three judges.[15] The decision of the
fjorðungsdómr, or quarter court, was regarded as unanimous
even if difference of opinion existed among the judges, if
the number of dissenting votes did not exceed six. If there
were more than six dissenting votes, a *véfang* arose. The
judges holding adverse opinions would then divide into two
groups, each group seeking to persuade the members of
the other. If the number dissenting still remained too large,
each group would render its decision, the one making the
other void, and both groups would take the *véfang* oath
that they had decided in accordance with what they considered to be just and lawful. The case could then be
appealed to the supreme court of the *fimtardómr,* after this
tribunal was established.

The *fimtardómr* seems to have been created not earlier
than 1004 nor later than 1009.[16] It is mentioned in the
"Íslendingabók," which states that Skapti Thorodsson,
lögsögumaðr 1004-1030, secured the passage of a law
establishing this tribunal. But according to the "Njálssaga"
this court was created in accordance with a plan proposed
by Njáll of Bergthorshváll, the ablest jurist in Iceland at
that time. Of the two accounts, that given by Ari Frodi in
the "Íslendingabók," though very brief, is undoubtedly the
more reliable, as the "Njálssaga" narrative on this point is
confused and self-contradictory. The century 930-1030 is
known as the *Söguöld,* or saga age, because the numerous
deeds of violence and reckless daring for which it is especially noted became the themes of the Icelandic family
sagas. It was a turbulent period of ineffective constitu-

[15] Some authorities hold that each quarter had only nine judges; thus
J. Arnesen, *Islands Rettergang,* p. 315; R. Keyser, *Norges Stats-og Rets-
forfatning,* p. 274; P. A. Munch, *Det norske Folks Historie,* vol. i, part ii,
p. 156. But K. Maurer, *Island von seiner ersten Entdeckung,* p. 174; J. E.
Sars, *Udsigt over den norske Historie,* vol. i, p. 219; and Páll Melsted,
Nýjar athugasemdir við nokkrar ritgjördir um altþingismáliʒ, p. 108 ff.,
hold that there were thirty-six judges, a view which has been generally
accepted. See also V. Finsen, *Om de islandske Love i Fristadstiden.*

[16] *Íslendingabók,* 8. *Njálssaga,* ch. 98. *Grágás,* ch. 43. Björn M. Olsen,
Um kristnitökunna árið 1000, p. 43 ff. K. Maurer, *Island von seiner ersten
Entdeckung,* p. 57, p. 175. R. Keyser. *Efterladte Skrifter,* vol. ii, p. 275 ff.
P. A. Munch, *Det norske Folks Historie,* vol. i, part ii, p. 423 f.

tional reforms and growing lawlessness. The incompetence of the Althing as a national government was so painfully apparent that only far-reaching changes could save the people from anarchy. In an effort to remedy conditions the chieftains decided to create a superior judicial tribunal, the *fimtardómr*, which could exercise greater authority than the older courts. The thirty-nine *goðar* of the principal *goðorðs* were to choose each one judge for this new tribunal, except in the northern quarter, where the twelve *goðar* should choose nine judges, making in all thirty-six for the thirty-nine old *goðorðs*. But nine *goðar* who had hitherto remained outside the *thing* organization because they had accepted Christianity were also to be admitted now that all the chieftains were Christians. These nine *goðar* were to choose also twelve judges for the new tribunal, making the total number forty-eight. But the law required that the plaintiff should reject six judges and the defendant another six, so that only thirty-six trial judges remained for any given case. The *fimtardómr* sat together with the *lögrétta*. The judges were bound by solemn oaths, which were again strengthened by co-jurors, and the proceedings of the tribunal were carried on with elaborate formality.[17] The importance of a high court of justice of such authority is quite apparent. The courts had often failed to settle important controversies, so that duel (*holmgangr*) and blood-feud were still resorted to as a final settlement of disputes. The establishing of the *fimtardómr* led to the disappearance of the duel as a primitive way of seeking justice. The duel between the scalds Gunnlaug Ormstunga and Hrafn Önundsson, fought at the Althing probably in 1006, was the last event of this sort in Iceland. The day after the duel the Althing passed an act making dueling unlawful.[18]

In the procedure of the *thing* the *kviðr* was a very prominent feature, constituting one of the chief characteristics of

[17] K. Maurer, *Island von seiner ersten Entdeckung*, p. 175.
[18] *Gunnlaugssaga Ormstungu*, ch. ii, p. 258 f. K. Maurer, *Island von seiner ersten Entdeckung*, p. 61. P. A. Munch, *Det norske Folks Historie*, vol. i, part ii, p. 445.

the old Icelandic legal system. The *kviðr*, which corresponded in the main to the Norwegian *dómr*, was a sort of jury consisting of neighbors of the plaintiff, appointed by the *goði* at his request to testify in his behalf. The *búakviðr*, or neighbor *kviðr*, consisting of nine members, or in smaller cases of five members, was the one most frequently used. The members of the *kviðr* would not need to know the facts in the case from personal observation, but would only declare under oath what they considered to be the main facts and circumstances connected with it. The *tylftarkviðr*, or *goðakviðr*, used especially in cases between the *goðar* and their *thingmenn*, consisted of twelve members, the *goði* nominating eleven, the twelfth being the *goði* himself. If he was a defendant, one of the two other *goðar* of that district was nominated by the plaintiff. The declaration of the *kviðr* was used in the trial as general evidence in connection with the testimony of other witnesses, but the defendant could meet the *kviðr* of the plaintiff with a *bjargkviðr*, consisting of five members chosen from the defendant's home district to testify in his behalf. These would make a declaration tending to modify or counteract that given in favor of the plaintiff.[19] He could also on legal grounds expel members from the plaintiff's *kviðr*, and new members would then be chosen. The declaration of the *kviðr* could be determined by a majority opinion. In case of a tie the *goði* would cast the deciding vote.

Even in cases of homicide or other grave crimes the parties to the suit could settle the matter privately by agreeing upon a suitable compensation to the injured party, fixed either by the plaintiff himself (*sjalfdœmi*) or by trusted persons chosen as arbitrators. If no such settlement was made, the plaintiff could bring the case before the court. A person who was convicted or held legally responsible for some great wrong-doing would be outlawed, in which case either partial or complete banishment would be imposed. Partial banishment, *fjörbaugsgarðr*, lasted three years, and the guilty person might be banished to

---

[19] *Grágás*, ch. 36. *Njálssaga*, ch. 141-145. Ebbe Herzberg, *Grundtrœkkene i den ældre norske Proces*, p. 233 ff. *Norges gamle Love*, glossary, "dómr."

some other district,[20] or sent into exile. On the payment to the *goði* of a fine, *fjörbaugr*, three places of safety were granted the outlawed person until he could leave home or find passage to some foreign land to spend the term of exile. Should he fail to pay this fine, the sentence was changed to complete banishment. No one was allowed to molest him in passing between the places of safety, or in going to the ship, and no shipowner could refuse him passage.[21] When he returned after three years, he was again a free man and was restored to his full rights as citizen. The severest punishment inflicted was complete banishment, *skóggangr*, when a man became *skóggangsmaðr*, or complete outlaw.[22] For minor offenses, *útlegðarsakir*, a fine of three *merkr* or less was imposed. In order to bring the sentence of banishment to execution a *féránsdómr*, or court of execution, consisting of twelve judges, had to be assembled by the *goði* at the home of the outlawed person two weeks after the close of the Althing. This court formally dispossessed the convicted person of his property, collected the fines due, paid his debts, and made provision for his dependents.[23] It is quite clear, however, that the severe punishment of complete banishment was seldom inflicted. The spirit of the old laws was opposed to a mode of punishment which resulted in personal injury to the individual, favoring settlement based on compensation to the injured party. Limited banishment was more frequently used in order to remove troublesome persons from the scene of conflict until peace and quiet could be again restored.

The lawmaking power of the Althing, as already mentioned, was vested in the *lögrétta*, which, besides the *lögsögumaðr*, and after the introduction of Christianity also of the two bishops, consisted of 144 members divided into

[20] *Hörðr Grimkelssonssaga*, ch. 20 f. *Hrafnkelssaga Freysgoða*, ch. 11. *Grágás*, 369; ii, 86. *Njálssaga*, 145.

[21] *Hœnsathorissaga*, ch. 15. *Njálssaga*, 74, 145.

[22] *Grettissaga. Gíslasaga Súrssonar.*

[23] *Grágás*, ch. 48 ff. K. Maurer, *Island von seiner ersten Entdeckung*, p. 195. Dependents and the poor, *úmagar*, were to be cared for by their own nearest relatives. If they had none, they were assigned to the homes of other people in the community who were able to keep them.

three groups or benches. The first group consisted of the thirty-nine *goðar* of the principal *goðorðs* together with nine additional members, three from each of the quarters having only nine *goðar*, chosen in order to give all the quarters an equal representation. These forty-eight members constituted the middle bench, and they alone had the right to vote on measures proposed.[24] Each member of this bench chose two assistants, in all ninety-six, who occupied the front and rear benches. They had no vote, and acted only in the capacity of counselors. The *lögrétta* alone had the right to interpret, change or enact laws, grant pardons, reduce prescribed punishments in given cases, and to issue permits of various kinds. When a measure had been adopted by a majority vote, all members had to give their assent. It was then formally proclaimed to the assembled Althing by the *lögsögumaðr*. In minor affairs a decree could be passed even if all members were not present, but in no case could a smaller number than forty-eight constitute a quorum. The *lögsögumaðr* was to be chosen by unanimous vote of the *lögrétta*. He received a salary of 240 *alnar* of woolen cloth (*vaðmál*), and he was also to have one-half of the fines imposed for minor offenses. After his election the *lögrétta* escorted him to the Mount of Laws, where he took his seat as presiding officer. The session of the Althing began on Thursday between the eighteenth and twenty-third of June, and lasted for two weeks. On Friday, after the *thingsköp*, or plan of procedure, had been announced by the *lögsögumaðr*, the *goðar* appointed the judges for the quarter courts, and all cases to be brought before these courts were announced to the assembled *thingmenn* on Friday and Saturday or on Monday following. On Saturday at noon the members of the *thing* marched in procession to the Mount of Laws, led by the *lögsögumaðr*, who was followed by the *goðar* and the judges whom they had appointed. Places were now assigned to the quarter courts, which remained in session every week-day throughout the *thing* period, except when the *lögrétta* met, or when the

---

[24] K. Maurer, *Island von seiner ersten Entdeckung*, p. 172 f. R. Keyser, *Efterladte Skrifter*, vol. ii, p. 263 ff., p. 270 ff.

lögsögumaðr summoned them to meet at the Mount of Laws. The *lögrétta* was to hold at least four meetings during the session of the *thing,* one on each of the two Sundays of the *thing* period, one on the first Friday of the session, and one on the day of the closing. But it might be convened by the *lögsögumaðr* at any time during the session of the *thing.*

Thingvellir, where the Althing met, is a lava bed of prehistoric origin sloping toward lake Thingvalla. This bed north of the lake has sunk in cooling, creating two large rifts, the Almannagjá to the west and the Hrafnagjá to the east of Thingvellir. The Almannagjá, which has a length of several miles, stretches from Armansfell to the lake. It has a flat bottom and perpendicular sides of lava, the western wall being about a hundred feet, the eastern from thirty-five to sixty feet in height. The little river Öxará falls into the rift, but soon crosses it and flows through the Thingvalla plain into the lake. The road to Thingvellir led into the Almannagjá along steep steps of lava. The people who visited the *thing* found pasturage for their horses on the grassy plain along the rift. A short distance from the Öxará, not far from the lake, a craggy portion of the plain has been cut off by fissures which surround it on all sides except in one place where a narrow entrance is found. This singular stronghold was long supposed to be the old Mount of Laws where the Althing assembled. It has later been shown, however, that the old Mount of Laws was not located here, but on the west side of the river Öxará.[25] At the opening of the session the thingstead was formally consecrated by the *alsherjargoði,* a descendant of the first settler, Ingolf Arnarson, who bore that title and had the right to perform this ceremony. From the highest elevation of the Mount of Laws the *lögsögumaðr* would proclaim the laws and decrees. From the same place all announcements to the assembly were also made by persons who for this purpose were allowed to ascend the Mount of Laws. Below was the place of the *lögrétta,* which no one but the members was allowed

[25] Kr. Kålund, *Aarbøger for nordisk Oldkyndighed.*

to enter. Around the *lögrétta* the *thingmenn* and visiting public were assembled. On the plain between the Mount of Laws and the Almannagjá booths, or temporary dwellings, were erected for the members of the *thing* and those who attended its sessions. These booths were simple four-cornered structures with gabled walls without roofs. Before the opening of the session they were covered with a temporary roof of woolen cloth, the walls were draped with cloth, and the booth was divided into separate chambers for the *thingmenn* in the same manner. The *goði* had to attend the Althing unless lawfully prevented, in which case the other *goðar* of his district chose an alternate. If a *goði* remained absent from the session of the Althing without due cause, he forfeited his *goðorð,* so also if he arrived at the *thing* later than the prescribed time, Thursday evening before sunset. A certain number of *thingmenn* from the *goðorð* had to accompany the *goði* to the Althing. At the meeting of the *várthing* he could choose one-sixth of their number either by oral agreement or by lot, but as many could go as wished to attend the *thing.* Those who were sent as representatives from the *goðorð* received board, lodging and free transportation to and from the *thing.*[26] They were also exempt for the year from paying the *thing-fararkaup,* a tax of ten *alnar vaðmál* assessed by the *goði* on all the *thingmenn* who did not attend the Althing.[27]

Besides this tax other dues were also payable to the *goði.* A temple toll, *hoftollr,* was collected for maintaining the temple and defraying the expenses connected with the public worship. A *fjörbaugr* of one *mörk,* together with a cow or a four-year-old ox, was paid him when the property of an outlawed person was seized by *féránsdómr,* and a *saudatollr,* or tax of one sheep from each *thingmaðr,* was levied in some districts, though it does not seem to have been universally established. Of considerable pecuniary value also was the free entertainment given the *goði* and his followers when he traveled about in his *goðorð.* His right to supervise trade also constituted a valuable source of income. When

[26] *Grágás,* ch. 33.
[27] *Ibidem,* ch. 59.

a merchant ship from Norway or elsewhere came to Iceland, the nearest *goði* would ride to the shore to inspect the goods and fix the prices for which they were to be sold. If no quarrel arose, he was usually asked to select what he desired of the goods, and the news from abroad was first told him by the merchants. In return for this courtesy the *goði* would invite the master of the ship with his men to his home, where the most liberal hospitality was shown them.[28] The income of the *goði* from these various sources was not large, and probably never fully covered the expenses connected with his public duties. He had to furnish the animals for the religious sacrifices, he was responsible for the upkeep of the temple, and during the sessions of the Althing he had to provide at his own expense free board and lodgings for his *thingmenn* at his own booths. As he had to display on all occasions the munificence becoming a chieftain, his expenses were often quite out of proportion to his limited income, hence the old laws state that a *goðorð* was not to be made subject to tithes, since "it is an office of power but not one of profit." [29]

The meeting of the Althing was the great event of the year, not only politically but also socially. All men of means and prominence would go to Thingvellir on that occasion, often accompanied by their wives and daughters, to meet friends and relatives from other settlements, to learn the news from abroad, listen to cases tried in the courts, and to take part in the games and amusements. The young men from all parts of Iceland would naturally flock to so eventful a gathering to witness the *thing* proceedings and indulge in the national sports. Marriages were contracted, as seen from the "Njálssaga" narrative about Gunnar of Hlidarendi and Hallgerda, or Hrafn Önundsson's wooing of Helga the Fair, told in the "Gunnlaugssaga Ormstungu." Expeditions to foreign lands were arranged, and invitations were extended for great feasts at which the conviviality of the Icelanders found its fullest expression.

[28] *Sturlungasaga*, iii, ch. 9, p. 131; ch. 20, p. 223 ff. *Njálssaga*, ch. 101, p. 157. *Landnámabók*, iv, ch. 4, p. 246.
[29] *Grágás*, ch. 255. *Landnámabók*, i, p. 9.

The old culture continued to flourish. The fine traits of
early aristocratic life suffered no impairment, as the new
state organization preserved with pious conservatism the
features of political and social life which had been evolved
in the mother country through a long national development.
But an uncompromising adherence to the old ways tended
to isolate the colonists from the forces of progress. They
had turned their backs on innovations and the new elements
of growth which gradually transformed political life in Norway. To them tradition had made even the unimportant
sacred. Custom, elevated into an unwritten law, had become a sufficient reason for maintaining features of social
life which were harmful and objectionable. The chieftains,
who were governed by the narrow self-interest characteristic
of a privileged upper class, shooed away every new idea and
clung to the past with a veneration which made Icelandic
society unprogressive. This became the more harmful because of the isolation of the country. Their limited intercourse with other nations so retarded the growth of new
ideas that the uncanny features of pagan life continued to
flourish without abatement even after the introduction of
Christianity. This is apparent as well in the people's attitude to their own laws and institutions as in their private
intercourse. With a highly developed jurisprudence and a
well organized system of courts they nevertheless failed to
maintain social order and to administer justice with efficient
impartiality. In the public mind the law lacked majesty
and authority. It was regarded as something for lawyers
to sharpen their wits upon; something to be evaded, or even
ignored. Civic life was not regulated according to the principles of law, but continued to be controlled by custom.
Cases growing out of homicide and other great crimes were
often not brought before the courts, but were settled in the
most primitive way by personal revenge. Even after the
reform of the judicial system in 965 blood-feud continued
to rage unabated, as it was still regarded by many as the
most manly and direct way of obtaining justice. Two systems may therefore be said to have existed side by side;
that of law acting through the courts, and that of custom

operating through personal revenge. In a progressive society the primitive method of personal vengeance would have been gradually discredited; the growth of higher ideals would have strengthened the sacredness and authority of the law; but in Iceland this old destructive custom continued to cast its shadow over social life. Often it developed into a mad fury which stands in striking contrast to their great legal knowledge and their well organized judicial tribunals. The sagas furnish abundant proof of this strange dualism in the early period of Icelandic history. The pivotal feature of nearly all of these stories is a blood-feud around which all other events are grouped. A chain of events may be wrought into a great epic like the "Njálssaga," where the wrongs and provocations, the plots and counterplots finally culminate in the slaying of Gunnar of Hlidarendi, the burning of Njáll and his family, and the bloody encounter at the Althing. The feud may constitute a single tragic plot, as in the "Gunnlaugssaga Ormstungu," where the interest centers in the rivalry of the scalds Gunnlaug and Hrafn for the hand of Helga the Fair; or a series of feuds may give rise to dramatic events more loosely connected, as in the "Eyrbyggjasaga" or the "Víga-Stýrssaga ok Heiðarvíga." But however the theme may be varied, it presents the same picture of social conditions. There is passion uncontrolled, bloody encounters which destroy whole families, and feed new fuel to the consuming flames of hatred and revenge. Strong men, beautiful and heroic women move through these stormy scenes like heroes and heroines in a Greek tragedy. Nothing could stay the avenging hand, as the courts were unable to restrain the wrongdoer or provide adequate remedy for the misdeed. The paragraphs in the code might be wise and equitable, but above them stood the sensitive, arrogant, martial spirit of the people, jealous of its honor, ready to sacrifice home, friends, law or life on the slightest provocation. Such was the spirit of early Iceland. The new political organization had failed to establish a strong state chiefly because the people were so little amenable to law. But it created a society so well suited to the character and temper of the people that their native genius could

freely unfold its creative and restless activity. The rich
intellectual life which blossomed forth on the barren moors
of Iceland was mainly due to an exuberant spirit proud of
its old freedom, unsaddened and unsubdued by irksome
political and social restraints.

4. Introduction of Christianity

From the time of King Harald Haarfagre, and probably
even earlier, the peoples of the North came under the influence of ideas hitherto foreign to the pagan native mind.
The Viking expeditions had brought the Norsemen into
close contact with the Christian nations of Europe; a lively
commercial intercourse had developed, and the Norse colonies established on the western islands served as a mart
where people of different faith and nationality could meet
and exchange ideas. This stimulating intercourse created
a new era of intellectual growth in which elements of Christian thought became noticeable long before Christianity
was finally established in Norway. We have seen that
many of the Icelandic settlers who came from the western
Norse colonies had accepted baptism, or had been deeply impressed by such features of the Christian faith and worship
as they had learned to know. On all sides the new faith
was advancing also into the North. Early in the ninth century Ansgarius was preaching Christianity both in Denmark
and in Sweden, and later the archbishop of Hamburg, supported by the German king, so successfully promoted
missionary efforts in Denmark that King Harald Gormsson
accepted baptism in 965. In Norway King Haakon the
Good, son of Harald Haarfagre, reared at the English Court,
had accepted the Christian faith and sought to introduce it
in his kingdom. Both in Norway and Iceland many of the
ablest and most earnest men devoted themselves to a con-
templation of life revealing doubt in the old deities, and
yearning for a faith which should give satisfactory answers
to their queries. The old mythology contained many lofty

ideas, but as a practical religion it was bound to the temple with its sacrifices, its sprinkling of blood, and its magic incantations to propitiate cruel divinities who had nothing to offer as consolation in death or hope for the hereafter. It could give the pondering mind no more comforting answer than the story of the fading of life into the joyless shadows of ghastly Hel. How different was the message brought by Christ who came to save, to console the sorrowful, to gather men from the tribulation of the world into his own kingdom, where they would enjoy everlasting bliss! As the Norsemen were fatalists believing that whatever happened was unavoidable, they did not feel inclined to wage any determined fight in behalf of their old deities. If Christ was destined to triumph, it was decreed by fate. Many already believed that the old gods were fighting a losing battle. There was a growing feeling that something new and better was coming. "All people now let Odin's tribe go. I am also constrained to part from the kin of Njörd," sings Hallfred Vandrædaskald. About Thorkell Máni, *lögsögumaðr* in Iceland, 970-985, the "Landnámabók" says: "In his last sickness he caused himself to be carried out into the sunshine, where he recommended himself to the god who had created the sun. But he also lived as pure a life as any Christian who has the purest morals." [1] The clash between Christian European culture and Northern paganism had already begun in this vague but irrepressible conflict of ideas. Only one step was still lacking. If the wall of paganism which isolated the farthest North could be broken at any point; if the growing interest in Christian ideas should culminate in an enthusiastic acceptance of the new faith by some influential leader, adherents would rally to his support, and the final combat between the two systems would be on. This was soon to happen both in Norway and in Iceland, the only remaining abodes of primitive Germanic life.

An Icelandic leader who openly espoused the Christian cause was Thorwald Kodransson the Fartraveler. He had visited many lands, and is said to have been baptized in

[1] *Landnámabók,* i, p. 9.

Germany, probably in 981. Of still greater importance was the conversion in England of Olaf Tryggvason, who in 995 ascended the throne of Norway. The work of Christianizing the North was soon under way. The rather passive opposition of the stolid masses as well as the more hostile resistance of a few determined chieftains had to be overcome, but because of the indifference and even the friendly attitude of many of the leading men, Christianity was established with remarkable ease and rapidity when we consider the almost total absence of missionaries who could instruct the people in the new faith. According to the sagas Thorvald was born in Vatsdal in northern Iceland. But his father, who was attached to the older brother Orm, did little or nothing for him. Finally the father was prevailed upon to give him a ship so that he could visit foreign lands like other young men of good family. Thorvald left his native country and spent many years as a restless roamer and warrior in foreign lands, at first in the service of the Danish king, Svein Tjugeskegg, and later as Viking chieftain in the North Sea and the Baltic. On his journeys he also reached Saxony, Germany, where he was converted to Christianity. Fired with great enthusiasm for the new faith which he had embraced he resolved to turn missionary. Accompanied by the same Bishop Frederick who had baptized him he returned to Iceland in 981 for the purpose of converting his people to the Christian faith. They came to Gilja to Thorvald's father, and remained there the first year. Since the bishop did not know the language, he could only act as assistant and adviser while Thorvald preached to the people. The saga says that Thorvald's father, Kodran, was so impressed by the Christian ceremonies: the singing, the ringing of bells, the burning of incense, the white vestments worn by the missionaries, that he and his wife, Jarngerda, accepted the new faith together with all their people. Thorvald's brother Orm, however, did not receive baptism. Many others were also turned to Christianity already the first winter, especially in the northern districts. In the spring the missionaries moved farther west to Vididal. Here Thorvald married and settled at Lækjamot, where they remained during the next four years.[2] Through their work many had been led to accept Christianity, and others who had not wholly abandoned the old faith became so indifferent to it that they ceased to worship the heathen gods and refused to pay the prescribed temple toll. This aroused bitter resentment, especially among the chieftains. Still greater became the ill-will when Thorvald appeared and preached Christianity at the Althing in 984. Hedin from Svalbard, one of the most determined opponents of the missionaries, stirred the people to such anger that they hired poets to make lampoons about them. This so exasperated Thorvald that he slew two of the lampoonists, but Frederick bore all with patience. Through continued labors new converts were gained in the northern districts, but so hostile a public sentiment had been aroused that the missionaries were outlawed and had to leave Iceland. They sailed to Norway in 986. While they were lying in the harbor, Hedin from Svalbard, their old opponent, arrived. Thorvald watched his opportunity and slew him while he was cutting timber in the woods near by. Because of this violent and unchristian act Bishop Frederick parted from him and returned to his native country. Thorvald became a merchant and traveled through many lands. Visiting Greece and Constantinople he finally died as a monk in Russia in a monastery which he is said to have founded.

These early missionary efforts, the example of baptized Christians in the days of colonization, and especially the conversion of the Northern kingdoms, made Christianity well known in Iceland and created a religious unrest which is clearly reflected in the sagas. The faith in the old gods was waning, although the chieftains did what they could to uphold the old worship so essential to their own power and authority. That a new age was approaching was instinctively felt by all who in any degree possessed the ability to forecast events. Many who returned from foreign

---

[2] *Kristnisaga*, ch. 1 ff. *Tháttr af Thorvaldi Viðförla, Biskupasögur*, vol. i, p. 37. *Olafssaga Tryggvasonar*, ch. 139 ff. *Vatsdælasaga*, xlvl. *Landnámabók*, iii; p. 4; p. 6. *Fornmannasögur*, vol. i, ch. 137 ff. K. Maurer, *Die Bekehrung des norwegischen Stammes zum Christenthume*, vol. i, p. 19.

lands as baptized Christians told of the wonders wrought by the new faith, and prominent men declared themselves in favor of Christianity from general conviction of its superiority even without having received instruction in its doctrine. Njáll of Bergthorshváll, widely known for his wisdom and legal learning, was a friend of the new faith. The "Njálssaga" says:

"It was also rumored that the people of Norway had changed religion, that they had discarded the old faith, and that King Olaf had Christianized the western colonies; Shetland, the Orkneys, and the Faroe Islands. Many said within Njáll's hearing that they thought it strange that people would abandon their old religion. But Njáll said: 'It seems to me that the new faith must be better, and that he is fortunate who possesses it. If the men who preach it come to Iceland, I shall assist them according to my ability.'"[3]

As soon as Thangbrand the missionary arrived, Njáll was baptized with his whole family. A similar predisposition to accept the Christian religion is told also of other prominent men. As a missionary field Iceland was, indeed, white unto the harvest, but the work was still to be done, as the power of the old faith was unbroken. The Icelanders might have remained for centuries in pagan isolation had not King Olaf Tryggvason undertaken to direct the missionary efforts here as in all the other Norse colonies.

About Olaf Tryggvason's early years very little is definitely known. When he finally emerges from the twilight of romance woven about his youth by numerous legendary tales, he enters the historical arena as a young man, "tall, beautiful, strong and athletic beyond all Norsemen ever mentioned," says Snorre. After spending many years as Viking chieftain, especially in the Baltic, he had organized a great Viking army with which he began the conquest of England, an undertaking in which he was joined by the Danish king, Svein Tjugeskegg. Everywhere these two great leaders were victorious, but even in the midst of their advance Olaf yielded to the persuasions of

[3] *Njálssaga*, ch. 100.

Bishop Ælfea of Winchester. He accepted the Christian faith, was confirmed by the bishop, and concluded a treaty by which he solemnly pledged himself never again to wage war against the English. A new ambition now inspired him to worthier undertakings. He would turn crusader, regain the throne of his fathers, and introduce Christianity in the North, a great undertaking probably suggested to him by Bishop Ælfea. In 995 Olaf sailed to Norway with a small fleet accompanied by a few missionaries, among whom were Stefni Thorgilsson and Thangbrand, who later became missionaries in Iceland. Olaf soon gained the throne of Norway, and entered upon his work of introducing Christianity with true crusading zeal. Not only was the Christian faith to be introduced in his own kingdom, but also in the western colonies and other distant settlements.

The independence maintained by the settlers in Iceland so strengthened the self-assertiveness of the chieftains that a new patriotism soon manifested itself. They considered themselves a distinct people and took pride in calling themselves Icelanders when they traveled in foreign countries, but the most intimate relation with the mother country continued to exist. Many leading men from Iceland visited Norway every summer as merchants, and young men sought the royal court as scalds and *hirðmenn* to win honor and distinction. Though all allegiance to the royal house had been severed, the kings of Norway still regarded the Icelanders as Norse colonists, an integral part of the nation for whom they continued to feel a deep paternal interest. But after the death of King Harald Haarfagre no attempt was made to exert any direct influence on affairs in Iceland until Olaf Tryggvason ascended the throne. In his zeal for the cause of Christianity he paid special attention to the visiting Icelanders, whom he sought by various means to convert to the Christian faith. Prominent among these were Kjartan Olafsson, the son of Olaf Pá of Hjardarholt, and his foster-brother, Bolli Thorleiksson. According to the saga narrative they bought part interest in a ship owned by Kalf Asgeirsson, and the three sailed to Norway in the summer. They landed at Agdeness, near Trondhjem,

where they learned that Olaf Tryggvason had ascended the
throne of Norway and sought to convert all the people to
Christianity. Many Icelanders were in Trøndelagen at this
time. The scald Hallfred Ottarsson and others had
anchored their ships at the wharves before Kjartan and his
companions arrived. The saga says that they had entered
into an agreement among themselves not to accept the
Christian faith. They also asked Kjartan to join in this
agreement, and he promised to do what the others considered best in the matter. The king was in Trøndelagen at
this time, engaged in erecting churches and other buildings
in the city of Nidaros which he had just founded. One fine
day in the autumn when Kjartan and the Icelanders went
to the river Nid to look at the swimming contests, they saw
a man who excelled all others. Kjartan asked Hallfred
Ottarsson and Bolli if they would risk a swimming match
with this man, but they would not attempt it. Kjartan
then undressed and went into the water, but in the contest
he proved much inferior to the athletic stranger, who ducked
him under several times until he had to acknowledge his
defeat. After they came ashore and dressed, the stranger
revealed his identity, saying that he was King Olaf Tryggvason. He praised Kjartan for his great skill as swimmer,
and gave him his own costly mantle as a token of his friendship. But the Icelanders were not well pleased because he
accepted the present, as they considered it a sign that he
had become the king's man. Not long afterward the king
summoned them to a *thing* and spoke to them of the
Christian faith. He made a special appeal to Kjartan, asking him if he would receive baptism. The Icelanders told
him to make such reply as he thought proper, and he said
that since the king had treated them so well, since he had
neither forced them nor threatened, he would accept the
new faith, and would show the god Thor little honor on his
return to Iceland. At Christmas both he and Bolli were
baptized and became members of the king's *hirð*.[4]

The scald Hallfred, mentioned in connection with Kjar-

[4] *Heimskringla*, Ólafssaga Tryggvasonar, ch. 81. *Fornmannasögur*, Saga
Ólafs Konungs Tryggvasonar, ch. 156 ff. *Laxdœlasaga*, ch. 40.

tan and Bolli, was in all respects a typical Viking. From youth he had been a lover of adventure, self-willed and combative, gifted as a scald, but of a saucy disposition and always ready for bloodshed at the first challenge. Before he came to Norway he had been involved in a feud with a rival, Gris Sæmingsson, who married Kolfinna, a lady of whom Hallfred was enamored. In settlement of this difficulty he had to promise to leave Iceland for a period, a punishment which must have been a favor rather than a hardship, since he was now of an age when he would naturally spend some years abroad to obtain suitable training and distinction. One day while he was staying in Nidaros, King Olaf Tryggvason met him and entered into conversation with him. When the king learned that he was a scald, he asked if he who was so brave and frank a man would accept the Christian faith. Hallfred answered that he would not receive baptism without some reward. The king asked what he desired. He replied that the condition should be that the king himself should be his sponsor. The king consented, and Hallfred and his companions were baptized. Hallfred was placed under the tuition of Jostein and Karlshofdi, who were to teach him the paternoster and the credo. Also Bárd Örvi, the sons of Breidarskeggi, and all the other Icelanders who were in Nidaros accepted the Christian faith, says the saga.[5] This system of conversion, consisting chiefly in baptism urged on pagans who were wholly unfamiliar with the Christian doctrine, could not effect any real change of heart in the new converts, as they had not even had the opportunity to associate with Christians, like some of the early settlers in Iceland who came from the western colonies. Their sojourn in Norway had been short, and even here Christianity was preached for the first time. When they accepted baptism, it was usually for some ulterior motive, or because they regarded it as an interesting adventure. The chief reason seems to have been that they wished to be on friendly terms with the popular and powerful King Olaf. If they humored him, he show-

[5] *Fornmannasögur,* Saga Ólafs Konungs Tryggvasonar, ch. 164. *Laxdælasaga,* ch. 40.

ered favors upon them, invited them to his court, and made
them his scalds and *hirðmenn;* if they opposed him, they
would be made to feel his displeasure, and might not even
be allowed to enter the harbors. To some baptism represented a sort of conversion to the new faith, to others it
might mean very little. But the king himself was so little
familiar with the inwardness and true character of Christianity that he regarded baptism as conversion, and imposed
no restrictions on the subsequent life and conduct of those
who had thus given their allegiance to the Christian church.
Hallfred Ottarsson is quite a typical representative of this
kind of baptized but unconverted pagans. After his baptism he was with the king and enjoyed his special friendship;
but about the Christian religion he knew little and cared
still less. One day he stepped before the king and asked if
he would listen to a song which he had made in his honor.
When the king declined, Hallfred said that if he would not
listen to it, he would abandon the new faith which he had
received, for that was not any more poetic than the song.
The king replied: "You shall be called Vandrædaskald
because you are hard to please, and I will listen to the
song." After Hallfred had recited it, the king was well
pleased and asked him to join his *hirð,* an offer which Hallfred accepted on the condition that the king should not dis-
miss him from the court for anything which he might happen to do. He had formerly been in Haakon Jarl's service,
now he became King Olaf's hirdscald, and was since known
as Hallfred Vandrædaskald. He continued to lead an adventurous life, and committed violent acts with the same
heartless nonchalance as before. In a quarrel he killed the
king's *hirðmaðr* Ottar, a deed punishable by death; but his
life was spared because the king was his sponsor. Not long
afterward the king gave him the unpleasant task of punish-
ing a personal enemy, Thorleif Spaki, whom Hallfred
attacked and blinded in one eye. An adventurous journey
finally took him to Sweden, where he married a lady by the
name of Ingibjörg, who accepted the Christian faith and
accompanied him to Nidaros. After her death he again
visited Iceland, where the feud with his old rival, Gris, broke

out anew. In order to disgrace Gris, he ravished his wife
Kolfinna, a deed for which he was sentenced to pay a fine to
his rival. In all his conduct there is not a trace of Christian
spirit. The only attractive quality shown by the scald is
the old pagan virtue of faithfulness to his lord the king.
When he learned of King Olaf's death in the battle of
Svolder in the year 1000, he hastened to Norway, and made
a song in his memory, in which he voiced the king's praise
and his own deep sorrow. There is a ring of real sadness in
these verses which shows how deep was the attachment
which he felt for the great king:

> Desolate are the Northlands
> now that the king has fallen.
>
> Break will the earth and the heavens
> ere a king as good
> as the glad Olaf
> shall again be born.

It is said that he attempted to kill Eirik Jarl, who had
fought against King Olaf at Svolder; that he was seized and
laid in fetters, but received his freedom as a reward for a
song which he made in the jarl's honor. Under these circumstances he could hope for no further favors in Norway.
He set out for Iceland, but died on the return voyage.
During his last moments he showed a certain Christian-
mindedness which had never come to light in his conduct.
Now, he said, he would gladly die if he knew that his soul
would be saved.

In 996 Stefni Thorgilsson, a descendant of Ketill Flatnef,
was sent as missionary to Iceland. He was an Icelander by
birth, but as a young man he had journeyed abroad, and
after receiving baptism in Denmark he had joined King
Olaf in the British Isles. He was brave and well-inten-
tioned, but as he lacked both Christian knowledge and true
piety he was ill prepared for so important a mission. When
he arrived in Iceland, shortly before the opening of the
Althing, he began to preach publicly with great zeal. Had
he possessed the necessary tact and self-restraint, his labor

might have borne fruit; but the opposition which he encountered aroused his anger, and as he was more skilled in
the use of arms than in the art of persuasion, he undertook
with the aid of his men to pull down the heathen temples
and burn the images of the gods. Toleration in religious
matters was still regarded as a well established principle of
personal freedom. The question of religious belief was
usually considered a private matter to be settled by every
person according to his own conviction, and few examples
are found of persecution or religious bigotry. But an open
attack on the established institutions naturally aroused
general resentment. When the Althing assembled, a law
was passed which condemned to punishment any one
who did violence to the temples or offered insult to
the gods. Stefni was outlawed and had to leave Iceland.[6] With nothing accomplished he returned to Norway, and the sagas state that he met his death in
Denmark at the hands of Sigvalde Jarl, one of King Olaf's
enemies.

Upon Stefni's return King Olaf sent his chaplain Thangbrand to preach Christianity in Iceland. The newly baptized Kjartan Olafsson had also been requested to undertake
this mission, but declined, as he feared that he might arouse
the enmity of his friends and kinsmen. Thangbrand, who is
said to have been the son of a German count, had been
compelled to flee from his native land because of a murder
committed in a quarrel. In England he too had met King
Olaf, and after taking holy orders accompanied the king to
Norway, where he became parish priest in the first organized
Christian parish on the island of Moster. His knowledge
of the Christian doctrine might have made him a valuable
man had not his violent temper and vicious habits rendered
him unfit for so sacred a calling. He not only squandered
the income of his parish, but he organized piratic raids to
replenish his depleted stores, an unchristian conduct for
which the king finally called him to account. Due repentance saved him from banishment, but he was sent instead
as missionary to Iceland. The story of Thangbrand's mis-

* *Kristnisaga,* ch. 6.

sion is told in several sagas with some variation in details.[7]
According to the "Ólafssaga Tryggvasonar" he was not well
received by the people of Iceland, possibly because of the
impression made by former missionaries. But the chieftain
Sidu-Hall of Thvotá, who was friendly disposed to the
Christian faith, welcomed him and invited him to his home.
A tent was raised in which religious services were conducted.
Hall is said to have spent much time talking with the
missionaries about Christianity. He supplied them abun-
dantly with all necessaries, and was finally baptized, together with his whole household. In the spring of 998
Thangbrand began more active work. Accompanied by
Sidu-Hall and his assistant he undertook an extensive missionary tour and seems to have had notable success. But
determined opposition was also encountered which kindled
the martial spirit of the combative priest. At Stafafell they
met a man by the name of Thorkell who was so violently
opposed to Christianity that he challenged Thangbrand to a
duel. The doughty missionary advanced to the combat
with a crucifix attached to his shield and slew his antagonist,
a sort of missionary work quite in his style, nor was it the
last time that he resorted to this sort of argument. At
Arnarstaksheid his assistant Gudleif Arason slew another
opponent, Galdra-Hedin, and at Fljotslid the poet Veter-
lidi, who ventured to compose lampoons about them, suffered the same fate. Thorvald Veili, who had gathered a
band and planned to attack them, was also slain. But in
spite of his violent methods, duels and homicides Thangbrand was able to continue his labors from 997 till 999, and
many leading chieftains were baptized. Besides Sidu-Hall
and Njáll of Bergthorshváll are mentioned Gizur the White,
Hjalti Skeggjason, Hilld the Old, Ingjald Thorkelsson and
others. On his first missionary journey Thangbrand traveled from Thvotá through the southern districts to Bergthorshváll and Grimsnes. When the Althing assembled, he

[7] *Kristnisaga*, ch. 6 ff. *Íslendingabók*, ch. 7. *Laxdœlasaga*, ch. 41.
Heimskringla, Ólafssaga Tryggvasonar, ch. 73, ch. 84. *Historia Norwegiœ*,
ch. 14. *Historia de Antiquitate Regum Norwagiensium*, ch. 12. *Ólafssaga
Tryggvasonar*, ch. 188, 216.

also appeared at the *thing* and preached Christianity. This he could now venture to do because the Christians had already become so numerous that even at the *thing* they appeared as a strong party led by such chieftains as Sidu-Hall, Gizur the White and Hjalti Skeggjason, who were able to hold in check the adherents of the old faith. His appearance at the *thing* caused the greatest excitement. The Althing outlawed him, and the relatives of those whom he had slain would have seized him had he not been defended by Njáll of Bergthorshváll and other influential Christian chieftains. After the Althing he accompanied Sidu-Hall to Thvotá. He made a trip into the northeastern districts, where he baptized a few persons; but because of growing opposition he could accomplish little, and he returned to his friend Sidu-Hall. The "Olafssaga Tryggvasonar" states that he now made ready to leave Iceland, but that his ship was driven by contrary winds to the Borgarfjord, where he was invited by Gizur the White, one of the leading Christian chieftains, to stay with him at Skálholt. Here he spent the winter 998-999. It seems more likely, however, that Gizur had given him such an invitation at the Althing in the summer of 998, and that his going to the Borgarfjord was not due to any such accident as mentioned by the saga. It is quite certain that while at Skálholt he baptized Gizur the White, his son-in-law Hjalti Skeggjason and other chieftains. That winter he is also said to have met Steinun, the mother of Skaldref. The saga says that she began to preach paganism to him, asking him if he had not heard that Christ had been challenged by Thor to a duel, and that he did not dare to fight. "I have heard," replied Thangbrand, "that Thor would be but dust and ashes if God would not let him live." As this incident is mentioned only in the "Njálssaga," it may be an invention of later writers. His ship lying in the Borgarfjord had been damaged by the winter storms, and while it was being repaired he made a trip into the western districts, proceeding as far as Hagi in Bardastrond, where Gest Odleifsson received the sign of the cross and aided him in his work. Gest advised him not to go farther west, says the saga, as the people there were hard to deal with. "If the new faith is to be introduced," said Gest, "it will be accepted at the Althing when all the chieftains are present." Thangbrand answered that he had preached Christianity at the *thing*, and that nowhere had he met stronger opposition. "You have nevertheless done the greater part," said Gest. "Even if it shall be granted someone else to have it formally accepted, it will then only go according to the old adage that the tree is not felled by the first stroke." New clashes occurred between the two parties at the Althing in the summer, when the skald Hjalti Skeggjason in open challenge to the yet heathen populace recited a song in which he called Odin and Freyja dogs, an unseemly outburst which could only hurt the cause which he was trying to further. For this insult to the gods he was sentenced to banishment for three years, and he and his father-in-law, Gizur the White, sailed to Norway. After spending some time in the southern districts Thangbrand visited his friend Njáll at Bergthorshváll. His ship was now ready, and in the summer of 999 he sailed to Norway accompanied by his assistant, Gudleif Arason.[8]

Upon his return Thangbrand represented conditions in Iceland in the darkest colors. King Olaf was angry and disappointed because this new attempt to Christianize the island had also failed. In a resentful outburst he ordered that all the heathen Icelanders in the harbor of Nidaros should be seized and put to death, but several influential Christian Icelanders, among whom were Kjartan Olafsson, and also Gizur the White and Hjalti Skeggjason, who had just arrived from Iceland, pleaded with the king to show greater forbearance. They promised that all heathen Icelanders in Nidaros should receive baptism, and undertook to have Christianity fully established in Iceland. This wise counsel appeased the king. The heathen Icelanders were baptized, and Gizur and Hjalti remained at the king's court

[8] According to the *Kristnisaga* Thangbrand spent three years in Iceland; but all other sources are quite well agreed that he stayed only from 997 till 999. This must, therefore, be considered the best established view. See Björn M. Olsen, *Um kristnitökunna árið 1000*, p. 33 ff.

till in the summer of the year 1000, when they returned
home to carry out their important mission. It is very likely
that they were acting as agents for the Christian party in
Iceland in soliciting aid from the king, as matters were sure
to come to a crisis between the two parties at the next meeting of the Althing. They so timed their voyage that they
arrived in Iceland while the Althing was assembled. Although Hjalti had been outlawed, they hastened at once to
the *thing,* where all their friends and followers were assembled. Being well aware of the resistance they would encounter they marched to the *thing* in battle array, says the saga.
The heathens rushed to arms, and a battle between the two
factions was averted with great difficulty. But the following day the priests who accompanied Gizur and Hjalti,
after singing mass to a great concourse of people, were
nevertheless allowed to march to the Mount of Laws in their
sacred vestments to burn incense, the fine odor of which
spread over the assembly. Hjalti and Gizur now began to
explain to the people very carefully their mission and what
King Olaf desired them to do. It is very likely that Olaf
sought to establish overlordship over Iceland in connection
with the introduction of Christianity and with the aid of the
Christian party, as he had done in the Orkneys and the
Faroe Islands under similar circumstances. No one could
doubt that behind the messengers who now spoke in favor
of the Christian faith and on behalf of the Christian party
stood the powerful and energetic King Olaf. They probably
made it clear what serious results it might lead to, if the
Icelanders continued to thwart the king in a matter which
he had sought so earnestly to further. A numerous party in
the assembly continued to make violent demonstrations and
sought to resist Christianity at all points, but Gizur's and
Hjalti's message, and their explanation of the situation
made a profound impression on all who had a better understanding of national affairs. Christianity had now been
established in all lands; in Norway and the western colonies
it was being introduced; even in Iceland a strong party
had declared in its favor. Since 965, when the new *thing*

organization was effected, some *goðar* who in some way had identified themselves with the new faith had remained outside of the state organization. Since they could not take the heathen oaths or take part in the sacrifices, they could not belong to the *things,* and they and their adherents were virtually outside of the law of the land. Some chieftains had been baptized by Thorvald Kodransson and Bishop Frederick, and several had been baptized by Thangbrand. Nine *goðar* now stood outside of the old state organization, the number of new converts was growing, and since these would use their legal right to sever their allegiance to the heathen *goðar,* and give themselves under the chieftains who supported Christianity, a complete division had taken place in the Icelandic state organization. The nine *goðar* and their followers were no longer satisfied to remain outside all law and social organization. They had now met in full force at the Althing to hear what message Gizur and Hjalti brought from Norway. They had chosen their leader Sidu-Hall as their own *lögsögumaðr,* and threatened to set up a state organization of their own, independent of that of the old *goðar.* The critical moment had come when the Icelanders would have to accept Christianity or face the responsibility of rejecting it. This explains also the rather curious circumstance that Hjalti Skeggjason, who was still under the sentence of banishment, was not only allowed to appear, but even to speak at the Althing. Both parties, no doubt, felt the gravity of the situation. Through the efforts of Sidu-Hall and other leading chieftains the *lögsögumaðr,* Thorgeir Ljosvetningagodi, was finally persuaded to agree to a compromise. Though still a heathen he ascended the Mount of Laws and made an eloquent plea in favor of Christianity to the assembled Althing. No one attempted to oppose him, and it was finally decreed that the Christian party should abandon the idea of establishing their own state organization with their own *lögsögumaðr,* and that Christianity should henceforth be the official religion in Iceland. The people who were yet heathens were to receive the sign of the cross and were to be baptized at the earliest opportunity.[9] All temples and images of the gods were declared unholy and were to be destroyed. But since the greater part of the people were yet unconverted pagans who had never heard or seen a Christian missionary, the official acceptance of Christianity was regarded mainly as a compromise between the two parties, and many heathen customs were suffered to remain. It was made a punishable offense to worship the heathen gods openly, but secret or private worship of the old deities was not forbidden, nor were such heathen customs as the exposing of infants and the eating of horseflesh to be interfered with. This compromise agreement probably saved the Icelandic state from disruption if not from foreign overlordship. What plans King Olaf Tryggvason had entertained with regard to Iceland, or what agreements he had made with Gizur and Hjalti never became known, as he fell in the battle of Svolder the same summer that they returned to Iceland.

The concessions made to non-Christians were possible only as a temporary arrangement, as Christianity could not fail to demand the official repudiation of paganism. This was soon to be accomplished through the influence of King Olaf Haraldsson (Olaf the Saint), who ascended the throne of Norway in 1016. He directed an appeal to the Christian *lögsögumaðr*, Skapti Thorodsson, that the Icelanders should purge from their laws such provisions as still permitted offensive heathen practices. This appeal was heeded. The last legal recognition of heathen customs was revoked, a step which marked, at least in an outward way, considerable progress towards the establishing of a Christian social order.[10] The king was so well pleased that he sent to Iceland a bell and timber for a church to be erected at Thingvellir. He also took steps to provide bishops for the Icelandic church. Bishop Bernhard, who had accompanied him from England, was sent to Iceland; probably also Bishop Rudolf, who is mentioned both by Ari Frodi and the

---

[9] *Fornmannsögur*, Saga Ólafs Konungs Tryggvasonar, vol. ii, ch. 229. *Íslendingabók*, ch. 7. Odd Snorrason, *Ólafssaga Tryggvasonar*, ch. 30. *Kristnisaga*, ch. 11.

[10] *Íslendingabók*, ch. 7. *Njálssaga*, ch. 105.

"Hryggjarstykki." This aid encouraged the struggling Christians, and won new support for the cause, but the progress toward real conversion was very slow. The enforcement even of a rudimentary observance of the rules of the church proved difficult. Burials and the celebration of church holidays retained the character of corresponding heathen festivals; feast days were not observed, and marriages were solemnized without regard for the church rules governing the permissible degrees of relationship. Few churches had been erected, as the building of churches had been left to private initiative. Chieftains who had received baptism, or were in any way disposed to further the cause of Christianity, built churches on their estates, as they had formerly built heathen temples, the assistance of the state being limited to the passing of regulations that the churches, once built, should be kept in a proper state of repair. The "Eyrbyggjasaga" states that the priests encouraged men to build churches by promising that as many would enter the kingdom of heaven as could find standing room in the churches which they built.. Through such private effort many had been provided, though the number was still inadequate. Snorri Godi built a church at Helgafell, and his relative Styr erected another at Hraun. Churches were also built at Skálholt, Froda, Thingvellir, Knapstadir, Borg and other places.[11] But the priests were few, and without anyone to preach the gospel churches were of little real value. Missionaries from the continent or the British Isles rendered such assistance as they could without the knowledge of the language, but it was evident that little could be accomplished before the Bible and other religious literature should be translated into Icelandic, and native young men could receive proper training in Christian schools. The fact that the churches had no endowments or fixed sources of income also made it difficult to provide the necessary means for active church work. But the main

[11] *Laxdœlasaga*, 51, 66, 70, 78. *Eyrbyggjasaga*, 51, 53. Pétur Pétursson, *Commentatio de Jure Ecclesiarum in Islandia ante et post Reformationem*, 2. K. Maurer, *Island*, 82. *Heimskringla, Saga of Olaf the Saint*, 124. R. Keyser, *Den norske Kirkes Historie under Katholicismen*, p. 87 ff.

difficulty after Christianity was officially established was
the lack of parish priests. In an effort to overcome this
obstacle two alternatives suggested themselves. The chieftains who built the churches could receive holy orders and
conduct religious services, thus adding the dignity of priesthood to that of chieftain, as in pagan times. Many chose
to increase their influence in this way though they were
wholly unfit for the calling. Others hired as priests for
their churches untrained young men who were willing to
work for a small compensation, and were joined to the
chieftain's household like other servants. Often the chieftains selected for this calling young boys, and kept them in
their families until they arrived at such an age that they
could be ordained by the bishop and attached to their home
church. In either case the priesthood became an office of
secondary importance, so low in rank and devoid of all
qualities of leadership that it could exercise but small
influence on the intellectual and social life of the people.
So little dignity attached to this office that even after they
had received holy orders the priests were often kept in a
strange state of dependence and inferiority verging on serf-
dom. According to the church code the chieftain could
demand that no one, on pain of being outlawed, should
harbor a priest who had run away from his church, and his
return could be demanded like that of any other slave.[12]
The Icelandic clergy continued to live in married state.
Some priests even kept concubines as in the days of paganism without offending prevailing public sentiment.

An important step towards the remedying of the most
serious defects in Icelandic religious and social life was the
appointment of native bishops and the establishing of
permanent dioceses. Isleif Gizursson, son of Gizur the
White who built the first church at Skálholt, was made
bishop in 1055,[13] being the first native Icelander elevated to
that important office. He had studied in Germany, and

[12] *Grágás*, ch. 3.
[13] *Islandske Annaler*, edited by Gustav Storm, p. 470. *Íslendingabók*,
ch. 9. *Kristnisaga*, ch. 12. *Hungrvaka*, ch. 2. *Tháttr af Ísleifi Biskupi*,
Biskupasögur, vol. i.

was installed in his office by Archbishop Adalbert of Bremen by order of the pope. No diocese had yet been organized in Iceland, but Isleif became a resident bishop, as he stayed on his father's estate at Skálholt, where he also organized a school for preparing young men for the priesthood. A small income was provided for defraying the expenses of his household, a *tollr*, probably a head tax levied on all the people of the island; but for the support of himself and his family he was, nevertheless, dependent chiefly on his own means. Several bishops, some of them impostors, appeared in Iceland in his time and created much trouble. But matters improved in the days of his son and successor, Gizur Isleifsson, who was bishop of Skálholt from 1082 till 1118. He possessed marked qualities of leadership, and loved to rule. He accepted the office of bishop only when the chieftains who elected him at the Althing promised to submit to all church regulations which he might make. "And so it came to pass," says an old writer, "that everyone had to sit and stand as he commanded, young and old, rich and poor, men and women; and it can be truthfully said that he was both king and bishop in the island as long as he lived." Gizur secured the passage of a law making Skálholt a permanent bishop's seat, and the Skálholt estate together with other lands and property was given as an endowment to the new diocese. In 1096 the system of tithes, giving the church fixed revenues, was introduced through his efforts.[14] For the proper administration of this measure the first enumeration was made of all the taxpayers in the land. They were found to number 4500, possibly representing a total population of about 50,000 people.[15] Gizur also gave his consent to the creation of a second bishopric of Hólar for the northern districts of Iceland. With the consent of the clergy and the people he selected the priest Jon Ögmundsson as the one to be elevated to this new diocese. Jon, who was consecrated bishop by the archbishop of Lund in Skåne in 1106, proved to be a pious and able

[14] *Diplomatarium Islendicum, Islenzkt fornbrefasafn,* vol. 1, p. 70 ff. *Kristnisaga,* ch. 12.

[15] *Kristnisaga,* ch. 13.

man, and was held in high esteem. He built the cathedral
church at Hólar, and also organized a school where young
men received instruction in Latin, poetry and music in
preparation for the priesthood.[16]   Bishop Gizur maintained
order in the church, and was able to exercise such authority
even over the turbulent chieftains that Ari Frodi says of
him that "he was more honored by his countrymen than
any other man whom we know to have lived in this island."
"So many tears were shed at the bier of Bishop Gizur,"
says another old writer, "that it will never be forgotten by
those who shed them as long as they live. All agree that
his death was an irreparable loss. It has also been the
opinion of all men of good judgment that because of his
rare gifts and unusual talents he was the greatest man in
Iceland both of laymen and clergy." [17]

The final step in the organization of the Christian church
in Iceland was the adoption in 1123 of a code of church laws
compiled by the bishops Thorlak Runolfsson of Skálholt
and Ketill Thorsteinsson of Hólar, the successors of Gizur
and Jon.[18]   A few years earlier a new civil code, the
"Hafliðaskrá," was compiled under the general supervision
of the able jurist and great chieftain Haflidi Marsson. Both
these codes are found as parts of a later digest, the
"Grágás."

The bishops were elected by the Althing, and were consecrated by the head of the church province of which Iceland formed a part, the archdiocese of Bremen-Hamburg,
later by the archbishop of Lund in Skåne, and finally by the
archbishop of Nidaros in Norway. As the priesthood occupied so inferior a social position, the bishops alone could
be said to exercise any religious authority. As members of
the *lögrétta* they were also able to influence lawmaking.
But the legislation for the church was done by the same
secular body which legislated for the state, and in all cases
except purely disciplinary matters the clergy was amenable
to the same laws, and subject to the jurisdiction of the

[16] *Jónssaga hins helga, Biskupasögur,* vol. i.
[17] *Hungrvaka,* ch. 7.
[18] *Grágás,* ch. 17. *Diplomatarium Islendicum,* vol. i, ch. 22.

same courts as other citizens. In this way the church of Iceland became strongly national, but the official position of the clergy, as well as the social standing and private lives of the priests, made it so wholly secular in spirit that it failed to curb prevalent evils, or to exercise any marked spiritual leadership. The priestly office, even when exercised by men of rank, was usually regarded as of secondary importance, and was combined with secular callings of various kinds. Priests would hold the high office of *lögsögumaðr* or would act as heads of *goðorðs*. Some were merchants or sailors, others managers of estates or overseers superintending the erection of buildings. The nickname of "half-priest" applied to one of them seems to have fitted them all, observes J. E. Sars.[19] In their moral life they rose little above the general social level. Even those of the highest standing and ability were tempted to yield to the old spirit of lawless violence. Ketill Thorsteinsson, who succeeded Jon Ögmundsson as the second bishop of Hólar, 1122-1145, was married to a daughter of Bishop Gizur of Skálholt. When a rumor was circulated that Gudmund Oddsson had attempted to lead his wife astray, Ketill, provoked to jealousy and forgetting the dignity of his ecclesiastical office, attacked Gudmund on the public highway, with the result that he was worsted in the encounter, and lost an eye. This episode seems to have calmed the spirit of the combative prelate. He was afterward as eager to show Christian forbearance as he had hitherto been violent and vindictive. When Gudmund at last lost everything and became dependent on others, Ketill offered to care for him as long as he lived.[20]

The outward religious forms which had been substituted for the old pagan faith had not yet become a force able to control public sentiment and morals. As a rule they were only an imperfect covering of a state of agnosticism and religious indifference which manifested itself in a low moral

[19] J. E. Sars, *Udsigt over den norske Historie*, ii, p. 56. K. Maurer, *Bekehrung des norwegischen Stammes*, ii, 464 ff. Finnur Jónsson, *Historia Ecclesiastica Islandiæ*, p. 112 ff.

[20] *Ljósvetningasaga*, ch. 31. *Sturlungasaga*, vol. 1, 24, 25.

tone, and in continued spitefulness and violence characteristic of pagan social life. It was through the impressive
ceremonies of the Catholic church, through its fasts and
penances, through its church laws, backed by the powerful
organization of the Roman hierarchy, rather than through
religious conviction and moral teachings that Christianity
exerted its first influence on the people of Iceland. A new
day was to dawn through the coming of Christianity; new
opportunities for intellectual and social progress were
created through the closer connection with all Christian
nations established by the church; but the leaven of the
Christian faith had to work for centuries before the pagan
mind of Iceland yielded fully to its spiritualizing and ennobling influence.

5. Climate and Natural Conditions in Iceland. Early Social Life

The rapid colonization of Iceland shortly after its discovery was mainly due to conditions which forced many
chieftains to leave Norway and the western colonies to seek
new homes in this far-away island. If circumstances had
remained favorable to the aristocracy, they would have
remained at home; only the poorer landless class would
have emigrated, and centuries might have passed before
the colony would have reached any degree of strength, as
the island possesses few features which could attract settlers. It lies in latitude 63° 30', so snug up against the
arctic circle that at midwinter the sun does not rise above
the horizon for a week in the northern districts, and in the
southern part the day is only three hours long from sunrise
to sunset. At the summer solstice the day in the southern
districts is twenty hours long, and in the northern part the
sun does not set for about a week. The average temperature is higher in Iceland than in corresponding latitudes
elsewhere except on the west coast of Norway; but because
of the high latitude the summer is short, and especially in
the northern districts the climate is generally raw and cold.

The Greenland Current, which moves from the frozen arctic regions in a southwesterly direction north of Iceland, often carries large floes of ice to the northern shores, accompanied by fogs and a chilly atmosphere. On the high plateau of the interior, which is covered in many places by immense glaciers, the climate is cold and stormy. Little vegetation is found on this barren waste; but when it is illuminated by the brilliant, many-colored northern lights prevalent in high latitudes, few regions of the earth equal it in wild grandeur. Frequently, too, the ice fields and snowy mountain summits are lit up by the lurid fires of the numerous active volcanoes which stud the plateau, for Iceland still hangs like a boiling caldron over the unextinguished subterranean fires to which it owes its origin. One hundred and thirty volcanoes have been counted in the island, of which twenty-five have been active within historic times. Among the largest and best known in southern Iceland are Katla, which since the time of colonization has had fourteen eruptions, and Hekla with a record of eighteen eruptions or more since 1104. Measured by the violence of the eruptions as well as the material ejected Hekla is probably the largest active volcano in the world. In the northern part, in the region of Myvatn, are also found a number of large volcanoes, among which are Krafla, Hverfjall, Leirhnukr, and Viti with a crater 1000 feet in diameter. In the east central part Askja, and near the southeasterly coast Öræfajökull tower prominently.[1] The southwestern part of the island is especially a center of volcanic activity. Great volcanoes abound in these districts, and in Arnessysla are also found numerous hot springs and geysers—fifty in all—of which the largest is Geysir, which ejects a column of boiling water to the height of 100 feet. Throughout the island numerous volcanoes both dead and active, solfataras, fumeroles, hot springs, hot waterfalls, rifts and lava beds bear evidence of the volcanic forces which have convulsed it, and which since the time of its first settlement have filled Icelandic history with many a woeful catastrophe. Numerous mountain

[1] *Lýsing Íslands, Ágrip eftir Th. Thoroddsen.* Eggert Olafsson, *Reise igjennem Island,* vol. ii, p. 225 ff.

streams have cut their paths from the high glacier-covered snow-capped interior, and leap in large waterfalls to the sea. They add to the scenic grandeur of the landscape, and in the future they may be destined to play an important part in a new economic development, when their hitherto unused forces shall be tamed to the useful labor of turning the wheels of industry. Among the most noteworthy waterfalls is the Dettifoss in the river Jökulsá in northern Iceland, the largest in the island. This great mountain stream makes a perpendicular plunge of 350 feet, forming an imposing cataract. The Gullfoss in the river Hvitá, in southern Iceland, is also a very large waterfall, as the stream plunges in two successive falls over a precipice about 190 feet high. The Skogafoss, south of the Eyjafjallajökull, has a fall of about 200 feet, but a smaller volume of water. Very noteworthy also are the Eldeyjarfoss, Godafoss and Ullarfoss in the river Skjálfandafljot in northern Iceland; also the Hengifoss in Flotsdal in eastern Iceland, 360 feet high, but with a relatively small volume of water.

The total area of Iceland is 40,426 square miles, but the inhabitable portion is limited to the valleys and lowlands fringing the coast. Here the climate is mild and pleasant, considering the high latitude, as the neighboring Gulf Stream greatly influences the temperature. This ocean current flows northward between Iceland and the British Isles. But south of Iceland a subsidiary stream, the Denmark Current, is shunted off, and passes along the southern and western coasts, up the Denmark Sound, between Iceland and the Greenland Current. In the eastern, southern and western districts the climate is so modified by these warm currents that the average temperature falls but little below the freezing point even during the coldest winter months, January-March, while in summer the heat may at times be quite intense. In eastern Iceland the thermometer is known to have registered 86° F. in the shade, though that is quite unusual. Eastern, southern and western Iceland have on the whole a genial insular climate with a relatively low summer temperature. The climate in northern Iceland, on the other hand, is of a distinct continental type, severe and cold. Great ice-floes are often carried to this part of the island by the cold Polar Current, which flows in a southwesterly direction toward the coasts of Greenland. Not only during the winter months but often far into the summer cold and foggy weather prevails, caused by the ice drift piled close against the shores. The average temperature in northern Iceland is, therefore, considerably lower than in other parts of the island. The following figures on the temperature of Iceland in the southwestern district of Reykjavik and the northern district of Eyjafjord have been compiled by Mr. Petermann in the "Journal of the English Geographical Society," vol. xxii: [2]

Reykjavik		Eyjafjord	
Feb.	28°.31 F.	Feb.	16°.50 F.
March	29°.86	March	20°.66
April	36°.46	April	27°.50
May	44°.80	May	36°.14
June	51°.58	June	43°.66
July	56°.19	July	46°.94
August	52°.86	August	46°.94
Sept.	46°.45	Sept.	43°.16
Oct.	36°.91	Oct.	34°.34
Nov.	30°.45	Nov.	35°.88
Dec.	29°.41	Dec.	18°.32
Jan.	29°.82	Jan.	25°.70

As the real productive summer heat is wanting, grain is not raised in Iceland. The sagas tell, indeed, about the early settlers that they were sowing grain. The "Njálssaga" speaks of the "yellow harvest fields," and the Icelandic writers both from the Middle Ages and from later periods state that grain was raised in former times in a few places.[3]

---

[2] *Lýsing Íslands.* Richard F. Burton, *Ultima Thule or a Summer in Iceland,* vol. 1, p. 60 ff.

[3] *Landnámabók,* part i, 6; part ii, 20; part iii, 3. *Njálssaga,* ch. 3. *Sturlungasaga,* vol. 1, 13. *Egilssaga,* 29. *Gullthorissaga* ch. 10. Abbot Arngrim of Thingeyrar, who died in 1361, writes: "Grain grows in a few places in the southern districts, but only barley." Björn M. Ólsen, *Um kornyrkja á Íslandi,* in *Bunaðarrit,* 1910. Eggert Olafsson og Bjarne Paulsson, *Reise igjennem Island,* vol. i, p. 6 f.; vol. ii, p. 182 ff. Arngrimur Jónsson, *Crymogæa,* p. 52. Th. Thoroddsen, *Landfrædissaga Íslands,* vol. ii, p. 137, 183 ff.

But the testimony of all these writers makes it clear that grain has never been raised in Iceland to any considerable extent, and in modern times it has ceased to be cultivated. The only agricultural products are turnips, some varieties of cabbage, and potatoes, which have been raised with success since 1759. With the almost total absence of grain, and the potato yet unknown, it is clear that Icelandic agriculture at that time was of no real importance. It may be said to have taken its beginning with the introduction of the potato, which has become a very valuable agricultural product. The food plants which grow in a wild state in Iceland are the huckleberry and the crowberry, which are found in great abundance. In some places strawberries are also found. In the mountain highlands is found the edible Iceland moss, and along the seacoasts grows the dulse (söl) and the lyme grass (elymus arenarius), a species of wild rye yielding a grain from which bread can be made. But the fine grass, mixed with beautiful and fragrant flowers, which abounds in the valleys and seacoast lowlands has always been the most important product of the soil in Iceland, as good grazing and a sufficient supply of hay has enabled the Icelanders to keep large flocks of domestic animals, which constitute one of their chief means of subsistence.

The raising of sheep has always been one of the leading branches of husbandry in Iceland. In early ages some chieftains are said to have owned flocks of 600 to 2400 sheep, though such cases must have been exceptional. Usually the more well-to-do owned from 200 to 400 head. In modern times the number of sheep has been constantly increasing until there are now over 600,000 head, and sheep skins, wool and tallow continue to be leading articles of export. Cattle have decreased in number, so that few homesteads now have twenty cows, while in early ages many had fifty, sixty or even a hundred head. In 1700 there were about 36,000 head of cattle in Iceland; in 1896 the number had fallen to 23,000, with the result that 136,000 pounds of butter had to be imported.[4] This decline is chiefly due to

[4] *Lýsing Islands*, p. 86 f. Absalon Taranger, *Udsigt over den norske Retshistorie*, p. 75 ff. *Landnámabók*, i, 14. *Eyrbyggjasaga*, 33 f., 37, 60, 151.

the development of sheep herding, which has proved more profitable. Even in early times horses were numerous and were often left to range in droves in the mountains both summer and winter. Since no vehicles could be used on the roadless lava beds, everything had to be transported on horseback, and each farmer needed a number of head. Some of the settlers had 150 to 200 horses. Great attention was paid also to the breeding of trotters [5] and fine saddle horses, and to the training of stallions for the horse fights, which was a favorite national sport.[6] The horse has continued to be one of the most important domestic animals in the country. In 1700 Iceland had 27,000 horses, in 1896 43,000. Not a few are now exported to England and Scotland, and of late years horse-flesh has come into general use as an article of food. Goats and hogs were also kept in considerable number by the early settlers.[7] At present hogs are found only in towns and trading places along the coast, but goats are found here and there throughout the whole island. Chickens, ducks and geese are also raised at present as in days of old, but not in sufficient number to be a factor of much importance in domestic economy.

From early ages the fisheries have been of great importance to the Icelanders, as fish and herring have been staple articles of export since the early part of the fourteenth century. The catching of sharks, from which train-oil is made, is also a paying pursuit, and the lakes and rivers yield a good supply of trout and salmon. In 1896 the fish export brought a total income of over a million dollars. But want of boats, ships and proper equipment has hitherto so handicapped the people that this important pursuit has not been developed to the margin of its possibility. The Icelandic

[5] *Njálssaga*, ch. 59.

[6] *Gullthórissaga*, ch. ix, says that Hauknef gave Thorir a Swedish trotter, which was fed with grain both summer and winter.

[7] "Helgi Magri came to Boar Cliff, where he put two hogs on land. The boar was called Sölfi. They were found three years later in Sölfadalr, and they had then multiplied so that there were seventy in all," *Landnámabók*, iii, 12. "It is also told that Ingimund lost some hogs. He did not find them till in the fall of the summer following, and they numbered then a hundred." *Vatsdœlasaga*, xv.

fisheries have been to a great extent in the hands of foreign
nations, especially the English and French, though of late
years an increasing number of the native population have
found occupation in this industry. In 1850 eighty-two per
cent of the people were engaged in agriculture and only
seven per cent in the fisheries. In 1890 sixty-four per cent
were farming and eighteen per cent were occupied in the
fisheries.

Wild animals are few in Iceland, but they are not wholly
wanting. Foxes are quite numerous, and the polar bear is
an occasional visitor, being carried to the island on cakes of
drifting ice.[8] The early settlers occasionally captured young
polar bears and tamed them, and they were then regarded
as precious pets, fit presents for kings. We read in the
"Vatsdælasaga" that Ingimund the Old gave bears as a
present to King Harald Haarfagre, and Isleif Gizursson,
who later became bishop of Iceland, brought with him a
polar bear and presented it to Emperor Henry III.[9] In
1563 the king of Denmark made the regulation that all
bear skins in Iceland should be sold to the king, and the
governor of the island was instructed to buy them for the
royal household. Reindeer, introduced from Norway in
1771, are now found in considerable numbers in the inland
wilds; but they have been of little economic importance, as
the problem of hunting them is connected with almost
insurmountable difficulties. Efforts have also been made
to introduce the rabbit, but without success. Along the
coast various kinds of seals are found, and walrus also
appears occasionally on the drifting ice-floes. Of other
aquatic animals the whale was for a time of such importance that the Norwegians maintained nine whaling stations in Iceland, which yielded handsome profits; but the
Icelanders did not devote themselves to this pursuit. Only
one Danish-Icelandic whaling establishment was found in
Dyrafjord in northwestern Iceland. At present there is
scarcely any whaling in Icelandic waters. Birds are found

[8] *Vatsdælasaga*, xv. *Hungrvaka*, ch. 2.
[9] *Vatsdælasaga*, xv. *Grágás*, 88. *Heimskringla, Harald Haardraadessaga*,
ch. 72. *Hungrvaka*, ch. 2.

in large numbers, especially along the coasts. Fulmars, guillmots, gulls, kittiwakes, puffins and other aquatic fowl inhabit the bird cliffs in such vast assemblages that the people derive a considerable income from the catch of birds, eggs and feathers. Eiderducks, ducks, geese and swans are also numerous, and gathering of the costly eiderdown is a paying pursuit. In 1880 7,600 pounds of cleaned eiderdown was exported. Inland the ptarmigan, a bird of the grouse family, is hunted extensively. In the Middle Ages the falcons, too, were much sought for the hawking sport carried on by lords and ladies in all lands. The Iceland falcons were regarded as superior to all other varieties, as they could be used for the hunt sometimes for the period of twelve years. If they were a pure white they were regarded as great treasures, and were usually secured for the royal family. King Christian IV of Denmark-Norway made the regulation that falcons could be exported from Iceland only with the king's permission, and every year he sent a ship to Iceland to bring home the necessary supply of these birds. When the hawking sport finally died out in the latter part of the eighteenth century, the falcons ceased to have any commercial value.

At the time of colonization Iceland was better forested than at present. Large areas seem to have been covered with woods, as many of the sagas, even the most reliable, emphasize that in early periods the island had extensive forest areas.[10] The "Íslendingabók" states that "at that time Iceland was covered with woods between the mountains and the sea." At present the forests of Iceland are very limited in area, and consist only of birch trees with here and there a mountain ash which seldom attains a height of twenty-eight or thirty feet. Other varieties, as willow and dwarf-birch, appear only as brush and shrubs. The ravages of grazing herds, fires and volcanic eruptions, as well as the forced use of the scant wood supply during periods of inadequate commercial intercourse, tended to denude the wooded areas, since the extremely slow growth

[10] *Íslendingabók*, i, 5. *Landnámabók*, i, ch. 1, 14; ii, ch. 2, ch. 21; v, ch. 1. *Eyrbyggjasaga*, ch. 26, 33, 35. *Fljótsdœlasaga*, ch. 2.

of trees in this latitude makes the forests unable to resist the inroads of destructive forces. On the other hand, it should not be overlooked that many of the sagas exaggerate the importance of woods found in Iceland in early times. It is quite evident that even in the period of colonization Iceland possessed no forests of any great value. The varieties of trees were the same as at present, and though they were undoubtedly found in larger quantities and also of larger size, there is nothing to show that either the flora or the fauna has been affected by any permanent change in the climate. Even the first settlers were dependent for the most necessary building material on the driftwood which is carried to the shores of Iceland by the ocean currents,[11] or they imported timber from Norway. We read in the "Vatsdælasaga" that Ingimund the Old went to Norway to get building timber, and brought two shiploads back to Iceland. Likewise the "Reykdælasaga" tells that two ships loaded with timber came to northern Iceland, and the settlers sought to outbid each other to procure it. The importation of timber is mentioned so frequently in the sagas that it is clear that a general want existed of this important commodity.[12]

Iceland is not rich in minerals. Some iron ore is found, but it is of poor quality, and for want of fuel no smelting furnaces can be operated. A limited supply of this mineral was obtained by the early settlers from the bog ore which occurs in many places. The "Egilssaga" states that Skallagrim was a great blacksmith, and that in the winter he was engaged in smelting iron, a process carried on by means of charcoal which was burned in the early forests.[13] Real coal deposits are few, but lignite occurs in considerable quantities, especially in the western part of the island, and peat is cut for fuel here and there in all parts of Iceland. The Iceland spar (silfurberg) is found in Helgustadsfjall in Reydarfjord. Many kinds of beautiful crystals also abound,

[11] Eggert Olafsson, Reise gjennem Island, vol. 1, p. 264, p. 271 ff. Gliemann, Beschreibung von Island, p. 66.

[12] Vatsdælasaga, ch. xvi. Reykdælasaga, ch. ix. Njálssaga, ch. 32. Laxdælasaga, ch. 13. Víga-Stýrssaga þk Heiðarvíga, ch. 3.

[13] Eyrbyggjasaga, ch. 26.

especially the almandite. Lime is found in considerable quantities in large mountain fissures, and rich sulphur deposits occur in some places, a product which was exported from Iceland quite early. According to the "Arni Biskupssaga" the archbishop of Nidaros in Norway had a monopoly on the sulphur export from Iceland in 1284. But the trade in this commodity, at one time quite extensive, has decreased in recent years, and is now of no importance.

No domestic trade of any importance was developed in Iceland in early ages, since inland travel and transportation were difficult, and the products were about the same in all districts. The "Hænsathorissaga" narrates as an unusual occurrence that a man by the name of Thorir in the summer time traveled from place to place selling in one district what he bought in another, and that in this way he acquired much property. At one time when he crossed the mountains he brought chickens from southern Iceland and sold them together with other goods in the northern settlements. From that time forth he was known as "Hænsathorir" (Chicken Thorir).[14] With such rare exceptions all trade was an import and export trade with foreign lands. Sometimes the Icelanders themselves would engage in this traffic, but as no native merchant class had been developed, it was usually in the hands of professional Norse traders who brought their wares from Norwegian and British seaports after they had first imported them from far-off foreign markets in France, Spain or Russia.[15] These merchant mariners usually crossed the sea only once each summer. When they arrived in Iceland, they raised a tent in the harbor and stored the goods until they could gradually be sold during the next twelvemonth. The ship was usually pulled ashore, as they intended to remain in the island over winter. The nearest *goði* was the first to visit the trader to inspect his wares and fix the prices for which they were to be sold. He could also select for himself such goods as he

[14] *Hænsathórissaga*, ch. 1. The *Njálssaga*, ch. 23, mentions Hedin the Peddler.
[15] *Landnámabók*, iii, ch. 1. *Njálssaga*, ch. 3.

might want, and the merchant, together with the ship's crew, was usually invited to spend the winter as guest at his home. The most common articles of import were: timber, flour, cloth, iron or iron ware, copper, weapons, tar, wine, beer, wax and honey; for which they would receive in return wool and woolen cloth, sheepskins, hides, pelts, meat and tallow, butter and cheese, train-oil, falcons, fish and sulphur. Among the Icelanders trade was usually coupled with travel in foreign lands, but only as a matter of subsidiary importance. All young men had to spend several years abroad to acquire the necessary training and culture. In order to defray the expenses of such travels the father would equip his sons with a supply of woolen cloth and other home wares which were to be sold in foreign ports. But the young man who possessed no business training, and had no desire to enter the profession of trader, usually showed little interest in this part of the enterprise. It was his ambition to enter the circles of the courts as scald or *hirdmaðr,* where he could win distinction by scaldic art and courtly bearing.[16] On returning home he married and settled permanently as a *bóndi* on the acres of his fathers.

In private life as well as in state organization and public institutions the Icelanders adhered with great fidelity to the ways of their ancestors. This conservatism, which had been adopted as a distinct program by the early settlers, was strengthened through the isolated location of the colony as well as through a natural environment which made innovations difficult. Some slight modifications were, indeed, necessitated by local conditions, but in all essential features Norwegian life and customs were more carefully reproduced and successfully perpetuated in Iceland than in any other Norse colony. In the erection of dwellings some new features were developed owing to the want of building material, but the general Norse plan was preserved as far as possible. In Norway, where timber was plentiful, each farmstead consisted of a number of separate houses, each one erected for a special purpose, the chief ones being the living and dining house proper (*stofa*), the sleeping house

[16] *Gunnlaugssaga Ormstungu,* ch. 3 ff. *Njálssaga,* ch. 3.

(*skáli* or *svefnbúr*), the kitchen (*eldhús*), and the store-house for food and provisions (*búr*). About these were grouped other minor houses for various purposes, and far-ther in the background were the stables for horses and cattle. In the modern dwelling several houses have been united into a single structure under the same roof, but in Iceland the system of a group of houses erected for different purposes has been maintained even to the present. They are not built entirely separate, but are arranged side by side in one or two rows, each house opening like a separate chamber into a transverse hall which extends the full length of the row from one end to the other. The roofs are of turf, and for want of timber, which is used only for framework, the walls are constructed of sod and rock. The more impor-tant rooms have wooden floors and are wainscoted on the inside.[17] In early times the *stofa* was often so large that feasts for several hundred guests could be held in it. In Norway it had an open fireplace in the middle of the floor, and on festive occasions the walls were hung with tapestries. The early Icelandic settlers undoubtedly arranged the *stofa* in the same way, but for want of fuel the custom of heating it was soon discontinued, and the Icelanders soon found it necessary also to reduce the size of the room to save the heat. On the larger farmsteads, however, separate festive halls (*veizluskáli*) were erected of timber imported from Norway.[18] These were usually large and beautifully deco-rated. Some of the leading families also had a bath-house furnished with a stone stove, which was heated until very hot, when water was poured over it to produce steam for the

[17] Hermann Paul, *Grundriss der germanischen Philologie*, vol. iii, Valtýr Guðmundsson und Kristian Kålund, *Skandinavische Verhältnisse*, p. 407 ff. R. Keyser, *Nordmændenes Privatliv i Oldtiden, Efterladte Skrifter*, vol. ii. Valtýr Guðmundsson, *Privatboligen pa Island i Sagatiden*. Daniel Bruun, *Fortidsminder og Nutidshjem paa Island*. Valtýr Guðmundsson, *Islands Kultur ved Aarhundredskiftet 1900*, p. 24 ff.

[18] In saga times some chieftains built their houses of timber, mostly imported from Norway. The *Njálssaga* states that the house of Gunnar of Hlidarendi was built of timber and had a board roof. According to the Laxdœlasaga Olaf Pá of Hjardarholt built a house mostly of timber cut in the home forests, and partly from driftwood. But such instances must have been quite exceptional.

vapor baths. Bathtubs were also used, and the numerous hot springs were much used for bathing. Two principal meals were served each day in the *stofa*, usually for the whole household, the *dagverðr* at 9 o'clock A.M., and the more elaborate *náttverðr* in the evening when the day's work was over. The head of the family would then occupy the high-seat, while the other members of the household would be seated on benches to his left and right, with another row facing him along the opposite side of the room, the place being regarded the more honorable the nearer it was to the high-seat. A small table (*skutill*), covered on festive occasions with a white linen tablecloth, was placed on trestles before each person, and was removed as soon as the meal was over. Fingerbowls and towels were passed by maid servants, as it was customary to wash the hands both before and after the meal. The food consisted of meat, fish, game and milk products, together with a limited supply of bread. Sour milk was the common every-day drink; but on festive occasions beer, mead and even imported wines were served. Wooden plates and spoons were commonly used; but forks were yet unknown, and the knife was carried in a scabbard suspended from the belt.

That the spirit of hospitality and love of festive social entertainment which always characterized the Norsemen should continue to flourish in Iceland is natural. This old custom not only gave zest to life in an otherwise bleak and comfortless environment, but it developed grace and skill in conversation, and fostered in the stern and apathetic popular character the traits of generous kindness which continue to distinguish the Icelandic people. Festivities of various kinds were of common occurrence especially in the leading families. During pagan times the yearly religious festivals were the *vetrnætr*, or beginning of winter (October 14), the *miðsvetrar-blót* (January 12), and *sumardagr*, or first day of summer (April 14), when sacrificial feasts usually took place in the temples accompanied by general social pastime.[19] Weddings and funerals were always elab-

---

[19] *Gíslasaga Súrssonar*, ch. 11, p. 115. *Fornmannasögur, Saga Olafs Konungs Tryggvasonar*, ch. 215. *Njálssaga*, ch. 35. *Laxdœlasaga*, ch. 45, 46.

orately celebrated. Occasionally, too, the *goði* and his
retinue had to be entertained for several days when he made
his tour through the district, and private parties were often
arranged for a large number of invited guests. On such
occasions the walls of the *stofa* were draped with woven
tapestries, fire was kindled on the fireplace, and cushions
were placed on the benches for the guests. Great quantities
of food were provided, as the tables had to display liberality
and plenty. Great care had to be taken to place the guests
according to rank and dignity at the proper distance to the
right and left of the high-seat, since mistakes on this point
might lead to serious misunderstandings.[20] The women
occupied the *pallr*, or *thverpallr*, a bench extending from one
wall to the other toward the rear end of the hall. But at
the drinking feast which followed the meal men and women
would often sit together by couples, and as mead and beer
were served in abundance, overindulgence in these strong
beverages was not uncommon. Over the mead cup the spirit
of conviviality gained full sway. Songs were declaimed,
sagas were recited, or sharp irritating word-duels were
indulged in, which often ended in quarrels and bloodshed.
At greater festivals it was customary for young men to
empty the *bragarfull*, or promise cup, and to make a solemn
vow to do some notable deed. At the termination of the
feast, which often lasted several days, the host would give
the guests presents, and accompany them on the way, where
the final formal leave was taken. The number of guests at
weddings, funerals and other festive gatherings was often
very large. The saga says that when Hallgerd, the daughter of Höskuld Dalakollsson, was married, not less than 100
(120) guests were invited.[21] But far more pretentious were
the funeral festivities arranged upon Höskuld's death by his
son Olaf Pá of Hjardarholt. "All the leading men who
promised to be present arrived at the appointed time,"
says the saga, "and there were so many that, according to
general opinion, there were fully 900 (1080). This was the
second largest festival ever held in Iceland, the largest being

[20] *Njálssaga*, ch. 34, 35.
[21] *Ibidem*, ch. 10. The hundred was the large hundred, 10 x 12 or 120.

the funeral which the sons of Hjalti celebrated at the death
of their father, when the guests numbered 1200 (1440)." [22]
As the guests had to journey on horseback even from far
away districts, they often traveled in imposing cavalcades
which attracted an attention not wholly unwelcome; for
love of display, connected with the proud class conscious-
ness and martial temperament of medieval Europe, characterized the leading Icelanders as well as the jousting knights
on the continent. Knight errantry had, indeed, not been
introduced, and in so bleak and barren a land life naturally
fell along simpler lines than in more favored countries, but
the time-spirit manifested itself here as elsewhere. The
native aristocracy of proud chieftains and highborn ladies
were no less fond of fineries and the customary trumpery of
rank and station than the Flors and Blancheflors in southern
lands. At festive social gatherings the ladies would usually
appear in costly gold-brocaded garments. The hair, which
was scrupulously cared for and treasured as a special adorn-
ment, fell loose over the shoulders, with only a ribbon tied
around the head to hold the locks in order. The men would
wear mantles of scarlet or other striking colors, and ornamented helmets and fine swords were greatly coveted as
special marks of distinction. The "Njálssaga" says of
Gunnar of Hlidarendi that one day when he rode from the
thing he saw a well dressed woman approaching. "When
they met she greeted him. He returned her greeting and
asked her what her name was. She said that she was
Hallgerda, the daughter of Höskuld Dalakolsson. She was
rather forward in speech, and asked him to tell her about
his travels. This request he did not refuse, and they sat
down and talked together. She was dressed in the following
manner: She had a red skirt well ornamented, and over it
a red scarlet mantle embroidered with gold. Her hair hung
over her bosom, and it was both long and beautiful. Gunnar
wore the scarlet clothes which King Harald Gormsson had
given him, and on his arm he had the ring of gold which he
had received from Haakon Jarl." [23] Making allowance for

[22] *Laxdœlasaga*, ch. 122.
[23] *Njálssaga*, ch. 33.

the fact that the saga writers are often guilty of the anachronism of picturing costumes and manners of their own time as if they belonged to past ages, it is nevertheless clear that on festive occasions the chieftains and ladies of Iceland wore the finest attire obtainable. The "Landnáma-bók" states that Glum Geirason cited the scald Ottar before the Thorskafjord *thing*. Odd's sons came to help their father, and they were so beautifully attired that the people thought that the gods themselves were coming. Skarphedin, the son of Njáll of Bergthorshváll, was dressed as follows at the Althing according to the saga: He had a blue mantle, blue striped trousers, and high shoes. He had a silver belt, and carried a large shield. In his hand he had the battle-ax Rimugygi with which he had killed Thráin. His hair was combed back behind the ears, and a gold embroidered silk ribbon was tied around his forehead.[24] About Gisli Sursson it is stated that he wore a blue mantle and was very beautifully dressed. "Thorleif Kimba," says the saga, "had a richly ornamented sword, a gold adorned spear, a dark blue shield richly decorated, and very fine clothes." Costly mantles were often given as presents by chieftains who wished to show their munificence and desired to do a friend special honor. The "Njálssaga" states that in the fall Höskuld went to Svinafell to visit Flosi. When he departed on his homeward journey, Flosi gave him a scarlet mantle embroidered with gold brocade to the waist. The custom of giving costly presents, like scarlet mantles, saddle horses or large sums of money, was quite universally practiced throughout Europe in the Middle Ages, and conformed, no doubt, to the conception of a liberality worthy of princes and men of high station. We read of Kjartan Olafsson that King Olaf Tryggvason gave him a costly mantle,[25] and the scald Gunnlaug Ormstunga received a scarlet mantle from Ethelred, king of England, as a reward for a song with which he had entertained the court. To receive such tokens of royal favor was the highest ambition of young Icelanders who traveled abroad. The display of

[24] *Njálssaga*, ch. 120. *Gíslasaga Súrssonar*, ch. 20. *Eyrbyggjasaga*, ch. 13.
[25] *Laxdœlasaga*, ch. 24.

such fineries was sure to attract attention on their return
home, and it was in keeping with the highest standards
of good manners when they themselves practiced a like
munificence.

Aside from the more formal pastime connected with festivities and social parties, the playing of chess and kindred
games was in great favor as private recreation, especially in
the winter when there was little opportunity for outdoor
amusements. The dance seems to have been unknown in
early ages, but it was introduced from the Scandinavian
countries, where it developed in connection with romantic
folk-songs in the twelfth century, and it soon became a
popular public amusement. Men and women would join
hands in a large circle, and would move with rhythmic steps
to the chanting of some favorite ballad. This pastime was
in all its features a distinctly new departure. Before the
introduction of Christianity even singing was unknown
except in magic incantations, and music, which was limited
to the simplest instruments, the harp, the flute and the
trumpet, was little practiced. These new social features of
foreign origin, music and the dance, as well as the singing
of romantic love songs, could gain entrance only in the face
of adverse public sentiment, but they heralded a time when
the chief interest should be transferred from the dueling
ground to the drawing room, when the old martial spirit
should be tempered with new social ideals. According to
the old conception all amusements were to subserve the one
prime purpose of strengthening the body and training the
mind for feats of arms by developing physical skill, courage
and martial spirit. Swimming, hunting, skating, ski-
running, wrestling, jumping, and training in the use of
weapons were regarded as the proper pastime for young
men, as bravery was the virtue most to be desired. The
same spirit also pervaded the distinctly national sports, the
playing of ball (*knattleikr*) and horse-fighting. The game
of ball was evidently very different from its present form,
though the details of the game are not known. Two men
were pitted against each other. A wooden ball was thrown
by one of the players and struck by the other with a wooden

mallet. Strength and agility rather than skill decided the outcome, and the temper of the players was often so aroused that the game developed into a violent personal encounter.[26] The "Gíslasaga Súrssonar" gives the following description of such a game:

"They now began to play as if nothing had happened. The brothers-in-law, Gisli and Thorgrim, were usually pitted against each other, and people did not agree as to who was the stronger, though the greater number thought that it was Gisli. They played ball at Siftjorn, where many people usually assembled. One day when there were unusually many people present, Gisli asked them to play the game by turn. This they agreed to do, but they also asked him not to hold back when he played against Thorgrim. 'It is rumored,' they said, 'that you are not exerting yourself when you play against him. But we should like to see that you win the honor if you are really the stronger.' 'We have not yet done our utmost in the contest,' said Gisli, 'but possibly we may now do so.' When they began to play, Thorgrim was unable to hold his own against Gisli, who threw him down and carried the ball away. Gisli sought again to take the ball, but Thorgrim held it fast. Then Gisli threw him down so violently that he skinned his knees and knuckles, and blood was running from his nose. Thorgrim arose slowly, looked towards the burial mound of Vestein and said: 'The sword pierced your heart, which is not to be complained of.' Gisli took the ball in one jump, threw it between the shoulders of Thorgrim so that he fell forwards, and said: 'The ball on broad shoulders broke, which is not to be complained of.' Thorkell said: 'We can now see who is the strongest and most agile. Let us now stop.' The game closed, but they were not as good friends as before."

Horse-fights seem to have been an especially favorite pastime among the chieftains, who raised and trained horses for this purpose. The "Njálssaga" gives the following description of this sort of amphitheatrical exhibition:

"People now rode to the horse-fight, and there were many people assembled. Gunnar and his brothers, the sons of Sigfus, Njáll and all his sons were present, also Starkad, Egill and their sons. They now told Gunnar to let the horses start the fight, and he let them do as they wished in the matter. Skarphedin

[26] *Gullthórissaga,* ch. 2. *Gíslasaga Súrssonar,* ch. 15, 18.

said: 'Will you, Gunnar, let me have charge of your horse?'
'No,' replied Gunnar, 'I will not.' 'But that would be the better
way,' said Skarphedin, 'there would then be valiant men on both
sides.' 'You would not say or do much before there would be
a fight,' said Gunnar. 'With me it is not so easy to start a
quarrel, though the outcome may be the same.' The horses
were now brought forward. Gunnar was ready to drive, and
Skarphedin led his horse. Gunnar wore a red mantle. He was
girded with a broad belt, and had a big horse-stick in his hand.
The horses rushed to the attack; no one needed to urge them,
and it caused the greatest merriment. Thorgeir and Koll had
agreed that when the horses reared for the attack, they would
rush forward and push their horse and thus throw Gunnar.
When, therefore, the horses reared to attack each other, Thorgeir
and Koll pushed against the back of their horse, but Gunnar
also pushed against his horse so hard that both Thorgeir and Koll
fell backwards and their horse on top of them. They jumped
up to attack Gunnar, but he jumped aside, grabbed Koll and
threw him to the ground so hard that he lay senseless. Thorgeir
struck Gunnar's horse and blinded him on one eye, but Gunnar
knocked Thorgeir down with his horse-stick, and bade Kolskegg
kill the horse, for he would not let it live now that it was maimed.
Kolskegg then beheaded the horse. Thorgeir was now on his
feet again, and sought to attack Gunnar with the sword, but
the people restrained him, and there was the greatest uproar.
'I am tired of this noise,' said Skarphedin. 'It is much better
that we fight with the sword.' But Gunnar was so cool that
one man held him, and he did not say a word. Njáll sought to
arrange a peaceful settlement; but Thorgeir said that he would
neither accept nor grant a peaceful understanding, that he
would see Gunnar dead first. Kolskegg replied: 'Gunnar has
stood too firm to be felled with words, and it will be hereafter
as it has been heretofore.' The people now rode home from the
horse-fight. No one dared to attack Gunnar, and so the winter
passed." [27]

The contest was, undoubtedly, viewed as a most successful event. Not only the strength of the horses, but the
courage and fighting spirit of the men were put to a test
which aroused the greatest excitement. It was a carnival of
conflict as well suited to awaken the martial joy of the

[27] *Njálssaga*, ch. 59.

spectators as the shivering of lances on the blood-stained lists of England and the continent.

The most strongly knit unit of social life in the Icelandic state as elsewhere among Teutonic peoples was the family, which embraced not only parents and children but all other persons of nearer and remoter kinship. Whatever might be the relation of the individuals to each other in daily life, they would act together in time of trouble, giving each other aid and support whenever some member or group of the family became involved in a feud. If one was slain, it was the duty of the remaining relatives to exact due reparation or to execute vengeance upon the slayer or his kindred. In a society where feuds were so common, and where the families through intermarriage were gradually united by some tie of relationship, the principle of loyalty of kinship could not always be maintained. It is evident that it was gradually weakened until in the Sturlung period, 1200-1265, even the nearest of kin would wage war upon each other. But in the earlier days this venerated principle usually remained inviolate. The relation between parents and children, generally friendly, was often so cordial that the sons would remain under the parental roof even after marriage. We read of Skarphedin, the son of Njáll, that his father asked for him the hand of Thorhild, daughter of Randve of Thorolfsfell. Skarphedin married Thorhild, but continued to stay with his father at Bergthorshváll. His younger brother Grim married a rich widow, Ástrid of Djupabakki, but he too remained at home with his father.[28] As in the case of Skarphedin, the son often left it to his father to select a bride for him, though this was always done with the son's consent. The right of the son to choose his own bride was unquestioned, but the courtship was not carried on by the young people directly, but between the bridegroom and his representatives and the bride's father or guardian. Only when all the details of the marriage contract, the amount of dowry and other stipulations, had been arranged was the bride asked to give her consent. At times the saga writers

[28] *Njálssaga*, ch. 25.

will picture with great skill the tender sorrows of true affection, some sad love tragedy where the human heart records its protest against the tyranny of established social custom with such vigor that the events growing out of it deeply influence the life story of the whole family or even of the whole community. Some impetuous scald, in defiance of the rules of good conduct, has made personal visits to his lady love, like the violent Thormod Kolbrunarskald in the "Fóstbrœdrasaga," who received the sobriquet of *Kolbrunarskald* because of the love songs he made to his beloved Kolbruna. Or he might seek the hand of his lady love in marriage from no other motive than pure affection, like Gunnlaug Ormstunga in the beautiful love story "Gunn-laugssaga Ormstungu," or like Kormak, the hero of the "Kormákssaga," the greatest lyricist among the scalds, who never forgot his beloved Steingerd, and refused to wholly give her up even after she was married to another. But such relations were exceptional and were always regarded as a misfortune. Marriage was a mere business affair into which no sentiment was allowed to enter. It was based wholly upon the idea that the contracting parties should be of equal worth and rank, that the marriage should be advantageous and profitable. A young woman might be given away in marriage even against her wish, though such instances seem to have been few. But in spite of the wholly unsentimental and businesslike way of entering into the married state, the sagas show that the majority of marriages were happy, and that the tenderest affection often existed between husband and wife. If woman had little to say as to the arranging of the marriage, she enjoyed extensive rights and privileges as wife. The management of the household was left to her, and to a large extent also the employment and control of domestic servants. As a sign of her authority in the home she carried in her belt a bunch of keys, as all stores and valuables were entrusted to her safekeeping. In the marriage contract it was stipulated how much of a dowry (*heimafylgja*) the bride should receive from her parents, and a like amount (*mundr*) had to be given her by the bridegroom. On the day after the wedding he also had to give her a *morgungjöf*, which seems to have corresponded to the modern wedding present. All the property thus specified in the marriage contract belonged to the wife, and could be held by her either jointly with her husband or in separate ownership, but in case of divorce it reverted to her under all circumstances.

In pagan times the husband might lawfully keep concubines, but he had to treat his wife with the kindness and respect due her as his wedded spouse. Any wilful discourtesy or violence against her person was regarded as just cause for divorce. The husband, too, might put away his wife for almost any trivial reason. No legal action was required to make the divorce effective. The only proceeding necessary was a public declaration renouncing the marriage relation. The following incident narrated in the "Vígastyrssage ok Heiðarvíga" shows how little sacredness still attached to the marriage bond:

"It happened one morning that they were both in the bedchamber. Bardi wanted to sleep, but his wife, wishing to keep him awake, took a small pillow and threw it in his face for fun. He threw it away, and they kept this up for a while. Finally he threw it back in such a way that he let the fist follow the pillow. This made her so angry that she grabbed a stone and threw at him. Later in the day, after refreshments had been served, Bardi arose and declared himself separated from Aud, stating that he would not tolerate any such treatment either from her or anyone else. It was useless to speak in opposition to it, and the matter was thus settled." [29]

In spite of the ease with which the bonds of matrimony might be severed, divorces seem to have been so rare as to attract quite general attention. Then as now true affection and mutual interests gave stability and protection to this important relation. Where these failed, the spirit of faithfulness and devotion to duty, yet so strong in early society, was the final sheet-anchor which saved many a marriage from threatening shipwreck. With the conspicuous faults

[29] *Viga-Stýrssaga ok Heiðarvíga*, ch. 41. *Njálssaga*, ch. 34. *Eyrbyggjasaga*, 14. *Laxdælasaga*, ch. 34.

which attached to moral life and also to the marriage relation, marriage was, nevertheless, highly respected, and fostered with remarkable success the tender attachments and lasting family ties which proved to be the chief strength of Icelandic social life.

The heathen ideals, which continued to live long after the formal acceptance of Christianity as a state religion, were maintained especially in the method of rearing the children and educating the youth. If the child was reared in the home, it was entrusted to the care of some servant or subordinate member of the household. But very frequently the boys especially were sent away to be reared by some friend of the family who in this way wished to show the parents a special favor. It was natural that the closest attachment should exist between the child and its foster-parents, and it was a common saying that a child thus reared favored its foster-father by one-fourth (*fjórðungi bregðr til fóstrs*). Children who were reared together acquired the same mutual affection for each other as children of the same family. Foster-brothers often clung to each other with a friendship so lasting and intimate that in imitation of it a similar relation, the *fóstbræðralag,* was established by special ceremonies between young men who wished to be closely associated for life. The children were given the greatest freedom. No effort was made to curb their self-will or to restrain their recklessness or cruel instincts. They had to read and carve runes, study the laws, and acquire skill in public speaking and the art of poetry; but the chief ambition of a young man was to become skilled in the use of arms, athletic, physically strong, able to endure hardships, hunger, wounds and pain, and to meet danger or death without flinching. For this reason the various sports as hunting, swimming, *glima,* or wrestling, and especially the violent *knattleikr,* or game of ball, were favorite pastimes. Any rash act, even homicide, was readily condoned. Young men were encouraged to all sorts of hazardous adventures, and he who could show the most arrogant self-reliance, and perform the most remarkable stunts of reckless daring would receive a nod of approval as a very hopeful lad. It is very natural that such a system of education should perpetuate the warlike Viking spirit which filled early Icelandic history with strife and bloodshed. But it developed also a race of bold adventurers and daring voyagers who visited all lands and spread their sails on every sea in quest of new exploits. To their courage and enterprise was due the colonization of Greenland, the first discovery of the American continent, the Vinland voyages and the establishing of the earliest transoceanic sailing routes between Europe and America, some of the greatest achievements in the history of navigation.

6. DISCOVERY AND COLONIZATION OF GREENLAND. DISCOVERY OF THE AMERICAN CONTINENT. THE VINLAND VOYAGES

THE strong individualism and impatient dread of restraint bred in the Norsemen by their social life and ideals were further intensified in the Viking Age through the excessive love of adventure which characterized that period. The great movement of emigration from the mother country, and the planting of overseas settlements was largely due to a restless national spirit which even in the western colonies continued to urge the more venturesome onward from one outpost to another. Hardly had the Icelanders thatched their first cabins in their new homes when they began to scan the sea, if, perchance, some new land might be found beyond the Ultima Thule of which they had taken possession. It was rumored that a man by the name of Gunnbjörn on a voyage to Iceland about 900 had been driven from his course, and that to the westward he had seen a new land which the settlers called *Gunnbjarnarsker* (Gunnbjörn Skerries).[1] It is not impossible that Gunnbjörn may have been driven so far to the west that he had seen the coast of Greenland, but he may have seen also only a mirage or a drifting ice-floe. The rumor, nevertheless, aroused an interest which

---

[1] *Grønlands historiske Mindesmærker,* vol. i, p. 71 ff.

led to the discovery of Greenland by Eirik the Red in 981.
About this doughty voyager the sagas give so detailed an
account that he is better known than most other early explorers. He belonged to a wealthy and powerful family in
Jædern in southern Norway, but because of some homicides
committed in a feud he and his father, Thorvald Ásvaldsson,
fled to Iceland, and settled at Drangar north of the Isafjord
in the northwestern district. When his father died, Eirik
married Thorhild or Thjodhild, the daughter of Jörund At-
lason, and settled at Eiriksstad east of the Hvamsfjord, one
of the best districts in western Iceland. While clearing land
here his slaves let a landslide fall upon the house of a neighbor by the name of Valthjof, killing him. To avenge his
death a relative of Valthjof, Eyjolf Saur, killed the slaves,
but the vindictive Eirik slew both Eyjolf and another neighbor, Holmgöngu-Hrafn. For this deed he was cited before
the *thing* and banished from the district. After changing
his residence a couple of times he finally settled at Eiriksstad in Öxney, but as he became involved in new feuds, he
was finally outlawed by the Thorsnesthing for a period of
three years. As he was now compelled to leave Iceland, he
resolved to attempt to find the land seen by Gunnbjörn. He
set sail from Snefellsjökull, continuing his voyage until he
approached the east coast of Greenland. Finding this uninhabitable because of vast glaciers he turned southward,
rounded Cape Farewell, and reached an island on the west
coast, which he called Eiriksey, in what was later known as
the Eastern Settlement. The following spring he entered a
fjord, which he called Eiriksfjord, where he established
his home. He spent the summer in exploring the coast as
far as 64°-65° N. L. The second winter he spent on an
island since called Eiriksholm, near the southern extremity
of Greenland. The following summer he proceeded still farther northward to a place called Snæfell, the location of
which is not known. He then sailed back to Eiriksfjord and
spent the winter there. He had now spent three years in
exploring that barren northern region, and as the term of
banishment had expired, he returned to Iceland the following summer. The land which he had discovered was called

Greenland, in the hope, as the saga puts it, that such a name would attract settlers, as it was his aim to bring out colonists and found a permanent settlement. The glowing account which he gave of the country seems to have appealed strongly to the adventurous spirit of the Icelanders. In the spring following his return twenty-five vessels sailed for Greenland from the western districts of Breidafjord and Borgarfjord. Fourteen of these reached their destination. Of the others some were shipwrecked and some returned home. Eirik established himself at the head of the Eiriksfjord on the southwestern coast of Greenland, 60°-61° N. L., in the present Julianehaab district, where he built a residence called Brattahlid. Most of the colonists also settled in this district, forming the Eystri Bygd, or Eastern Settlement. But some proceeded farther along the coast to 64°-65° N. L., where the Vestri Bygd, or Western Settlement, was established, in the present district of Godthaab.

In spite of the cold climate and the dangers connected with navigation in these northern seas the colonies continued to grow until the Eastern Settlement had 190 farmsteads, twelve churches and two monasteries. The Western Settlement had ninety dwellings and four churches. Together the two settlements probably had at the time of their greatest prosperity about 2,000 people. The settlers found no native inhabitants in Greenland, though numerous traces of human habitations convinced them that the country was inhabited. The old Icelandic historian Ari Frodi says: "They found remnants of human dwellings both eastward and westward in the land, stone weapons and fragments of boats, from which it was evident that the same people who inhabit Vinland, and whom the people of Greenland call Skrælings, had also sojourned here." [2] But the Skrælings, or Eskimos, who inhabited this region must have moved to other hunting grounds, as they did not return until a later period. The climate and general conditions in Greenland were found to be much the same as in Iceland. The winters are long and cold, and the sea is usually strewed with icebergs even late in the spring, but in the summer a green belt

[2] *Íslendingabók,* ch. 17.

of vegetation stretches along the western coast. During this season of the year the weather is agreeable and the scenery beautiful. No woods exist, but there is an abundance of grass, flowers, berries and brush of dwarfed birch trees. The clear air and blue fjords, the glaciers and snow-covered mountains give the region in summer time a serene and tranquil beauty equal to that of any region of the far North. Fish are found in great abundance in the streams as well as in the sea; and seals, walrus, polar bears and furbearing animals are plentiful. Cattle, sheep, goats and horses thrived well and were kept in goodly numbers by the settlers. For want of other building material the houses were erected of stone, and as the dwellings were usually structures of considerable size, with separate stables for sheep, horses and cattle, many remnants are still to be seen in Greenland of the buildings erected by the early settlers. In the Eastern Settlement the ruins of several churches and of about one hundred dwellings have been found.[3]

The Icelandic colonists in Greenland established a social organization, copied, as might be expected, without innovations from that of their homeland. The Icelandic laws were introduced, and a general *thing* was assembled every summer at Gardar, the present Igaliko, situated not far from Brattahlid on a neck of land between Eiriksfjord and Einarsfjord. The *lögrétta,* consisting of the chieftains and their assistants, the *goðordsmenn,* exercized the lawmaking power. The usual judicial tribunals were established in connection with the *thing,* which was presided over by the *lögsögumaðr,* who recited and interpreted the laws.

At first the old pagan worship with the customary religious ceremonies and sacrifices prevailed, but Christianity was introduced so soon after the founding of the colony that we hear nothing about the erection of heathen temples. This event, which took place at the time when the Christian faith was being established in Norway and Iceland through the efforts of King Olaf Tryggvason, was due chiefly to the energetic leadership of the family of Eirik the Red. Eirik had three sons: Leif, Thorvald and Thorstein, and the illegi-

[3] Daniel Bruun, *Erik den Røde og Nordbokolonierne i Grønland.*

timate daughter Freydis. The three brothers were great
sailors and explorers, but Leif Eiriksson, famous as the discoverer of Vinland, or the mainland of North America, was
especially prominent as the greatest navigator of his age.
Hitherto the route to Greenland had been by the way of Iceland, but in 999 he struck boldly across the Atlantic, sailing
directly from Greenland to Norway. This was the first direct
transoceanic voyage, an achievement not repeated later by
voyagers of other seafaring nations till in the time of Columbus.   En route Leif is said to have stopped a while in the
Hebrides, where he became enamored of a young lady by
the name of Thorgunna, who, according to the saga, bore
him the son Thorgils, who later came to Greenland. But
Leif could not marry her, as her relatives opposed the match,
neither did he dare to carry her away against their will, since
he had only a few men with him. When he arrived in Norway, he was cordially received by King Olaf Tryggvason,
and remained at court during the winter. The king, who
was actively engaged in Christianizing his kingdom and all
its dependencies, soon prevailed on Leif Eiriksson to receive
baptism and to undertake the task of introducing Christianity in Greenland. Leif sailed from Norway the following summer, but on the return voyage he was driven out
of his course, and came to a land which he had not before
seen. He found there self-sown wheat fields, grapevines,
and also a tree called *mösurr*, says the saga. "Of all these
things they took some samples; some trees were so large
that they used them for house beams." This country could
only have been the coast of America. "They also found some
men on a wreck, whom they rescued and brought back to
Greenland. He had shown great highmindedness and good
qualities: he brought Christianity to the country, and saved
the men on the wreck, and he was henceforth known as Leif
the Lucky. He landed in Eiriksfjord and came home to
Brattahlid, where he was well received." He immediately
began the work of Christianizing the people of Greenland,
according to the promise which he had given the king. His
father, Eirik the Red, refused to accept the new faith, and
did not hide his antagonism to the movement. "The two

things may be regarded as equalizing one another," he is said to have stated to his son, "that you saved the men on the wreck, and that you brought hither this hypocrite,' meaning the priest. He does not seem, however, to have openly resisted the work for Christianity. Leif is said to have brought several priests with him to Greenland, and the conversion of the people, at first a purely formal matter, was soon accomplished. His mother, Thjohild, erected a church, called the Thjohild church, at Brattahlid, and parted from her husband because he refused to accept the Christian faith. The Church of Greenland, like that of Iceland, was at first placed under the supervision of the archbishop of Bremen, later under the archbishop of Lund in Skåne in southern Sweden, at that time a Danish province. But when a new archbishopric was established at Nidaros in Norway in 1152, Greenland, as well as Iceland, was joined to this archdiocese.[4]

Leif Eiriksson's voyage, and the introduction of Christianity, established also permanent connections between Greenland and Norway, so important to the new colony which had to import many necessaries of life from abroad. The "King's Mirror" (*Konungs skuggsjá*), written in Norway about 1250, mentions the trade with Greenland, which had then flourished for 250 years: "Some go to Greenland because of the renown which they gain by exposing themselves to dangers," says the writer, "others go to satisfy their curiosity, but some for the sake of profit. The Greenlanders have to import nearly all things needed in the colonization of the country: iron, building material, and other necessaries; but they sell hides, seal skins, walrus tusks and rope of walrus hide."[5] Among other necessaries grain was also a leading article of import.

The trade which the new colony carried on with Iceland must have been small, as the products of both countries were about the same. But the sagas show that goods which had been imported to Iceland were again exported to Greenland, and that intercourse between

[4] *Eirikssaga rauða*, ch. 5.
[5] *The King's Mirror*, ch. 17.

the two colonies was maintained. The "Eirikssaga rauða" gives an interesting description of a trading expedition to Greenland by Thorfinn Karlsefni and his companions in 1002. He was of a well-to-do and influential family, the son of Thord Hesthöfda and his wife Thorun, living at Reynines in Skagafjord. His chief assistant in the undertaking was Snorri Thorbrandsson.

"One summer he fitted out his ship for a voyage to Greenland," says the saga. "Snorri Thorbrandsson from Alptafjord accompanied him, and there were forty men on the ship. Bjarni Grimolfsson from Breidifjord and Thorhall Gamlason from eastern Iceland also prepared their ship to sail to Greenland, and they, too, had forty men. As soon as they were ready, both ships set sail. How long they remained at sea is not known, but it is said that both came to Eiriksfjord in the fall. Eirik and many of the settlers rode to the ships, and a pleasant trade was soon established. The masters of the ships invited Eirik to take what he might want of their goods. But he showed himself equally generous, for he invited them and their men to spend the winter with him at Brattahlid. The traders accepted this invitation, and the goods were brought to Brattahlid, where there was no lack of good houses to store them in. The traders were much pleased with their stay at Eirik's home during the winter. But when Christmas approached, he grew more gloomy than usual. One day Karlsefni spoke to him and said: 'What troubles you, Eirik? It seems to me that you are more reticent than you have been. You have been very hospitable to us, and we should like to reward it according to our means, if you will only let us know what makes you sad.' Eirik answered: 'You have been very friendly and easily satisfied. Now, I am not afraid that you shall have the greatest advantage of your stay here, but it is rather this which troubles me, that it may be rumored that you never spent a duller Christmas than the one which now is approaching.' Karlsefni said: 'That shall never happen. We have malt, flour and grain on the ships, and you have the right to take what you may desire. Prepare then a Christmas feast as sumptuous as you deem proper.' This offer he accepted, and a Christmas feast was prepared so fine that people thought that they had never seen a finer one."

Later in the winter when Karlsefni married Gudrid, the daughter of Thorbjörn Vifilsson, the festivities were re-

newed, and there was much merriment at Brattahlid that
winter. Other expeditions are also mentioned. The "Floa-
mannasaga" tells of Thorgils Orrabeinsfostri, who sailed
from Iceland to visit Eirik the Red at Brattahlid. Thorgils
had come to Iceland from Norway; but he had known Eirik,
and when he received an invitation to visit him, he sold his
home and sailed for Greenland accompanied by his wife
Thorey, the manager of his estate, Thorarin, and many slaves.
Encountering stormy weather they were driven about on the
sea until they finally landed far north on the east coast of
Greenland in the fall. Here Thorey gave birth to a son,
and they had to spend the winter there. Before spring most
of the slaves had died, and even when summer came they
were unable to get away because of the pack-ice. Thorey
was slain by the slaves, but Thorgils with his son and a few
other survivors finally reached Brattahlid after four years
of adventures and suffering. Though much in this saga is
undoubtedly fabulous, there may be a kernel of truth in the
story of Thorgils' unlucky voyage. Disasters of this kind
must have happened frequently to the early navigators who
had to sail the polar seas without compass and in open boats.
Much more reliable, however, is the account given in the
"Fóstbrœdrasaga" about expeditions to Greenland, and of
conditions there. One of the leading men in the Eastern
Settlement was Thorgrim Einarsson Trolli. In 1022 he
went on a trading expedition to Norway, Denmark and England. On his return he stopped for a time in Iceland, where
he slew Thorgeir Hávarsson and brought his captured ship
with him to Greenland. When Thormod Kolbrunarskald
learned that his foster-brother had been killed, he resolved
to avenge the deed. He went to Norway, where he found the
Greenlander Skuf ready to sail on his return voyage. Thormod accompanied him, arriving in Greenland in the fall.
After wreaking vengeance upon the slayers of Thorgrim, he
sailed again to Norway and entered the service of King Olaf
the Saint as hirdscald. He fell in the battle of Stiklestad
in 1030.

It is natural that the Greenlanders, who were so dependent
on seafaring for many necessaries of life, should devote

themselves also to the exploration of their own land and the neighboring coasts. In the summer they sailed northward to a place called *Norðrsetur* to hunt and to gather the driftwood carried thither from Siberia and the coasts of America. How far north they penetrated is not known, but a runestone found in 1824 on the island of Kingigtorsuak, 72° 55′ 20″ N. L. shows that they reached that latitude. Booths or huts for hunters and seamen who visited Norðrsetur were erected at Greipar and Krogsfjarðarheiði, probably in the present region of Holstenborg, as most of the driftwood gathers there. These icy regions were called *Óbygðir* (Wilderness) by the settlers, and are represented as lying far to the north of the Greenland colonies. A Vestri Obygð is also mentioned, which Eirik the Red is said to have visited during his first stay in Greenland, but the location of this land is not known.[6]

The voyages between Greenland, Norway and Iceland led also to the discovery of Vinland, or the mainland of North America. In the "Eirikssaga rauða," Leif Eiriksson is credited with this discovery. But in the "Flateyjarbók" Bjarni Herjolfsson is said to have been the first discoverer of Vinland. He belonged to a good family in Iceland, took to sea early, and became a noted trader and voyager. One winter while Bjarni was in Norway, his father, Herjolf, emigrated to Greenland, and settled at Herjolfsnes. When Bjarni found, upon his return, that his father had left Iceland, he did not unload his cargo, but resolved to follow him, if his men would undertake the voyage. This they agreed to do, and they soon put to sea again. After they lost sight of Iceland, the weather became so foggy for several days that they strayed far from their course. When they were again able to make nautical observations, they continued to sail in a westerly direction until they finally came in sight of land. But they saw that it was not Greenland, as it was forest-covered. Turning northward they followed the coast for some time, and at last they succeeded in reaching Greenland, where Bjarni was welcomed by his father at Herjolfsnes. According to the same source Leif Eiriksson bought Bjarni's

[6] Andrew Fossum, *The Norse Discovery of America*, p. 48 f.

ship, and set out to explore the land which had thus been discovered. He persuaded his father, old Eirik the Red, to become the leader of the expedition. After some hesitation he consented, but when they rode to the ship his horse stumbled and he was thrown off, hurting his foot. This he evidently regarded as an unfavorable omen. "It appears," he said, "that I am not destined to find any more lands than the one which we now inhabit, and that we may not all travel together any farther." He returned to Brattahlid, and Leif had to undertake to lead the expedition. With a crew of thirty-five men, among whom was his foster-father, Tyrker, he set sail. "They found first the land which Bjarni had seen last," says the saga. They sailed to land, lowered a boat and went on shore. But they found no grass there. The higher part of the land was covered with ice and snow, and from the shore to the glaciers seemed to be but one flat rock. The land seemed useless, and they called it Helluland (Stoneland). This description fits the region of northern Labrador. They continued their voyage, and soon found another land, where they also went on shore. This land was forest-covered with low, sandy shores. They called it Markland (Woodland), probably southern Labrador. They now hastened to their ships, says the saga, and sailed away with a north wind. They were out two *doegr* (two days' sail) before they saw land. They came to an island which lay to the north of the land, went on ashore and looked about in fine weather. They noticed that there was dew on the grass, and it seemed to them that they had never tasted anything so sweet. Thereupon they embarked and sailed into a sound that lay between that island and the ness. Here they landed at a place where a stream fell into the sea from a lake, says the saga. They built booths, or temporary huts. But later, as they decided to stay, they erected a large house there. They found the climate so mild that they thought that the cattle would not be in need of fodder during the winter. They also observed that night and day were of more equal length there than in Greenland. In exploring the country they found wild grapes. They cut a cargo of timber with which they loaded the ship, and after filling the ship's boat with grapes they sailed back to Greenland. Leif called the country Vinland because of its products.[7]

That the discovery of a forest-covered land to the southward should arouse great interest among the settlers in Greenland is natural, and when the "Flateyjarbók" describes several attempts made by them to explore and colonize the new land, it accords with what we might expect them to do under the circumstances. But the population of the Greenland settlements was so small, and their means so limited that these undertakings would have proved difficult even if the new region had been uninhabited. On the American coast, however, they encountered a warlike native population against whose fierce attacks the small bands of Norsemen must have been well-nigh helpless, as firearms were not yet in use. In Greenland the settlers had been able to maintain a foothold in an unfavorable environment, because the land, upon their arrival, was uninhabited. But it is probably true, as shown also by the saga narratives, that further extension of colonization to the American mainland was prevented mainly by the natives, whose resistance the Norsemen lacked the means to overcome. According to the source already mentioned there was much talk in Greenland about Leif's voyage to Vinland after his return. His brother Thorvald was of the opinion that the country should be explored still further. Leif offered him his ship for a Vinland voyage, and Thorvald made ready, sailing from Greenland with a crew of thirty men. He seems to have followed as closely as possible the route established by Leif. Striking out across the sea from the Eastern Settlement to Helluland, or northern Labrador, they came to Leif's booths in Vinland, and spent the winter there. The following summer was spent in exploring the country. In the spring Thorvald sent a few men westward with a boat to search out that region. In the summer he with the rest of the crew sailed

[7] *Flateyjarbók*, vol. i, p. 429. *The Flatey Book and Recently Discovered Vatican Manuscripts Concerning America as Early as the Tenth Century,* Published by the Norroena Society, London and New York, p. 11 ff. The documents dealing with the colonization of Greenland and the discovery of America are found in *Antiquitates Americanæ,* edited by C. C. Ravn, Copenhagen, 1837.

eastward and to the north of the land. Hard weather came upon him and his men off a ness. His ship was damaged, losing its keel, and some time had to be spent in repairing this damage. On the highest point of the promontory they raised the old ship keel, evidently as a guide to later voyagers, calling the place Kjalarnes (Keelness). On continuing their voyage they found three skin boats and three men under each boat. They killed eight of the men, but one escaped, and soon they were attacked by a large band of natives. Thorvald was mortally wounded by an arrow, and died soon afterward. They buried him, according to his wish, on a jutting promontory, placed crosses on the grave, and called the place Krossanes. They then sailed back to Leif's booths to their companions, spent the winter there, and returned to Greenland the following summer.

The "Flateyjarbók" tells also of an unsuccessful attempt by Thorvald's brother Thorstein Eiriksson to sail to Vinland. Because of storms he lost his way, and was driven back. Later he went to the Western Settlement, where he died of an epidemic shortly afterward. A brief account is also given of Karlsefni's attempt to colonize Vinland, and finally the story is told of the brothers Helgi and Finnbogi who had gone from Norway to Greenland, evidently on a trading expedition. Eirik the Red's daughter Freydis persuaded the brothers to join her and her husband Thorvald in an expedition to Vinland. The voyage seems to have been undertaken for the purpose of gain; chiefly, perhaps, for securing timber, which was very valuable in Greenland. But they seem also to have had in mind the planting of a colony, as a number of women went along. Freydis and her husband entered into a sort of partnership with the two brothers, according to which they were to share equally in all the good things which they might secure. They were to have an equal number of men, thirty on each ship, besides the women, and Leif Eiriksson granted them the use of his cabins while they were in Vinland. From the outset Freydis showed her selfishness and evil disposition. Contrary to the agreement she had thirty-five men on her ship, evidently for the purpose of having an advantage over Helgi and Finnbogi, who did not discover this breach of good faith before they reached Vinland. As they arrived first, they unloaded their supplies and stored them in Leif's booths. But when Freydis came, she compelled them to withdraw and build a cabin of their own. One morning early she came to see Finnbogi. She asked him if he would trade ships with her, as he had the larger ship, and she wished to sail back to Greenland. Finnbogi said that he was willing to remain behind and let her have the ship. But her evil mind was maturing a dark plot to get possession of both ships with their cargoes. Upon returning to her cabin she pretended to be greatly offended, claiming that Finnbogi and Helgi had struck and abused her. She succeeded in so stirring up her husband that he fell upon the brothers, and they were killed together with all their followers, both men and women. In order to hide the crime she threatened with death any one of her followers who should venture to say a word about what had happened. The ships were then loaded, and Freydis and her followers returned to Greenland. But in spite of her threats the news of her crime leaked out. When her brother Leif heard of it, he took three of her men and forced them to make a full confession. When he had learned the whole truth, he said that he would not treat his sister as she deserved, but he prophesied that her offspring would not fare well.

Such voyages to Markland and Vinland, or the coast of North America, as those here described must have been made frequently by the Greenland settlers for the purpose of bringing home timber, of which they were in great need. Of this we have quite positive evidence also in an entry in the "Skálholt Annals" for the year 1347:

"There came also a ship from Greenland smaller in size than the smallest vessels which sail to Iceland. It came to the outer Straumfjord. It was without anchor. There were seventeen men on board. They had sailed to Markland, but afterward they were driven hither."

Since these annals were written not long after this event occurred, there is no reason to doubt the truth of the statement. But such voyages made for commercial reasons by men of no great note were not regarded as exploits, and would not attract the attention of the sagamen, who were interested mainly in preserving the traditions of the leading families.

The account of the Vinland voyages found in the "Flatey-jarbók" seems to be based on the tradition about the discovery and exploration of Vinland as it was preserved in Greenland, as it describes the part played by the Greenland colonies in these events. Another form of the tradition is found in the "Eirikssaga rauða," which represents Leif Eiriksson as the discoverer of Vinland, and describes only one attempt at exploration and colonization, that of Thorfinn Karlsefni.[8] We have already seen that Karlsefni came to Greenland as a trader together with his companions, and that he spent the winter as Eirik's guest at Brattahlid, where he married Eirik's daughter-in-law Gudrid. They spoke much about Vinland, says the saga, and thought that it might prove very profitable to go thither. The result was that Karlsefni and Snorri prepared their ship for a voyage to Vinland in the summer. Gudrid accompanied her husband on the expedition. Bjarni and Thorhall also prepared their ship and made ready to accompany them with the men who came with them from Iceland. Freydis, Eirik's daughter, her husband Thorvard and many others also accompanied them with a ship manned by a crew from Greenland. Thorhall the Hunter, who had accompanied Eirik on expeditions many summers, and was well acquainted with the sailing routes, also accompanied them. Together they had on the three ships 160 men. Instead of following the route established by Leif Eiriksson, Karlsefni sailed first to the Western Settlement and the Bjarneyjar, whence he turned southward to Helluland and Markland. After leaving the Bjarneyjar they first came to a land where they found large flagstones and many foxes, says the saga, and they called it Helluland. They then sailed two *doegr*,[9]

<hr>

[8] *Eirikssaga rauða.* This saga is found in English translation in *Original Narratives of Early American History*, Scribners Sons, New York, 1906.

[9] The word *doegr* used as a nautical term means a day's sailing, usually the distance sailed in twelve hours.

veering to the southeast, and found a land which was well
wooded and had many deer. This land they called Markland. When they had sailed two more *doegr,* they sighted
land, and sailed under the land. There was a promontory
where they first came. They followed the coast having the
land on starboard. It was without harbors, and the shores
were long and sándy. They tacked along the coast, having
the land on the starboard. They went on shore in boats,
and found there on the promontory a ship's keel, and called
it Kjalarnes (Keelness). The shores they called Furdustrandir because it took a long time to sail by them. South
of the Furdustrandir the coast was indented by bays. Sailing into one of these Karlsefni put on shore two runners
which he had received from Leif Eiriksson, the man Haki
and the woman Hekja. He ordered them to run southward
and examine the land, and return before three days had
passed. He cast anchor and waited during their absence.
When three days were passed,

"they came running down from the land. One of them had
grapes in his hands, and the other had self-sown wheat. Karlsefni said that they seemed to have found a fertile country.
They sailed along the coast and came to anchor in a fjord.
"There was an island outside, and round the island strong
currents. They called it Straumsey. There were so many birds
there that one could hardly put one's foot between the eggs.
They held up the fjord and called it Straumsfjord, and unloaded
the ships, and established themselves there. They had with
them all kinds of cattle, and sought to make use of the land.
There were mountains there, and fair was the prospect."

While they were staying at Straumsey they ran short of
food, and were forced to eat the flesh of a dead whale which
drifted ashore. Thorhall the Hunter was much disappointed
with the outcome of the expedition, as it was evident that
they had not found Vinland. He quarreled with Karlsefni,
and wished to go northward in search for Vinland, while
Karlsefni wished to continue southward. With one ship and
nine men Thorhall left the expedition, and proceeded northward. But they were caught in a storm which carried them

out into the ocean. They drifted to Ireland, says the saga, where they were sold as slaves and ill-treated. "There Thorhall lost his life, as merchants have reported."

Karlsefni with Snorri, Bjarni and the rest continued southward along the coast.

"They sailed a long time, until they came to a river, which flowed down from the interior into a lake, and thence into the sea. There were great sandbars before the mouth of the river, so that it could only be entered at high water. Karlsefni and his people sailed to the mouth of the river, and called the country Hóp (i.e., a small land-locked bay). There they found self-sown wheatfields, where the land was low, but vines wherever they saw heights. As every brook was full of fish, they dug trenches on the shore below high-water mark, and when the tide went out, there were halibuts in the trenches. In the forests there was a great number of animals of all kinds. They were there half a month amusing themselves, and suspecting nothing. They had their cattle with them. But early one morning, when they looked about them, they saw nine hide-boats, and wooden poles were being waved on the boats, making a noise like thrashing-flails, and they were moved with the sun. Karlsefni's men took this to be a token of peace, and bore a white shield towards them. Then the strangers rowed towards them, and wondered, and came ashore. They were small (or black) men and ugly, and they had ugly hair; their eyes were big, and they were broad across the cheeks. They stayed there a while, and wondered, then rowed away and went south of the headland.

"Karlsefni had built their houses above the lake, some nearer, and some farther off. Now they stayed there that winter (1004-1005). No snow fell at all, and their cattle were out at pasture.

"When spring came, they saw early one morning a number of hide-boats rowing from the south past the headland, so many that it seemed as if the sea had been sown with coal in front of the bay, and they waved wooden poles on every boat. Then they set up shields and held a market, and the people wanted most to buy red cloth; they also wanted to buy swords and spears, but this was forbidden by Karlsefni and Snorri."

The Skrælings gave them untanned skins in exchange for the cloth, and the trade was proceeding briskly when "an ox which Karlsefni had ran out of the woods and began to bellow. The Skrælings were scared, and ran to their boats, and rowed south along the shore. After that they did not see them for three weeks. But when that time was past, they saw a great multitude of Skræling boats coming from the south, as though driven on by a stream. Then all the poles were waved against the sun, and all the Skrælings howled loudly. Then Karlsefni and his men took red shields and bore towards them. The Skrælings leaped from their boats, and then they made towards each other and fought; there was a hot exchange of missiles. The Skrælings also had catapults (*valslöngur*). Karlsefni and his men saw that the Skrælings hoisted upon a pole a great ball about as large as a sheep's paunch, blue in color, and slung it from the pole upon the land over Karlsefni's people, and it made a great noise when it came down. At this, great terror smote Karlsefni and his people, so that they had no thought but of getting away and up the river, for it seemed to them that the Skrælings were assailing them on all sides; and they did not halt till they had reached certain crags. Then they made a stout resistance. Freydis came out and saw that they were giving way. She cried out: 'Wherefore do you run away from such wretches, ye gallant men? I thought it likely that you could slaughter them like cattle. Had I but arms, I believe that I should fight better than any of you.' None heeded what she said. Freydis tried to go with them, but she fell behind, for she was with child. She nevertheless followed them into the woods, but the Skrælings came after her. She found before her a dead man, Thorbrand Snorrasson, and a flat stone was fixed in his head. His sword lay unsheathed beside him, and she took it up and defended herself with it. Then the Skrælings came at her. She then took her breasts out of her sark and wetted the sword upon them. At that the Skrælings became afraid, and ran away back to their boats, and went away. Karlsefni and his men met her and praised her happy device. Two out of Karlsefni's men fell, and four of the Skrælings; but nevertheless, Karlsefni had suffered defeat. They then went to their houses to bind up their wounds, and to consider what swarm of people it was that came against them from the land. It seemed to them now that there could have been no more than those who came from the boats, and that the other people must have been glamour.

"The Skrælings also found a dead man, and an ax lay beside him; one of them took the ax and struck at a tree, and so one after another, and it seemed to delight them that it bit so well. Then one took and smote a stone with it; but when the ax broke, he thought it was of no use, if it did not stand against stone, and he cast it from him.

"Karlsefni and his men now thought that they could see that although the land was fertile, they would always have trouble and disquiet with the people who dwelt there before. Then they prepared to set out, and intended to go to their own country. They sailed northward and found five Skrælings sleeping in fur-jerkins, and they had with them kegs with deer's marrow mixed with blood. They thought that they could understand that these were outlaws, and they killed them. Then they found a headland and a multitude of deer, and the headland looked like a crust of dried dung, from the deer lying there at night. Now they came back to Straumsfjord, and there was abundance of everything. It is reported by some that Bjarni and Gudrid remained behind there, and a hundred men with them, and did not go farther; but they say that Karlsefni and Snorri went southward with forty men, and were no longer at Hóp than barely two months, returning the same summer.

"Karlsefni then set out with one ship in search of Thorhall the Hunter, but the greater part of the company remained behind. They sailed to the northward around Kjalarnes, and then bore to the westward, having the land to the larboard. The country there was a wooded wilderness as far as they could see. When they had sailed a long time, they came to a stream that flowed from east to west into the sea. They laid the ship along the south bank in the mouth of the stream. One morning Karlsefni and his men saw something that glittered in the forest above a clearing. They called to it, and it moved; it was a Uniped. It hopped down to the bank of the river, where they lay, and shot an arrow into the entrails of Thorvald Eiriksson, who sat at the helm. A little later Thorvald died of this wound. The Uniped ran away northward. They hurried after him and thought that they saw him now and then, but he seemed to get away, and at last he ran out upon a bay. Then they turned back. They then sailed away northward, and on the way they thought they saw the land of Unipeds; but they did not want to risk the lives of their people. It appeared to them that the mountains that they saw here and those they had seen at Hóp were the same, and that from Straumsfjord here and to Straumsfjord at Hóp was the same distance. They returned, and stayed at

Straumsfjord the third winter. There was disagreement, and the people divided into two parties. Karlsefni's son Snorri, who was born the first fall that they were at Straumsfjord, was now three winters old, when they went away."

The narrative of the "Eirikssaga rauða," or "Karlsefnis-saga," describing the discovery of America by Leif Eiriksson, and the attempt of Thorfinn Karlsefni to colonize Vinland, evidently rests on traditions preserved in Iceland regarding these events, as it describes the part played by the Icelanders in these voyages. Regarding the relative merit of the two traditions, and the value of these sagas as historical sources, no unanimity exists among historians. But all agree that the mainland of North America was discovered by Norse colonists and voyagers from Iceland or Greenland. This is proved by reliable accounts outside of these saga narratives. The entry in the "Skálholt Annals" for the year 1347, stating that a ship carrying seventeen men came to Iceland from Markland, has already been mentioned. The seventeen men on board the ship could give the annalist full information, the correctness of which can not well be questioned. Another entry in the Icelandic annals (Annales Regii) for the year 1121 states: "Eirik, the bishop of Greenland, went to search for Vinland." This is the last record of voyages to Vinland. Eirik may have been the first bishop of Greenland. He must have lost his life on the expedition, as nothing more is heard of him, and in 1122 and 1123 the Greenlanders were making efforts to secure a new bishop. In his work "Íslendingabók" (1120-1130) the old and reliable Icelandic historian Ari Frodi says:

"The land which is called Greenland was discovered and colonized from Iceland. Eirik the Red, a man from Breidafjord, went thither, and took land in a place called Eiriksfjord. He gave the land name, and called it Greenland, saying that it would entice people to go there, if the country had a fine name. They found human dwelling places both east and west in the land, remnants of boats, and stone implements, from which they could judge that the same people had wandered about there, which inhabit Vinland, and which the Greenlanders call Skrælings. But he began to colonize the country fourteen or fifteen winters before Christianity was introduced in Iceland, according to what was told Thorkell Gellison in Greenland by one who had accompanied Eirik thither."

Vinland is mentioned also in the "Landnámabók" about 1250. A most interesting reference to Helluland, Markland and Vinland is found also in an old Icelandic geography, thought to have been written in part at least by Abbot Nikulas Bergsson of Thverá, who died in 1159.

"South of Greenland," he says, "lies Helluland, then comes Markland, and not very far from there lies Vinland the Good, which some believe to be connected with Africa; but if this is the case, then the great ocean must come between Markland and Vinland. It is said that Thorfinn Karlsefni chopped a tree for a *húsa-snotra* (an ornament on a building), and that he afterwards set out to find Vinland the Good, and came to a place where this was supposed to lie; but he was not able to explore it, and did not establish himself there. Leif the Lucky first discovered Vinland, and he rescued some merchants whom he found in the sea in great danger. He also introduced Christianity in Greenland, which so prospered that a bishopric was established at Gardar."

Vinland is mentioned also in the "Eyrbyggjasaga," in the "Heimskringla," and in several other sagas from the classical period. Vinland is first mentioned by Adam v. Bremen about 1070 in the fourth chapter of his church history of the archbishopric of Hamburg, the "Gesta Hammaburgensis":

"He (the king of Denmark) mentioned also another island which has been discovered by many in this ocean, which is called Winland, because grapevines grow wild there, and yield the best wine."

The discovery of the American continent by the Norse traders and voyagers was, furthermore, so natural an event that no ground can exist for questioning this varied and reliable testimony. After the Norsemen had established permanent colonies in southern Greenland, and had opened routes of trade from Norway to Greenland by way of Iceland, and from Norway to Greenland directly across the

Atlantic, it would indeed be strange if some voyager should not also find the neighboring American coast while groping his way in these foggy and dangerous waters. But admitting, as we must admit, that the mainland of North America was discovered by the Norsemen, what should stand in the way of accepting as fairly reliable such features of the saga narratives as stand supported in part also by other evidence: the repeated trips to Markland and Vinland to get timber, the efforts to colonize the coast, the trade with the natives, the battle with them, in which the Norsemen were defeated and forced to abandon the projected colonization? These features are as realistic and natural as any other page of American colonial history.

The question of the location of Vinland remains a matter of controversy.[10] All original sources agree that Markland was the name given to the first forest-covered region found by the Norse voyagers as they sailed southward along the coast. This enables us to determine approximately the location of this land. But where was Vinland? No discussion of this question can here be entered into. It should be remembered, however, that the Greenland colonists had but few ships, and lacked the materials for building new ones. The population of the colonies was small, and their resources were in every way very limited, a circumstance which would scarcely encourage the settlers to undertake voyages of discovery on a large scale by sailing to the distant coast of New England, or even still farther along the American seaboard. After all, the statement of the old geographer Nikulas Bergsson of Thverá that not far from

[10] Many writers, notably R. B. Anderson, *America not Discovered by Columbus,* and William Hovgaard, *The Voyages of the Norsemen to America,* hold that Vinland was located on what is now the coast of New England. Prof. Gustav Storm, *Studier over Vinlandsreiserne,* places Vinland on the coast of Nova Scotia. Dr. Andrew Fossum, *The Norse Discovery of America,* places it to the south of the mouth of the St. Lawrence river. Prof. H. P. Steensby, *The Norsemen's Route from Greenland to Wineland,* Copenhagen, 1918, locates Helluland and Markland on Labrador, and Hóp at the mouth of the St. Lawrence river. G. H. Gathorne-Hardy, F. R. G. S., *The Norse Discoverers of America,* recently published, regards Long Island Sound as Straumsfjord, and the estuary of the Hudson River as Hóp.

Markland lies Vinland sounds very natural. The Norwegian historian Gustav Storm in his work "Studier over
Vinlandsreiserne" places Vinland on Nova Scotia. Dr.
Andrew Fossum in his work "The Norse Discovery of
America" places it at the mouth of the St. Lawrence river;
and Professor H. P. Steensby in a recently published work,
"The Norsemen's Route from Greenland to Wineland,"
places Helluland and Markland on Labrador, and Hóp at
the mouth of the St. Lawrence river. These writers agree
in so far as to limit the activities of the Norsemen on the
American coast to the basin of the St. Lawrence bay, a
feature which commends itself to a thoughtful reader. But
the question regarding the location of Vinland has not been,
and probably never can be, definitely settled.

The Greenland colonies continued to flourish so long as
the intercourse with Iceland and Norway was maintained.
Greenland became a bishopric in 1110, though Arnald, who
was ordained in Lund in Skåne in 1124, is the first bishop
of Greenland known to have been ordained. A cathedral
was erected at Gardar, of which ruins are still found. In
1261, in the reign of King Haakon Haakonsson, Greenland
became a Norwegian dependency, or crown colony. Traffic
between Norway, Iceland and Greenland was quite well
maintained till in the fourteenth century, but great harm
was done when the trade with the colonies was made a
royal monopoly, so that no trade with these distant settlements could be carried on except by a few vessels in the
king's service. The Black Death, which reached Norway in
1349, and carried away over one-third of the population of
the country, gave the traffic with the colonies a blow from
which it never recovered. When the Hanseatic merchants
gained control of Bergen, the chief Norwegian commercial
city at that time, and swept Norwegian commerce from
the sea, the colonies in Greenland were cut off from all
communication both with Norway and Iceland. At this
time the Eskimos also seem to have returned from the north
to their old haunts in Greenland and to have attacked the
settlers. In 1341 Ivar Baardsøn went to Greenland, returning in 1370. According to his report he went to the Western

Settlement with a small force to aid the settlers, but he found no one there either Christian or heathen, only a few almost wild sheep and cattle. The colony had been entirely destroyed. The Icelandic annals for the year 1379 contain the following notice:

"The Skrælings attacked the Greenlanders, killed eighteen of them, and carried away two boys, whom they made slaves."

Throughout the fourteenth century some efforts were made in Norway to maintain communications with the Greenland settlements. In 1367 Bishop Alf came to Greenland after the people had had no bishop for nineteen years. He was the last bishop in Greenland, and died there in 1377. After 1385 an old priest is known to have acted as bishop. In the beginning of the fifteenth century all communication with Greenland ceased. In 1406 a ship sailing from Norway to Iceland strayed from its course, and finally came to anchor in Greenland, where it remained till 1410, when it returned to Norway. This is the last definitely recorded visit to Greenland. The last mention of the colonies is found in a letter issued by Pope Alexander VI in 1492, the same year that Columbus set out for the new world.[11] "For eighty years, or thereabouts," says the pope, "absolutely no bishop or priest has governed that church (of Greenland) in personal residence. The result has been that most of the inhabitants have fallen away from the Christian faith." The letter indicates that news from Greenland had been received not many years previous to the publication of the letter, an assumption which is rendered almost a certainty by a recently discovered letter in the government archives in Copenhagen. This letter shows that in 1475 an expedition was sent out under the leadership of the voyagers Pining and Pothorst to search for new lands. From a station on the mountain of Hvitsark in Greenland, says the writer, Pining fought with the Greenland sea-robbers

[11] The letter is found both in the original and in translation in *The Flatey Book and Recently Discovered Vatican Manuscripts*, Norroena Society, London and New York; also in *Original Manuscripts of Early American History*.

which infested the seas, which indicates that the expedition must have reached Greenland. But the Norse colonies on the island disappeared. When John Davis in 1585 reached the coast of Greenland, the "Land of Desolation," he found no white settlers, and thought that he was the first discoverer of the country. What was the ultimate fate of the Norse colonists is not known. Cut off from all communication with the rest of the world they could exist in that region only by adopting the mode of life of the surrounding native tribes. Norse loan-words and traditions found among the Eskimos indicate that the colonists finally joined them. An entry in the "Gisli Oddsson's Annals" written in Iceland in 1637, says: "The people of Greenland fell away from the true faith, and after having lost all good customs and true virtue they returned to the American people." This can only mean that they adopted the ways of the native inhabitants; but the statement is probably unhistorical. Their fate remains shrouded in mystery, but numerous ruins of churches and dwellings in both settlements which they founded still bear evidence of their life and activity in Greenland.

7. Development of Scaldic Song and Saga Literature

The rapid advance of the Norsemen during the Viking era, their conquests and naval exploits, their activity in trade and colonization shaped their early history, and revealed the basic traits of their character in practical pursuits. Their intellectual life manifested itself chiefly in their mythology and their scaldic poesy which gave expression to the pagan spirit of the North after it had reached the height of self-conscious vigor through the stirring events of the Viking Age. In the motherland Norway the scaldic art had flourished long before the discovery of Iceland.[1] The names of many scalds prior to the period

[1] Finnur Jonsson, *Den oldnorske og oldislandske Literaturs Historie;* Hermann Paul, *Grundriss der germanischen Philologi,* vol. ii, p. 71 ff. Th. Wisén, *Carmina Norroena.* Karl Müllenhoff, *Deutsche Alterthumskunde,* vol. v. Rasmus Flo, *Gamle Skaldar og Kvad.*

of King Harald Haarfagre have been preserved, but it was especially his illustrious reign and his own interest in scaldic poetry which caused it to blossom into new growth. Inspired probably by the example of Charlemagne and Alfred the Great he showed special fondness for the scalds, making them members of his *hirð*, where they could lead a life free from care in full enjoyment of royal favor. Several scalds are known to have been connected with King Harald's *hirð*, as Thjodolf of Hvin, Thorbjörn Hornklofi, Ölver Hnufa and others. These hirdscalds who lived in the attractive court circles and became devotedly attached to their royal patron would naturally extol his valor and achievements in *drápas,* or laudatory songs. Such expressions of gratitude and esteem became part of their vocation as court poets. In time, as the royal *hirð* gradually became the center of literary life, a new kind of poetry developed, the hirdscalds poetry, martial in spirit, narrative historical in contents and characterized by the very intricate verse-form, the *drottkvætt* strophe, or *drottkvæðr háttr,* in which it was produced.

The number of scalds who could stay at the king's court was naturally limited. Many who had no opportunity to court royal favor continued to cultivate their art in the old way, uninfluenced by the new departure of the hirdscalds. They still used the older and simpler verse forms: *fornyrðislag, málaháttr,* and *ljóðaháttr,* and turned into poetry the old myths and heroic traditions, the most cherished intellectual heritage of the people. Their greatest achievement is a collection of old songs known as the "Elder Edda," the greatest work in Old Norse poetic literature. None of the authors of these poems have become known to posterity, probably because they were not connected with the court circles, but chiefly perhaps because they regarded their songs, not as new creations to which they could lay claim of authorship, but as a common national inheritance which they had only been instrumental in preserving in poetic form. In this way two distinct branches of scaldic song had been developed; the "Elder Edda" group, which is of chief interest as mythology and poetry, and the scaldic songs proper by known authors, which are chiefly of historical contents, constituting the first recorded history of the North.

The last great Norwegian hirdscald was Eyvind Finnsson, known as Eyvind Scaldaspillir, who stayed at the court of King Haakon the Good and fought in the battle of Stord where the king fell. It is evident that scaldic poetry continued to flourish also in Norway, as the greater number of the Elder Edda songs must have been written there from the ninth to the eleventh century. But after Eyvind Skaldaspillir's time a general decline seems to have made itself felt in Norse scaldic poetry, as the hirdscalds both in Norway and elsewhere after that time were almost exclusively Icelanders. The leadership in literature was passing to the colony, though the influence of the mother country was still strong. Many of the early Icelandic scalds were of Norse birth or parentage. As scaldic song was their heritage from the homeland, the poetry which blossomed forth in Iceland was but the continuation of an old art of song already so well developed that it underwent no subsequent change even in an era of vigorous growth in a new environment. The *drottkvæðr háttr,* in which the scaldic songs were generally composed, had reached a stage of intricacy and artificiality which to the modern mind makes the stanzas appear like puzzling word riddles difficult to decipher. All principal ideas are set forth figuratively through metaphoric expressions, *kenningar,* which presuppose an intimate knowledge of mythology and other elements of thought employed in the comparisons. That the expression *the dragon's bed* means gold is evident enough when we know the Fafnir myth. So we can also analyze the expression *brynie-thing's tree* and see that it means a hero, since *brynie-thing* means the meeting of the brynies, or battle, and the tree of the *brynie-thing* is the hero who stands in the battle as a tree stands in the storm. But the analysis of such figures is rendered still more difficult by the fact that the words do not follow each other in the natural order, but are thrown about promiscuously in such a way that it is often difficult to determine to what part of the sentence or to what sentence the word belongs. To compose lengthy poems in meter so involved and artificial was a difficult task. A *drápa* had to consist of at least twenty stanzas, and often they were much longer, numbering forty or fifty stanzas. The work of composing these long and intricate songs, in which the historical events dealt with also had to be told with the greatest accuracy, seems to have been done chiefly at night when the scald could be undisturbed in his labor. We read of the great scald Egill Skallagrimsson that in one night he was able to compose the great song "Höfuðlausn," by which he saved his life when he fell into the hands of his enemy King Eirik Bloodax. On another occasion his younger contemporary Einar Skálaglam paid him a visit, and as he was not at home, he left a shield at his door. At this Egill became angry, saying: "Does he think that I will sit up nights to compose a poem about his shield?" This he nevertheless did. He wrought a song about the shield in which all the figures in the decorations are carefully described. "About my renowned lord I make a song while others sleep," says Einar Skálaglam. The second great task of the scald was to commit his poem to memory so that he could recite it with vigor and effect. Considering the length of the *drápas* and the intricacy of the met r it is clear that the task of composing them and committing them to memory was an arduous one, requiring both patience and talent. The scald naturally considered a well-made *drápa* an achievement worthy of praise and reward. Bitter must have been his disappointment, if, after his painstaking labor, his royal patron should fail to appreciate the song, or even refuse to hear it, as King Olaf Tryggvason did with Hallfred Vandrædaskald. Against this slight Hallfred protested so vigorously that the king consented to hear the song, and rewarded the scald liberally for it. Few scaldic songs have been preserved in complete form. For the most part only fragments are found as quotations in later prose works, so that, according to Finnur Jonsson, not over a one-hundreth part of the old scaldic poetry has been preserved. These fragments deal principally with historical events, the warlike achievements of the kings and chieftains in whose honor the songs have been written. But it is clear that the interest of the scalds was not limited to this general theme, though the laudatory martial verses give the general tone and character to scaldic poetry. Not infrequently did the scalds devote their entire poems to quite different themes, as did Egill Skallagrimsson in his "Sonatorrek" and Ulf Uggason in his "Húsdrápa." Lovesongs, though condemned by the social etiquette of those times, were nevertheless composed by many noted scalds like Kormak Önundsson, Thormod Kolbrunarskald and Björn Hitdælakappi. Often the scalds would encourage their hearers to wisdom, moderation, justice, faithfulness and other manly virtues. They taught the young men what virtues were to be admired and what vices would bring dishonor and contempt. At times they were able also to strike more tender chords which gave expression to the deepest emotions. Their art projected itself into every field and stirred the national spirit to daring and adventure. It became a conventional mode of public utterance, giving expression to the people's thoughts and sentiments—a force so great that even kings would bow before it in silence.

The scalds were of importance not only as poets but as men of prominence who played a leading part in public affairs in shaping the national life of their people. Through extensive travels abroad they became the representatives through whom the Icelanders as a nation remained in close touch with European life and culture. Other chieftains would also travel in foreign lands, but few became so well known or maintained so close relations with rulers and men of note as the scalds, who, in many instances, exerted a marked influence even on the affairs of foreign countries. When they returned home, they naturally made a great impression on their own local circles through their proud bearing and the display of costly presents which they had received from royal patrons. The spirit of adventure and restless energy, the proud self-assertive vigor which characterized the Icelanders during the period of their national independence was largely fostered by the scalds, who were

the exponents of whatever was most typical in Northern
social and intellectual life. For centuries they remained
the chief representatives of their people's intellectual culture, and often the leading actors in those events which
made the deepest impression on the public mind. It is natural that the hirdscalds as a rule should be the best known,
as they were found in the entourage of ruling princes,
and often played a conspicuous part in public affairs.
Their connection with the court would not of itself prove
that they were more gifted than others who had won less
distinction, but it showed that, aside from their poetic
talents, they possessed personal qualities which enabled
them to win the favor of rulers, and the esteem of the
highest circles everywhere. They were high-spirited men
jealous of their honor, equal in polish and courtly etiquette
to the best men who graced the royal halls in all lands. As
they were welcomed by the rulers, they appeared at every
court where language did not stand in the way. We find
them in England, Ireland, Scotland, Denmark and Sweden
as well as at the courts of the ruling jarls in the western
Norse colonies. But from reign to reign their best representatives were usually grouped about the throne of the
kings of Norway.

A martial figure who carried his helmeted head high
above all other Icelandic scalds and chieftains in his day
was Egill Skallagrimsson, born at Borg in Borgarfjord about
900.[2] His grandfather Kveldulf Bjálfason of Firdafylke in
Norway was a chieftain of the old school, a giant in stature,
ugly and morose, but possessing to some degree the gift of
song which seems to have been a family heritage. He had
two sons, Thorolf and Skallagrim, Egill's father. We are
told that Thorolf, who was a friendly and fine appearing
man, joined King Harald Haarfagre's court as *hirðmaðr*,
but Kveldulf and Skallagrim persisted in their opposition
to the king. When they finally had to flee, they brought
their families and household goods on board the ships and
sailed for Iceland. Kveldulf died on the voyage, but Skallagrim reached his destination, and settled in the western

[2] *Egilssaga*, edited by Finnur Jonsson.

districts, where he built a residence called Borg, from which the Borgarfjord derived its name. The saga narrative makes it clear that Egill resembled in all respects his father and grandfather. He was very tall and broad-shouldered, with a big head and homely features. The following description is given of him as he sat in King Aethelstan's hall in England: "He had a big face, high forehead and bushy brows, a thick and not very long nose. The bearded part of his face was prominent, he had a broad chin and cheeks, a heavy neck and broad shoulders. When angry he looked very fierce. He was well built and taller than all others. His hair was thick and of a wolf-gray color, but he grew bald very early. He had dark eyes and black eyebrows." With great physical strength Egill combined a restless and violent temper, productive of bloodshed and contention throughout his whole career. While a child of seven he slew his playmate. At twelve he killed the manager of the estate in revenge because his father had caused the death of his governess. Wherever he went, trouble was sure to follow; but as a poet he stood unexcelled, and he must be classed as one of the greatest of all known scalds. At the age of twenty he went to Norway in company with his brother Thorolf, but as trouble soon arose between the brothers and King Eirik Bloodax, who had been elevated to the throne by his father, King Harald Haarfagre, Thorolf and Egill had to flee. After spending some time on Viking expeditions they entered the service of Aethelstan, king of England, who was at the time engaged in a war with the combined forces of Scots and Vikings. In a great battle with these forces Thorolf fell. But Egill is said to have received from the king two rings of gold and also two chests filled with silver, which he was to divide with his father and other relatives in compensation for their loss. The event seems to have so endeared Egill to the king that he was invited to spend the winter at the court. The following summer he went again to Norway, where he married his brother's widow, and after an absence of many years he returned to Iceland with his wife and treasures. On a second trip to Norway, which he undertook in order to secure some property to which his wife had fallen heir, the quarrel with King Eirik was renewed. The king was probably too preoccupied with weightier matters to pay much attention to the rather insolent chieftain, as he was soon driven from the throne by his brother Haakon the Good. But fortune once more brought the two face to face under altered circumstances. Eirik had to flee to England, where he became ruler of Northumbria as King Aethelstan's vassal. While he sat at York, Egill was shipwrecked on the Northumbrian coast, and had to surrender himself into his hands. He was condemned to death, and would have been speedily executed, but through the intercession of his friend, the powerful Arinbjörn Hersi, who was King Eirik's chief adviser, a respite was granted till the following day. In the night he composed the song "Höfuðlausn" in praise of the brave and gallant Eirik, which so pleased the king that he spared his life, and allowed him to depart unharmed. After his fortunate escape from King Eirik Egill again went to King Aethelstan of England, and later to Norway. On the island of Hereidland on the coast of Søndmøre, he visited the widow Gyda, a sister of his friend Arinbjörn Hersi, who lived here with her daughter and a son called Fridgeir. A rude Viking warrior by the name of Ljot, a Swede by birth, who was pressing an unwelcome suit for the daughter's hand, had challenged Fridgeir to a duel because he opposed the match. When Gyda told Egill her plight, he promised to meet Ljot in the duel. In his arrogance Ljot formally challenged Egill, but lost his life in the encounter. After another successful duel with Atli Skammi Egill gained possession of his wife's inheritance and returned to Iceland. For many years he continued as before in hazardous undertakings. But when he grew older he finally abandoned life of adventure, remaining quietly at home. In spite of his warlike appearance and his love of strife and adventure Egill was at times moved by great feelings which reveal a tenderness of heart strange in a man so inured to danger and bloodshed. While dwelling quietly at Borg he had the misfortune to lose his favorite son, Bödvar, who was drowned in the Borgarfjord not far from home. Shortly after the accident he found the body and interred it in his father's burial mound. But he was so overwhelmed with grief, says the saga, that he shut himself up in his room, refused food and drink, and would allow no one to see him. Finally his daughter Thorgerd persuaded him to take nourishment and to compose a song in memory of his sons. In this poem, "Sonatorrek," [3] he pours forth his grief with a depth of lyric sentiment quite marvelous when we consider how seldom real sentiment found expression in early Germanic song. Poetry had not yet risen to be an expression of man's inner life. It was not poesy in the modern sense, but an art of narrative setting forth in an objective way, in well wrought and properly ornamented form, such traditions and events as might be of general interest. Egil, however, was too strong a personality, too gifted and original a poet to be confined within the narrow limits of oppressive rules. In his song "Sonatorrek" his sorrow overflows the conventional borders like a mad torrent, and he composes a tearladen song full of the tenderest emotion. Egill died at the ripe old age of over eighty years. He was not a hirdscald, as his strong individuality rendered him as unfit as he was unwilling to serve any one in any capacity. When not engaged in perilous adventures he chose to stay at home as a powerful magnate on his own estates, as did many other chieftains and poets of less note. He was of importance not only as scald but as a typical Icelandic chieftain whose personality and achievements are written large in the annals of his people.

Of special importance at the beginning of the eleventh century were the two scalds and chieftains Gunnlaug Ormstunga and Hrafn Önundsson, whose tragic rivalry is narrated in the "Gunnlaugssaga Ormstungu." According to this saga Gunnlaug, the son of Illugi Svarti of Gilsbakki, was betrothed to Helga the Fair, a granddaughter of Egill Skallagrimsson. He had already arranged to go abroad to spend some time in foreign lands. But an agreement was made with the bride's father and relatives that he should return and consummate the marriage within three years,

[3] *Egilssaga*, p. 362 ff.

or the engagement should be considered canceled. Gunnlaug went to Norway to the court of Eirik Jarl, where he met other Icelandic scalds who were members of the jarl's *hirð*, among others Halldor Okristni and Skuli Thorsteinsson, Helga's brother. Skuli took a friendly interest in him and introduced him at court; but through his arrogant behavior the haughty Gunnlaug so offended the jarl that he had to leave Norway. He sailed to England, where he was well received by King Aethelred, who seems to have had a special fondness for Icelandic scalds and chieftains. A song which Gunnlaug composed in his honor so pleased the king that he gave him a scarlet mantle, and made him a member of his *hirð*. Through these royal favors his success as hirdscald was assured, and he remained at court during the winter. In the spring he went to Dublin to King Sigtrygg Silkbeard, where he was cordially received. Here his songs were no less liberally rewarded, as he received from the king a scarlet mantle and an arm ring of gold. From Dublin he went to Sigurd Lodveson, jarl of the Orkneys; and shortly after he sailed to Sweden, and spent the winter at the court of Sigurd Jarl of Götaland. The following spring he arrived in Upsala. At the royal court, where he found a welcome, he met his rival Hrafn Önundsson, who had spent the summer in Norway, and had arrived in Sweden in the fall. Their rivalry is described with dramatic vividness in the saga narrative. Both sought eagerly to win the king's favor, and asked to recite songs in his honor. Hrafn asked the privilege to appear first in the contest, as he had been longest at the court; but the king decided that Gunnlaug should have the first opportunity, as he would become angry if he could not have his own way. He then stepped forward and recited a *drápa* to the king. "What do you think of the song, Hrafn?" said the king. "Well, my Lord," answered Hrafn, "it is boastful, and not very beautiful; just like Gunnlaug's own character." "Now you recite your song, Hrafn," said the king. Hrafn did so. When he had finished, the king said to Gunnlaug: "What do you think of the song?" "It is pretty, but very insignificant," said Gunnlaug, "just as Hrafn himself is a handsome man." [4]   Their rivalry soon led to open enmity. Hrafn told Gunnlaug that since he had insulted him in the presence of the court, he would henceforth do what he could to harm him. Hrafn became a member of the *hirð,* and received valuable gifts from the king. The following spring he went to Trondhjem, Norway, returning to Iceland in the summer. Gunnlaug seems to have been less successful. The saga says that he, too, received gifts from the king, but what these were is not stated, neither does it appear that he became a member of the *hirð*. He returned to England to King Aethelred, where he remained during the summer and the following winter. The next summer he went to Norway, and found opportunity to sail with Hallfred Vandrædaskald to Iceland late in the fall. As his three years' leave of absence had long since expired, his rival, Hrafn, who knew his pledge, had used the opportunity to sue for the hand of Helga the Fair. Against her will she was given him in marriage, the wedding being solemnized shortly after Gunnlaug's return. In sullen gloom the wronged and outwitted scald had to nurse his wrath in his parental home during the winter, but the following summer he challenged Hrafn to a duel. This was fought at the Althing without decisive results. Since it was apparent that a new encounter would soon follow, a law was passed by the Althing forbidding duels in Iceland. The two rivals then repaired to Norway, where duelling was not yet prohibited, and in a final contest both lost their lives. Helga later married a good and well-to-do man, the scald Thorkell Hallkelsson. But in this otherwise happy marriage she never forget her love for Gunnlaug.

"It was her greatest pleasure," says the saga, "to look at a scarlet mantle which Gunnlaug had given her. At one time there was much sickness in Thorkell's home, and many were ill for a long time. Helga, too, had become sick, though she was not in bed. One Saturday evening as she sat in the living room leaning her head upon her husband's knee, she sent for the scarlet mantle. When it was brought she spread it out and looked at it a while, sank back in her husband's arms and died."

[4] *Gunnlaugssaga Ormstungu,* ch. 18.

As Egill Skallagrimsson distinguished himself as a war-like chieftain, and Gunnlaug and Hrafn as courtiers and hirdscalds, Sighvat Thordsson, usually known as Sighvat Scald, distinguished himself especially as statesman and counselor. He had been reared in Iceland, but at the age of eighteen he came to Norway, where he met his father, Thord Sigvaldascald, at the royal court in 1015. Through a poem which he composed to the king he won his special favor. Upon nearer acquaintance there grew up between King Olaf and the scald a friendship so intimate that Sighvat slept in the king's own apartments, and acted as his counselor in cases which no one else ventured to bring before him.[5] When Olaf sent his men to collect the *land-aurar* tax from the Icelanders who were staying in Norway, they went to Sighvat Scald, and asked him to help them, says the saga. Sighvat's noble character, his even temper and good judgment so endeared him to the king that in spite of his youth he was sent on important missions as the king's own representative. In 1018, when twenty years of age, he was dispatched on a difficult diplomatic errand to Ragnvald Jarl of Vestergötland, as the Swedish king had broken his agreement with Olaf regarding his marriage to the Swedish princess Ingigerd. King Olaf had gone to Konghelle, where the wedding was to be celebrated; but the bride did not appear, and it was learned later that her father had promised her in marriage to Grandduke Jaroslaf of Gardarike (Russia). This wanton breach of faith made King Olaf very angry, and it became Sighvat's task to bring about a settlement by which the king might be appeased and war averted. At Ragnvald's court he met the beautiful princess Astrid, Ingigerd's sister, and entered into negotiations with the jarl about a possible marriage between her and King Olaf. When he had obtained Astrid's consent and the jarl's promise of assistance, he returned to King Olaf. He told him of the beautiful princess, and praised her charms so highly that the king forgot his dudgeon. His marriage to Astrid was celebrated at Sarpsborg in 1019. This new proof of tact and ability placed Sighvat so high in

[5] *Heimskringla, Saga of Olaf the Saint*, ch. 43 ff.

the king's esteem that he was elevated to the position of *stallar*, the highest office within the *hirð*. In 1025-1026 he traveled in England and France. When he returned, King Olaf expressed his displeasure because he had visited his enemy King Knut the Great of England. To this Sighvat replied in a song: "Knut asked me if I would be his man as I had been yours, but I answered truthfully that it was proper for me to have only one lord at the time." This pleased the king, and Sighvat was reinstated in the office of *stallar*. In 1029 he made a pilgrimage to Rome in company with Bersi Skaldtorfuson. In August the following year he began the homeward journey, but on the way he received the news that King Olaf had fallen in the battle of Stiklestad. When he reached Norway, the Danish king, Swein Alfivason, who had seized the throne, invited him to join his *hirð*, but he refused. His deep sorrow for his friend King Olaf he has expressed in numerous songs. In one of these he says: "The high mountains throughout the land seemed to smile while Olaf lived. Now the dreary mountain-sides are no longer beautiful!" Sighvat remained with Olaf's widowed queen, Astrid, and joined the party which planned to drive the usurper, King Swein, from the throne. This was successfully carried out in 1035. Swein was driven away, and Olaf's son Magnus was placed on the throne. Sighvat now returned to court, and resumed once more his former position as chief counselor to the king, an office in which he rendered his young patron the most valuable services. Before he had been elevated to the throne, King Magnus had given a promise that he would not persecute those who had fought against his father at Stiklestad. But during the early years of his reign he seemed disposed to break his word on this point. Sighvat was then asked by the magnates to admonish the king. This he did in a song called "Bersöglisvisur" (i.e., plain speaking song). He reminded the king of his promise; told him of the enthusiasm with which the people had elevated him to the throne; that they felt as if they had grasped heaven with both hands when they got Magnus, the son of Saint Olaf, for their king. But now they did

not know whether to rejoice or feel sad, since he had broken
his pledge. A king especially, says the poet, ought to keep
his word. But now the people complain that he deprives
them of their *odel* by seizing their property through unjust persecution. These words sank deep into the young
king's mind. From that time forth he began to rule so well
that he was known as Magnus the Good. Not long after
this Sighvat died. His work was finished. For the second
time he had averted war, and had rendered the greatest
service to his royal friend and patron. Sighvat's reputation did not rest wholly on his poetic talents, as others undoubtedly equaled if they did not surpass him in the exercise of the scaldic art. It was not less his personality and
lofty character, his wisdom and prudence through which
he won the confidence of the king which made him one of
the most conspicuous figures in public life in his own day,
and transmitted his name with special veneration to succeeding ages. With the gifts of a poet he combined the
high qualities of a leader, and the clear vision of the proper
course of conduct under trying circumstances, qualities of
real greatness which raised him high above those who had
little but their poetic gifts to recommend them to their
own generation or to preserve their names to posterity.

Prominent at the court of King Olaf Haraldsson was
also Thormod Kolbrunarskald Bersason, one of the best
known hirdscalds, whose life story is told with interesting
detail in the "Fostbrœdrasaga." Thormod was born at
Isafjord in northern Iceland in 997. From youth up he
was very courageous and active, of middle size, with dark
curly hair, says the saga. He entered into the closest
friendship, *fostbrœðralag,* with Thorgeir Hávarsson, and
the two indulged in all sorts of reckless deeds until they
parted because of some misunderstanding, as Thorgeir's
heartless arrogance seems to have known no bounds.[6]
Thormod returned to his parental home, but Thorgeir continued his life of adventure till he was slain by a Greenland
merchant. One of the most interesting episodes in Thormod's career was his infatuation for the beautiful Thor-

Fostbrœdrasaga, ch. 2 ff.

björg Kolbruna, the daughter of a widow in Isafjord. To
her he composed a number of lovesongs which earned for
him the sobriquet of Kolbrunarskald by which he was since
known. The same restless spirit which characterized his
youth led him to undertake a voyage to Greenland, where
he took a cruel revenge for his fallen friend Thorgeir Hávarsson. Before his voyage he had spent some time at the
court of King Olaf Haraldsson. On his return to Norway
he was again attached to the king's *hirð*, where he remained
until King Olaf fell at Stiklestad in 1030. Thormod and
all other Icelandic hirdscalds at the king's court took part in
that battle and fought valiantly under the royal standards.
Many Icelanders also served in the king's army in that
memorable battle. Snorri Sturlason says that before the
battle began an enemy reconnoitering detachment of thirty
men under Hrut of Vigg was attacked by the Icelanders and
destroyed.[7] This shows that they must have been present
in the royal army in considerable force. Thormod was
mortally wounded, and died at the close of the battle.
Much of his renown is due to his brave conduct and heroic
death at Stiklestad, through which his name has become
associated with King Olaf's last heroic struggle on that
memorable field.

This brief account of men like Egill, Gunnlaug, Hrafn,
Sighvat and Thormod will serve to illustrate the general
character of Icelandic scalds, and the influence they exerted at home and abroad. A great number of talented
Icelanders devoted themselves to the scaldic art, especially
during the Viking Age. Fifteen are known to have remained at the Norwegian court during the reigns of Magnus
the Good and Harald Haardraade. But after the Norman
conquest of England in 1066 scaldic poetry suffered a rapid
decline. For the kings and nobles of the North the opportunity for further conquests now disappeared, and with it
faded away the glories of warlike expeditions to foreign
lands. The lively intercourse which hitherto had been
maintained between Norway, Iceland and England was to a
large extent interrupted, since Olaf Kyrre, who succeeded

[7] *Heimskringla, Saga of Olaf the Saint,* ch. 209.

his father, King Harald, on the throne, not only inaugurated
a distinct peace policy, but was almost exclusively interested in codifying and revising the laws of the realm.
Scaldic poesy was no longer in harmony with the prevailing spirit of the times. Its decline was due primarily to
fundamental changes in the cultural life in the North
wrought by the development of new social ideals. But the
art itself had limitations which in a period of intellectual
growth soon rendered it archaic and hastened its decay.
It had not sought to give a comprehensive picture of life
even of the aristocratic upper classes. It had dwelt on the
heights, dealing mostly with isolated contemporary events
and persons of rank and renown. In versification it had
reached the limit of artificiality, and as the most intricate
of all, the *drottkvætt* strophe, had gradually been established as the standard poetic form, in which nearly all
poems were composed, there was little opportunity for
creative originality. In early times this art had reflected
clearly the soul of a primitive age, but to younger generations born after the introduction of Christianity it gradually lost much of its original charm. No longer versed in
the details of the old myths, people found difficulty in understanding the vague allusions, the curiously turned
phrases and artificial verses of the scalds. The need was
felt of a more popular form of literary art. This was found
in the developing saga literature.

The early settlers in Iceland brought with them from the
mother country the knowledge of prose narrative as they
had brought that of scaldic song, though this form of literary expression existed at that time only in a primitive and
rudimentary form of development. Prose narrative in some
form had flourished in Norway from very ancient times,
but it was in the Icelandic colonial settlements that it first
developed into a distinct literary art, giving rise to the great
prose literature known as the sagas. It is true that in the
period during which the sagas were produced prose composition was no less highly cultivated in Norway than in
Iceland, but with comparatively few exceptions the sagas
as we now possess them are of Icelandic origin. The reasons

for this rather anomalous literary development may be many and difficult to trace, but the explanation must be sought chiefly in the peculiar environment surrounding the Icelandic settlers, and in the intellectual renaissance which developed in Iceland after the introduction of Christianity. In the isolation of colonial life the love for the homeland and the old ancestral traditions was often intensified among the colonists. News from abroad, every rumor of what happened in their old home districts or elsewhere in Norway, was eagerly sought for and as eagerly repeated. Storytelling, which in Norway had been largely confined to the kitchen or the nursery, became in Iceland a chief source of information, as well as a favorite entertainment in the home and at festivals and public gatherings. In such an environment the story teller would gradually assume a quasi-professional character similar to that of the scald, but his activity would be limited to his own environment. The tales told by returning traders and travelers furnished an abundant supply of interesting material, and it is natural that this form of literary entertainment should grow in favor, as it was well adapted to the public wants, far better suited to the simple cabins and rural life of Iceland than the more formal and pretentious scaldic poetry.

The sagas were at first developed as oral narrative, especially during the period 930-1030, known as the *Söguöld*, or saga age. This was a period of great unrest in Iceland, filled with numerous bloody feuds among the war-like chieftains. Active overseas communications with foreign lands were maintained, and the news of violent upheavals in Norway, accompanied by frequent overthrow of rulers, helped to intensify the general unrest. Stories about all sorts of interesting events multiplied rapidly. "Wise" men and women who knew the old traditions were actively engaged in preserving the family genealogies in new and more carefully constructed tales about leading men. A rich store of prose narrative was thus created, a folk literature of oral tradition which bore as yet no imprint of distinct authorship. In the succeeding period, 1030-1118, the so-called *Friðaröld*, or peace period, it became possible to view past events in a more undisturbed perspective, as the internal struggles subsided, and greater tranquillity began to prevail in political and social life. In this period *fróðir* or learned men appeared, who had studied in schools both at home and abroad, and possessed the necessary literary ability to gather the ready narrative material and give it permanent form in written sagas. Iceland had now been a Christian state for several decades. Pagan ideas were yet firmly enough imbedded in the public mind, but the effect of increasing communication with the rest of the Christian world was beginning to show itself in the development of learning and a new literary spirit. The Icelanders were entering upon an epoch of intellectual growth, an era which culminated in the literary golden age of the twelfth and thirteenth centuries, when the greater part of Icelandic history writing and other prose literature was produced. The leaven of Christianity had finally wrought its changes. Under its influence young Icelanders were now flocking abroad, not as scalds and warriors, but as students seeking the learning of European universities, and the distinction which could be won through scholarly attainments. A new type of national leaders appeared—schoolmen, historians and high officials in the Christian church—replacing the scalds who had hitherto been the chief representatives of the people's higher social and intellectual life. Not only bishops and higher ecclesiastics studied abroad. Many learned Icelanders of distinguished ability who could find no suitable positions in the church entered the monasteries, or lived as private men on their own estates, where they worked as teachers and devoted themselves to literary work. Learning was assiduously cultivated, and schools were organized, not only in connection with the cathedral churches and at the monasteries, but also by private individuals. This love of scholarship, the schools at home, and the number of young men who studied abroad, placed Iceland ahead of the other countries of the North in higher intellectual culture, and launched the people upon a new national development.

We have already observed that Isleif Gizursson, the first

native bishop, had studied in Germany, and had visited Rome; that after his consecration as bishop he organized a school at Skálholt, where he prepared young men for the priesthood.[8] Two of his pupils later became bishops; Koll in southern Norway, and Jon Ögmundsson, who became the first bishop in the northern Icelandic diocese of Hólar. Isleif's son and successor, Gizur, studied in Germany, visited Rome, and was consecrated bishop at Madgeburg. Jon Ögmundsson, bishop of Hólar, also organized a school at his bishop's seat. The "Jónssaga helga inn elzta" says:

"When Jon had been bishop but a short time, he erected a school west of the church. It was well and carefully built, and remnants of the buildings are still to be seen. To manage this school, and to instruct young men who came there, he took one of the best and ablest clerics, Gisli Finnason from Götaland." [9] "Bishop St. Jon took many young men as pupils, and set good teachers to instruct them: Gisli Finnason, already mentioned, as teacher of grammar, and the priest Rikinna, his friend and chaplain, as teacher of song and poetry, as he was a very able scholar."

Teit Isleifsson, another son of the bishop, who had also studied abroad, was a man of learning and recognized ability, though he held no position in the church. In his "Íslendingabók" Ari Frodi acknowledges his special indebtedness to him for much of the reliable knowledge of early Norwegian and Icelandic history which he has embodied in that work. After his return to Iceland Teit lived at Haukadal, where he organized a school, and worked as teacher.[10] Sæmund inn Frodi Sigfusson, 1056-1133, was a grandson of the Christian chieftain Sidu-Hall, one of the leading men in Iceland. At an early age he went abroad to study, and became so well versed in Latin learning that he seems to have surpassed all his contemporary countrymen in that line. This circumstance led the old writers to regard him as a sort of learned wizard who knew every-

---

[8] *Hungrvaka*, ch. 2. *Lýsing Íslands*, p. 99. Jón Sigurdsson, *Um skóla á Íslandi, Ný félagsrit*, vol. ii, p. 67 ff.

[9] *Jónssaga helga inn elzta*, ch. 11, 14; *Biskupasögur*, vol. i.

[10] *Biskupasögur*, vol. i, p. 153.

thing and wrote most of the great literary works, among others also the "Elder Edda." He was even considered able to practice the black art. Such fictions belong in the realms of legend, but after his return to Iceland he became very influential, and his assistance was sought in matters of great importance. He was one of the prime movers in the introduction of the system of tithes in 1096, and he also helped to frame the system of church laws adopted in 1123.[11] Sæmund took holy orders and settled at Oddi. There seems to be no reason to doubt, though it is nowhere expressly stated, that he was the founder of the school established there, the most noted of all early Icelandic institutions of learning. He married Gudrun, daughter of Kolbein Floason, and had several children. According to the "Thorlákssaga" his son Eyjolf became head master of the school at Oddi, which was then in a flourishing condition.[12] Another son, Lopt, was the father of the great chieftain Jon Loptsson, the foster-father of Snorri Sturlason. These early schools created a general love of learn-

---

[11] *Biskupasögur*, vol. i, 320. *Grágás*, part i, p. 36. *Hungrvaka*, ch. 6. According to popular tradition Sæmund lived in the South with a celebrated master, by whom he was instructed in various occult arts. But thereby he forgot all that he had learned before, even his own Christian name. At last St. Jon (the later Bishop Jon Ögmundsson of Hólar), while traveling in the South, heard where he was, and sought him out. When asked for his name he said that it was Koll. But Jon finally told him that he knew him to be Sæmund Sigfusson, who was born at Oddi in Iceland. When he persuaded him, Sæmund recovered recollection of himself, and determined to escape with his countryman. In order to deceive his master Jon remained for a time in the same town, and often visited Sæmund. At last on a dark night they fled. Then follows the story how they eluded their pursuer by means of magic. It is also related that in the Middle Ages there existed a school of black art (*Svartaskóli*), which by some is said to have been in Germany, by others in Paris. The school was supposed to have been kept in a subterranean chamber, into which no ray of light could enter. The pupils were compelled to stay there until they had finished their course, which was from three to seven years, without seeing the daylight. A gray shaggy hand entered every day to give the pupils their food. They learned their lessons from books written in letters of fire so that they might be studied in darkness. There were no real teachers, but the devil himself kept the school. This school Sæmund had attended, according to popular belief. Jon Arnason, *Íslenzkar thjóðsögur og æfintyri*, i, p. 485 ff. Konrad Maurer, *Isländische Folkssagen der Gegenwart*.

[12] *Biskupasögur*, vol. i, p. 165.

ing and fostered, not only able church leaders, but also gifted authors, who produced the great literature of Iceland. The monk Gunnlaug says that all the leading priests in the northern quarter who were remembered in his generation had been instructed for some time at Hólar; some from childhood, others at mature age. Of these he mentions Isleif Grimsson, who, but for his early death, might have become Bishop Jon's successor. Also Jon Svarti; Villmund, the first abbot of Thingeyrar; Hrein, the third abbot; Bjarni Bergthorsson; the young lady Ingun, who served as teacher, especially of Latin grammar; Björn, the third bishop of Hólar, and many others.[13] The subjects taught were undoubtedly those common to all schools at that time, but at least in one important particular did the Icelanders make a notable improvement on the established curriculum. In Iceland as in Norway the mother tongue became the language of literature as well as of the church. Careful instruction must have been given in it since the Icelanders were able to produce their great prose literature in their own vernacular at a time when Latin was still the universal literary language.

After the election of native bishops and the establishing of permanent dioceses monasticism was also introduced in Iceland. The monasteries built by the different orders maintained schools with able teachers, and became the centers of literary life. The Benedictine monastery of Thingeyrar, founded in 1133, became especially the seat of history writing.[14] Towards the close of the twelfth century the monks Odd Snorrason and Gunnlaug Leifsson wrote here their Olafssagas under the direction of the learned abbot Karl Jonsson, himself the author of several important works. The monastery of Thverá (Munkathverá) was of special importance because of its abbot Nicolas Bergsson, who died in 1159. He had traveled extensively in foreign lands and wrote the "Leiðarvísir"

[13] *Biskupasögur*, vol. i, p. 240 f.
[14] Jon Jonsson, *Um klaustrin á Íslandi, Timarit*, vol. viii, p. 174 ff. Jon Thorkelsson, *Om Digtningen paa Island*, p. 4. Richard F. Burton, *Ultima Thule or a Summer in Iceland*, vol. i, p. 96 f.

or "Itinerarium ad Terram Sanctam," the first original geographical work written in Iceland. The Benedictine Order founded also the monastery of Reynistadir in 1295. A monastery of Hitardal is also mentioned, but little is known about it. In the thirteenth century there existed also the monastery of Saurbær, in the district of Eyjafjord, but it was soon discontinued. The Order of St. Augustine established the monastery of Thykkvabær, where the learned Brand Jonsson became abbot in 1247. Thorlak Thorhallsson, who had studied in Paris and Lincoln, and finally became bishop of Skálholt, was prior and later abbot of this monastery. A later abbot, Runolf Sigmundsson, was also an able scholar. Dr. Kálund thinks that the "Njáls-saga" in its final form was written here.[15] The first attempt to translate the Bible into Icelandic was also made in this monastery. The Flatey monastery, founded by the same order in 1172, was moved to Helgafell in 1174. Here the learned Hall Gizursson, who is thought by some to have been the author of the "Eyrbyggjasaga,"[16] was abbot from 1221 till 1225. He had formerly been *lögsögumaðr* from 1201 till 1209. The monastery of Videy, founded in 1226, and that of Mödruvellir, 1296, also belonged to the Order of St. Augustine. At Kirkjubær was founded a cloister for nuns in 1186, the first of this kind in Iceland. The last monastery founded in Iceland was that of Skrida in Fljots-dal, erected in 1493. Besides the new learning which followed in the wake of Christianity, the Latin alphabet was also introduced through the schools and monasteries. The cumbersome runic alphabet was soon replaced by the new art of writing on parchment, so important to the new literary development.

The greatest achievement of the Icelandic scribes was their history writing, a field in which they had little serious competition in contemporary European literature. They were pre-eminently the historians of their age, although history writing had begun to develop also in Norway and

[15] Kr. Kålund, *Beskrivelse af Island,* vol. ii, p. 327.
[16] Eugene Mogk, *Geschichte der norwegisch-isländischen Literatur,* p. 758.

elsewhere in the North. In Denmark Saxo Grammaticus
(1140-1206) wrote his "Historia Danica," comprising the
history of the Danish kingdom till 1185. In Norway literature did not flourish as it did in Iceland, due in part, perhaps, to the bloody civil wars waged by the numerous pretenders to the throne. But three historical works nevertheless appeared, all of them written in Latin. The "Historia Norwegiæ," which probably dates from 1170, narrates the history of Norway and its dependencies, but is a
production of little literary merit. The "Historia de Antiquitate Regum Norwagiensium," by the Norwegian monk
Theodricus, is a history of Norway during the period 878-
1130, probably written in the years 1177-1180. The "Historia de Profectione in Terram Sanctam," written by an
unknown Norwegian author, gives an account of a crusade
undertaken by Danes and Norwegians after Saladin had
captured Jerusalem in 1187. Fortunately the growing
patriotic sentiment soon led to the discarding of Latin as a
literary language in the North. The writers began to make
use of their own mother tongue, in which they developed
so excellent a style in their sagas and other prose works.

The fathers of Icelandic history writing were the two
scholars Sæmund inn Frodi Sigfusson and Ari Thorgilsson
inn Frodi (1067-1148). Sæmund had become interested
in chronology and turned his attention especially to the
genealogies of the Norwegian kings and the events connected with their reigns. For the early period of Norwegian
history he established the Christian chronology up till 1047.
He evidently wrote in Latin, but of his works nothing has
been preserved. One of his works, however, the "Noregs
Konungatal," must have been translated into Norse, as it
was well known both in Norway and in Iceland.[17] Some
time later, about 1190, an unknown Icelander turned
Sæmund's work into verse in a poem called "Noregs Konungatal," with continuation after Sæmund's time.

Ari Frodi was of good family. He spent most of his
youth at Helgafell with his grandfather, Gellir, as he had

---

[17] Halvdan Koht, *Den fyrste norske nasjonalhistoria, Edda,* vol. xii, p.
90 f.

lost his father in early childhood. Later he came to Haukadal, where he associated for some time with Teit Isleifsson, the son of the bishop, who gave him much valuable historical information. He wrote his work "Íslendingabók" in his own native tongue. In this book he gives a survey of the early political and church history of Iceland, including the colonization, the founding of the Althing, the establishing of the early courts of law, the discovery of Greenland, and the introduction of Christianity. The dates of these important events he has fixed carefully according to Christian chronology, and the information given is based on the most trustworthy sources. The work, which is very reliable, became a basis and pattern for Icelandic history writing.

In the monasteries learned monks were everywhere cultivating the new literary art. Eirik Oddsson wrote the "Hryggjarstykki" shortly after 1160, a work on Norwegian history covering the period 1130-1160. The work is lost, but we know of it indirectly through later works, especially the "Morkinskinna" and the "Heimskringla," whose authors have used it as a source. A little later Karl Jonsson, abbot of Thingeyrar, while staying at the court of King Sverre of Norway, wrote the "Sverrissaga," under direct guidance of the king. The original is lost, but we possess a later copy of the work by Styrmer inn Frodi. A continuation of the narrative is found in the "Böglungasögur," or "Sagas of the Three Kings," by an unknown author. Odd Snorrason and Gunnlaug Leifsson, monks in the monastery of Thingeyrar, in Karl Jonsson's time, both wrote sagas of Olaf Tryggvason in Latin. The "Olafssaga" by Odd Snorrason is the shorter and better of the two, and is the author's only literary work of which we have any knowledge. Gunnlaug Leifsson wrote, besides his "Olafssaga," also biographies of the bishops Jon Ögmundsson and Thorlak Thorlaksson, the "Jónssaga helga" and the "Thorlákssaga." The sagas of many other bishops were also written, usually by unknown authors, and are found incorporated in the great collection known as the "Biskupasögur," which, together with the "Kristnisaga," constitute the early church

history of Iceland. These men and others like them, whose
names as authors of important literary works have been
clearly established, show distinctly the type of men who
produced the Icelandic saga literature. But in a great
number of cases no knowledge of authors, even of the most
important works in this literature, has come to posterity.
A very important work dealing with the early history of
Iceland is the "Landnámabók," which gives the genealogies, and to some extent the stories of the early settlers
down to the thirteenth or fourteenth century. Neither the
work of the original unknown author nor a later version
by Styrmer inn Frodi now exist. But we possess versions
by Sturla Thordsson (†1284), the "Sturlubók," and Hauk
Erlendsson (†1334), who combined Styrmer's and Sturla's
versions in his "Hauksbók."

The Icelandic writers devoted special attention to the
history of Norway. About 1190 appeared a brief history
of the Norwegian kings, written in the mother tongue by
some unknown Icelandic author under the title "Ágrip af
Noregs Konugasögum." To the material found in Ari
Frodi's and Sæmund's works he has added many unhistorical accounts which rest on no other authority than
on traditions current among the people. The work is a
series of individual sagas rather than a connected history.
"Morkinskinna," another history of Norway, written by an
unknown Icelander about 1220, covers the period from the
reign of Magnus the Good till about 1177. It is a rather
uncritical compilation from various sources, and possesses
relatively little value as an historical production. The
writer has been well acquainted with scaldic songs and has
included many of them in his work, but he has not been
able to use them properly as historical material. The
"Fagrskinna," another history of Norway, written by an
unknown Icelandic author in the period 1230-1240, covers
the period from the time of the father of Harald Haarfagre
to 1177. The sagas of the Norwegian kings follow one
another without much inner connection, but the events of
each reign are told in an interesting way. The writer has
known how to use the scaldic songs as source material. He

has carefully avoided all stories, myths and popular traditions, even where they might have served to give life and
color to his narrative.   He shows strong Norwegian-
Icelandic sympathies, but he has not been inspired by any
leading constructive thought, and his literary style is rather
dull and colorless.

High above all other Icelandic historians stands Snorri
Sturlason, author of the "Heimskringla," a history of Norway from the earliest times to the battle of Ré in 1177.
Snorri (1178-1241) was also a poet and scholar, and played
a prominent part in the events of his own time as lawman
and diplomat.   In his historical writings he developed his
own critical method, according to which he examines and
evaluates his material.   Although he inserts things which
will not stand the test of modern criticism, he sought to
eliminate all fables, and to give a truthful and realistic account of persons and events, based on the most reliable
sources.   In speaking of the "Heimskringla," the German
scholar Eugene Mogk says:

"Snorri is an historian in the modern sense, not a tiresome
annalist of historical events.   His persons speak and act, and
in his dramatic conception of history he surpasses even Thucy-
dides.   One is attracted by him and is tempted to read on.   And
then there is the pure and noble language; no intricate sentence
construction; none of the clumsy expressions over which we often
stumble in later historians; no useless elaboration of details;
nothing which draws the attention from the main theme, or
hinders a vivid character portrayal; his language is classical
in the best meaning of the word." [18]

With his ability as writer he combined also that of
critical scholar.   Towards the end of his work, as he ap-
proaches his own time, he makes more and more use of oral
tradition and the writings of well-informed and reliable
men.   But whenever it was possible he used as his chief
source the scaldic songs, which, he says, he considers most
reliable when they are well made and clearly understood.

[18] Hermann Paul, *Grundriss der germanischen Philologi*, vol. ii, p. 128 ff.

"It was indeed customary for the scalds," he observes, "to praise highly the men about whom they composed their songs, but none dared to tell things which everybody, themselves included, would know to be falsehood and irresponsible talk. That would not be praise but mockery."

This critical method was Snorri's greatest achievement, and enabled him to write an historical work which belongs to the centuries. Also in other fields he was able to achieve great things. In scaldic poetry he was a recognized master, although this old art was already falling into disuse in his time. It was especially through his scholarly prose work, the "Younger Edda," or "Snorri Edda," that he rendered this dying art his greatest service. This is a scientific treatise in which he gives a complete analysis of scaldic versification with copious illustrations from the songs of the leading scalds. The book also contains a survey of Norse mythology, one of the best sources of our knowledge of this old religion. Snorri evidently wrote his work as a handbook for young poets to infuse new vigor into the decaying art of scaldic song.

Styrmer Kárason inn Frodi, Snorri's contemporary, was a diligent but not very gifted writer. He was lögsögumaðr for a time, and died as prior of the monastery of Videy in 1245. He wrote a saga about King Olaf the Saint, and also a version of the "Landnámabók" and a "Sverrissaga," both of which works are lost.

As historian Snorri found a worthy successor in his nephew Sturla Thordsson, the son of Thord Sturlason, Snorri's brother. Sturla was not only a learned and able writer, but a peaceful man of noble character, who loved his country, and sought as long as possible to preserve its independence. He also held his great uncle, Snorri, in high esteem, and did much to preserve his memory untarnished through the bitter feuds in which the family was constantly involved. One of Sturla's greatest literary works is his "Islendingasaga," which constitutes the chief component part of the large historical work known as the "Sturlungasaga." [19]

[19] B. M. Ólsen, *Um Sturlungu, Safn til Sögu Íslands*, vol. iii, b.

This collection of sagas wrought into a single work, probably by Thord Narfason (†1306), deals with the history of Iceland in the thirteenth century. Sturla's "Íslendingasaga," being the pivot of this great work, is the chief source of Icelandic history during this critical period. Sturla was also a noted scald, possibly less gifted as a poet than his older brother, Olaf Thordsson Hvitaskald, but the two are the last masters in this old art of song. In 1250 Sturla was elected *lögsögumaðr,* but retired in a few years to private life. In 1263 he went to Norway, and remained for many years at the court of King Magnus Lagabøter, who employed him to write a history of his father's reign, the "Hákonarsaga Hákonarsonar." This work is based on letters and documents of the royal archives placed at his disposal by the king, and is the chief source of the history of the Scandinavian North in the thirteenth century. In 1271 Sturla returned to Iceland with a new code of laws, but in 1278 he again went to Norway, where he was employed to write King Magnus' own saga, the "Magnúsarsaga Hákonarsonar," of which only a few fragments have been preserved. As Sturla was the last of the scalds, he was also the last real historian of the old period. Of the many works which appeared after his day many were copies or compilations of older works, like the "Hrokkinskinna," the "Eirspenill" and the "Flateyjarbók." But some valuable contributions to historical literature appeared in the form of sagas about the Norwegian colonies: the "Eirikssaga rauða" and the "Grænlendinga tháttr," dealing with the colonization of Greenland and the discovery of America by the Norsemen, the "Færeyingasaga" and the "Orkneyingasaga," dealing with the history of the Orkneys and the Faroe Islands. Sagas dealing with the history of Denmark, the "Knutssaga gamla," the "Skjoldungasaga" and the "Knytlingasaga," were also written.

Through the diligent labors of the Icelandic scribes a Norwegian national history had thus been written, together with important historical accounts of the Norse colonies and other countries. A national Icelandic history was also produced, but this was more fragmentary in character, as political and social life in Iceland found no center in an efficient national government. It was still the stories of individual scalds and chieftains, the dramatic incidents connected with the leading families which constituted the most interesting features of Icelandic history. Since these traditions were too local in character to be wrought into a connected historical narrative, the scribes developed them as individual family sagas more highly adorned with fictitious elements supplied by the writers' own imagination than the more critically written historical works. But in vivid character portrayal, in simplicity and force of diction, in dramatic power, in somber realism of description and finished skill in narrative many of the family sagas belong to the most enduring works of literary art. Only in rare instances can any conjecture be ventured as to the authorship of these sagas. Even the reason for this strange anonymity is wholly enigmatic. The old writers have given us their works, but with a certain proud disdain they have left us no clue to their origin or to their own personal identity.

In the western districts of Iceland appeared many family sagas of high excellence, as the "Egilssaga" about Egill Skallagrimsson and his family, one of the best written and most reliable of the family sagas; the "Gunnlaugssaga," about the scalds Gunnlaug Ormstunga and Hrafn Önundsson; the reliable and important "Eyrbyggjasaga," which narrates the history of a whole district; the "Hardarsaga og Holmverja"; the "Bjarnarsaga Hitdælakappa," which tells the story of the scald Björn Hitdælakappi, his love for Odny Light of the Island, and his feud with his rival Thord Kolbeinsson; also the "Laxdælasaga," written about Ketill Flatnef's influential family. The "Hænsathorissaga," also from this district, deals with the feud between the plotting and greedy chieftain Hænsathorir and Blundketill of Örnulfsdal, which finally culminated in the burning of Blundketill in his own house. Revenge for this deed was sure to follow. Blood-feud raged till the death of Hænsathorir finally led to a reconciliation of the two contending parties.

All districts had their popular heroes and interesting
local events, which were described in numerous sagas written by diligent monks in the Icelandic monasteries. Of
special interest were the bloody feuds, which often involved
so many families that they developed into a petty warfare
of the bitterest and most vindictive sort. Such events were
of more than local importance, as they made a deep impression throughout the whole land, helped to give national
life in Iceland its distinctive features, and remained for
all times indelibly imprinted on the annals of the people.
The sagas describing them are not only interesting stories,
but valuable historical documents throwing light on social
conditions through centuries of Icelandic history. Of
tragic local events which have grown into such national
importance that they have occupied the imagination and
swayed the feelings of the people through all subsequent
times, the "Njálssaga" from the southern districts furnishes
most striking illustration. In epic-dramatic power and
psychological character portrayal, as well as in mighty
sweep of descriptive analysis of early Icelandic life, this
work surpasses all other sagas. It is the prose "Iliad" of
Viking life, a narrative masterpiece unexcelled in Northern
literature. Gunnar of Hlidarendi, the most knightly figure
pictured in the family sagas, and Njáll of Bergthorshváll,
learned in the law, and a very noble character, are the two
leading figures in the narrative. Gunnar is of special interest as the beau-ideal of Icelandic heroes, being in this respect to the Icelanders what King Olaf Tryggvason was
to the Norwegians. "Gunnar," says the saga, "was a man
of great stature, strong and very able in all sports. He
could wield the sword or use the bow with either hand as
he liked. With the sword he could play so dexterously
that one seemed to see three in the air at the same time.
He was the best bowman, and could hit everything he
aimed at. He could leap more than his own height fully
armed, and equally far both backward and foreward. He
could swim like a seal, and there was no play in which anyone could compare with him, so that it was said that he
never had an equal. He was beautiful in appearance, with

a fair complexion. His nose was well formed, with the tip bent slightly upward. He had bright blue eyes, ruddy cheeks, and a rich growth of blonde hair which was very becoming. He was courteous in manners, manly, fearless, kind and faithful to his friends, but very critical in the selection of them." He traveled extensively in foreign lands, where he won great distinction. When he returned to Iceland he rode to the Althing in a scarlet mantle and gilt helmet, girded with a beautiful sword, and wearing on his arm a heavy ring of gold. Here he met Hallgerd, the sister of Olaf Pá of Hjardarholt, tall and beautiful, attired in a red gold-brocaded garment and a scarlet mantle, with a growth of hair so rich that she could wrap herself in it. Courtship and marriage followed close upon their acquaintance. But Hallgerd was as wicked as she was beautiful, and set her mind on nothing but mischief and the stirring up of feud. She had already been married twice, but with a fatal charm she had used her blandishments as a wily coquette only to abandon her husbands and admirers to death and ruin with the most cynical heartlessness. To Njáll her betrothal to Gunnar was no welcome news. "She will only cause trouble here," he remarked. "But our friendship she shall never destroy," answered Gunnar. Bergthora, Njáll's wife, an able and upright, but haughty and self-assertive lady, who would brook no affront, soon became the special object of Hallgerd's spite. The strife between the two began at a festival at Bergthorshváll, where they bandied angry and insulting words. Soon after the festival Hallgerd sent a servant to Kirkjubær to steal provisions, as it seems, with well planned intent to create trouble. When Gunnar learned that she had compromised his honor in this way, he became so irritated that he gave her a box on the ear, saying: "It would be unfortunate if I should also become the harborer of stolen goods." "This you shall remember," she cried, and ran out of the house. The violent blood-feud which was now set on foot by the two women spread among the relatives, servants and younger members of the two families, and Bergthora knew well how to retaliate when her people fell victims to Hall-

gerd's evil plots. In the midst of these growing difficulties
Gunnar, guided by Njáll's wise counsel, was able to arrange
peaceful settlements. The two men seemed to draw
closer in their friendship as the feud deepened. Gunnar
was often attacked by large bands of enemies, but he defended himself heroically, and slew or defeated them in
every encounter. Finally his adversaries were able to win
a suit against him at the Althing, causing him to be banished for the period of three years. Njáll advised him to
go abroad. "If you violate this decision, it will be your
death," he said, "but if you go abroad, you will have more
honor of this journey than from all your Viking expeditions." Gunnar made ready to leave, but on riding to his
ship his horse stumbled, and he fell from the saddle. Look-
ing back at his home he said: "Beautiful are the mountain-
sides. So beautiful I have never seen them. The meadows
are yellow, the hay around home is cut,—I will ride home
again. I will not go abroad." Fate seemed to have halted
his steps. It was the first time that he had refused to follow
Njáll's wise counsel. His enemies, led by Geir Godi and
Gizur the White, father of the later bishop Isleif Gizursson,
now renewed their attacks upon him with increased determination. From his brother-in-law Olaf Pá of Hjardarholt
he had received the dog Sám, so intelligent that he would
bark at the approach of enemies, but never at friends. As
his adversaries knew that they could accomplish nothing
against Gunnar so long as Sám lived, they forced one of
the neighbors to kill the dog. They now swept down on
Gunnar's house, which was built of timber; but he defended
himself so heroically that many lost their lives, and the
assailants made no progress. Finally one of them was able
to cut his bowstring with the sword. Gunnar then asked
his wife, Hallgerd, to twist him a new bowstring from a
lock of her hair, but she refused, saying: "I will now remind you of the box you gave me on the ear, and I care not
how long you are able to defend yourself." "People have
different ways of gaining notoriety," said Gunnar; "I shall
ask you no favors." His enemies now closed in upon his
house, and he fell after a most heroic struggle.

After Gunnar's death the tragedy only deepened. Njáll's oldest son, the redoubtable Skarphedin, and Gunnar's son Högni assumed leadership of their party, and slew many men in revenge for Gunnar's death. Finally Thráin Sigfusson was also slain by Njáll's sons. This made the feud flame up with new intensity. Especially tragic was the slaying of Höskuld Hvitnesingagodi by the sons of Njáll, who were led to this deed by the evil machinations of Mord Valgardsson. "This one thing touched Njáll so nearly," says the saga, "that he could never speak of it without shedding tears." When his sons asked him what he thought would be the result of it, he said: "My death, and the death of my wife and of all my sons." An attempt to bring about a reconciliation at the Althing failed. Under the leadership of Flosi Thordsson the enemies of the sons of Njáll assembled in great numbers, and proceeded to Bergthorshváll, where they surrounded Njáll's house on a windy autumn night. Women and children were offered quarters, but no fighting man was allowed to escape. "Go thou out, housewife," Flosi said to Bergthora. "Far be it from me to let thee burn within." But she was a wife worthy of her husband. "Young I was when I was given to Njáll," she replied, "and we have promised that one fate should befall us both." [20] The old couple lay quietly down in their bed with their little grandson, the son of Kári Solmundsson, between them, spread an ox-hide over themselves, and perished together when the enemies burned the house. Njáll's sons perished in the fire, among them also Skarphedin. But his son-in-law, Kári Solmundsson, managed to escape, and lived to take a summary vengeance on some of those who had assisted in the burning of Njáll and his family. The feud finally ended with a reconciliation between Flosi and Kári, after both had made a pilgrimage to Rome, where they did penance and received absolution for their sins. The events of the saga cover the period 930-1016. In its present form it dates from about 1250, but the author has undoubtedly made use of older narratives about Gunnar and Njáll.

[20] English translation by George Webbe Dasent, Edinburgh, 1861.

Many other sagas about scalds and leading chieftains are of great historical value, as the "Vatsdælasaga" from northern Iceland, and the "Hrafnkelssaga Freysgoða" from the eastern districts; also the "Gislasaga Surssonar," the "Hallfrædarsaga" and the "Kormakssaga" written about the scalds Gisli Sursson, Hallfred Vandrædaskald and Kormak Önundsson. But the fictitious romantic elements were increasing in the family sagas under the influence of the literary taste prevalent in Europe in the Middle Ages. In many of these stories the historical nucleus became so small that the narratives assume the character of historical romances, of importance as works of literary art, but of little value as historical documents. In this class belong such stories as the "Grettissaga," one of the most dramatic and interesting of saga narratives, dealing with the tragic life and death of the outlawed Grettir Ásmundsson, the most interesting of all Icelandic outlaws. Also the "Bandamannasaga," the "Svarfdælasaga" and others belong to this sort of narratives. Such stories form the transition to the purely imaginative and fictitious tales, the romantic sagas, dealing with early heroic Germanic tradition, or the romantic fiction of knight-errantry imported from England and the continent. As these tales were written only for entertainment, they mark the decay of saga literature. Legal books and religious works of various kinds continued to be written by the monks in the quiet retreats of the monasteries, but history writing was no longer cultivated except in the form of annals, which continued to appear even to the sixteenth century.

8. CIVIL STRIFE IN ICELAND. CONDITIONS IN THE CHURCH. SNORRI STURLASON

THE introduction of Christianity was followed by a period of peaceful development known as the *Fridaröld*, 1030-1118. During this period the bloody feuds subsided, churches and schools were built, and an intellectual life blossomed forth which elevated Iceland to the position of

literary leadership in the North. Even the formal acceptance of the Christian faith must have helped to turn the
minds of the people to more peaceful ways, though their
progress toward true conversion was so slow that the
church at first could exercise but little intellectual or moral
guidance. Its teachings were imperfectly known and little
heeded, but indirectly it exercised great influence, especially
through the early bishops. As these were members of
the leading families, talented and able men who could play
a prominent part in all public affairs, the two bishops' seats,
Skálholt and Hólar, soon became the centers of a new governing authority to which even the chieftains yielded some
degree of submission. The local churches also helped to
foster a spirit of peace. The Icelandic church, though still
weak, was a part of the great Church of Rome, subject to
its guidance and supported by its authority. When the
chieftains, as often happened, took holy orders in order
to serve as priests in their home parishes, their sacred office
made them amenable to the disciplinary authority of the
Roman Church, and it became necessary for them to maintain at least a semblance of Christian conduct. Many,
also, who went abroad to study returned to found schools,
or to devote themselves to literary pursuits. In many ways
Christianity was completing its peaceful conquest, while
the Icelandic people were emerging from a primitive colonial condition into a mature intellectual and national life.

The peaceful development so auspiciously begun might
have welded the loosely knit Icelandic society into a well
organized state if it could have continued uninterrupted.
But the absence of the stabilizing influence of a central
government, together with new evils growing out of faults
inherent in the social system, enabled the spirit of discord
to flame up anew with such violence that it finally broke
down all legal and religious restraints, wrecked the established state organization, and destroyed the peoples' national independence.

Since the Icelandic state system was founded on the
goðorðs, its stability naturally depended on the permanence of these fundamental units. Their number was finally

fixed by the law of 1004, but they were of too indeterminate a character to form a satisfactory basis of political and social organization. We have already seen that they had no fixed boundaries, but consisted of the *goði's* personal adherents, who could transfer their allegiance from one *goði* to another as they might feel inclined. Under these conditions the original equality of the *goðar* could scarcely have been maintained even if the *goðorðs* had been strictly inalienable. Popular chieftains could find adherents everywhere, even in remote districts; jealous rivalries would follow until a few powerful leaders could lord it over all the rest. This danger was further increased by the fact that legally the *goðorð* was a private possession which could be divided, donated, sold or inherited like other property, and that no limit was placed on the number of *goðorðs* which might be held by a single chieftain. As armed conflict was still the final argument in so many controversies, the *goðar* were naturally eager to gain possession of new *goðorðs* whenever possible, in order to increase the number of their *thingmenn*. How this method was used to satisfy personal ambition at the expense of the existing state organization is clearly seen in the case of the Sturlungs in western Iceland, who rose in this way to the greatest power, though at first they probably did not even possess a *goðorð*.[1] The real prominence of this family began with Sturla Thordsson, or Hvamm-Sturla, so called from the estate Hvamm which he had purchased.[2] In his marriage with Gudny, daughter of Bödvar Thordsson of the Myramen family, Sturla had three sons who became famous in Icelandic history: Thord Sturlason (1165-1237), Sighvat Sturlason (1170-1238), and Snorri Sturlason, the great historian (1178-1241). Through marriage Thord secured the estate Stad at Snæfellsnes, together with one-half of the Thorsnesinga *goðorð*, which

[1] Hvamm-Sturla's father, Thord Gilsson of Mánljot, was a grandson of Snorri Godi. He inherited the Snorrunga *goðorð*, which since remained in the Sturlung family. Thord was probably the first member of the family who really possessed a *goðorð*. The Sturlungs sprang from good ancestors, but did not belong to the leading families. *Sturlungasaga*, vol. i, 47, 55. K. Maurer, *Island*, 103.

[2] *Sturlungasaga*, ch. 12, p. 60.

belonged to it. The other half he received as a present from the priest Thorgils Snorrason.[3] Sighvat bought one-half of the estate of Stadarhol upon the death of Einar Thorgilsson in 1185, and secured also the possession of Einar's *goðorð*.[4] He likewise obtained both the Saurbæinga and the Reyknesinga *goðorðs*, which belonged to Einar's father. Snorri Sturlason received from his uncle one-half of the Lundarmanna *goðorð*, and from Thorstein Ivarsson he received the Ávellinga *goðorð*, which belonged to northern Iceland.[5] Seven *goðorðs*, and, possibly, even more, had thus come into the possession of a single family, an accumulation of power in the hands of a few leading chieftains which was proceeding rapidly all over Iceland. In the northern districts Gudmund Dyri Thorvaldsson already possessed the Mödruvellinga *goðorð*, but in 1187 Jon Ketillsson and his brother Ásgrim surrendered to him also the Fljotamanna *goðorð*, in order to secure his aid against their personal enemies.[6] About Kolbein Tumasson (†1208) the saga states [7] that he was the most powerful man in the northern districts, and held all the *goðorðs* west of Yxna-dalsheidi to the Ávellinga *goðorð*. North of Yxnadalsheidi Ögmund Sneis and Hall Kleppjarnsson possessed *goðorðs*. "Thorvald, the son of Gudmund Dyri, gave the *goðorðs* which his relatives had possessed to Sigurd Ormsson, but he gave them to Tumi Sighvatsson, who thus came to possess them in his time." This throws sufficient light on the way in which *goðorðs* passed from hand to hand until they finally came into the possession of the most powerful and ambitious chieftains.

The *thing* organization, according to which three *goðorðs* with their *goðar* and *thingmenn* were united into a *thing* district, was also seriously disturbed through the alienation of the *goðorðs*. It became more and more customary

---

[3] *Sturlungasaga*, vii, ch. 41, p. 198.
[4] *Sturlungasaga*, iii, ch. 39, p. 114; ch. 41, p. 197.
[5] *Sturlungasaga*, iii, ch. 22, p. 227. *Biskupasögur*, vol. i. *Guðmundarsaga*, ch. 51.
[6] *Sturlungasaga*, iii, ch. 12, p. 138.
[7] *Sturlungasaga*, iii, ch. 22, p. 227. *Biskupasögur*, i, *Guðmundarsaga*, ch. 51.

to change the place for the assembling of the *thing,* as this was not forbidden. The *thing* districts could also be divided, or two districts could be united if the chieftains, after reaching an agreement, obtained the consent of the people, and made the change publicly known. Since the *thing* districts were divisible, it became possible for any self-willed or dissatisfied *goði* to secede from it and establish a *thing* of his own. But whether a single chieftain held possession of several *goðorðs* within the district, or divided it to suit his own convenience, the courts would be under his personal control and would be so manifestly unable to render impartial justice that they could only be viewed with general contempt. Respect for the law was destroyed in the same degree that the courts were deprived of their ability to act as impartial judicial tribunals, and arrogant chieftains gained such power that they could defy the courts and commit lawless acts with impunity. Instead of being the pillars of the state as members of the *lögrétta* of the Althing, as presiding judges in the local courts and privileged leaders in their communities, the *goðar* often became dangerous exponents of lawlessness, cynical flouters of all authority who shrank from no violence in their pursuit of selfish aims.

Already upon the death of Bishop Gizur of Skálholt, 1118, a serious conflict arose between the two chieftains Haflidi Marsson of Hunafjord in northern Iceland and Thorgils Oddsson from Breidafjord in the western districts. A violent and quarrelsome man by the name of Mar, a relative of Haflidi, had killed many men, and Thorgils finally cited him before the *thing.* Haflidi defended Mar, but was able to obtain only a compromise verdict, according to which Mar was to pay a heavy fine. Among the adherents of the two chieftains the feud continued. Many were killed on both sides, and in 1120 the case was again brought before the Althing, where both chieftains appeared with large bands of armed followers. Haflidi sought to drive Thorgils and his followers from the *thing,* but in the armed clash which ensued he was wounded in the hand and had to abandon the attempt. For shedding blood on the consecrated ground of the *thing* Thorgils was outlawed, but he paid no attention to the decree. On returning home he gathered a large force of armed men, and defended the mountain passes so well that Haflidi, who was advancing with a large band to carry into execution the decision of the court, had to return home with nothing accomplished. The following summer Thorgils appeared again at the Althing with an armed force of 800 men in open defiance of the decree which had been passed against him. His antagonist Haflidi came with no less than 1400 men. For a while it looked as if a pitched battle was to be fought on the thingstead itself, a calamity which was finally averted through the intercession of Bishop Thorlak of Skálholt, Sæmund Frodi and other influential men. As the bishop threatened Haflidi with the ban of the church if he did not desist from his purpose, he finally agreed to a compromise by which order was again restored.[8]

The size of the armed bands employed by these chieftains shows that the power had already passed from the *goðar* and the old aristocracy into the hands of a few powerful and ambitious magnates. Strife increased, as did also the moral laxity, the violence and heartlessness, the disregard for law and religion which always accompany bloodshed and armed conflict. Feud was rife everywhere, and more serious clashes occurred from time to time, revealing a constantly growing bitterness, and general disregard for the established judicial tribunals. A long conflict was thus waged between the two chieftains Einar Thorgilsson, son of Haflidi Marsson's opponent Thorgils Oddsson, already mentioned, and Sturla Thordsson, or Hvamm-Sturla, father of the historian Snorri. Their quarrel had been before the *thing* repeatedly. Both had been sentenced to *fjörbaugs-garðr*, or minor banishment, for the period of three years, but neither of them paid any attention to the decision of the *thing*. One summer while Sturla was on his way to the Althing, Einar surrounded his houses with an armed band, and burned them to the ground. Through the inter

[8] *Sturlungasaga*, i, ch. 5-27, Supplement to the *Landnámabók*, 1, from the *Skardsárbók*.

cession of Bishop Klæng of Skálholt they were finally persuaded to agree to a peaceful settlement, but the reconciliation was not lasting. As Sturla, who was dissatisfied with the terms of the agreement, failed to pay the compensation for past wrongs which the bishop, acting as arbitrator, had awarded his opponent, the feud blazed forth anew. This time Einar and his band went to the home of Ingjald, Sturla's son-in-law, and seized all his cattle. This led to a bloody fight between the two chieftains at Sælingsdalsheid in 1171, in which Ingjald and many other men fell. Sturla, however, was entirely victorious, and Einar had to beg for peace, which was granted him. A final settlement was now arranged between the two with the aid of the great chieftains Jon Loptsson and Gizur Hallsson. Hvamm-Sturla had gained new power and prestige through this victory over his opponent. The decrees of the Althing he had successfully set at naught. Only when friendly arbitrators arranged a settlement agreeable to him did he consent to terminate the struggle.[9]

In 1163 occurred a most violent clash between the warring chieftains, to which a brief reference is made as well in the "Sturlungasaga" as in the Icelandic annals.[10] At this time an armed conflict was waged in the very *lögrétta* of the Althing. The priest Halldor Snorrason was slain, and in the mad fury of the fight stones were thrown of such size that people afterwards were scarcely able to lift them, says the saga. This summer was since known as the "Stone-throwing Summer." It is probable that the priest Halldor died fighting valiantly in this bloody riot which desecrated the thingstead. The church had now become so secular in spirit, so wholly subservient to the state organization that it was no longer able to exercise any real restraint on the warlike spirit of the chieftains. Often the priests themselves would join, sword in hand, in the bloody feuds, like Odd, Lufina and others, only to give the otherwise dark picture of social and political life a still more forbidding aspect. It should be observed, however,

[9] *Sturlungasaga*, iii.
[10] *Ibidem*, iv. G. Storm, *Islandske Annaler*, year 1163.

that Iceland was in no way an exception to the conditions generally prevailing in Europe at this time. The strife and bloodshed which rent Icelandic society differed only in magnitude from the Hundred Years' War in France, the constant conflicts between French kings and nobles, the bloody struggles between Guelfs and Ghibellines in Germany, the incessant feuds between Italian *condottieri* and petty despots, and the wars between numerous pretenders, powerful nobles and weak kings which plunged Norway for centuries into anarchy and civil strife.

Among the chieftains who, together with the two bishops, may be regarded as the leaders of public affairs in Iceland about the middle of the twelfth century, Jon Loptsson of Oddi in the southern districts, the foster-father of Snorri Sturlason, was one of the most prominent. He was noted not only for his wealth and power, but also for his learning and love of peace and order. He was numbered also among the clergy, as he had been consecrated deacon, or assistant priest, and belonged as such to the third major order of the church. Gizur Hallsson, who was regarded as the most learned man in Iceland in his day, was another powerful chieftain in this district. In his youth he had traveled extensively abroad, and for some time he had been *stallari* at the court of King Sigurd Mund in Norway. The latter part of his life he spent quietly at home in his native land, where he died in 1206. In the western district Thorgils Oddsson of Stadarhol and his son Einar were the most powerful leaders. Of equal importance was also Thord Thorvaldsson in Vatsfjord, who had married the daughter of Haflidi Marsson. Sigurd Ormsson of Svinafell in eastern Iceland, Tumi Kolbeinsson in Skagafjord, and Önund Thorkellsson in Eyjafjord in the northern districts were also very powerful. The Sturlungs also rose to be numbered among the foremost leaders. So great became the power of this family, and so prominent a part did they play in the disastrous events which led to the loss of Icelandic independence that the years 1200-1265 are known as the *Sturlung Period*.

After Hvamm-Sturla had defeated his rival, Einar Thorgilsson, he soon became involved in new struggles. In many controversies he met with humiliation and defeat in the form of sentences passed upon him by the Althing, but with nonchalant disregard for court decisions he pursued his course of feud and contention with a certain diabolic good cheer. When his turbulent illegitimate son Svein abducted Valgerd, daughter of the priest Olaf Solvason of Helgafell, shortly after her beautiful mother Hallgerd had also been abducted by the chieftain Paul Thordsson, the people were greatly aroused, as Olaf and his brother Paul, the priest at Reykholt, belonged to the most prominent families. Jon Loptsson, who was closely related to the two ladies, now took a hand in the affair, and brought about an adjustment agreeable to all. But Hvamm-Sturla, who again had been compelled to agree to a reasonable settlement, soon found new opportunity to quarrel. This time he started a controversy with the priest Paul of Reykholt about an inheritance, and showed such cynical heartlessness that in a heated argument with him the priest's wife cried out: "If you are like Odin (i.e., cunning and heartless), I will make you like him also in appearance." She struck at him with a knife in an effort to blind him on one eye, but only succeeded in cutting an ugly gash in his face.[11] This situation threatened to become very disagreeable for the priest. In his anxiety to settle the matter as soon as possible he yielded to Hvamm-Sturla on the points in controversy, and left it to him personally to fix the compensation to be paid him for the wound which he had received. This mode of settlement pleased the greedy chieftain. He named a sum so exorbitant that the priest was forced to refuse to settle on such terms. The case was then brought before the Althing, where Jon Loptsson again compelled Hvamm-Sturla to accept a reasonable settlement. But in order not to humiliate him by any appearance of personal defeat, Jon offered to rear his son Snorri Sturlason, the later historian. This generous offer helped to appease the saucy old chieftain. He brought the three-year-old boy

[11] *Sturlungasaga*, i, p. 112 ff, published by Det kongelige nordiske Oldskrift Selskab, Copenhagen.

to Oddi, where he remained for fifteen years until Jon
Loptsson's death in 1197.[12] It was especially fortunate for
a youth with Snorri's talents to find a home where the
interest in history and scaldic art was cultivated, where
large collections of books and manuscripts were found, and
where he could devote himself in peace to intellectual pursuits in this period of storm and stress. His father, Hvamm-
Sturla, died at the age of sixty-seven, shortly after his controversy with the priest Paul, in 1182.

The lack of efficient organization which gradually enabled lawless violence to undermine the state was felt to
some extent also in the church. Moral laxity and open disregard for the most fundamental Christian teachings were
everywhere apparent. The common clergy continued to be
of a distinctly inferior type, and disciplinary authority
was so feebly exercised that prevailing practices often de-
viated sharply from established church polity. Celibacy
of the clergy had not been introduced in Iceland. The
choice of bishops, which after the Second Lateran Council
in 1139 had been left principally to the cathedral chapters,
was here exercised by the Althing with the advice and
assistance of the bishops, an arrangement which virtually
placed the choice of bishops in the hands of the aristocracy. Priests would often assume the management of cases
brought before the Althing, and took so active a part in the
bitter quarrels that they were in danger of becoming hostile
partisans rather than spiritual advisers and preachers of
the gospel. A stricter general supervision was begun in
1152, when Iceland was joined to the new archdiocese of
Nidaros in Norway. The gifted and powerful Norwegian
archbishop Eystein Erlendsson (1157-1188) inaugurated
a policy of reform. He sharpened church discipline, and
sought to eradicate flagrant abuses, but even he was able
to accomplish but little in the face of the insolent opposition of the chieftains. In letters to the Icelandic
bishops he vigorously assailed the prevailing violence and
immorality.

[12] *Íslendingasaga,* 2.

"It has come to my knowledge," he says, "that there are men among you who have beaten, wounded and even killed priests, while some have driven away their wives and have taken concubines instead. Some keep both their wives and concubines in their homes, and live licentious lives which tempt all Christians to sinfulness. And if the bishops attempt to reprove them, they take pride in defying them, and refuse to submit to any punishment for such offences. . . . The reason that such abuses continue so long in your land is that those who conduct themselves in this manner are chieftains, both learned and unlearned. I could mention the names of many who are guilty of such great sins, but I will not at present expose them to the public. But I want to state that I will not long bear the responsibility for their sinful lives, now that I know their misdeeds and the names of the offenders.' [13]

He forbids anyone who has slain a person to conduct religious services of any sort. He also forbids priests to assume the management of suits in the courts, except in behalf of poor relatives, orphans or defenseless women; and even then only for God's sake and not for profit,

"as it is contrary to God's ordinance, and many among you have lost both temporal and eternal life through assembling of partisan bands, and the perpetration of deeds of violence. From all such things the clergy should abstain, as they ought to show no less obedience than they demand of the unlearned. The greater the punishment imposed for their ill-treatment, the more the clergy ought to avoid everything which results in eternal harm to both parties; for he who does bodily harm to any member of the clergy is under the ban of God and the pope; and no one can obtain absolution for the slaying of a priest or a monk except from the pope himself, or for wounding or striking such a person only of us. But among you there are many who are in this sad plight, and still they act as if they did not care. Now I summon all who are under the ban for these things to come from your land hither to me; and I forbid all and everyone to sit together with them at the table or in the church, or to greet them on the highway, unless they should be proceeding on a journey to obtain absolution. But if they show insubordination and will remain under the ban rather than receive absolution, then both

[13] Finnur Jonsson, *Historia Ecclesiastica Islandiæ*, vol. i, p. 237 ff.

those who have committed these wrongs which have made them subject to this punishment, and those who have continued in intercourse with them, will all alike be under the ban from Olaf-mas following the publication of this command. If the people shall be unwilling to heed this salutary admonition, then I command the bishops in God's name to discontinue all religious services to which their consecration gives origin, after said Olafmas. And if they are unable to do so because of the opposition of unreasonable men, then they should appeal to the king and to us." [14]

In other letters he makes it punishable with the ban to bury in consecrated soil anyone who has robbed churches or cemeteries, or has committed deeds of violence against pilgrims or persons who have sought safety in churches. He also sought to abolish private ownership of churches, and he forbade anyone to receive priestly orders who held the office of *goði*, as these practices had helped to keep the Icelandic church in a state of subserviency to the secular authorities.

As Bishop Klæng of Skálholt was now so old and sickly that he could no longer give proper attention to the duties of his office, Archbishop Eystein had given the people of his diocese permission to elect a new bishop. At the meeting of the Althing in 1173 three candidates were proposed: Abbot Ögmund Kalfsson of Helgafell, the priest Paul, and Abbot Thorlak Thorhallsson of Thykkvabær. The choice was left to Bishop Klæng, and he selected Thorlak, who was a general favorite. Born at Hlidarendi in southern Iceland, Thorlak had been reared and educated at Oddi under the supervision of the priest Eyjolf Sæmundsson. When he had taken holy orders, he went abroad to study, and spent many years in Paris and Lincoln. On his return home he became prior and later abbot of the newly established monastery of Thykkvabær. After his election as bishop he moved to Skálholt, but Klæng remained in charge of the diocese until his death in 1176.[15] "The people would not

[14] The letter seems to have been addressed to Bishop Brand of Hólar.
[15] *Biskup Thorlákssaga.* Thorlak's predecessors were Isleif Gizursson, Gizur Isleifsson, Thorlak Runolfsson, Magnus Einarsson, and Klæng Thorsteinsson.

let Thorlak go abroad to be consecrated," says the saga, "because of the hostility between Norway and Iceland, since the controversy arising from murders and robberies had not been settled." [16] When Klæng died, however, he proceeded to Norway, where he was cordially received by the archbishop.

At this time the old aristocracy, under the leadership of the great noble Erling Skakke, aided and supported by the church, had gained control in Norway. A child king, Magnus, the son of Erling, had been placed on the throne by the hierarchy, and since no legitimate claim to the crown could be urged in his behalf, he was sure to be a pliant tool in their hands, the real ruler being Erling himself, who acted as the king's guardian. It was rumored that he was not favorably inclined to the consecration of Thorlak as bishop of Skálholt, and Archbishop Eystein would not perform the consecration without his consent. It is not probable that in a purely ecclesiastical affair Erling should have deemed it expedient to oppose the great archbishop, who had been his supporter, had been instrumental in placing his son Magnus on the throne, and had been able to dictate terms to Erling regarding the weightiest matters of government. It was, no doubt, only a shrewd maneuver on the part of the archbishop, calculated to impress on the mind of the bishop elect that Iceland was to be regarded as a dependency under the Norwegian crown. It must have been through his influence also that Bishop Brand of Hólar, and the great chieftain Jon Loptsson had come from Iceland to attend the coronation of Magnus Erlingsson in 1164. The policy of placing Iceland under the crown of Norway would be in full harmony with the views of the pope and the Roman hierarchy, who regarded monarchy with a king anointed by the church as the only legitimate government. In his efforts to eradicate the prevailing evils in the Icelandic church, and to bring the unruly chieftains to submission, the support of the king of Norway would

---

[16] *Biskup Thorlákssaga*, ch. 10. The strained relations between Norway and Iceland at this time are referred to also in a letter by Archbishop Eystein.

also be of the greatest value, as had been shown at the time of the introduction of Christianity in the reign of King Olaf Tryggvason. After a short delay Erling Skakke's consent was obtained, and the consecration was duly performed at Nidaros in the presence of the bishops of Bergen and Stavanger, July 2, 1178.

Bishop Thorlak, who was a very gifted and earnest man, shared fully the archbishop's views in regard to general church polity. On his return to Iceland he sought to restrict the right of private ownership of churches and church lands, but this attempt, as well as his efforts to exercise the disciplinary authority of the church, soon brought him into conflict with the chieftains. The powerful Jon Loptsson, one of the most peaceful and rightminded of them all, who, as already noted, had even been consecrated deacon, kept the bishop's own sister Ragneid as concubine. On refusing to terminate this illicit and offensive relation the bishop placed him under the ban of the church, but Jon revenged himself by taking position with an armed band in front of the church door at Skard, barring the bishop from entering. To the question what this should mean he replied that he was retaliating because the bishop had placed him under the ban. Thorlak explained that he had not yet pronounced full excommunication upon him, hoping that he would repent of his sins, but now that such hope seemed to be vain, he would exercise with full severity the authority of the church. Jon retorted that, though he might deserve such punishment, the ban would not convert him. Only God's grace could change his heart and mind. In due time he would part with the bishop's sister, but only of his own free will, not upon command of the bishop. An armed clash was averted with difficulty; but shortly afterward Jon sent Ragneid away, and was in turn freed from the excommunication. Thorlak's attempt to exercise excommunication and to introduce celibacy of the clergy was also doomed to fail because of the opposition offered by the chieftains, who resented all attempts of foreign authorities to limit their liberties in any way whatever. When the bishop appealed to the authority of Archbishop Eystein, Sigurd Ormsson of Svinafell replied that Norsemen and foreigners had no right to limit the privileges of the country's own inhabitants.[17] In the face of so determined an opposition on the part of the laity the bishop was forced to abandon his hierarchic plans. His attempt at reform bore little fruit, but the people held him in so high esteem because of his learning and purity of life that after his death in 1193 he was venerated as a saint. In 1198 his remains were enshrined and placed on the altar of the cathedral church at Skálholt. In the same year a like honor was shown the remains of Bishop Jon Ögmundsson of Hólar, who died in 1121, though neither of them was ever formally canonized. Thorlak's successor, Bishop Paul Jonsson, a son of Jon Loptsson and Thorlak's sister, Ragneid, pursued a more conciliatory policy, as did also Bishop Brand Sæmundsson of Hólar. The controversy with the chieftains subsided, but only because the bishops had failed to maintain their authority on very vital questions of church polity.

Upon the death of Bishop Brand the priest Gudmund Arason, a man of humble birth, became his successor in the bishopric of Hólar. He had won a reputation for piety and purity of Christian life, but he proved to be very self-willed and arbitrary. He did not hesitate to attack the privileges of the chieftains who had done most to further his election, and as he traveled about with a large band of followers of evil repute who pretended an outward piety only to exploit people's hospitality, he became a real scourge to the parishes of his diocese. With vain display of authority he not only used the churchly weapons of excommunication very freely, but he suffered his rude followers to wield the sword in bloody combats with the angry chieftains. In one of these clashes Kolbein Tumason, the most powerful chieftain in northern Iceland, lost his life, 1208. So bitter became the struggle that the chieftains seized the bishop's residence and deprived him of nearly all his power. He was finally summoned to Norway by the archbishop to answer for his conduct, and remained abroad for several years. On his

[17] Finnur Jonsson, *Historia Ecclesiastica Islandiæ*, vol. i, p. 289 ff.

return in 1218 he continued his former conduct until he was again driven from his bishopric by the chieftains. After some time he was able to return to his bishop's residence, but he kept such a rabble about him that the people appealed to the chieftains for protection. They gave him a solemn warning to part with his lawless followers; but he fled instead from Hólar, and Tumi, the son of Sighvat Sturlason, took possession of the bishop's seat. Gudmund and his band had retired to an island in the Skagafjord, and on a dark and stormy winter night they attacked Hólar and slew Tumi Sighvatsson. With a hundred followers he now fled to a more distant island, but Sighvat, Tumi's father, pursued him with three hundred armed men and forced him to flee to Norway. His case was now brought to the attention of the pope, who advised him to resign, but this he refused to do. In 1226 he returned to Iceland, only to pursue his former tactics. The chieftains finally dispersed his band of followers, and kept him as a prisoner at Hólar for two years. From that time forth he was again allowed to wander around with his band. In 1233 he made a pilgrimage to Rome to do penance, but no noticeable change occurred in his relation to the people of his diocese. Old and blind, and despised by all respectable people, he continued to rule over a band of motley followers of both sexes, though wholly unable any longer to perform even the simplest duties of his office. The pope finally issued an order for his suspension from office, but Gudmund died at Hólar in 1237 before the order could be executed.[18] In the same year died also Bishop Magnus Gizursson of Skálholt, a man of very different character, who resembled his worthy predecessors. Magnus, who belonged to one of the best families of Iceland, had been educated by Bishop Thorlak. He took no part in the feuds and quarrels of the chieftains, but used his influence as far as possible to allay strife. He too was summoned to Norway by the archbishop because of some changes which he had introduced in the church service, but his absence of several years only enabled Bishop

[18] Finnur Jonsson, *Historia Ecclesiastica Islandiœ*, vol. i, 335 ff. *Biskupasögur, Guðmundarsaga.*

Gudmund to carry his activities also into the diocese of Skálholt.

After Hvamm-Sturla's death his three sons, Thord, Sighvat and Snorri, became his chief heirs, and succeeded in time to the position of leadership which he had created. Thord, the oldest of the brothers, was now eighteen, Sighvat thirteen and Snorri six years of age. The older illegitimate son, Svein Sturlason, had gained notoriety as an unruly factionist, who had taken a prominent part in many feuds and escapades, but was otherwise of no great importance. The quarrels of jealous rivals continued with increasing intensity, but a few prominent leaders had extended their sway over so many families that they were able to rally to their support the armed yeomanry of extensive districts. In a quarrel between Kolbein Tumason, the most powerful chieftain in northern Iceland, and one of Thord Sturlason's *thingmenn,* both parties arrived at the Althing with large forces of armed followers. Great commotion arose in which one man lost his life, and a bloody conflict was averted only through the effort of Bishop Paul of Skálholt, who was able to arrange a temporary settlement, 1196. The following year Gudmund Dyri and Kolbein Tumason collected a large band, and burned one of their opponents, Önund Thorkelsson of Langahlid, in his own house. The party hatred grew so violent that a general fight between the two factions at the Althing the following summer was avoided only through the influence of the aged Jon Loptsson, who was able once more to calm the angry opponents, and arrange a peaceful settlement.

Upon Jon's death in 1197 his son Sæmund Jonsson inherited the family estate of Oddi. He did not possess his father's literary interests, but he maintained a sumptuous household, and was regarded as the leading chieftain of the southern districts till his death in 1222. The Sturlung brothers had also acquired great wealth and influence. Through marriage and in other ways they had become owners of large estates, and were related to the most prominent families. Thord, who lived at Stad in Snæfellsnes, was considered the most powerful man in southern Iceland. In

the northern districts Sighvat had risen to equal prominence, as he had become very wealthy, and was related to
Kolbein Tumason and Sigurd Ormsson of Svinafell through
marriage. Snorri Sturlason was now nineteen years of age.
He possessed no estate of his own, but through marriage
with Herdis, the only daughter of the rich priest Bersi
Vemundsson of Borg, he became the possessor of Egill
Skallagrimsson's famous seat.[19] From his mother he also
received the estate Hvamm as a wedding present for his
bride. During the year following his marriage (1199-1200)
Snorri remained at Oddi, but upon the death of his father-
in-law in 1201 he moved to Borg, where he stayed till
1206. In that year he bought the estate Reykholt, where
he since resided. His marriage, which seems to have been
a wholly unsentimental business affair, brought him little
happiness. Two children were born to them, but Herdis
did not accompany him to Reykholt. Though never formally divorced, they lived apart from that day forth, and
Herdis continued to reside at Borg till her death in 1233.
But since wealth and power had become his, Snorri was
now able to assume the rôle of a leader. "He became a
great chieftain, says the saga, "for he did not lack money.
He was also a very thrifty manager of his estates. But he
was very incontinent, and he had children with many
women besides Herdis." [20] Shortly after he settled at Borg
he acquired also one half of the Lundarmanna goðorð with
the rank and title of goði. Fortune had so favored him
that his manifestation at this time of the haughty spirit
which usually characterized the chieftain class seems almost
pardonable. The brusk display of superiority, so tempting
to a wealthy and gifted youth, is seen especially in his dealings with some Orkney merchants who had arrived in the
Borgarfjord with a cargo of flour. The master of the vessel,
Thorkell Rostung, a nephew of the bishop of the Orkneys,
had been invited to spend the winter at Borg. But he soon
had a serious quarrel with his host, as Snorri in his office

[19] *Sturlungasaga*, vol. i, p. 48, 241.
[20] *Sturlungasaga*, vol. i, p. 274. *Saga Guðmundar Arasonar Hólar-Biskups
hin elzta*, ch. 51.

as *goði* demanded the right, according to old custom, to fix the price at which the cargo was to be sold. When the skipper objected to this interference, Snorri seized the cargo and sold it at the stipulated price. Thorkell felt deeply aggrieved, and the following summer, before sailing away, he slew one of the men who had assisted at the sale. This wanton act of vengeance so aroused Snorri that he summoned his brothers to join him in an attack on the traders, who were still in the Borgarfjord. They came to his assistance, but Thorkell made good his escape. In the fall, when he was again driven to Iceland in a storm, he sought the protection of Sæmund Jonsson at Oddi, where he spent the winter. Snorri sent men to slay him, but the attempt miscarried, and the following summer Thorkell was able to leave Iceland unharmed. The event shows an unnecessary vindictiveness on the part of Snorri, though it must be admitted that he acted in the main within his right. In the first flush of youthful pride as chieftain and *goði* he was only too eager to assert his authority. No other importance seems to attach to the incident, which throws little light on Snorri's real character. Self-assertive and strong of will he undoubtedly was; but he respected justice, and was usually ready to listen to counsel as to what was regarded as fair and equitable. Like his father, Hvamm-Sturla, he was avaricious and hard to deal with. Judged by modern standards his faults were conspicuous enough; but the sinister traits of character attributed to him by some biographers remain wholly unproved by evidence of historical events properly interpreted. In mental power he towered so high above all his contemporaries that the Icelandic intellectual and literary renaissance found its culmination in him, and he possessed to some extent the wisdom, moderation and breadth of view which are usually associated with so superior an intellect. As he excelled in all lines of literary activity, he was also very learned in the law, and served with distinction as *lögsögumaðr* for a number of years. In political life he was not only a prominent leader, but a farsighted patriot, who loved peaceful development and social order, and he must have viewed with serious misgivings the growing spirit of strife and lawlessness which more and more endangered the existence of the state.

The years 1206 to 1214 seems to have been rather un-eventful so far as Snorri was personally concerned. In 1209 he took part in an expedition against Bishop Gudmund, but the following winter he kept the eccentric bishop in his own home and treated him well. He is also said to have saved the life of a priest on the same expedition. His peaceful disposition is shown also in his relation to a feud waged at this time between the men of Vatsdal and Midfjord. He took no part in these hostilities, but used his influence as *goði* to terminate the strife. In 1215 Snorri was elected *lögsögumaðr*, but he had already won great fame as scald, and at the expiration of his term of office in 1218 he found an opportunity to visit Norway, where he remained for two years enjoying the highest favor of King Haakon Haakonsson and Skule Jarl. The relations between Norway and Iceland at this time were very strained, due to events which had created misunderstanding and bitter feel-ing. The policy of the Norwegian kings, who had built a colonial empire embracing all the western island groups, and on many occasions had wielded great influence even in purely Icelandic affairs, had also made the chieftains appre-hensive of their own independence. King Harald Haar-fagre had always regarded Iceland as a quasi-Norwegian dependency. He sent Uni Oborni, a son of the discoverer Gardar, to Iceland, promising to create him jarl, if he could bring the colony under Norwegian dominion.[21] The plan failed, but the colonists agreed to pay the *landaurar* tax for unrestricted intercourse with Norway. They also ap-pealed to him as arbitrator in the question of the size of landholdings among the early settlers, showing thereby a disposition to regard him as their friend, though they would not own him as their ruler. In his zeal for the cause of Christianity King Olaf Tryggvason had treated the Ice-landers as if they were Norwegian subjects, and King Olaf Haraldsson had made very determined efforts to bring Ice-land under Norwegian rule. In 1022 he entered into an

[21] *Landnámabók*, iv, p. 176. *Njálssaga*, ch. 19.

agreement with the Icelandic chieftains, known as "The Institutions and Laws Which King Olaf Gave the Icelanders." [22] According to this agreement the Icelanders should enjoy in Norway the same rights as free native citizens in case of personal injury. They should have the right to inherit property in Norway, and they were to pay no taxes except a small contribution to the watchmen in the cities, and the *landaurar* tax, established in the time of King Harald Haarfagre. In return for these concessions the king's men should have the same rights in Iceland as native citizens, and suits at law in which they were involved should be brought before the courts without previous notice. In time of war the Icelanders who happened to be in Norway owed the king military service, and could not leave the country. Two out of every three should then join the royal standards, but they could only be called upon to serve in defensive war within the borders of the kingdom. In 1024 King Olaf submitted a definite proposal to the Althing to recognize him as ruler. The Norwegian laws should be adopted, and the Icelanders should pay a head tax of one *pening* per person. He also demanded the cession of the little island of Grimsey in the Eyjafjord. When this request was refused, he invited several leading Icelanders to Norway in 1026. One of these, Gellir Thorkellsson, he sent back to Iceland with a renewal of his request, the others were retained as hostages. But again the proposal was rejected. His wars with King Knut the Great of Denmark, his flight from the kingdom, and subsequent death in the battle of Stiklestad, 1030, prevented further attempts on his part to establish Norwegian dominion over Iceland. The warlike and ambitious King Harald Haardraade seems to have cherished similar plans, but his war with England, where he fell in the battle of Stamford Bridge, 1066, prevented their execution. His successor, Olaf Kyrre, devoted himself exclusively to the pursuits of peace, and during the period of destructive civil wars, which lasted from 1130 till the reign of King Haakon Haakonsson, no attention

[22] Diplomatarium Islandicum, vol. i, no. 16, p. 54; no. 21, p. 64 ff. "The laws and regulations here written King Olaf gave the Icelanders."

could be paid to this phase of Norwegian colonial policy.
In 1152, as already noted, Iceland was joined to Norway
in ecclesiastical affairs as a part of the archdiocese of
Nidaros, a very important step towards the establishing of
full sovereign dominion over the colony. Not only Icelandic priests and bishops, but other prominent men were
now repeatedly summoned to Norway by the archbishop,
who not only asserted his own power as head of the archdiocese and representative of the pope, but even appealed,
though indirectly, to the authority of the king. Snorri
himself was among those who had thus been summoned
to Norway by the archbishop, but from patriotic motives
he and other prominent leaders had refused to heed the
summons.

When Snorri arrived in Norway, the young King Haakon
Haakonsson, who ruled from 1217 till 1263, had ascended
the throne. In his reign the bloody civil wars were terminated, and Norway reached the zenith of her political
power. In international affairs this able and gifted ruler
enjoyed high esteem. He guarded with wise forethought
all the interests of his realm. He also devoted careful attention to the colonies, and sought to link them more firmly
to the mother country. In Iceland unceasing strife prevented the development of a united patriotic sentiment.
The growing turmoil could only create situations which
invited the constant intervention of Norwegian authorities; and as the struggle between rival leaders grew more
bitter, the spirit of independence was able to assert itself
but feebly within the umbra of the approaching crisis.
Chieftains who through defeat or otherwise had lost their
power and influence would be inclined to welcome the
supremacy of the Norwegian king rather than submit to
the whims of their successful rivals. Even among those
who were most farsighted and patriotic some would favor
submission of the king of Norway as the only escape from
lawlessness and anarchy.

The strained relations between the colony and the mother
country at the time of Snorri's visit were occasioned by the
death of Paul, a son of the chieftain Sæmund Jonsson of

Oddi, who was accidentally drowned in Norway. When the father heard of this sad happening, he grew furious and blamed the people of Bergen for it.[23] He seized some Bergen merchants who were lying with their ships at Eyrar, and demanded that they should pay such an indemnity as he himself should fix. His brother Orm sought in vain to persuade him to modify this unreasonable demand. The merchants were forced to pay 900 marks of silver, an enormous sum in those days. Some Norwegian traders who arrived with a ship from Greenland were also forced to contribute to this indemnity. In revenge they slew Orm Jonsson, Sæmund's brother, a deed which further complicated the case.[24] In Norway people now demanded redress because of Sæmund Jonsson's high-handed acts; in Iceland they insisted on the payment of indemnity also for the death of Orm Jonsson. So great became the excitement that Skule Jarl, now Duke Skule, planned a military expedition to Iceland, as he undoubtedly found the moment opportune for an attempt to subjugate the island. The more fairminded leaders, however, would not rush to arms. Snorri Sturlason, who had remained with the Duke as his guest, had accompanied him on a visit to Sweden, and at Christmas time the following year had been made *skutilsveinn* by King Haakon, counseled moderation and peaceful measures. It was probably through his influence that Skule was persuaded to abandon the attack on Iceland. Snorri argued that nothing could be accomplished by force. It would be better, he said, to secure the friendship of the most influential men in Iceland. It would then be an easy

[23] Paul descended from King Magnus Barefoot, as his grandfather, Jon Loptsson, was a son of Magnus' daughter. When he came to Norway he seems to have carried himself rather arrogantly. The saga narrates the incident as follows: "At that time Paul Sœmundsson went abroad, and when he came to Bergen, the people made fun of him, and asked if he came there to become king or jarl over Norway. Some thought it dangerous to wait until he perhaps should gather a rebel force. Because of this jest he made ready to sail in a boat to Trondhjem to King Ingi. Aslak Hauksson was in one of the boats. They sailed past Stadt, but there the boats foundered, and all on board were lost. When his father, Sæmund, heard this, he became very angry, and claimed that Paul had perished because of the acts of the people of Bergen." *Sturlungasaga*, vol. i, p. 329.

[24] P. A. Munch, *Norges Konge-Sagaer*, vol. ii, 278.

matter to persuade the chieftains to submit voluntarily to
the Norwegian king, especially after the death of Sæmund
Jonsson, since he himself and his brothers would then be
the leaders.[25] Why he suggested such a plan is not clear,
but in light of subsequent events it seems to have been only
a diplomatic artifice by which he sought to avert the im-
pending stroke. On Snorri's suggestion Skule abandoned
the plan of an expedition to Iceland. But in order to avoid
the appearance of fickleness on his part he persuaded the
Icelanders to ask the king to mediate. This was done, and
at a conference assembled for this purpose King Haakon
said: "Sir Jarl, the plan of undertaking an expedition to
Iceland, which has been considered this summer, seems to
the Council to be inexpedient, partly because of the long
and difficult voyage, and partly also because that country
was colonized from here, and our forefathers and relatives
Christianized it. To this must further be added that the
Icelanders as a whole have done us no harm, though certain individuals have ill-treated our thanes. It would be
harmful to us all if the country should be harried by war,
and I therefore ask, Sir Jarl, that on my request you drop
this plan." [26] Many supported the king, and Skule at once
consented. In return Snorri undertook to guarantee safety
for Norwegian merchants in Iceland. He also had to enter
into a secret agreement with the king and the jarl by which
he promised to use his influence to bring Iceland under
the dominion of Norway in a peaceful way. As a further
guarantee that the agreement would be faithfully carried
out, Snorri was also to send his son Jon Mutri to Skuli
Jarl as a hostage. The king in turn sought to win his
friendship by making him a *lendermaðr*, an honor not be-
stowed on an Icelander since the days of King Olaf Haraldsson. Snorri now set sail in a ship given him by Skule,
and after a stormy voyage he reached Iceland late in the
fall. Through skilful diplomacy he had averted a war
which under all circumstances would have proved disastrous to his country. He had received presents and

[25] *Sturlungasaga*, vol. i, p. 339.
[26] P. A. Munch, *Norges Konge-Sagaer*, vol. ii, 279.

honors both from the king and from Skule Jarl, but his cheerful acceptance of their friendship was undoubtedly essential to the diplomatic game which he was playing, and was otherwise in keeping also with the old usage of prominent Icelanders who traveled abroad. His countrymen, however, who failed to understand the nature of his services, met him on his return with hostile ill-will. They thought that he was in the service of the king, and that he had only tried to favor his Norwegian friends at the expense of his own people. They ridiculed his new title, parodied the songs which he had composed in honor of Skule, and showed in every way their unqualified disapproval of the course which he had pursued. No one showed more undisguised hostility than Björn Thorvaldsson, a son-in-law of Orm Jonsson. When Snorri upon his arrival accepted the hospitality of Bishop Magnus of Skálholt, and entered the bishop's residence with his men, Björn arrived with an armed band, and demanded if he would deny Orm's heirs their rightful indemnity. Snorri replied that this was not his intention. But Björn persisted in his accusations, and the two parted as bitter enemies. Snorri's promise to bring Iceland under Norwegian dominion was not known, nor did he make any attempt to fulfil it. It seems to have been a part of a diplomatic move to placate the warlike Skule Jarl. But the promise, which he also had given, to protect Norwegian merchants in Iceland was faithfully carried out. "He did not succeed in carrying out his plan with regard to the Icelanders," says the saga, "neither did he make any attempt to do so. But the Norwegian merchants enjoyed at that time perfect peace in Iceland." [27]

9. THE STURLUNG PERIOD OF CIVIL WAR

IF the Icelanders had been united under an efficient national government, their independence would not have been endangered by foreign aggression, which now began to

[27] *Hákonarsaga Hákonarsonar*, ch. 58.

loom on their political horizon. But since all power had
become lodged in the hands of rival chieftains who aimed
at nothing but self-aggrandizement, the country's safety,
like its judicial system and its social order, was recklessly
sacrificed in the growing domestic feuds. After Snorri's return in 1220 the strife waged by rival leaders developed into
a civil war involving nearly all parts of the island. In this
struggle the Sturlung brothers stood divided, and became
the leaders of the hostile factions which they organized in
their support. Snorri continued to reside at Reykholt, and
took steps to fortify and improve his estate. He surrounded his houses with stone walls, and built also a famous bath, the *Snorralaug,* of which remnants are still
found. Politically he allied himself with the powerful
Oddaverjar family of Oddi in southern Iceland, as Jon
Loptsson, the greatest of the Oddi chieftains, had been his
foster-father. Sighvat Sturlason became related to the
powerful Kolbein Tumason of northern Iceland through
marriage with his sister Halldora. He had been able to add
one estate to the other until he was very wealthy. He also
entered into formal alliance with his brother-in-law Kolbein, and Sigurd Ormsson of Svinafell, the most influential
leaders in northern and eastern Iceland, the three forming a
very strong confederacy. Thord Sturlason, the oldest and,
perhaps, the most peaceful of the brothers, had become so
influential that he was regarded as the leading man in the
southwestern districts, but he attempted to maintain a
neutral attitude between the hostile groups supported by
his two brothers.

Björn Thorvaldsson, who had shown Snorri such affront
on his arrival at Skálholt, was killed shortly afterward by
his brothers-in-law, the sons of Sæmund Jonsson, in a
quarrel over their inheritance. For this deed the brothers
were banished, and as Sæmund himself died in 1222, the
power of the Oddi chieftains was broken. Snorri and
Thorvald Gizursson, Björn's father, remained leaders in
southern Iceland. As Thorvald himself soon sought peaceful retirement in the monastery of Videy, Snorri found it
necessary to strengthen himself in his rather isolated posi-

tion. For this purpose he married Hallveig, the widow of
Björn Thorvaldsson, at that time the richest heiress in
Iceland. He also won to his side the turbulent Thorvald
of Vatsfjord, who married his daughter Thordis. His other
daughter, Ingibjörg, was married to Gizur, the son of his
friend Thorvald Gizursson. He was also able at this time
to win the support of his brother Thord, with whom he had
not hitherto maintained very cordial relations. In 1222 he
was again elected *lögsögumaðr,* and was reëlected in 1231.
As matters stood he was now undoubtedly the richest and
most influential man in southern Iceland. A grouping of
opposing forces had thus been effected which would give
a new conflict a more serious aspect than had hitherto
characterized Icelandic feuds. The easily foreseen struggle
was precipitated by the rather insignificant event of a
minor family quarrel. The Snorrunga *goðorð,* which was a
Sturlung family possession, had not been granted to Thord,
the oldest brother, but to Sighvat, who in turn had given
it to his son Sturla. As both Snorri and Thord had failed
to obtain what they considered their share, they agreed to
lay claim to it, and Snorri was now so powerful that at the
meeting of the Althing he made a formal demand that the
Snorrunga *goðorð* should be surrendered by Sighvat. The
case was not decided by the Althing. A bitter controversy
now arose between Snorri, Sighvat and Sturla, with the
final outcome that Snorri seized the *goðorð* by force and
summoned the *thingmenn* to swear him allegiance. During
this controversy the violent Thorvald of Vatsfjord supported his father-in-law Snorri, but he met his death at
the hands of the sons of Hrafn Sveinbjarnarson, whom he
had slain. Hrafn's sons Thord and Sturla, who in all
respects ·resembled their father, directed their attacks
against Sighvat and his son Sturla, whom they blamed for
his death. One night they made a most brutal attack on
Sturla's home, robbed and plundered, and killed even women and children, but they failed to find Sturla, who happened to be away from home. It seems certain that Snorri
was wholly innocent of any part in this outrage. The relations between him and Sturla from this time forth grew

more cordial, until they finally arranged a complete settlement of their difficulty in 1230. The following year Sturla stayed with Snorri, and was especially interested in providing for the copying of the books which Snorri had written. Friendly relations were also established between Snorri and his brother Sighvat, Sturla's father, and for a period peace again prevailed throughout Iceland. But it was of short duration. Sturla Sighvatsson offered the Vatsfjord chieftains a peaceful settlement for the attack made upon his home. An agreement was reached, but one of the brothers, Thord, mocked him because he was willing to make such a settlement. This insult added to previous injury, and the insolent conduct of the two brothers so exasperated Sturla that he broke his agreement, gathered an armed force and slew them both, whereupon he departed on a pilgrimage to Rome in 1232. To the people of the Vatsfjord district the death of the two brothers must have been a welcome riddance, but it brought no permanent relief. Snorri's illegitimate son Urökja, a dissolute and violent youth, took possession of the Vatsfjord *goðorð* only to continue the vile practices of his predecessors with increased recklessness. He kept a large band of armed followers, and levied forced contributions upon the neighboring districts for their support. From time to time he would send out armed bands to plunder and ill-treat the people, and seize everything which he might desire, like the arrogant robber knights on the continent. Kolbein Ungi, another saucy young chieftain, also joined him in offering affront to Sighvat Sturlason, the two remaining very defiant until Sighvat finally gathered an armed force of sufficient size to cow them into submission. He forced them to accept the agreement of Flatatunga, according to which the controversy should be arbitrated by Bishop Magnus at the next meeting of the Althing. Peace, however, remained but an evanescent hope, as Urökja continued his exploits with the same unbridled violence as before.

On his return from Rome Sturla Sighvatsson spent some time in Norway. He had heard about Urökja's violence,

and had many conversations with King Haakon Haakonsson and Duke Skule about affairs in Iceland. To an
inquiry from the king whether it would be difficult to bring
the country under Norwegian rule so that peace and order
could be maintained there, he answered that it would not
be difficult if the one to, whom the task was entrusted had
sufficient power and authority.[1] His aggressive attitude
and undisguised ambition must have led the king to think
that he would be more willing to further the interests of
the crown in Iceland than Snorri Sturlason, who was no
warrior, and who was too patriotic to support any scheme
against his country's independence. Sturla was restrained
by no such scruples, as it appears from his later conduct
that he acted from purely selfish motives in an effort to
vanquish all rivals, and gain full sway in the island. Without hesitancy he promised to subjugate Iceland, a service
for which he was to receive the title of *jarl*. The king, who,
aside from his own ambitious plans, really desired to establish peace and order in the island, warned him that he
should use no violent means, that he should kill none of
the leaders, but that he might send to Norway those whom
he wished to get rid of. To these terms Sturla readily
agreed, but the king's warning he suffered to go unheeded.
His treason soon led to violence and civil war.

On his arrival in Iceland in 1235 Sturla, with the aid of
his father Sighvat, began to collect military forces for an
attack on Snorri Sturlason, of whom they demanded full
reparation for the damages done by his son Urökja. Snorri,
who seems to have understood the nature of the threatening
danger, asked Urökja to hasten to his assistance, a request
to which the young chieftain immediately responded. He
gathered a force of 720 men, and advised his father to attack Sturla before he could organize an invincible army.
But Snorri did not desire to wage war against his own
relatives. The Easter holidays were approaching. At such
a time, he said, he could not enter into armed conflict with
his brother. Urökja had to disband his force, and Snorri

---

[1] *Hákonarsaga Hákonarsonar,* ch. iv., p. 344 f.   *Sturlungasaga,* vol. i,
ch. iv., p. 344 f.

made no further attempt to resist the attack. He left
Reykholt, retiring to Bessastadir in the Faxafjord. Upon
Sturla's approach with an army of 1,000 men he continued
his flight to the eastern districts of Iceland. Thord Sturlason had tried in vain to arrange a peaceful settlement of
the controversy. Sturla was implacable. Immediately after
Snorri's departure he seized Reykholt, took possession of
all his belongings, and forced the chieftains of the district
to offer their submission. Urökja and Sturla Thordsson,
the historian, fled to Ædey, where they began to gather a
fleet of ships with which they intended to sail to the Borgarfjord, but Sighvat and Sturla harried the seacoast districts and killed many of their adherents. No decisive results, however, could come from this desultory fighting.
The people soon grew so tired of the struggle that they demanded peace. A preliminary agreement was also entered
into by Sturla and Urökja. But lasting peace could not be
concluded, as Sighvat failed to appear at the conference,
evidently according to a secret understanding with Sturla.
With incredible treachery Sturla soon broke the agreement, seized Urökja and ordered him to be maimed and
blinded. It seems that the men who were to execute this
wicked deed yielded only partial obedience to the command,
as Urökja was not blinded, but was allowed to escape to
Norway. Sturla's conduct finally aroused even Snorri to
resistance. With the aid of Thorleif of Gardar he raised
an army of 480 men, but Sturla met them with a superior
force and defeated them at Bær in a bloody battle. Snorri
was not in the battle, but Thorleif of Gardar and Olaf
Thordsson, the leaders of the force, were taken prisoners,
and were compelled to leave Iceland. It was probably due
to a desire of ending this conflict that King Haakon at this
time issued a summons to the *goðorðsmenn* of Iceland to
come to Norway. In answer to this summons Snorri Sturlason as well as Sturla's younger brother, Thord Kakali,
accompanied Thorleif and Olaf on their voyage. Sturla
Sighvatsson had now almost accomplished his purpose of
making himself lord of all Iceland. Snorri Sturlason had
fled, Thord Sturlason died, and most of the leading chief-

tains had been reduced to a state of dependency, or they had been harried out of the land. Only Kolbein Ungi and Gizur Thorvaldsson were yet able to offer resistance, and against them he now directed his attacks.

The extent of Sturla's ambition is most clearly revealed in a conversation which he is said to have had with his father, who now began to think that he was carrying matters to dangerous lengths. In a joking way Sighvat asked him where he intended to reside. "Next to the bishops' seats," he said, "I know of no better estates than Oddi and Mödruvellir, but I suppose you do not consider them very satisfactory." "I like them both quite well," said Sturla, "but I suppose they can not be seized at once." "But for your big household," continued Sighvat, "you need a good steward and stewardess. For these positions I know of none better than your brother-in-law Halfdan and your sister Steinvor, his wife." Sturla said that he was of the same opinion. "And then," said Sighvat, "you must have a good and quick-footed shepherd. For this position you can get Björn Sæmundsson, and for personal attendants who can follow you in and out I can secure your brothers Thord Krok and Markus." "That might be well enough," thought Sturla. "But since the household is very large," continued Sighvat, "you ought to have people well trained in hunting and fishing, skilled with hammer and ax, and able to repair ships, etc. I know who would be best qualified for such positions. It would be Bödvar of Stad (son of Thord Sturlason) and Thorleif of Gardar." After a little hesitation Sturla thought that they might be chosen. "And then to mind the horses, and to decide which ones are to be used on each occasion you should take Lopt, the bishop's son, and Bödvar of Bær," said Sighvat. Sturla, who now began to understand the irony of the conversation, replied: "It is not to be expected that all people should serve me. This is idle talk." "Now there are not many places left in your household," continued Sighvat, "but a couple of men are needed who can manage trading expeditions, purchase the necessary supplies, arrange routes of travel, etc. For these positions you might select Gizur

Thorvaldsson and Kolbein Ungi." Sturla now became
angry and left the room.[2]

In his victorious career Sturla could not long postpone
the final struggle for overlordship in Iceland. Under some
pretext he seized the estates of the wealthy Koll Arnason,
and marched into southern Iceland with a large force.
Gizur Thorvaldsson was summoned to meet him for the
purpose, as it was stated, of assisting in the division of
Koll's estates, but he was instead made prisoner with his
whole escort, and had to take an oath that he would leave
the country. Sturla also seized many of the estates of the
Odda chieftains, the sons of Sæmund Jonsson, although
he was married to their sister Solveig. It was now so evident that all the chieftains would share the same fate that
if any effective resistance was to be offered, quick and
united action would be necessary.

As soon as Sturla left the southern districts, which he
now considered subdued, several chieftains hastened to
form a league against him. Hjalti Magnusson, son of the
bishop of Skálholt, and Kolbein Ungi, who well knew that
he would be the next victim, were the leaders of this movement. They were joined also by Gizur Thorvaldsson, whom
they soon liberated from the captivity in which he was held.
Armed forces were gathered in all districts until the con-
federates had an army of 1680 men. At Örlygsstadir they
joined in battle with Sighvat and Sturla, and defeated them
after a bloody conflict. Sighvat fell in the battle, and
Sturla and his brothers Kolbein and Thord were taken
prisoners and executed. Sturla Thordsson, the later historian of this period, son of Thord Sturlason, who was also
one of the leaders of Sighvat's and Sturla's forces, was
fortunately spared. Had he shared the fate of the others,
the events of this period of Icelandic history might never
have become known to posterity. It soon became evident,
however, that the victory at Örlygsstadir had only substituted new tyrants for the old. Kolbein Ungi and Gizur
Thorvaldsson had overthrown Sighvat and Sturla only to
seize all power and lord it over their neighbors with an

[2] *Sturlungasaga*, vol. i, ch. v, p. 498 f.

equally arrogant pride. Henceforth the selfish and calculating Gizur began to play the rôle of Sturla. In his efforts to lay all Iceland at his feet he used even more heartless and unscrupulous methods than his ambitious predecessors.

The report of Sighvat's and Sturla's defeat and death aroused the greatest interest in Norway. The king's plan of establishing supremacy over Iceland was thereby shattered, and new hope was revived among the Icelanders who had been driven into exile. The evil incubus which had threatened them with complete ruin had suddenly disappeared, but Snorri Sturlason, who was still in Norway, did not give himself over to any sudden rejoicing, probably because his thorough knowledge of Icelandic affairs enabled him to foresee the violent struggles which were still to shake his troubled country. It is noteworthy that his first recorded utterance regarding these events is a pathetic song addressed to Sighvat's son, Thord Kakali, in which he expresses his sorrow for his fallen brother. Snorri had now spent two years in Norway as a guest of Duke Skule, the king's powerful father-in-law, who was soon to raise the standard of revolt in an attempt to seize the crown. It was natural that he should welcome the friendship of this intriguing rival of King Haakon Haakonson, since the king had entered into an agreement with Sturla, and had been aiding and abetting him. He could have no choice but to seek support among the king's enemies so long as he opposed his plan of subjugating Iceland. The purpose of his visit in Norway at this time seems to have been to gain the support of Skule and his party in an effort to frustrate the king's plans and the ambitious schemes of Sturla. The old writer Styrmer Frodi calls him *folgsnarjarl* (i.e., secret jarl), as it was believed by some that Duke Skule had conferred on him the title of *jarl* with the understanding that if the duke won the Norwegian crown in his contest with King Haakon, Snorri should become his representative and rule Iceland as a Norwegian dependency.[3] But this assump-

[3] "It was stated by Arnfin that the duke had given Snorri the title of *jarl*, and Styrmer Frodi says: '*ártið Snorra folgsnarjarls*'; but none of the Icelanders would admit it." *Sturlungasaga*, vol. i, ch. vi, p. 540.

tion is supported by no acceptable evidence. Even if Snorri did receive this title from the duke, as he had already accepted that of *lendrmaðr* from the king, he undoubtedly did so from no other motive than that of diplomatic courtesy. Since he opposed the king's plan of subjugating Iceland, he could have no incentive to support Skule, if, in case he should win the throne, he should pursue a similar policy. He had already on a previous occasion prevailed on the duke to abandon an expedition against Iceland, and there is nothing which indicates that he had in any way changed his patriotic attitude. As King Haakon entertained no illusions with regard to Snorri's position, he took drastic measures to render him harmless. He summoned Duke Skule to meet him in Bergen, issuing at the same time an order that the Icelanders who were then in Norway should not be allowed to leave the country until the nature of their errand should be fully ascertained. This was clearly an infringement on their well established rights, since, according to old agreements, they were guaranteed free intercourse with Norway, except in time of war. A situation was thus created which gave Duke Skule a welcome opportunity to thwart the king, as he felt justified in disobeying the royal order by granting the Icelanders permission to sail. When the king's command was repeated to the Icelanders as they lay ready to depart from Munkholmen in the harbor of Trondhjem, Snorri's only comment was: "Home I will go." Without delay he sailed for Iceland, but the king soon set forces in motion which accomplished his destruction.

On his return home Snorri again took possession of his estate Reykholt, and he lost no time in bringing to book those who had assisted in attacks upon him. He summoned Sighvat's and Sturla's *thingmenn* to meet him at Dal, where he arrived accompanied by Urökja, Thorleif of Gardar, and other returned exiles. At this conference it was agreed that the punishment to be imposed should be determined by Snorri himself. He demanded restitution in the form of fines to be paid by those who had assisted in robbing his estates and despoiling his friends. No charge of injustice can be brought against him for settling the affair in this way. In the hour of triumph he abstained from bloodshed and other violent measures, demanding only what the law allowed. Had he shown greater leniency, his warlike enemies would, undoubtedly, have interpreted it as weakness and vacillation.

In his plans with regard to Iceland King Haakon found a strong ally in the Roman Church, which also sought to bring this distant and loosely governed island more firmly under its control. At this time the archbishop of Nidaros inaugurated a new policy which greatly aided in linking the colony more closely to the mother country. When the eccentric Bishop Gudmund of Hólar and Bishop Magnus Gizursson of Skálholt died in 1237,[4] their successors had already been chosen in order to avoid any prolonged vacancy in their office. Magnus Gudmundsson was elected to succeed Magnus Gizursson as bishop of Skálholt, and Björn (Kygribjörn) Hjaltason was to become bishop of Hólar.[5] Both priests went to Norway in 1236 to be consecrated by the archbishop of Nidaros, but he would not sanction their election. For this refusal he could find ample pretext, as the method of choosing bishops in Iceland did not conform to established usage. Björn proceeded to Rome, evidently for the purpose of laying the case before the pope himself, but he seems to have failed in his efforts, and he died on the homeward journey. Magnus returned home in 1239, and lost his life by drowning the year after. If it had been the purpose of the archbishop merely to introduce a reform in the method of choosing bishops, he would have created cathedral chapters in the Islandic bishoprics to carry out the election according to the rules of the church. But he made instead the regulation that the bishops of Iceland henceforth should be chosen by the archbishop and the cathedral chapter of Nidaros. This could only mean that Norwegian churchmen who were fully in sympathy with the archbishop's policy and the king's political ambitions would be placed in charge of the Icelandic dioceses. In

[4] Gustav Storm, *Islandske Annaler*, p. 65.
[5] *Ibidem*, p. 130.

1238 two Norwegian ecclesiastics were consecrated bishops
for Iceland; Sigvard Tittmarsson, abbot of Selja, as bishop
of Skálholt, and Botolf, canon of Helgeseter, as bishop of
Hólar.[6] The monk Hildibrand Gunnarson was sent to Iceland with letters from the archbishop, evidently to announce the consecration of the new bishops, and to prepare
for their proper reception. On their arrival they seem
to have taken possession of their diocese without any
opposition.

The ambitious Gizur Thorvaldsson found it advantageous from the outset to support Bishop Sigvard of Skálholt
and the Norwegian dynastic interests in Iceland. In order
to gain full control in the island he planned to overthrow
his erstwhile father-in-law, Snorri,[7] and, if necessary, to
destroy the whole Sturlung family. King Haakon, who
was now able with the aid of the new bishops to keep well
informed regarding affairs in Iceland, made Gizur his representative. He had already been appointed *skutilsveinn* on
a visit to Norway in 1229, and greater honors were in store
for him, if he could carry out the king's plans. Duke Skule
finally rose in rebellion against King Haakon, and was
hailed as king by his own party, but met with defeat and
death after a short struggle. Whatever hope of support in
Norway Snorri might have entertained disappeared, and
the intimate relations which he had maintained with the
rebellious duke so aroused the king's resentment that he dispatched messengers to Iceland with orders to Gizur to
send Snorri to Norway, or else to slay him as a traitor. This
gave Gizur the desired opportunity. For some time he did
not let the king's order become known, as he evidently
planned to capture Snorri by a secret stratagem, which was
attempted at the time of the meeting of the Althing.
Gizur's associate, Kolbein Ungi, arrived at the *thing* with
an army of 600 men, but Snorri and his followers, who
suspected treacherous designs, fled to the church, where
Kolbein did not venture to attack them. Later in the sum-

[6] *Sturlungasaga*, vol. i, ch. vi, p. 541. G. Storm, *Islandske Annaler*, p. 188.
[7] Gizur had married Snorri's daughter Ingibjörg, but they disagreed and
were later divorced. *Sturlungasaga*, vol. i, ch. ii, p. 49; ch. v, p. 426 f.

mer Gizur called his friends to a secret conference, read to
them the king's orders, and laid plans for a sudden attack
on Snorri. With seventy men he secretly proceeded to
Reykholt in the night, and gained entrance to Snorri's
home while the people were sleeping. Snorri, who was
awakened by the noise, attempted to hide in the cellar.
Here he was soon discovered, and could easily have been
made prisoner, but the treacherous and relentless Gizur
sent five men led by his servant Simon Knut to slay the
defenseless old man. At the hands of these assassins
Snorri lost his life at the age of sixty-three, September 22,
1241.

Snorri's nearest male heir at the time of his death was
his illegitimate son Urökja. But Gizur seemed to ignore
him. He paid him no wergeld for his father, but seized
instead the estate Reykholt and gave it to Klæng Bjarnarson, Snorri's stepson. Urökja, who had not forgotten the
personal wrongs which he had suffered at Gizur's hands, was
the more eager to avenge his father. At the head of an
armed force he attacked Reykholt, captured Klæng Bjarnarson and put him to death. After recruiting additional
forces he turned against Gizur himself, who, having been
warned, hastened to Skálholt, where Bishop Sigvard gave
him protection and support. A battle was fought in which
the bishop himself took an active part, but as the combat
was indecisive, peace was concluded, and Urökja retired
to the Borgarfjord district to take possession of his father's
estate of Reykholt.

It was not Gizur's intention, however, to abide by the
agreement thus forced upon him. He was determined to
destroy his dangerous opponent. As soon as he found opportunity to strengthen his forces, he raised a new issue by
claiming that no settlement had been made for the death
of Klæng Bjarnarson, and new negotiations were begun.
In order to dispel all suspicion these should be conducted
by Gizur's ally, Kolbein Ungi, who was Urökja's brother-in-
law. A conference took place at the river Hvitá, where the
two parties stationed themselves at opposite ends of a
bridge leading across the stream. Kolbein arrived with a

large armed force, accompanied by Bishop Sigvard and
Abbot Brand Jonsson, but a little later Gizur and Orm
Bjarnarson, Klæng's brother, also arrived. Urökja did not
trust Gizur, and had refused to negotiate with him, but he
was finally persuaded by Bishop Sigvard and the abbot
to cross the bridge. Immediately Gizur cut off his retreat
and made him prisoner, in spite of the most energetic protest of the bishop and many of his own men. Both Urökja
and Sturla Thordsson the historian were forced to pledge
themselves under oath to leave Iceland. Urökja was sent to
Norway, but Sturla was later released by Kolbein Ungi,
and was allowed to remain at home.

Law and order had gradually disappeared in Iceland.
The Althing was powerless; the local courts were under the
heels of chieftains, who so utterly flouted all authority that
they even refused to abide by their own promises given
under oath. Anarchy could not be more complete. The
settlers, who had hitherto been independent freeholders enjoying their ancient rights under the old laws, were becoming oppressed victims of lawless magnates who seized at
will all the estates of the island, and imposed on the people
their arbitrary demands at the point of the sword. The
need of some form of governing authority was so urgent,
and the hope of salutary reforms in social conditions was so
remote that the people could not much longer hesitate to
accept even foreign overlordship as a welcome deliverance.
Even Urökja and Gizur felt obliged to appeal their case to
King Haakon, an evidence that he was already acknowledged as the highest authority in Icelandic affairs. Gizur
himself was summoned to Norway, where he was retained
for two years, evidently because the king was dissatisfied
with his conduct, and feared that he might establish himself as a despot in Iceland. Urökja was treated with fairness and consideration, but he too had to remain in Norway, where he died in 1245.

With the death of Snorri Sturlason and the banishment
of Urökja the influence of the Sturlung family disappeared
for a time. Gizur Thorvaldsson of the Haukdœlir family,
who traced their lineage from Isleif, the first bishop of

Skálholt, became sole leader in southern Iceland, and Kolbein Ungi held sway in the western and northern districts.
Kolbein seized Sighvat Sturlason's estates and distributed
them among several leading men in order to gain their support. Sighvat's heirs, thus deprived of their inheritance,
were treated in an arbitrary and despotic way. His wife,
Halldora, and her son Tumi were compelled to leave their
estate Grund and move to Thverá in Skagafjord. Sturla
Sighvatsson's wife and children emigrated to Norway.
None of the Sturlungs were any longer able to offer resistance. Thord Kakali, the oldest of Sighvat's two living
sons, was still held in friendly custody by King Haakon.
Thord Sturlason's only legitimate son, Bödvar of Stad,
was married to Kolbein's sister, and was, therefore, inclined
to favor his brother-in-law. Of Thord's illegitimate sons
Sturla Thordsson had played a conspicuous part as chieftain, but both he and his brother Olaf Hvitaskald were
chiefly interested in literary pursuits. Through their own
feuds the Sturlungs had lost their great leaders, and had to
submit to ambitious rivals like Gizur and Kolbein. But
they had been so far chastened by misfortune that old
enmities were forgotten, and they now stood reunited in
sentiment and common interests.

In 1242 Thord Kakali was finally allowed to return to
Iceland after many years' absence, to the great satisfaction
of the Sturlungs, who saw in him a new leader of their
family. When Kolbein heard of his arrival, he sent word
to the leading men of the district that they should seize
him and deliver him up as prisoner. Many people flocked
to Thord's ship to trade, among others also many prominent
men who had been the friends of his father Sighvat. His
mother, Halldora, and other relatives also came to see him.
But the joy of meeting him soon vanished, says the saga,
when people thought of the power of his enemy Kolbein.
None of the leading men, not even Thord's own relatives,
ventured to join him, and people were so afraid that no
one would even talk to him except publicly so that all could
hear it.[8] When Thord saw that he could gain no support,

[8] *Sturlungasaga,* vol. ii, ch. vii, p. 5.

he went to Grund to visit his sister Sigrid and her husband.
But he was soon warned by the abbot of Thverá not to
prolong his visit, as Kolbein might send men to slay him.
Following the advice of his relatives he then went to
southern Iceland to Halfdan Sæmundsson, who was married to his sister Steinvor. With them he discussed his
plan of avenging his father and recovering his inheritance.
Steinvor gave him enthusiastic support. "Hitherto," she
said to her husband, "you have never exhibited any warlike spirit, neither have I encouraged you to take part in
great feuds. But now I declare that there will be little
cordiality between us, if you do not assist my brother
Thord. If you refuse to do so, the strange thing may come
to pass that I may carry arms and gather warriors, and
leave to you the keys for the storehouse and the cellar."
Halfdan remained silent until she had ended her angry
harangue, and then replied: "So far as I can see, it re-
quires more than mere excitement, if Thord's plan is to
succeed. I know myself best, and feel that I am not well
qualified to take part in great feuds, besides I am now somewhat advanced in years. It appears, too, that those who
join Thord will be opposed by nearly all the people of the
land. I would therefore like to see what help he can secure
among friends and relatives in other places before I decide
the matter. If he returns with a respectable force, I shall
not refuse to aid him." [9] It was then agreed that Thord
should try to win support in the western districts, and he
advanced with a force of thirty men, accompanied by his
brother Tumi. Kolbein Ungi dispatched a force to capture
him, but he was able to elude his pursuers, and many of
Urökja's old adherents joined him. Even Sturla Thordsson,
who resided at Stadarhol, promised to support him, but
would not join him outright until he had secured a larger
following. Thord made all possible efforts to persuade the
people to join him. The chieftains of Eyrar, and other
prominent leaders promised hearty cooperation; but so few
actually joined his forces that when he returned to Stadarhol, Sturla shook his head and said that he would do noth-

[9] *Sturlungasaga*, vol. ii, ch. vii, p. 8.

ing against the powerful Kolbein until affairs looked more
promising. A similar answer was given by his brother-in-
law Halfdan Sæmundsson. He would give him no aid,
though his wife Steinvor sought zealously to promote his
cause. Kolbein's assistants now gathered a force of 700
men, and occupied the bishop's seat of Skálholt, where the
bishop gave them all possible assistance and encouragement.
As Thord Kakali had yet only 240 men, his undertaking
seemed doomed to failure. But he had the courage of a
leader, and resolutely marched against Skálholt to try con-
clusions with his opponents even under these discouraging
circumstances. Some of the leaders of the opposing forces
now proposed that peace should be arranged, since all had
to admit that Thord, whose father had been killed, and
who had been deprived of his inheritance, had a just griev-
ance. The bishop and Steinvor were chosen arbitrators.
They granted Thord a large indemnity, with the understanding that peace should be kept till Gizur returned from
Norway. Through this agreement Thord received the
necessary means for supporting his followers, and he also
gained the additional advantage that for a time he would
not need to fear any hostile move in the southern districts.

Thord Kakali now went to the Borgarfjord in western
Iceland, but Kolbein Ungi had gathered a force of 700 men,
and marched across the Tvidoegra Heath in order to be sure
to capture him. It was already the month of November.
On the march across the mountains many men perished
from cold, and many more were overcome by suffering and
exposure. Thord had watched Kolbein's movements, and
knew the condition of his army, but he had so few men that
he did not venture an attack. For him there was no alternative but flight. This was at once undertaken, but Kolbein's men pursued him with such vigor that escape seemed
impossible. The chase lasted several days, and only with
the greatest difficulty was Thord able to evade his pursuers.
Through the winter no further attempt was made to capture Thord, but the following summer Kolbein prevailed on
the Althing to outlaw him. Thord, however, did not leave
Iceland, but fled to some islands, where he gathered a fleet

of thirty ships, a naval force which his adversaries did
not venture to meet. Kolbein harried the southwestern districts where Thord had received some assistance. He even
dispatched a force to Stadarhol to slay Sturla Thordsson.
But he had been warned, and they were only able to plunder
his estates. Such depredations could only serve to arouse
peoples' ill-will, especially since they knew that even the
decree of the Althing had been rendered under pressure
from Kolbein without any real cause. Public sentiment in
the raided districts was turned in favor of Thord. Even
Sturla Thordsson openly espoused his cause. In a short
time he raised an army of 1440 men, and though he could
undertake no active operations of importance that year
because of approaching winter, it was now evident that
he was gaining general support, and was recognized as a
great leader. A minor expedition of his brother Tumi,
resulting in the capture of two of Snorri Sturlason's slayers,
Simon Knut and Thorstein Gudinason, also gave great encouragement to Thord's friends. Simon was executed, and
Thorstein, who admitted that he had inflicted a fatal
wound on the great historian, was sentenced to lose his
right hand. The fact that Thord, according to the decree
of the Althing, was still an outlaw created no anxiety, nor
was any attention paid to it. Court decisions might still
have weight among the common people, but the chieftains
had ceased to yield obedience to the civil authorities.

Even before the winter had passed Thord made preparations for a new attack on Kolbein. That wily chieftain
was now suffering from serious injuries received in an
accident, which confined him to his bed, but he was able to
save himself by a clever stratagem. He sent two messengers
to Thord to offer terms of peace and reconciliation. To
one of these he stated privately that if no other terms would
be accepted, he was willing to grant Thord the whole northern quarter and leave Iceland. Thord was unwilling to
consider any peace offer, but when these generous terms
were proposed, he was prevailed upon by his adherents to
accept them. In the final settlement, however, Kolbein
refused to keep his promise. He boldly declared that he

had given his messenger no authority to offer such terms, and Thord was unable to force the issue, as his army had already been disbanded. No new campaign could be begun that winter, and Kolbein, who was slowly recovering from his injuries, was able to make the needed preparations. As soon as he was well enough, he gathered forces for a new expedition to the western districts. On a sudden foray Tumi Sighvatsson, Thord's brother, was taken prisoner and beheaded, Sturla Thordsson's home was plundered, people were killed and property was destroyed throughout the districts. But although great damage was done, it was a mere raid, and not a victory of any importance. Thord now resolved to gather a fleet for an attack on Kolbein, since a march overland to northern Iceland was very difficult. He was able to secure fifteen small vessels, and sailed with a band of 220 men, leaving the defense of the home districts to Sturla Thordsson. But Kolbein, who was informed of his plans, met him with a larger fleet and superior forces in the bay of Hunafloi, and defeated him after a severe engagement.[10]

At this time Gizur Thorvaldsson, who had spent two years in Norway, returned to Iceland. It is probable that he too came as the king's representative, since Thord Kakali had failed to make any definite progress. Gizur at once sought to effect a reconciliation with Jon, the son of Sturla Sighvatsson. The question of a proper indemnity for the slaying of Sturla after the battle of Örlygsstadir was submitted to King Haakon for arbitration, an indication that Gizur really acknowledged the king as overlord of Iceland. Though Kolbein Ungi had been victorious in the naval battle with Thord Kakali, he was not optimistic as to the final outcome, if the struggle should continue. He was, however, troubled with ill health and was, therefore, willing, even in the hour of victory, to enter into negotiations with his adversary. It was agreed that both should go to Norway, and submit the whole controversy to the king for arbitration.[11] The agreement could not be car-

[10] *Sturlungasaga*, vol. ii, ch. vii, p. 61 ff.
[11] *Ibidem*, p. 83.

ried out, as Kolbein was soon confined to his bed by a fatal illness. He summoned Gizur, and offered to transfer to him and Brand Kolbeinsson all his *goðorðs,* but Gizur said that he was not in a position to accept the offer. Thord Kakali was then called, and a peace agreement was entered into, according to which Thord was reinstated in full possession of his inheritance, which embraced especially the estates in the Eyjafjord district. Brand Kolbeinsson should hold the districts of the Skagafjord, Hunafjord, Midfjord, and Hrutafjord, and he and Gizur agreed to support each other.[12] Kolbein Ungi died July 22, 1245. Thord Kakali was now one of the wealthiest and most popular of the great chieftains of Iceland. But his ambition was not yet satisfied. He aimed to become lord over all northern Iceland, and, if possible, of the whole island. He soon found a pretext to quarrel with Brand Kolbeinsson, and marched into the Skagafjord district with a force of 600 men. At Haugnes Brand had taken a strong position with an army of 720 men, but he was outmaneuvered and defeated after a bloody conflict, April 19, 1246. Brand was captured and put to death, and the victorious Thord seized all the northern districts, as he had planned.[13] Gizur, Brand's friend and ally, was now preparing to take the field against Thord. He arrived at Stad, Brand's home estate, with a force of 480 men, and the inhabitants of the district of Skagafjord, who were opposed to Thord, pledged him their allegiance and joined his forces. Thord was able to gather an army, but his men were so opposed to a renewal of the campaign that he finally consented to negotiate with Gizur. They agreed to submit their quarrel to King Haakon's decision, and both sailed to Norway in the fall of 1246.

Thord Kakali and Gizur met King Haakon in Bergen and accompanied him to Trondhjem, where he was to spend the winter. The king called a special meeting, probably of his *hirð,* to hear their case.

---

[12] Brand Kolbeinsson was the son of Kolbein Kalldaljos, who married Margaret, a daughter of Sæmund Jonsson of Oddi. *Sturlungasaga,* vol. i, ch. ii, p. 49.

[13] *Sturlungasaga,* vol. ii, ch. vii, p. 89. *Hákonarsaga Hákonarsonar,* ch. 248.

"At this meeting," says the saga, "Thord caused a long written exposition to be read of the quarrel between the Haukœdlir and the Sturlungs, and it was shown that many of his friends and relatives had been killed. The king asked Gizur what he had to reply to these charges. He answered that although he did not have any written document to read, he had several things to offer in reply, though he would admit that Thord's exposition was in every way truthful. All said that they had never heard two parties plead their case with greater clearness; nor did one attempt to contradict the other, or to question the truthfulness of his statements." [14]

At first the king seemed inclined to favor Gizur, but he would not decide the case that winter. Both Thord and Gizur remained at court. In the spring they accompanied the king to Bergen, where he was to be crowned by Cardinal William of Sabina. It seems that he wished to use this occasion to establish definitely his overlordship over Iceland, and to have it sanctioned by the pope through his personal representative. The cardinal cordially supported the king's plan, as it harmonized in every way with the views of the Roman Curia regarding the nature of legitimate government. He issued an address to the people of Iceland commanding them to submit to King Haakon, declaring that it was improper for them not to be governed by a king, like all other nations."[15] As successor to Bishop Botolf of Hólar, who died in 1246, Heinrik Kárason, a Norwegian ecclesiastic, was chosen. He was a man of energy and ability, who, undoubtedly, was selected for this position for the purpose of furthering the king's plans. Thord Kakali sought at once to gain the favor of the new bishop, and he in turn supported Thord in his controversy with Gizur, with the result that the cardinal advised Haakon to send Thord to Iceland as governor of the island, while Gizur was to remain in Norway, in order to avoid new conflicts. Thord and Bishop Heinrik were, accordingly, sent to Iceland with a letter from the cardinal to the Icelanders, and with a request from the king that they should submit to his author-

[14] *Sturlungasaga*, vol. ii, ch. vii., p. 100.
[15] *Hákonarsaga Hákonarsonar*, ch. 257.

ity and pay him taxes. Several prominent Icelanders, among others Thorleif of Gardar, were retained by King Haakon as hostages.

Thord Kakali soon gained control over a large part of Iceland. The Sturlungs recognized him as their leader, and in 1248 Hrafn Oddsson and Einar Thorvaldsson came from the Vatsfjord district in northern Iceland to pledge him their allegiance. In the spring of that year he traveled through the northern quarter, and all the people offered their submission. Sæmund Ormsson of Svinafell also sought his protection, and the two became still more closely united through Thord's marriage to Ingun, a daughter of Sæmund's brother Sturla.[16] The southern districts, which still adhered to Gizur, were forced to submit, and had to pay a fine. The king's request, as well as the direct command of the cardinal, undoubtedly exerted a great influence. Since the bishops also supported Thord as the king's representative, the opposition of the people was gradually overcome. Thord Kakali was now in fact lord of all Iceland. As he acted under a royal mandate, King Haakon's overlordship was virtually established, though not yet fully recognized. Reforms in Norwegian and Icelandic jurisprudence at this time also reflect the influence of the cardinal and the council of Bergen. Ordeal was abolished in both countries and with regard to Iceland the regulation was made that anyone who encroached on other peoples' rights or property should be punished by excommunication.

Thord Kakali's ambition soon brought him into conflict with Bishop Heinrik, as it became evident that he was not seeking to further the king's plans, but aimed to establish his own personal authority. In 1249 the bishop returned to Norway, but Thord, who had been summoned by the king, did not accompany him. The following year Thord, who was the king's sworn *hirðmaðr*, finally obeyed the royal summons, and went to Norway accompanied by Bishop Sigvard of Skálholt. Neither he nor the bishop was allowed to return. King Haakon sent instead Gizur Thorvaldsson, who during his stay in Norway had made a pilgrimage to

[16] *Sturlungasaga*, vol. ii, ch. vii, p. 100.

Rome, where he had received absolution for his sins. Accompanied by Bishop Heinrik he now returned to Iceland to continue the work of bringing all parts of the island under the king's rule. A number of prominent Icelanders were still kept in Norway by King Haakon, probably in order to weaken their influence at home, and to attach them more closely to the crown, as a distinct policy was inaugurated to create in Iceland a party of king's friends, who might give the royal cause their energetic support. Those who showed a distinct inclination to promote the interests of the crown, like Gizur Thorvaldsson, Thorgils Skardi, Finnbjörn Helgason and other royal favorites, were allowed to return home, and were given charge of large districts which they were to hold as royal grants.[17] Others, who still showed a spirit of opposition, were retained at court. They were often made to feel the royal displeasure, like Harald Sæmundsson and his brother Philip of the Oddaverjar family, who had to surrender their *goðorðs* to the king. By seeking to become heir to Snorri Sturlason's extensive possessions King Haakon also attempted to establish in Iceland a private royal domain, which according to the views of the times was an essential attribute to royal power. If this could be accomplished, it would increase his influence and bring his rule into closer conformity with monarchic principles.

The task of establishing a fully recognized royal overlordship in Iceland was not an easy one. Thord Kakali, who had sought to strengthen his own power rather than that of the king, had left his own adherents in charge of various districts, and was still able to encourage them to resistance against Gizur, the king's new representative. The people would not consent to the distribution of districts among royal favorites, neither would they sanction the king's claim to the possessions of Snorri Sturlason. Thorgils Skardi had received the whole of the Borgarfjord district, and immediately upon his arrival he summoned the chieftains to a conference at the home of Olaf Hvitaskald. But when he attempted to read to them the royal letters patent, energetic

[17] *Hákonarsaga Hákonarsonar,* ch. 272 ff. *Sturlungasaga,* ch. vii, p. 132 ff.

protest was made. Thorleif of Gardar said that he did not doubt that King Haakon had granted Thorgils the district, but he doubted very much that he had any right whatever to do so. The other chieftains were of the same opinion. Only when Thorgils threatened them was he allowed to read the royal letters, and the chieftains finally yielded a reluctant submission. How little real authority he was able to exercise within the domain granted him soon became apparent. The general ill-will, undoubtedly caused in part by his own arrogant conduct, developed into so hostile an opposition that the chieftains under the leadership of Sturla Thordsson and Hrafn Oddsson gathered an armed force and took him prisoner at Stafaholt, where he was visiting Olaf Hvitaskald. He saved his life only by taking an oath that he would join his captors in an attack on Gizur Thorvaldsson. This undertaking was immediately set on foot, but Thorgils, who wished to remain faithful to the king's cause, broke his oath, and escaped to his friend, Bishop Heinrik of Hólar. On learning of his defection the Borgarfjord chieftains abandoned their expedition. But Hrafn Oddsson assumed control of affairs in their district, and kept an armed force to guard against surprise. Bishop Heinrik undertook to negotiate a settlement between Thorgils and his opponents, but no agreement could be reached, as Thorgils demanded possession of the district which the king had granted him, while the chieftains refused to recognize any right on the part of the king to exercise dominion over Icelandic territory. Thorgils moved to his father's estate Stad, and since Gizur gave him no support, he was unable to maintain his claim to the district of the Borgarfjord.

Thorgils and Bishop Heinrik were earnest in their support of the king's cause, but Gizur's aim now as before was self-aggrandizement. This soon became so evident that a feeling of enmity and distrust separated the leaders of the king's party. Gizur took active steps to form an alliance with Thorgils' opponents. In the summer of 1253, after the meeting of the Althing, he met Hrafn Oddsson and Sturla Thordsson at Breidabolstad in the district of the Hrútafjord, where an alliance was entered into. In order to cement their friendship still more firmly Sturla's daughter Ingibjörg was promised in marriage to Gizur's son Hall. A regrouping of forces had thus been accomplished. Gizur had given up his allegiance to King Haakon, and Hrafn and Sturla had abandoned Thord Kakali, in order to form what might seem to be a strong anti-royal confederacy. The only real supporters of the king's cause were now Thorgils Skardi, Bishop Heinrik of Hólar and Abbot Brand Jonsson, who was acting as vicar for Bishop Sigvard of Skálholt. But Thorgils found it difficult to support his followers at Stad, and as his friends urged that he should seek a reconciliation with Hrafn Oddsson and his uncle Sturla Thordsson, he found it expedient to follow their advice.[18] He met Sturla on an island in the Faxafjord. The two entered into a secret agreement, promising each other friendship and support. But it was to be considered only as a family compact. Thorgils did not renounce his allegiance to the king, nor did Sturla sever his relations with Hrafn and Gizur. If a united patriotic sentiment had existed, a union like the one formed between Hrafn, Gizur, Sturla and Thorgils would have rendered Iceland secure against foreign dominion. But with the exception of agreements like that between Sturla and Thorgils based on family feeling, the confederacies formed rested on no foundation but mutual fear and personal ambition. Even the most solemn covenants were easily broken. No one could be trusted to remain faithful to an ally any longer than he found it to his own personal advantage. Confederacies would melt away like castles in the air with every regrouping of the changing factors of self-interest. To what degree the chieftains now could stoop to the most unashamed perfidy is seen in the attack on Gizur's home at Flugumyr shortly after his agreement with his former opponents.

Eyjolf Thorsteinsson, who had been driven from the Skagafjord district by Gizur, was his sworn enemy, and plotted revenge. He gained the support of Bishop Heinrik of Hólar, Kolbein Grön, Ari Ingimundsson, Hrani Kodransson and other leaders in the district, and a conspiracy was formed to

---

[18] Thorgils was the son of Bödvar of Stad, son of Thord Sturlason, and brother of Sturla Thordsson.

attack Gizur at the time when the wedding of his son Hall to Sturla's daughter Ingibjörg was to be celebrated. Among the guests invited to this festival at Flugumyr was also Hrafn Oddsson, Gizur's confederate. On his journey to the wedding Hrafn stopped at Vidimyr, where Eyjolf's brother Asgrim revealed to him the plot against Gizur, stating that it was the plan of the conspirators to burn Gizur's home, if they could not capture him in any other way. He also invited Hrafn, Gizur's guest and ally, to join in the attack, evidently because he knew him to be more ambitious than upright. Hrafn, it is said, did not favor this wicked plan, and as Gizur's guest he could not take part in it, but he promised not to reveal it. Saturday evening the guests to the number of 120 began to arrive at Flugumyr, and were cordially received by Gizur. When all had been seated, he arose to bid them welcome, and expressed his joy that so many prominent men were now assembled under his roof in peace and good understanding after the serious controversies which had hitherto separated them. It was his hope, he said, that their agreement would be faithfully kept, but for safety's sake he would nevertheless establish peace for the occasion by solemnly reading the peace formula. The following day Hrafn and Gizur's son Isleif sat side by side, kissed each other as friends, and drank from the same silver goblet. All this Hrafn could do, though he knew that at that very moment Gizur's enemies were hiding in the neighborhood, that at any time the house with all its occupants might be attacked and destroyed. Even Sturla Thordsson, the bride's father and Hrafn's closest ally, knew nothing of the perfidious plot. The festival continued also Monday, when Ari Ingimundsson came and revealed to Hrafn the conspirators' whole plan. But not even now did he warn Gizur. When he left the wedding, Gizur gave him two fine horses. In order to ease his conscience he now told Gizur to be careful, but to the question if he knew of any particular danger, he returned only an evasive answer. On Tuesday most of the guests departed, among others also Sturla Thordsson. In the night Eyjolf and his associates with a band of fifty-two armed men made their well planned

attack. They were unable to enter the house, as the doors
were barred and the entrances guarded. Finding that their
plan of surprise had failed, they set fire to the building,
which was soon wrapped in flames. Gizur stood surrounded
by his guests and his family, among whom were his wife,
Groa, and the beautiful bride, Ingibjörg, who had run from
her room attired only in her night robes. The assailants
offered Ingibjörg free exit, but she preferred to share the
fate of the rest. Kolbein Grön then leaped forward, seized
her in his arms and carried her to the church. Groa perished in the house, likewise Gizur's two sons Isleif and
Ketilbjörn. Hall, the bridegroom, made an effort to escape,
but was mortally wounded, and was brought to the church,
where he soon expired. Twenty-five persons found their
death in the burning building, but Gizur managed to save
himself in a most remarkable way. When all hope was
passed, he bade his wife an affectionate farewell, and made
his way into the provision house, which was not yet on
fire. Here he plunged into a large vat of whey, and remained there in such perfect hiding that his enemies failed
to discover him. All felt certain that he, like the rest, had
perished in the fire, but when the assailants departed, he
was able to make his way to the church, though he was so
exhausted from suffering and exposure that his life was
saved with great difficulty. When he was able to examine
the ruins of his home, where he found the charred remains
of his wife, sons and relatives, he was so overcome with
grief that tears rolled down his cheeks. Eyjolf Thorsteinsson
and his associates hastened from the scene of their vile deed
to Hólar, where Bishop Heinrik received them with open
arms, and immediately absolved them. Here they also met
Hrafn Oddsson, who now openly joined them and became
their leader.[19]

As soon as the incendiaries learned that Gizur was still
alive, they took steps to protect themselves, but he pursued them relentlessly. Many were captured and put to
death. Before a year had passed twelve had been slain,
among others two of their principal leaders, Kolbein Grön

[19] *Sturlungasaga*, vol. ii, p. 192.

and Hrani Kodransson. Eyjolf himself and fifteen of his associates were outlawed by the Althing. Bishop Heinrik sought to shield the incendiaries by placing Gizur under the ban of the church, which made it necessary for him to move to southern Iceland. When the rumors of these happenings reached Norway, Bishop Sigvard, accompanied by Sigurd Silkiauga, the king's personal representative, was dispatched to Iceland.[20] Gizur was summoned to Norway by King Haakon. He sailed from Eyrar in August, 1254, after placing Odd Thorarinsson over the Skagafjord district, and committing to him his case against the incendiaries. Gizur was well received by the king, but had to remain in Norway, like his rival, Thord Kakali. The king sent instead his treasurer, Ivar Englason, to promote his interests in Iceland.

Odd Thorarinsson, Gizur's friend, was welcomed by the people of Skagafjord, and he undertook at once to execute the decree of the Althing against the outlawed incendiaries. He seized the cattle of Thorstein Jonsson of Hvamm in Vatsdal, but since he did not observe the legal formality of *feránsdómr*, the act had to such an extent the character of robbery, that Bishop Heinrik, who was still shielding his outlawed friends, excommunicated him. In revenge for this act Odd arrested the bishop, and incarcerated him in a stronghold which had been erected by Kolbein Ungi. But the prelate was soon liberated, as it was evident that he could not long be kept a prisoner. Word had already been sent to Hrafn Oddsson and Eyjolf Thorsteinsson, the bishop's chief supporters, who, with the aid of Sturla Thordsson and Thorgils Skardi, raised an army of 1000 men and invaded the Skagafjord district, only to find that Bishop Heinrik had already been set at liberty. That this expedition did not express any unity of sentiment among the chieftains who took part in it was quite evident. Eyjolf and Hrafn, the leaders of the incendiaries, could hope for no real friendship from Sturla Thordsson, whose son-in-law had been slain at Flugumyr. Thorgils Skardi so hated Hrafn, that even before the expedition ended they engaged in a bitter

[20] *Hákonarsaga, Hákonarsonar*, ch. 283.

quarrel, in which Thorgils was supported by Sturla, to whom he was bound by secret agreement.

Shortly after this expedition Odd Thorarinsson renewed his attack on the incendiaries, but he was captured by Eyjolf and Hrafn and put to death. His brother Thorvard Thorarinsson appealed to Thorgils Skardi to aid him in avenging his brother's death. To this he agreed on the condition that the district of the Skagafjord should be ceded to him. Sturla Thordsson was also persuaded to join them, and Abbot Brand Jonsson expressed his cordial sympathy with the undertaking. The three chieftains gathered an army and marched into the Skagafjord district, where they met Hrafn and Eyjolf and defeated them at Thverá in Litla after a sharp engagement. Hrafn fled, and Eyjolf fell with many of his men. At first Bishop Heinrik showed his sympathy with the defeated leaders of the incendiaries by excommunicating Thorvard and Thorgils, but he finally granted them absolution, becoming very friendly with Thorgils, who earnestly championed the king's cause, and now held undisputed sway in the whole district of the Skagafjord.

During these events Bishop Sigvard and the king's representative, Ivar Englason, remained at Skálholt without taking any part in political affairs. In the spring of 1256 Ivar went to the Skagafjord district, where the people were assembled in a general *thing*. Both Bishop Heinrik and Thorgils gave him hearty support when he presented the king's request for the payment of taxes to the crown. The people of the whole northern quarter were persuaded to grant the request, and to pledge the king their submission. The success thus achieved in the negotiations was chiefly due to the influence of Bishop Heinrik, who had always been a faithful supporter of the royal cause. This prelate had shown himself intensely partisan and unscrupulous as to the means used for reaching desired ends; but he was a tower of strength, and aimed steadily at achieving definite results in the strife and turmoil of Icelandic political life. Now that the people of his diocese had finally acknowledged the king's supremacy, he must have regarded his real mis-

sion in Iceland as ended. In the summer he returned to
Norway. The king treated him as a special friend by retaining him at court as a royal councilor on Icelandic affairs.
Immediately upon the return of Ivar Englason and Bishop
Heinrik, King Haakon dispatched Ivar Arnljotsson to Iceland with a message to Thorgils Skardi, whom he appointed
governor of the northern quarter. Thorgils treated the people very generously, and soon won their loyal attachment.

Thord Kakali and Gizur Thorvaldsson remained in Norway, where they were created royal *syslumenn*, or governors
of administrative districts. Thord, who was placed over the
Skiens *sysla* in southern Norway, distinguished himself also
on a military expedition to Halland in southern Sweden.
One evening in the fall, while seated at a banquet with his
men, word was brought him that the king would now permit
him to return to Iceland, that he would be made the foremost man, probably royal governor of the whole island.
This message caused great rejoicing, and Thord was much
elated. But even before the banquet was over he was seized
with a fatal illness from which he died, October 11, 1256. [21]

In Iceland Thorgils Skardi's influence continued to grow.
Thorleif of Gardar had become his friend, and when Thord
Kakali died, no one seemed to have a better claim to the
highest position of trust in the island than Thorgils, who
was at this time thirty-two years of age, and experienced
in everything pertaining to leadership. None of the great
chieftains had been so faithfully devoted to the king's cause,
or had sought more earnestly to promote it. If matters had
not taken an unforeseen turn, he might have been made the
chief royal representative in Iceland. But the jealous and
plotting Thorvard Thorarinsson, whom he had aided and
befriended, attacked and slew him, January 22, 1258.

[21] *Sturlungasaga*, vol. ii, ch. ix, p. 300 f. Jacobus Langebek, *Scriptores
Rerum Danicarum*, vol. ii, p. 516.

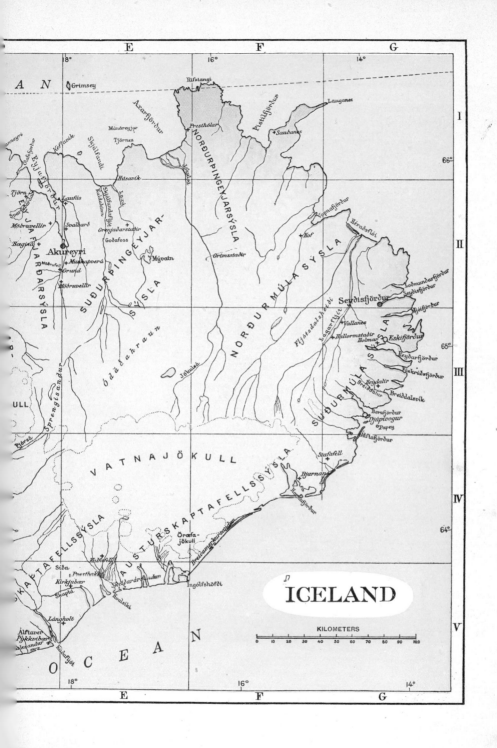

ICELAND

KILOMETERS

0 10 20 30 40 50 60 70 80 90 100

10. Union of Norway and Iceland. Growing Ascendency of the Clergy

THE opposition to the king's designs in Iceland was gradually weakened by influences which created a new public opinion. According to medieval thought royal rule was a divine institution to which all Christians owed submission. The Icelandic state system, which stood as a relic of a pagan past, could find no support in the prevailing ideas of the times. In literature and art the glorification of royalty was making its advent. In Norway the St. Olaf cultus had given kingship a special consecration. Hundreds of pilgrims flocked yearly to Nidaros, and the legends about the miracles wrought at the shrine of the sainted king became favorite popular reading even among the Icelanders. It is noteworthy also that the "King's Mirror," an eloquent panegyric on royalty, written in Norway in the reign of King Haakon Haakonsson, was nowhere read with greater interest than in Iceland. The Norwegian kings, who had been the champions of Christianity and the unity of the realm, had become national heroes and the leaders of the people, not least in the opinions of the Icelanders, who glorified their achievements in great historical works. Royal rule could no longer be viewed even by the chieftains as an illegitimate encroachment on ancient liberties. To the common people, who had lost their freedom, and were subject to the arbitrary will of the great lords, it could only bring new hope of peace and improved social conditions. The resistance to the growing influence of the king did not at this time spring from patriotic sentiment or conscious national aspirations on the part of the people, but was wholly due to the intense individualism and love of power of the chieftains. But even they had maintained the closest relations with the king. They had never hesitated to bind themselves to him in personal service under oath as *hirðmenn, skutilsveinar, lendrmenn* and other officials under the crown. Whenever they found it to their own personal advantage, they were ready to barter away their country's independence, and assume duties as the king's representatives; and this they could do without incurring any reproach from their fellow countrymen for treasonable acts.

After the death of Thord Kakali and Thorgils Skardi the king again appointed Gizur Thorvaldsson his chief representative in Iceland. He created him jarl,[1] and placed him over the southern and northern quarters together with the Borgarfjord district, undoubtedly with the understanding that he was to act as royal governor of the whole island as soon as the people could be prevailed upon to swear allegiance to the king. Since experience had shown great fickleness on the part of the Icelandic chieftains in their adherence to the royal cause, Thorvald Hviti was appointed special commissioner to accompany him to Iceland, probably for the purpose of observing his conduct.[2] On his arrival Gizur chose thirty *hirðmenn,* and established himself with all the dignity of a jarl, but the people were slow in submitting to his authority. He won the friendship of Sturla Thordsson and Sighvat Bödvarson, a brother of Thorgils Skardi, by promising them aid against Thorgil's slayer, Thorvard Thorarinsson. This promise was not fulfilled, but he made Sturla his *lendrmaðr;* and Ingibjörg, Sturla's daughter, whose husband had lost his life in the bloody wedding at Flugumyr, was given in marriage to a prominent young chieftain, Thord Thorvardsson of Saurbær. The wedding was celebrated at Gizur's home, as he still regarded her as his daughter-in-law. It seems, however, that even at this time he was more concerned about his own private affairs than in promoting the king's cause. As reports were received in Norway that he treated the royal interests with indifference and only sought to further his own aims, the king sent Ivar Arnljotsson and Paul Liinseyma to Iceland with letters under royal seal requesting the people to submit to the king and pay him taxes. These letters were read at the Althing. Gizur supported the request, at least in a formal way, but it was rejected, and the royal representatives had to return to Norway with nothing accomplished. Under

[1] G. Storm, *Islandske Annaler,* p. 257.
[2] *Hákonarsaga Hákonarsonar,* ch. 297 ff.

these circumstances Gizur sought to soften the king's growing displeasure by exhibiting greater zeal for the royal cause.
Immediately after the close of the Althing he assembled a
meeting at Thingskálar, in Rangárvellir, in the southern
quarter, where the poeple of that district seem to have
pledged their allegiance to the crown. But the king remained so distrustful that upon the return of his commissioners he dispatched Hallvard Gullsko to Iceland to remind
the jarl of his duties. He remained in Iceland over winter,
and succeeded in bringing about a reconciliation between
Thorvard Thorarinsson and his opponents. Hrafn Oddsson
was placed in charge of the Borgarfjord district, to the great
dissatisfaction of Sturla Thordsson, who had attached himself to Gizur in the hope that he could retain control of this
district, where he owned a number of estates. It became
more and more evident that the jarl was only seeking his
own advantage by secretly trying to harm the king's cause.
He assembled the people of the northern districts and told
them that the king demanded an enormous indemnity because they had not already submitted to him, and had paid
him no taxes. He seems even to have hinted that an armed
expedition might be sent to Iceland. Many became so
alarmed that they offered to pay large sums to avert the
threatened danger. When Hallvard Gullsko heard of these
things, he hastened to assure the people that the king did
not intend to oppress them, that he only requested them to
pledge him allegiance and to grant him such taxes as they
might be able to pay without feeling it as a burden. In
return he would improve their laws and grant them other
privileges. From this time forth Hallvard abandoned all
hope of cooperation with Gizur, and began active negotiations with his opponents to secure their support at the
Althing.

The drift of events had placed Sturla Thordsson in a
rather embarrassing position. Gizur Thorvaldsson was unpopular, as his new title of jarl had given general offense.
Now that the chieftains understood that the independence
of their country was destroyed, they would rather own allegiance to the king than serve Gizur, who had been their own

equal. Sturla also felt constrained to support the royal cause, but because of his relations with Gizur he was pushed aside by the king's representative. It was now felt that the fate of Iceland would be decided at the next Althing, and Gizur sought by secret intrigue and diligent propaganda to gather support against Hallvard Gullsko and the leaders of the king's party. His final appeal to the people's love of independence was so successful that he appeared at the Althing with an army of 1440 men, while his opponents had only half that number. But armed conflict does not seem to have been his plan. He undoubtedly felt restrained by the situation of the country and the attitude of the chieftains. With the advice of his adherents he himself took the initiative, and submitted the king's request to the Althing. He spoke earnestly in support of it, declaring that a refusal to accept it would be equivalent to his death warrant. To this appeal the people finally yielded. The *lögrétta* of the Althing, on behalf of the people, took the oath of allegiance and entered into the following agreement with King Haakon, known as the "Gamli sáttmáli, 1262:

"This is the agreement of the people of northern and southern Iceland, that we grant King Haakon and Magnus under oath land, thanes, and eternal taxes, twenty *alnar* [3] for every man

[3] In early ages cattle and various natural products were used as money; in Norway especially *vaðmál* or woolen cloth. The unit of value was the cow, or *kúgildi*. Later the *öln vaðmál*, or for larger sums *hundrað alnar* (120 ells) became the unit, the *hundrað alnar vaðmál* being equal to a *kúgildi*, or the value of a cow. 1 *hundrað* = 120 *alnar* = 1 *cow* = 6 *sheep* = 240 fish = 5 rigsdaler specie. Twenty *alnar vaðmál*, the tax to be paid the king by every farmer whose duty it was to attend the Althing, would, therefore, be equivalent to the value of a sheep. Precious metals were also used as money, the weight unit being the *mörk*, equivalent to 215.8 grams.
8 *eyrir* (plu. *aurar*) = 1 *mörk*.
1 *eyrir* = 3 *örtogar* or 10 *þveiti*.
120 *eyrir* = 1 *hundrað* (120).
In the twelfth and thirteenth centuries the rates of silver to *vaðmál* was about 7.5 to 1; hence the value of the royal tax in silver would be 2⅔ *aurar*. See Hermann Paul, *Grundriss der germanischen Philologie*, vol. iii, p. 473 ff. A. Taranger, *Udsigt over den norske Retshistorie*, p. 127 ff. Seebohm, *Tribal Customs in Anglo-Saxon Law*, p. 233. Marius Hægstad og Alf Thorp, *Gamalnorsk Ordbok*, mörk. *Dansk historisk Tidsskrift*, 6te række, vol. iv, p. 569.

who pays the tax of *thingfararkaup*.[4] These taxes are to be collected by the *heppstjórar*, brought to the ship, and delivered to the royal officials, after which there is to be no further responsibility for them. In consideration hereof the king is to let us enjoy peace and the Icelandic laws. Six ships are to sail from Norway to Iceland every summer during the next two years. From that time forth this matter shall be arranged in such a way as the king and our best men shall deem most serviceable for the country. Any inheritance which falls to Icelanders in Norway is to be given them, however long it may remain due. so soon as the rightful heirs, or their legal representatives, appear to claim it. The *landaurar* tax is to be abolished. Icelanders are to have in Norway the most extensive rights which they have ever enjoyed there, and which have been promised them in your letters. You (King Haakon) are also to maintain peace for us, as God may give you strength to do so. The jarl's authority we will acknowledge so long as he keeps faith with you and peace with us. This agreement we and our descendants will keep in good faith so long as you also faithfully keep it, but we consider ourselves released from all obligations, if, in the opinion of the best men, it shall be broken. To this end I place my hand on the Holy Bible, and call God to witness that I grant King Haakon and Magnus under oath land, thanes and eternal taxes according to the conditions here named, and as the written agreement bears testimony. May God so be merciful to me as I keep this oath, unmerciful if I do not."[5]

Only the *thingmenn* of southern and northern Iceland were present at the Althing in 1262 when the oath was taken. The people of the Borgarfjord district took the same pledge at the Thingnesthing, but when Hallvard Gullsko, shortly after the adjournment of the Althing, left for Norway, the chieftains of the eastern districts had not been heard from. They yielded, however, to the persuasion of their friends, especially to the advice of the popular Abbot Brand Jonsson, who now became bishop of Hólar. At the

---

[4] *Thigfararkaup*, the expenses of the *thingmenn* incurred in attending the Althing. These expenses had to be defrayed by the people who remained at home. In time it developed into a definite tax, and as it was collected by the *goðar*, or chieftains, themselves, it was often very extortionate.

[5] Jon Thorkelsson og Einar Arnorsson, *Ríkisréttindi Íslands*, p. 1 f. *Diplomatarium Islandicum*, vol. ii, p. 602 ff.

Althing in 1263 the southern districts east of the Thjorsa
pledged their allegiance, and in 1264 the remaining eastern
districts yielded their submission to the king.[6]

The agreement by which Iceland was formally brought
under Norwegian rule created only a confederate union, and
did not materially change the status of the Icelandic chieftains. They were now to hold their rights from the king,
and were forbidden to wage war on each other; but since
the Icelandic laws were still in force, the union agreement
really involved only an acknowledgment of the king's sovereignty, and the payment of a small tribute to the crown.
It appears from the Icelandic code, the "Jónsbók," adopted
in 1280, that the taxes to be paid were very moderate, as
the twenty *alnar vaðmál* payable by each freeholder for himself and his household, and by unmarried persons who owned
property to the value of ten hundred unincumbered by
debts, included also the old tax of *thingfararkaup*. Only one-
half of the whole sum was to be paid to the king. The other
half was to be kept in Iceland for the payment of the usual
taxes.[7] To the common people the union with Norway
brought the distinct advantage of the termination of the
bloody conflicts in which they had been forced to take part.
Peace was established, and the conviction that henceforth
the government would safeguard life and property must have
created a new sense of security and well-being. Freedom
from lawless terror, established by the altered relation to the
mother country, must have been welcomed by the people in
general as a new freedom rather than as foreign oppression.

But whatever advantages the union with Norway might
bring, it produced no new era of development. Intellectual
life continued to flourish, and numerous literary works were
written, but a distinct decline in the quality of literary production becomes noticeable, especially towards the close of
the thirteenth century. The old vigor and originality was
dwindling, as the growing Christian medieval time-spirit,

[6] G. Storm, *Islandske Annaler* (Annales Regii, year 1263-1264). Arngrim
Jonsson, *Crymogea*, p. 199 ff.

[7] *Den islandske Lov Jonsbogen*, Copenhagen, 1763, part ii, ch. i. *Norges
gamle Love*, vol. 1, p. 460 f.

which was only strengthened through a closer relation with Norway, was fostering a love for legends and chivalric romances which encouraged copying and translation rather than creative production and original scholarship. Trade and economic conditions continued as before without any distinct manifestation either of progress or decline. The destructive civil wars of the Sturlung period had undoubtedly done much to weaken the people's strength, and had hampered somewhat their intercourse with foreign lands, but the more peaceful era inaugurated by the union with Norway brought no perceptible change in prevailing conditions. Some scholars have considered the provision in the union agreement that six ships should be sent to Iceland every year as evidence that the commerce with Iceland at this time was declining, but K. Maurer has shown that this conclusion is erroneous.[8] For various reasons few ships would arrive in Iceland during some years, but the same happened also during the most vigorous period of Icelandic national life, as in 1187 and 1219, when the Icelandic annals record that no ships arrived in Iceland. Various national disasters also occurred at this time. In 1258 a contagious disease in the district of Midfjord carried away 400 people. In 1233 and again in 1261 great ice-floes beleaguered all the coasts of the island so densely that they did not disappear during the whole summer, and it is quite certain that now, as on later occasions, this severity of climate must have caused famine and extreme suffering. But the same had happened at intervals during all previous Icelandic history There is no evidence at this time of any distinct depression in the public spirit, but the general decadence which fell upon the whole North during the later Middle Ages was, nevertheless, approaching also in Iceland. The old spirit of maritime enterprise was dying out among the Icelanders, as among all the Scandinavian peoples. No progress was made in trade or ship-building, and the Hanseatic merchants had already made their appearance as competitors for the control of Scandinavian commerce. The only event which

[8] K. Maurer, *Kaflar úr verslunarsögu Íslands* (Ny félagsrit, xxii, p. 100 ff). Thorvald Thoroddsen, *Landfrœdissaga Íslands*, vol. i, p. 101 ff.

still reflects some of the old spirit of daring and enterprise
at sea was the finding of a new land west of Iceland in 1285
by the priests Aðalbrand Helgason and his brother Thorvald. The new land was called "Nýland" (Terra Nova),
sometimes also "Duneyjar," but its location is not given.
The discovery must have attracted considerable attention
since it is recorded in the Icelandic annals. In 1289 King
Eirik Magnusson sent a navigator, Hrolf, or Landa-Hrolf, to
seek the new land, which may have been Newfoundland or
the coast of North America. He went to Iceland and sought
to persuade sailors to join his expedition, but with what
success is not recorded. The only thing known about his
later career is that he died in 1295.[9]

The leading writer in Iceland at this time was Sturla
Thordsson, second only to Snorri himself as historian.
Hrafn Oddsson's appointment as governor of the Borgarfjord district had made him so dissatisfied that against his
better judgment he was persuaded by his son Snorri, a violent youth, to join him in an expedition against Hrafn. This
proved a failure, as he had predicted. Snorri was captured,
and Sturla himself was forced to leave Iceland, 1263.[10] He
went to Norway with some misgiving, fearing that he might
be made to feel the king's severest displeasure, since he had
always been a strong supporter of Icelandic independence.
But he was somewhat cheered up by the news that at this
time King Haakon was absent on an expedition to Scotland,
and that his son Magnus was ruling as viceroy, assisted by
Gaut of Meli, who had always been a friend of the Sturlungs.
When he arrived in Bergen, Gaut invited him to be his
guest. He was told that his enemies had slandered him, but
Gaut promised to do what he could to have him received at
court. As soon as he found an opportunity, he presented
Sturla to King Magnus as a noted Icelandic scald, but the
king would not receive him. Gaut renewed the attempt the
following day, and finally persuaded the king to accept him
as a member of the crew of a ship which was to carry the
king and queen southward along the coast. On the voyage

[9] G. Storm, *Islandske Annaler* (Skálholt Annaler, year 1265).
[10] *Ibidem* (Gottskalks Annaler, year 1263).

he soon won favor among the sailors by his skill in story-telling. The queen's attention was attracted to him, and whenever they lay at anchor during periods of calm weather, he was invited to entertain the royal pair with his stories. The queen was especially well pleased. Even the king's ill-will disappeared after Sturla had been permitted to recite a song which he had composed in his honor. One evening the king called him, filled a goblet of wine, brought it to his lips and gave it to Sturla saying: "Wine one shall drink to a friend." "God be praised that it is so," said Sturla. "So it shall be," said the king, "and now you may recite also the song which you have made about my father." Sturla did so, and when he closed, it was praised by all, especially by the queen. "I believe you can sing better than the pope," said the king. He now entered into conversation with Sturla, asked him the reason for his coming to Norway, and was told of his conflict with Hrafn Oddsson in Iceland. "I have now heard your songs," said the king, "and know that you are a great scald. This I will now reward by asking you to remain with me in peace and friendship. When my father returns, you will have to settle your affairs with him, but I shall use my influence in your behalf." [11] The king became very attached to Sturla, and often sought his advice, especially in Icelandic affairs. Not only was he made *hirð-maðr* and *skutilsveinn*, and employed as royal historiographer to write the history of King Haakon Haakonsson as well as of King Magnus' own reign, but he also aided the king in preparing a new code of laws for Iceland. On his return home he was appointed to the important office of lawman.

During the first years following the establishment of the union conditions in Iceland remained quite unchanged. The *goðorðs* were still in the hands of the leading chieftains. Gizur, who was to exercise the highest authority as jarl, was unpopular, and his power was very limited. Royal commissioners were sent to Iceland to exercise control with or without his consent, and he had to share his nominal authority with the powerful Oddaverjar chieftains of southern

[11] *Sturlungasaga,* vol. ii, ch. x, p. 323 ff.

Iceland, Hrafn Oddsson of the Borgarfjord district, and Orm Ormsson of eastern Iceland. The king regarded him with suspicion; the chieftains hated him because of his rank and title; opposition and difficulties confronted him everywhere. Even his own character and previous record rendered him unfit to maintain peace and order, which was his principal official duty. He was unable to see the need of any change in the general régime, and the last chapter of his stormy life formed a fitting close to the drama of bloody feuds in which he had played so conspicuous a part. Shortly after the meeting of the Althing in 1264, while visiting in southern Iceland, he was suddenly attacked by Thord Andrisson, the head of the Oddaverjar family. With great difficulty he escaped from his assailants, and after gathering an army of 750 men he cruelly ravaged the Rangarvalla district, where the Oddaverjar chieftains were dwelling. This summary vengeance seemed to make him feel that the score was quit. He invited Thord and his brothers to a peace conference, but when they came, he pursued his usual tactics and made them prisoners. They were disarmed and condemned to death, but the pleadings of his own men finally moved him to spare the lives of all except Thord, who was executed. Such treachery and violence could only make him still more unpopular. At last the people's hatred and opposition grew so intense that he resolved to retire and enter a monastery. He had already made an agreement with Bishop Jörund of Hólar to take the monastic vow of the Order of St. Augustine, but he died January 12, 1268, before the final arrangements could be consummated. His estate Stad, at Reynines, he gave to the church with the understanding that a monastery should be erected there. This condition was finally fulfilled in 1296, when the cloister for nuns at Reynines and the monastery at Mödruvellir were founded by Bishop Jörund of Hólar.[12] After Gizur's death no new jarl was appointed, and for a time there was no real head of Icelandic affairs. In 1267 Orm Ormsson and Thorvard Thorarinsson went to Norway, Hrafn Oddsson following in 1268. Both Hrafn and Orm seem to have aspired to succeed Gizur, but

[12] G. Storm, *Islandske Annaler* (Annales Regii, year 1296).

the king found it advisable not to elevate another chieftain
to the rank of jarl, as the title had been very unpopular.
After some delay, and probably with the advice of Sturla
Thordsson, he gave both rank as *hirðmenn* and placed them
in charge of Icelandic affairs with no other title than that of
valdsmaðr, or royal magistrate. Hrafn was to govern the
western and Orm the eastern districts.[13] Hrafn assumed the
duties of his office, but Orm was drowned shortly after his
appointment, probably on the homeward voyage.

It was quite evident that peaceful conditions could not be
maintained in Iceland without important changes in the
framework of government and a careful revision of the antiquated system of jurisprudence. King Magnus Lagabøter,
who was devoting special attention to the framing of a new
code of laws for his kingdom, considered it necessary to bring
the Icelandic administration into closer harmony with that
of Norway. The stipulation in the "Gamli sáttmáli," or
act of union, that the Icelanders should keep their own laws
was wholly ignored, and Magnus undertook to frame a new
code of laws for Iceland based on those of Norway,[14] a work
in which he was assisted by Sturla Thordsson. The new
code, the "Jarnsíða," erroneously called "Hákonarbók," was
brought to Iceland in 1271 by Sturla, accompanied by the
king's *hirdmaðr* Eindride Böngull.[15] The code was a hasty

[13] In the margin of the Oddaverjar annals is written: "Giordi Magnus
Kongur Rafn Oddason Orm Ormsson son Orms Svinafellings handgeignu
menn syna og skipadi þeim allt Island."

[14] The *Guðmundar Biskupssaga,* ch. 76, says: "In the evening Thord
Sturlason seated himself on a bench and called his son Sturla, who was
later knight at the court of King Magnus Haakonsson, lawman, and with
the king's assistance and advice wrote the first code of laws for Iceland,
after the country came under Norwegian rule. This book was brought to
Iceland by Thorvard Thorarinsson of the Eastfjords, and remained for
fifteen years, until aforesaid King Magnus wrote-another code with the
advice of Jon Einarsson." The last mentioned work was the "Jónsbók,"
brought to Iceland in 1280. The one brought by Thorvard Thorarinsson
fifteen years before must, then, have been the first version of the
"Jarnsíða." The Icelandic annals state that Thorvard came to Iceland that
year, and the "Sturlungasaga," vol. ii, ch. x, p. 327, says that the king gave
Sturla Thordsson permission to return to Iceland. So little is known about
events in Iceland during the years 1265-1271 that the uncertainty obscuring
these matters can not be removed.

[15] G. Storm, *Islandske Annaler* (Annales Regii, year 1271).

compilation of Norwegian laws, containing many provisions wholly unsuited to conditions in Iceland, while important chapters of the Icelandic code seem to have been overlooked. Because of these defects and the great changes in the system of government which it would entail, the people strenuously resisted its adoption. Some of the most important parts of the code were, nevertheless, sanctioned already in 1271, as the *thingfararbölkr,* or constitution of the *thing,* the *thegngildi,* or laws governing the payment of fines to the king in cases of murder of freemen, and a part of the *arfabölkr,* or laws about inheritance.[16] The remaining portions of the code received sanction in 1272 and 1273. The introduction of this code wrought a fundamental change in the Icelandic constitution and jurisprudence. Norwegian law had been substituted for the old Icelandic code, the "Grágás"; the *goðorðs* were abolished, so also the characteristic features of the Althing: the *fjorðungsdómar,* the *fimtardómr,* and the office of *lögsögumaðr.* The *thing* system was reorganized according to Norwegian pattern. The *valdsmaðr* should choose a certain number of men from each *thing* district, 140 in all, to constitute the *thing,* and from these the lawman should select three from each *thing* district, in all thirty-six, to sit in the *lögrétta.* Instead of the *lögsögumaðr* there should be a lawman, after 1277 two lawmen, as in Norway. Royal officials and representatives of the crown should preside over the Althing and take part in its decisions. The judicial powers were lodged in the *lögrétta;* the legislative functions should be exercized by the Althing and the king conjointly. Both the *thing* and the crown might take the initiative in legislation. As the king now acted as lawgiver, the legislative functions of the *thing* were greatly reduced, and it became principally a judicial tribunal like the Norwegian lagthings. The laws were no longer recited from the Mount of Laws, and as the Althing now consisted of chosen representatives, who were soon further reduced in number, it lost its popular character. As the general public ceased to attend

[16] G. Storm, *Islandske Annaler* (Annales Regii, 1271).

its sessions, its significance as a center of national and social life disappeared.

It may have been the many faults of the "Jarnsíða" which led King Magnus Lagabøter to prepare a new code for Iceland, the "Jónsbók," which was brought to Iceland in 1280 by the lawman Jon Einarsson and the royal commissioner Lodin Lepp. It is possible that Jon Einarsson, and possibly also Hrafn Oddsson and Thorvard Thorarinsson assisted the king in preparing this code, as they were in Norway in the year 1278-1279. Hrafn Oddsson, who received the title of royal *merkismaðr* (standardbearer), was now to exercise authority over all Iceland. Some of the provisions in the new code met with opposition, but after much discussion it was adopted in 1281, the revision of the objectionable articles being left to the king's own good will. The new law reduced the number of members of the Althing to eighty-four, and established the title of *sýslumaðr* for the royal district magistrates in Iceland. It adhered as closely as possible to the new Norwegian laws, the "Code of Magnus Lagabøter," prepared a few years previous. The work was greatly superior to the "Jarnsíða." It proved to be very satisfactory, and remained in force till in the nineteenth century.[17]

These new codes wrought a fundamental change in the conception of positive law as well as in legal practice in Iceland. The old court procedure with its intricacies and formalities was replaced by the simpler Norwegian system. The king as ruler and lawgiver was regarded as the source of justice, and behind the laws now stood the royal authority, ready to execute the decrees of the courts even against the most powerful offenders. Violation of the law was no longer viewed as a private affair to be settled by the offender and the party injured, but as a crime for which the wrong-doer had to answer to the government. The fines to be paid and other punishments to be inflicted were still to be determined by twelve men according to ancient usage. The old punishment of banishment for serious offenses was retained, but

[17] *Hin forna lögbók Íslendinga sem nefnit Jarnsíða aðr Hákonarbók*, edited by Th. Sveinbjörnsson, Copenhagen, ch. ii ff. The *Jarnsíða* is also found in *Norges gamle Love*, vol. i.

fines payable to the king were instituted in numerous cases, and capital punishment was to be inflicted for grave crimes, like murder, robbery, rape, counterfeiting, forgery, and seduction. Other severe punishments were also established.

"If one wounds another with a dagger," says the code, "the plaintiff shall bring the offender before the *thing*, and there the royal magistrate shall take the knife which he used and run it through his hand. Thus shall he purchase the king's peace, if he lives. But he himself shall be responsible for the wound, however it may go. But if he who was injured dies from his wound, then his assailant shall be put to death." [18] "Anyone who slays another, or wounds him, or commits other acts for which he is liable to lost life or limb, shall be seized and bound and brought before the *syslumaðr* by those who are nearest to the scene of the crime and have the first opportunity to do so. . . . The *syslumaðr* shall bring him before the *thing*, but the *bœndur* (freeholders) shall sentence him according to law, after which the *syslumaðr* shall cause him to be punished according to the sentence imposed." [19]

There breathes through the "Jónsbók" a stern spirit of legal justice well suited to inspire a wholesome respect for law and government. But care had been taken by the lawgiver to guard against hasty action and undue harshness in the treatment of wrong-doers. In a chapter about legal decisions he advises the judges to consider carefully truth, justice, patience and mercy, in order that their decisions may not bear the marks of cruelty and hatred. "For we are to hate evil deeds," he concludes, "but love men by natural instinct as our fellow Christians, but most of all their souls." The first lawmen appointed under the new laws were Sturla Thordsson and Jon Einarsson. The first royal magistrates who received the title of *syslumaðr* were Hrafn Oddsson in western Iceland, Thorvard Thorarinsson for the southern and eastern districts, and Asgrim Thorsteinsson in the southwestern districts. Others may have been appointed, but their names are not known. In 1279 Hrafn Oddsson became

[18] *Jónsbók* (Mannhelgi-bölkur, ch. xiv).
[19] *Ibidem* (Mannhelgi-bölkur, ch. xvi).

royal *merkismaðr* with authority over all Iceland, as already noted.

At this time important changes also took place in the Icelandic church. For some time the bishops in Iceland had been Norwegian ecclesiastics, but in the latter part of Haakon Magnusson's reign the Icelander Brand Jonsson became bishop of Hólar, and when he died a year later, his countryman Jörund Thorsteinsson succeeded him in 1267, after a long vacancy in the office. As the Norwegian born Bishop Sigurd of Skálholt was now so old and feeble that he could no longer perform his official duties, Bishop Jörund assumed supervision also over the Skálholt diocese by placing the popular priest Arni Thorlaksson in charge of it. Arni, who was a relative of Gizur Thorvaldsson of the powerful Haukdœlir family, had early distinguished himself by studious habits and brilliant intellectual gifts. In 1262 he had accompanied Brand Jonsson to Norway, where he became acquainted with King Haakon Haakonsson, as well as with his son Magnus, with whom he formed an intimate and lasting friendship. When Bishop Sigurd died in 1268, the diocese petitioned Archbishop Jon of Nidaros to appoint Arni as his successor, but the archbishop ignored the request and chose instead a Norwegian priest, Thorleif, evidently because he wished to continue the practice of placing Norwegian ecclesiastics over the Icelandic dioceses. As Thorleif died shortly after his election, the archbishop was prevailed upon, probably by King Magnus himself, to elect Arni, who was consecrated bishop June 21, 1269. Upon his return to Iceland Bishop Arni, assisted by Bishop Jörund of Hólar, summoned the people of his diocese to a general council at Skálholt, where he proposed several measures of reform, among others that the churches should be made ecclesiastical property under the control of the bishops. As nearly all churches in Iceland were privately owned, this would involve a change in property rights to which the people would not readily consent. The able and popular Bishop Thorlak Thorhallsson had failed in a like attempt. But circumstances were now more favorable, since the king's assistance could be invoked. Arni pursued his course with great energy. With threats of ban and excommunication he so intimidated the lesser landowners that they suffered the smaller churches to pass under ecclesiastical control. But the chieftains who owned the larger churches resolutely resisted. This was especially the case with the churches of Oddi and Hitardal, two of the largest in Iceland. Their owners refused to surrender them; but the bishop caused a decree of transfer to be promulgated at the Althing, threatening the owners with the ban if they resisted. Led by Hrafn Oddsson the chieftains appealed to the king, claiming that he would not sanction such arbitrary confiscation of property and the use of the ban. Arni wrote both to the archbishop and the king, described his difficult position and pleaded for aid. The archbishop encouraged him to persevere in his efforts until the desired reforms could be carried through. The king also promised him protection if he would work for the adoption of the new code, the "Jarn-síða," which had just been brought to Iceland. Arni earnestly supported the king in all matters which did not infringe on the authority of the church, and the adoption of the new code was largely due to his efforts. In 1273 King Magnus summoned a council to meet in Bergen to consider a new code of church laws proposed by Archbishop Jon of Nidaros, and to deal with other questions touching the relation between church and state. At this council Bishop Arni, Hrafn Oddsson and the Icelandic chieftains also appeared. In the trial of their case the king was inclined to favor the chieftains, but the archbishop rendered a decision in Arni's favor. His victory was so complete that upon his return home he began to prepare a new code of church laws for Iceland, based on principles suggested to him by Archbishop Jon. The code was adopted at the Althing in 1275 with the understanding that it was later to be ratified by the king and the archbishop.[20]

Bishop Arni's popularity and his successful management of church affairs soon made him so influential that he was able to exercise the authority of the church with the greatest vigor. The rule respecting celibacy of the clergy was so

Arni Biskupssaga, ch. 5.

rigorously enforced that even subdeacons who had been married for many years and had several children were compelled to separate from their wives. With like energy he preached the crusade to the Holy Land which had been urged at the Council of Bergen. People were prevailed upon to pay an extra tax of one *öln vaðmál* a year for the period of six years to defray the expenses of the undertaking. Bishop Jörund of Hólar was also encouraged by Arni's example to collect all sorts of dues for the church, and to enforce the provisions of the church laws. Bishop Arni gradually assumed the rôle of ruler in Iceland. In many cases he even opposed the *sýslumaðr* Thorvard Thorarinsson, so that the people at the Althing appealed to the decision of the bishop in purely secular matters, contrary to all law. Of these things complaints were made to the king. "His power is now so great that your officials can scarcely show the resistance which one should think they would have the courage and heart to do," wrote Thorvard Thorarinsson. "At the *thing* this summer Hrafn and the bishop were the leaders, but they were only in moderately good accord. The *lögsögumaðr* (should have been lawman) (Sturla) was confused, and referred most cases to the decision of the bishop or other men, as it might be convenient, and the *lögrétta* rendered us little service." [21] The people were still unfamiliar with the new laws and court procedure, Sturla was getting old, and the aggressive conduct of Bishop Arni helped to make the *thing* a scene of incompetence and confusion.[22] In 1277 the king sent Eindride Böngull a second time to Iceland as his commissioner, accompanied by the Icelander Nicolas Oddsson. They brought letters addressed both to the *sýslumaðr* and the bishop forbidding any appeal to the bishop in cases brought before the Althing. The king had already written to the people warning them not to accept any law before he and the archbishop had considered the measure, as the right to alter the laws of the church or any other statute belonged to them alone. The church code given by Bishop Arni was

[21] *Arni Biskupssaga,* ch. 14.
[22] *Ibidem,* ch. 19.

accordingly rejected, and although the king continued to address the bishop in the kindliest terms, the people felt that the royal government was henceforth the supreme authority in the land. This was made especially manifest by the new procedure introduced at this time of summoning people to Norway for trial. The first instance of this odious and oppressive practice grew out of a quarrel between the *sýslumaðr* Asgrim Thorsteinsson and a man by the name of Björn, reported to the royal commissioner by Bishop Arni. Both were summoned to Norway to plead their case, but when it became evident that the two men had committed no serious wrong, the summons was revoked, and they were allowed to remain at home, after renewing their oath of allegiance to the king. The king's officers also traveled about collecting the royal revenues with greater severity than had hitherto been customary. They reproved the people for appealing to the bishop, and in some cases forbade them to pay as large church dues as the bishop had demanded. But since no attempt was made to interfere seriously in affairs properly belonging under the jurisdiction of the church, Bishop Arni continued to be the king's friend and supporter. In 1277, when Eindride Böngull left Iceland, the *sýslumenn* Hrafn Oddsson and Thorvard Thorarinsson, as well as the lawman Sturla Thordsson, had sailed for Norway, probably at the request of the king. They were shipwrecked and had to spend the winter in the Faroe Islands, but the following spring they reached their destination. Sturla had to answer to various complaints with regard to his services as lawman. It appeared that in his old age he was too weak and timid to perform properly the duties of his office. On his return to Iceland he gradually withdrew from political conflicts. In 1283 he resigned his office and retired to the island of Fagrey in the Borgarfjord, where he died July 30, 1284, at the age of seventy years.

The Council of Bergen, which placed the churches of Iceland under ecclesiastic control, proved to be only another abortive attempt to settle the difficult question of the relation between church and state. In Norway a new controversy arose between the nobility and the clergy upon the death of King Magnus Lagabøter in 1280. The arrogant Archbishop Jon of Nidaros sought to make the church wholly independent of the state. He even attempted to dictate the coronation oath to be taken by King Magnus' successor, but the nobles acting as a council of regency during the minority of the crown prince, Eirik Magnusson, drove the archbishop and two of his leading supporters from the realm. These events could not fail to encourage the Icelandic chieftains in their opposition to the aggressive policy of Bishop Arni. When the question of accepting the new code, the "Jónsbók," was brought before the Althing, Arni, supported by a strong party led by his nephew Lopt Helgason, objected to various provisions in it, and refused to accept it until these should be revised. As this well organized opposition was strong enough to block the measure, the royal commissioner, Lodin Lepp, sought to win the people's support by picturing the excessive burdens of the tithes which the Icelanders had to pay to the church. The stratagem succeeded. The opposition was broken up, and the code was ratified by the Althing against nine dissenting votes. Lopt and the others who had opposed the ratification were treated as traitors, and had to go to Norway to submit their case to the king. This was a severe defeat for Bishop Arni, as the chieftains saw that in Iceland as in Norway they could defeat the church party by co-operation and energetic action. Now that they felt sure of support from King Eirik and the Council of Regency, they were no longer afraid to join issue with the bishops regarding the question of ownership of churches and church property. The *sýslumaðr* Asgrim Thorsteinsson led the new opposition against the church authorities. He collected the tax of *thingfararkaup* from the members of the bishop's own household at Skálholt in spite of energetic protest. Lopt was compelled to go to Norway for trial, and the *sýslumaðr* sought to prejudice the king against him. Increased impetus was given the new movement when Hrafn Oddsson in 1283 returned from Norway, where he had supported the Council of Regency in its quarrel with

Archbishop Jon. With him came also Erlend Olafsson, who
had been appointed lawman. They brought royal letters
addressed to the people of Iceland encouraging them to
resist the bishops. All church property which had been
unjustly seized was to be returned to the laity,[23] and the
church laws as they had been in King Haakon Haakonsson's time were to be in force. Bishop Jörund of Hólar
immediately yielded to these demands, but Bishop Arni
resolved to resist to the utmost. He yielded on many minor
points, but he would not surrender the principle of freedom
from taxation for the clergy, and full control of ecclesiastical
property by the church. In 1285-1286 the quarrel grew
so intense that the chieftains threatened Arni with the
same fate which had befallen Archbishop Jon in Norway.
They would place the property of the bishop's seat under
the supervision of laymen, forbid him to make tours of
inspection, and outlaw those whom he might make managers of church estates contrary to instructions contained
in the royal letters. These extreme measures were averted
only through the hesitation of Hrafn Oddsson, and the
declaration of Arni that he would await the decision of the
king and the archbishop. A change in the attitude of the
Norwegian government now gave the bishop some hope of
ultimate success. Both the king and the Council were
anxious to secure a new archbishop after Jon's death in
exile in 1282. Strained relations with Denmark and the
Hanseatic cities also gave cause for uneasiness and inclined
them to favor an adjustment of domestic difficulties. Jarl
Alf Erlingsson of Thornberg, who was now the most influential member of the Council, even turned to Iceland to
secure military aid for the realm. It was decided that for
the defense of the kingdom 240 men should be sent from
Iceland, together with those who were otherwise bound to
the king's service.[24] It was a small assistance, scarcely of
more than nominal value, but the Icelanders regarded it as
a new burden to be imposed upon them, contrary to the

[23] *Diplomatarium Islandicum*, vol. ii, p. 240 ff.
[24] *Arni Biskupssaga*, ch. 57. G. Storm, *Islandske Annaler* (Annales Regii,
year 1286).

union agreement, and Hrafn Oddsson vigorously opposed
the measure. Bishop Arni supported it, undoubtedly for
the purpose of winning the favor of the government. The
plan was soon abandoned by the Council, but Arni had
earned the king's good-will by his loyal attitude. Lopt
Helgason, his nephew, who had now remained in Norway for
some time, had also won the king's favor. He had become
royal *hirdmaðr,* and was able to exert great influence in
Arni's behalf. When a new archbishop, Eindride, was
finally chosen at Nidaros, Bishop Arni took new courage.
He revived his claim to all churches and church property,
and excommunicated those who, since the beginning of the
controversy, had taken possession of any part of it. The
people, led by Hrafn Oddsson and the lawman Erlend
Olafsson, offered determined resistance. The men whom
the bishop placed in charge of the church estates were outlawed by the Althing, and Hrafn Oddsson declared those
innocent who had been placed under the ban of the church.
The bishop retaliated with further excommunications, declaring that both Hrafn and Erlend had fallen under the
ban, though he would not excommunicate them.

In 1288 two royal commissioners, the king's *stallari* Olaf
Ragneidsson and the Icelander Sighvat Halfdansson, arrived in Iceland. At the Althing Hrafn expected that they
would give him their unqualified support in his controversy
with Bishop Arni, but they had been sent to arbitrate the
difficulty, and were anxious to bring about a compromise.
The *stallari* gave the bishop a very friendly letter from the
king. When the question about the church property was
brought up, he persuaded both parties to submit the controversy to the decision of the king and the archbishop.
The men in charge of the estates should remain until the
matter had been decided, while those who had been excommunicated should be freed from the ban. In accordance
with the request of the king's commissioners both Hrafn
and the bishop agreed to go to Norway in the fall. Before
leaving Iceland Arni received letters from Archbishop
Jörund, Eindride's successor, confirming Archbishop Jon's
decision of 1273 regarding church property, and asserting

that Bishop Arni's code of church laws should remain in
force in Iceland. Many of the bishop's friends now urged
him to remain in Iceland, but he and Hrafn Oddsson sailed
to Norway in the fall, as they had agreed. Hrafn sought
the king in Bergen, and Arni remained in Nidaros during
the winter as the guest of Archbishop Jörund.

The first task to which Jörund devoted his attention after
receiving the pallium was the punishment of the nobles who
had driven his predecessor from his archdiocese. Since
Hrafn Oddsson had assisted the Council in its attacks on
Archbishop Jon, the two prelates soon agreed on joint
action against him. Jörund cited him to trial for wrongs
committed against the archbishop, and Arni summoned him
to answer for his activities against the church and clergy
in Iceland. They called upon Bishop Narfi of Bergen to
excommunicate him, a demand which was granted without
any protest from the king. Bishop Jörund of Hólar was
encouraged to travel about in the Skálholt diocese, and
force the people under threats and intimidations to surrender the church estates, as if the case had already been
decided. But the Norwegian nobles, who still directed the
policy of the young and weak King Eirik Magnusson, persuaded him to retain Bishop Arni in Norway until the case
could be finally settled. In the summer of 1289 both he
and Hrafn Oddsson had to accompany the king on a military expedition to Denmark. On their return they were
summoned to Nidaros for a final hearing of their case.
Hrafn was unable to appear, as he was suffering from a
wound received in the campaign, from which he died
November 22 of the same year. In his absence the lawman
Erlend Olafsson represented the laity in the trial, but
Bishop Arni conducted his case so well that the judges were
inclined to accept his view. Erlend was obliged to ask for a
continuance of the case to avoid an adverse decision. The
case was postponed till the following year, when Erland
promised to appear again before the tribunal of the archbishop at Nidaros. This he later refused to do because
Bishop Jörund of Hólar had been instructed by the archbishop to seize the church property in the Skálholt diocese

prior to the decision of the court. Bishop Arni remained in Norway till 1291, when he had to return to his diocese without a final decision in the case about the status of church property in Iceland.

The church estates which still remained in the hands of the laity were surrendered to the bishops shortly after Arni's return to Iceland. But this attempt to forestall a final settlement proved to be of little value. In 1292 royal commissioners were sent to Iceland with instructions from the king stating that with regard to churches and church property the conditions existing prior to the union should be restored, that church estates should be returned to their lay owners. Both bishops resented the royal orders, but the people, led by Thorvard Thorarinsson, seized many estates, and the controversy was renewed. In 1295 Thorvard went to Norway to plead the cause of the people. In his absence Bishop Arni forced twelve men to surrender in behalf of the people all the churches of the diocese. Thorvard died in Norway, but Gudmund Skaldstekil, who succeeded him as *sýslumaðr*, came to Iceland with orders from the king summoning the twelve men to Norway to be tried for disobeying royal orders. Bishop Arni accompanied them abroad, and the case was finally settled by a compromise embodied in a royal document of September 13, 1297. It was agreed that all the churches in which the lay people owned a share amounting to at least one-half should belong to them without any curtailment of property rights. All other churches should be surrendered to the bishops.[25] Bishop Arni did not return to Iceland. He remained in Norway over winter, and died in Bergen in 1298 at the age of sixty-two. The Skálholt diocese remained without bishop till 1304, when his nephew, Arni Helgason, was finally chosen as his successor.

In the bishopric of Hólar the struggle between church and laity was less intense but of a similar character. Bishop Jörund died in 1313, and was succeeded by Audun Raudi,

---

[25] *Arni Biskupssaga*, ch. 79. The Icelanders called the case *staðarmál*, the word *staðr* meaning church with parsonage, monastery, bishop's residence, etc.

a member of the cathedral chapter at Nidaros. Audun, who was a friend of the king, had served as his *féhirðir*, or treasurer, and had been very active in the defense of the city of Nidaros in the wars of 1309. It is stated that he had a daughter, but whether he had been married or lived in concubinage is not known. He was consecrated bishop November 25, 1313, but did not arrive in Iceland till 1315. He was already advanced in years, but he ruled his diocese with great energy and authority, maintained a fine household and practised the greatest hospitality. The cathedral church was improved, new buildings were erected at the bishop's seat, and the cathedral school was kept in a high state of efficiency, as he took pains to secure able teachers. But the expenses incurred exceeded the income of the diocese, and he was forced to increase his revenues by augmenting the public burdens. He began to carry through the same system in his diocese which Bishop Arni had sought to introduce in southern Iceland. This created such an ill-will that the people addressed a letter of complaint to the king, stating that "foreign bishops had been forced upon the country contrary to ancient usage." [26] The king returned a very kindly answer, saying: "We will in no wise tolerate that such wrong and injustice be done. Therefore we forbid the bishops and learned men to oppress our thanes, contrary to the laws and old usage." [27] But little real benefit came from these fair words, as no steps were taken to curb the power and arbitrary conduct of the bishops. The clergy had established an ascendency which no existing authority in Iceland could successfully control. Gradually the people sank helplessly under the sway of foreign-born bishops, who in their efforts to extend their power and increase their revenues destroyed the people's freedom, exhausted their limited resources, and hastened Iceland's national downfall.

[26] *Diplomatarium Islandicum*, vol. ii, p. 491.
[27] *Ibidem*, vol. ii, p. 495 ff.

11. GROWING INFLUENCE OF THE NORWEGIAN GOVERNMENT. GREAT CALAMITIES RESULTING IN GENERAL DISTRESS. DECLINE OF INTELLECTUAL LIFE AND LITERARY ART

THE royal executive authority and the new efficiency of the courts of law created through the union with Norway terminated the bloody feuds which had hitherto raged between the Icelandic chieftains. An uneventful era of peace followed the turmoil of the Sturlung period. Even the struggle between church and state was now adjusted so that economic life and the pursuits of peace could receive the undivided attention of the people. But the few sources which deal with political conditions in Ice and during the years following the death of Bishop Arni show that conditions created by the union were causing dissatisfaction and unrest. The chief cause of public discontent was the unsatisfactory arrangement with regard to commerce, the insufficient Norwegian exports to Iceland, together with the policy pursued by the Norwegian government of bringing Icelanders to Norway for trial, and of appointing Norwegians as *syslumenn* and lawmen, contrary to the spirit of the union agreement. The chieftains undoubtedly had thought that their political and social organization would be left undisturbed under the union; that they would only be required to pledge their allegiance to the king, pay him taxes, and receive a jarl as his personal representative, as the union agreement expressly stated. But the most far-reaching changes had been wrought. The *goðorðs* had been abolished, the Althing had been reorganized, Norwegian jurisprudence had been introduced, Norwegians had been appointed to the leading public offices, and Icelanders had been summoned abroad for trial. The Norwegian government had shown an unmistakable disposition to treat Iceland as a dependency. Even the economic advantages which were expected had not been obtained. In 1281 the question of accepting the "Jónsbók" as the new code for Iceland precipitated an animated debate in the Althing.

It appears that the chieftains at that time made a specific demand that only Icelanders should be appointed to the higher offices, a condition which seems to have been granted by the Council of Regency in King Eirik Magnusson's reign, though no specific provision to that effect was incorporated in the Icelandic laws. The *sýslumenn* appointed by King Eirik were Icelanders, but the lawman Erlend Olafsson was Icelander only on the mother's side. The same was the case also with Hauk Erlendsson, who served as lawman in 1295 and again in 1304 and 1306.[1] The provision that six ships should be dispatched to Iceland every summer for two years had also been changed so that six ships should continue to sail yearly. This provision does not seem to have established any specific obligation on the part of the Norwegian government to send so many ships to Iceland every year, but was probably inserted here as in the original act of union only to prevent the king from laying an embargo on Icelandic trade or on articles especially needed by the Icelanders.[2] Norwegian commerce was still flourishing. Traffic was maintained with Flanders, northern Germany, southern Sweden, the island of Gothland and other places, but especially with England, where Lynn was a Norwegian trade center.[3] Though few ships might at times arrive in Icelandic harbors, many Norwegian merchantmen usually visited Iceland every year. The Icelandic annals state that in 1340 eleven ships came to Iceland, in 1345 twelve ships, in 1357 eighteen ships besides two which foundered on the voyage. Seagoing vessels were also built in Iceland.[4] Many Icelanders owned ships with which they undoubtedly carried on trade, as had always been their custom, though most of the commerce was now in the hands of Norwegian merchants.[5] But the

[1] Finnur Jónsson, *Historia Ecclesiastica Islendiæ*, vol. i, p. 401.
[2] K. Maurer, *Kraflar ur verslunarsögu Íslands* (Ný félagsrit, vol. xxii). Jon Thorkelsson og Einar Arnorsson, *Ríkisréttindi Íslands*, p. 30.
[3] A. Bugge, *Studier over de norske Byers Selvstyre og Handel før Hanseaternes Tid.*
[4] Th. Thoroddsen, *Landfrædissaga Íslands*, vol. i, p. 101 ff.
[5] B. Th. Melsted, *Hverjir raku verzlun milli Íslands og annara landa á dögum hins íslenska þjóðveldis* (Búnadarrit, vol. ix, p. 52 ff.).

import trade, which had always been small, could not supply the growing needs of the people. The Icelandic annals show that at times there must have been great need of imports, since it even happened that the mass could not be celebrated for want of wine. During years when no ships came to Iceland, or when only one or two arrived each year, the need of articles for which people were wholly dependent on imports must have been very great. Still more deplorable was the inadequacy of imports during periods of famine and other great calamities, when little aid could be given the stricken population. Under ordinary circumstances commerce was probably sufficient to supply the people with the necessary articles, but the meaning of the provision regarding commerce inserted in the "Gamli sáttmáli," and constantly repeated in the union agreement, seems to have been that the Norwegian government should not suffer commerce at any time to fall below the specified minimum amount.

King Eirik Magnusson died in 1299, and was succeeded by his brother Haakon Magnusson. Before taking the oath of allegiance to the new sovereign the Icelanders demanded redress of grievances, especially with regard to commerce, the appointment of Norwegians to higher offices, and the removal of Icelanders to Norway for trial. The king would not accede to these conditions, but demanded that they should take the oath of allegiance unconditionally. What grievances they might have could be considered at some later date. He sent Alf of Krok with royal letters to Iceland requesting the people to take the oath of allegiance, without taking any steps to redress the wrongs of which they complained. The two lawmen were replaced by two Norwegians, Lodin Bakki and Bard Högnason, who should have separate jurisdiction, each over one-half of the island, and two new *sýslumenn* were also appointed. At a council assembled in Bergen in 1302 he made the regulation with regard to commerce that only Norwegian merchants could trade with Iceland.[6] This step was probably necessitated

⁶ *Diplomatarium Islandicum,* vol. ii, p. 332.

by the encroachments of the Hanseatic merchants on Norwegian trade, but the provision would undoubtedly tend to decrease the intercourse with Iceland. This arbitrary procedure could not fail to arouse bitter feelings among the already discontented Icelanders. In 1303 the people assembled at the Althing and pledged their allegiance to the king, but only on condition of redress of grievances enumerated in a written remonstrance to which the oath was attached.

The document says:

"This was accepted and agreed to by the people at the Althing, and by all men in the king's service with unanimous consent, that with perfect good-will we offer our services to our worthy lord, King Haakon, crowned King of Norway, and promise to have and keep the code of laws which the blessed King Magnus sent us. We will keep also our oath to the kingdom on the conditions agreed to by the king and the thanes who inhabit our land. In the first place we will pay taxes and *thingfararkaup*, twenty *alnar*, as the laws specify, and we will do our full duty as citizens within the limits prescribed by the code. In return we ask that, because of the poverty of the country and the need of the people, the promises given us by the king be fulfilled; for it seems clear to us that our country can not long exist on account of poverty, if much goods are exported, and little or nothing is received in return. But the promises were that the *sýslumenn* and lawmen in our country should be Icelanders, and that, unless lawfully hindered, six ships should sail from Norway to Iceland every year, laden with such goods as would be of benefit to our country and to us. Summons abroad for trial we will not answer in excess of the limits prescribed by the code, for this has wrought us such grievous harm as we do not feel able to bear. As for the announcements which would place on us more grants and burdens than hitherto, we find ourselves in no wise able to bear the same because of the poverty of our country. Still less do we dare for the sake of our Lord Jesus Christ to decrease those sacred gifts which hitherto, with the blessing of God, we have given for the salvation of our souls. We further ask earnestly our worthy Lord, the crowned King Haakon, and all other good men not to burden us with heavier taxes than the law allows. The Lord Jesus Christ grant that this our counsel may be to the glory of God, the praise and honor of the saints, the benefit of the king and his true councilors, and to our peace and salvation, amen."[7]

This remonstrance was attached to the union covenant of 1262, the two documents constituting the act of union in the form to which the Icelanders had now pledged themselves under oath. It was brought to King Haakon Magnusson probably by Alf of Krok, who now left for Norway accompanied by other royal officials of Norwegian birth, pursuant to the provision that only native-born citizens should hold office in Iceland. But the king resented this manifestation of a spirit of independence on the part of the Icelanders, and paid little attention to the remonstrance. Three Icelandic lawmen were, indeed, appointed: Thorlak Narfason for the northern districts, and Gudmund Sigurdsson and Snorri Markusson for southern Iceland. But the following year the Norwegian Bárd Högnason again became lawman, and Erlend Olafsson and other prominent royal officials returned to Iceland. In 1303 many prominent Icelanders were summoned to Norway, among others Bishop Jörund of Hólar, and Abbot Runolf, who had served as vicar in the diocese of Skálholt after the death of Bishop Arni. The king's purpose seems to have been to obtain their advice regarding changes in the Icelandic code of laws which had been demanded, possibly also to secure their consent to new taxes to be levied in Iceland. The Icelandic annals for the year 1304 state that in that year the king collected Peter's pence (*Roma skattr*) in Iceland.[8] The supplement to the code resulting from this conference is dated June 23, 1305.[9] It contains provisions dealing with Iceland, but it does not touch the issues bearing on the relations between the two countries. These issues do not even seem to have been considered, but the Icelandic leaders probably consented to the levying of new taxes.

The attitude of the Norwegian government, and the

[7] *Diplomatarium Islandicum*, vol. ii, p. 333 ff. *Norges gamle Love*, vol. i. Jon Thorkelsson og Einar Arnorsson, *Ríkisréttindi Íslands*, p. 12.

[8] G. Storm, *Islandske Annaler* (Annales Regii, year 1304).

[9] *Lovsamling for Island*, vol. i, p. 17. The provisions of King Haakon's supplementary laws are also found in various chapters of the *Jónsbók*.

determination of the king to treat their country as a dependency, so increased the dissatisfaction of the Icelanders that in 1304 the people of the western and northern districts even refused to attend the Althing. They created two *heraðsthings* in each quarter, where they settled their own affairs.[10] Only representatives from the southern and eastern districts attended the Althing, where great excitement prevailed. The Icelandic annals state that the three lawmen, Gudmund Sigurdsson, Snorri Markusson and Hauk Erlendsson, each set forth a different law regarding taxation.[11] The king must have been well aware of the growing discontent; but instead of righting the wrongs complained of he imposed new burdens on the people, and turned a deaf ear to their remonstrances. Alf of Krok was again sent to Iceland with royal letters revoking all privileges granted the Icelanders by the royal council since the death of King Magnus Lagabøter. The king also made the regulation that all persons owning property to the value of five hundred or more should pay to the king a tax of one *öln vaðmál* for each hundred.[12] This arbitrary increase of public burdens, and the arrogant conduct of the king's representative, Alf of Krok, who was placed over the eastern and northern districts contrary to the remonstrance of 1303, roused a storm of resentment. Alf traveled about in the districts to publish the king's orders, and declared many to be outlawed because they had refused to attend the Althing. Both at the Oddeyrarthing and at the Hegranesthing he was attacked by the populace. At the latter *thing* his life was saved only through the efforts of Thord of Mödruvellir and other chieftains. Under Thord's protection he left the *thing* and retired to Dynhagi in Hörgárdal, where he died the following winter.[13] The Althing decided that the people should resist the king's unjust demands.[14] Shortly after the close of the *thing* a document was drawn up at Skálholt entitled, "A Covenant between the Best Men and

[10] G. Storm, *Islandske Annaler* (Flatø-annaler, year 1304).

[11] *Ibidem* (Gottskalks-annaler, year 1308).

[12] *Ibidem* (Skálholts-annaler, year 1305).

[13] *Ibidem* (Flatø-annaler, year 1305).

[14] *Ibidem* (Skálholts-annaler, year 1305).

Common People of Iceland," in which they reiterated their demand that the *sýslumenn* and lawmen should be native Icelanders, and that the people should not be carried to Norway for trial in cases which could be submitted to the lawmen and *sýslumenn* of Iceland.[15] The king finally understood that further attempts to carry through his demands for increased taxes against so violent an opposition would be futile, and he quietly dropped the matter without granting the demands of the Icelanders. The excitement gradually subsided, but the Althing was not regularly assembled. In 1313 the king addressed a letter to the Icelandic people, in which he took them severely to task because no Althing had been assembled for nine years.[16] This reminder had the result that in 1315 a full representation again met at the Althing from all parts of Iceland. In 1314 he issued a new supplement to the Icelandic code,[17] in which he sought to right some of the wrongs complained of in the remonstrance submitted by the Althing. Regarding the bringing of Icelanders to Norway for trial, the law was made to conform to the remonstrance. A provision was inserted stating that such a step should be taken only if the *sýslumenn* and lawmen were unable to try the case. The demand for new taxes was definitely dropped. But nothing was said regarding the appointment of native Icelanders to office; nor was any assurance given that six ships would be sent to Iceland every year, though this matter was now of greater importance than ever, since the trade with Iceland had become a Norwegian monopoly. No guarantee existed that the king would respect the provisions in the union agreement. Hitherto he had shown a disposition to place Iceland on the level with the Norwegian dependencies. What the future relation between the two countries was to be seemed as much as ever an unsettled question.

A despotic Norwegian overlordship was naturally feared

[15] *Safn til Sögu Íslands*, vol. ii (Árnesingaskrá), p. 168. Espolin, *Árbækur*, part i, p. 18 ff.

[16] *Diplomatarium Islandicum*, vol. ii, p. 386 ff.

[17] *Lovsamling for Island*, vol. i, p. 27. *Diplomatarium Islandicum*, vol. ii, p. 390 ff.

under these circumstances, but it was the weakness rather
than the strength of the Norwegian rulers which proved to
be Iceland's misfortune. King Haakon Magnusson had
been unnecessarily arbitrary in his dealings with Icelandic
affairs, but like his predecessors he had a real interest in
the country and its people, and meant to rule well. He took
energetic measures to maintain the efficiency of the Althing
as a supreme judicial tribunal, leading Icelanders were
called to Norway for consultation regarding matters pertaining to Iceland, valuable amendments were made to the
Icelandic laws, and the will of the people was so far respected that their remonstrances against the carrying of
citizens abroad for trial was finally heeded. The proposal to
levy new taxes was also dropped when met by their energetic protest. In some ways the king had even lent the
country a helping hand. When the cathedral church of
Skálholt was destroyed by fire in 1308, Bishop Arni Helgason went to Norway to solicit aid for rebuilding it. In 1310
he returned "with church timber and many other valuable
things which King Haakon and his queen and many leading
men in Norway had given to the bishop's seat of Skálholt,
so that it is a common opinion that no one had ever made a
more successful trip to Norway since the country was
settled," says the annalist.[18] With the death of the king
in 1319 the Norwegian royal house became extinct in the
male line. The crown went to foreign-born and incompetent rulers. Norway was united with Sweden, later both
with Sweden and Denmark, and finally with Denmark
alone, a union which lasted till 1814. During this period
of national decadence Norway fell under Danish rule. The
Hanseatic League destroyed her naval power and commerce,
and the galling royal monopoly established by the Danish
kings almost destroyed the intercourse with the distant
Norwegian colonies. The weak and exposed Greenland
settlements disappeared. In Iceland the courage and fortitude of the people were tried to the utmost by recurring
epidemics, violent volcanic eruptions, famine and poverty.
For centuries the Icelanders had to wage a struggle for

[18] G. Storm, *Islandske Annaler* (Flatø-annaler, 1310).

existence which brought into relief the noblest traits of
their character. Their national life became a combat with
adversity, in which they showed the most enduring courage
and patient devotion to the homeland.

King Haakon's sole heir at the time of his death was his
daughter Ingibjörg, who had married Duke Eirik, son of the
Swedish king. Her son Magnus Smek, born and reared in
Sweden, was then three years of age. Since he was the
nearest heir to the vacant thrones both in Sweden and
Norway, the two kingdoms were united under his rule. A
council of twelve members, assisted by his mother, was to
act as a council of regency during his minority. In 1320 the
Icelandic bishops and chieftains were summoned to attend
a council in Bergen, evidently for the purpose of giving
advice regarding Icelandic affairs.[19] But when Gunnar
Raasvein, the representative of the Norwegian government,
appeared before the Althing with the summons, and asked
the people to swear allegiance to the new king, they refused, and drew up instead a memorial to the Norwegian
government in which they reiterated their former demands
regarding the union agreement. The document says:

"To all wise councilors and guardians of the Kingdom of Norway the farmers and people of Iceland send greetings. We wish
to make known that Gunnar Raasvein announced to us at the
Althing with humble good-will to the kingdom, as he ought to
do, your demand that we should swear to Junker Magnus,
nephew of the crowned King Haakon, such taxes (*thegnskylda*)
as we granted his worthy ancestors and their descendants perpetually, and that in return for our taxes the king should send
hither six ships every summer laden with useful articles, two to
the northern, two to the southern, one to the eastern and one to
the western districts, and that the lawmen and *sýslumenn* and
all magistrates in the country shall be Icelanders. There is to be
one lawman in northern and one in southern Iceland, and neither
of them is to have a *sýsla*. Since we do not wish that the
responsibility of breaking any agreement shall fall on us, we
have granted and will grant him all the taxes which we owe

---

[19] The *Laurentiussaga* states that the bishops, the lawmen, six men in the
king's service and six *baendur* were summoned. See also G. Storm, *Islandske
Annaler* (Flatø-annaler, year 1318).

him according to aforesaid agreement, until you may take such wise counsel that we may obtain what has formerly been promised us, and that new agreements may be entered into. For you must know for certain that we consider ourselves released from all the obligations which we swore King Haakon the Elder (Haakon Magnussen) if next summer we do not receive what he promised us, and which we will here enumerate, namely, that no more codfish be exported from our land during periods of famine than the merchants need for their table. Summons abroad we will not obey, beyond what is specifically provided in the code. Magistrates we will have none, except those chosen by the people. We will take the oath when the Council of the Kingdom have given us their letter with appended seal, so that we may see their good-will, and not before. The Lord Jesus Christ grant that in this and all other matters you may take such steps that it may redound to the benefit of the blessed king's soul, the honor and glory of Junker Magnus, and the peace and joy of us all, now and forever, amen." [20]

Though the memorial is written in a sharp and aggressive tone, it could not be construed to mean that the Icelanders wished to assert their independence of Norway. The union had become so well established that secession was no longer contemplated even by the leaders who acted as public spokesmen. The summons to the chieftains and other prominent men to attend the council in Bergen was promptly obeyed. Ketill Thorlaksson, the lawman Snorri Narfason and other leading men, as well as Bishop Arni of Skálholt, sailed to Norway the same summer, while Bishop Audun of Hólar planned to go the following year. Neither of the bishops were present at the meeting of the council, as Bishop Arni died shortly after his arrival in Norway, and Bishop Audun was driven back to Iceland by a storm, but the Icelanders had other able representatives who could plead their cause to the council. What steps were taken to redress their grievances is not known. But their demands must have been granted, since the "Laurentiussaga" as well as the Icelandic annals state that in 1320 Ketill Thorlaksson came to Iceland with letters under royal seal, and that the people took the oath of allegiance to the king.

[20] Jon Thorkelsson og Einar Arnorsson, *Rikisréttindi Islands*, p. 14 ff.

In the church the patriarchal relation which had once existed between the bishops and laity had wholly disappeared at the beginning of the fourteenth century. Many of the ecclesiastics who at this time were elevated to the highest position in the Icelandic church were of foreign birth. In the period 1236-1465 thirteen of the bishops of Skálholt were foreigners, while only five were native Icelanders.[21] But whether foreigners or native-born they had usually acquired the greed and love of power which everywhere characterized the Roman hierarchy. They had ceased to be truly patriotic, and regarded themselves only as high church officials whose chief concern it was to swell their revenues and lord it over the people. Without regard for the welfare of the country they often resorted to extortionate practices to increase the income of their dioceses, while the people were sorely tried by great national calamities and steadily growing poverty. About Grim Skutuson, who became bishop of Skálholt in 1320, the annals state that during the three months in which he served as bishop he spent the sum of three hundred *hundrað*.[22] Such extravagance must have been the more offensive, since at that time there was famine in Iceland, and a number of people died of hunger. These oppressive practices of the leaders of the church gradually created among the people a hostile opposition to the selfish ecclesiastical officialdom which forms a distinct trait in Icelandic church life throughout the Middle Ages.

Upon the death of Bishop Audun of Hólar, 1321, a native Icelander, Laurentius Kalfsson, was chosen as his successor in 1323. He was highly praised for his learning and also for his piety and purity of life, though he had an illegitimate son before he was consecrated bishop. He had served as teacher in the monasteries of Thverá and Thingeyrar, and as bishop he devoted special attention to the schools and the education of the priests. Because of his popularity the "Laurentiussaga," one of the last historical works in the

[21] *Safn til Sögu Íslands*, vol. i (Jon Sigurdsson, Biskupatál á Íslandi). *Diplomatarium Islandicum*, vol. ii, p. 496 ff.

[22] Gustav Storm, *Islandske Annaler* (Oddveria Annall, year 1320).

Old Icelandic literature, was written about him about 1350, probably by his friend Einar Haflidason. On his death-bed Laurentius recommended to the archbishop that native priests should be chosen as bishops in Iceland. This advice was also followed in the selection of his successor, the native-born Egill Eyulfsson. But when he died in 1341, another Norwegian ecclesiastic, Orm Aslaksson, became bishop of Hólar. Orm's contemporary, Jon Sigurdsson of Skálholt, was a native Icelander, but both treated the people very harshly and laid heavy burdens upon them. Orm was able to remain on friendly terms with the king, but the people finally became so embittered against him that they lodged complaints with the government. This complaint he was called to Norway to answer in 1347. He was accompanied by Bishop Jon, who was almost as unpopular as himself. Jon returned to Iceland the following year and sought to effect a reconciliation between Orm and the people of the Hólar diocese. The attempt failed, and he had to return to Skálholt, where he died in 1348. Under the circumstances Orm did not venture to return to his bishopric. For a time there were no bishops in Iceland, a circumstance which the people seem to have felt as a relief. Finally, after receiving letters of protection from the king, he returned to Iceland in 1351, but he encountered such opposition that he again went to Norway three years later. His chief aim at this time was to obtain royal sanction for the enforcement of Archbishop Jon's code of church laws, especially with regard to the payment of tithes and other church dues. This code was almost identical with that of Bishop Arni of Skálholt, which granted the church extensive privileges. The king's consent was given in a royal letter issued October 19, 1354, commanding that the church laws in force in southern Iceland should also be in operation in the Hólar diocese. For the first time this code of church laws had now received the formal sanction of the king. Orm did not return to his diocese, but remained in Norway, where he died in 1356. He was succeeded by Jon Eiriksson Skalli, who had been chosen bishop of Gardar in Greenland, but was permitted to take charge of the Hólar diocese, as he claimed to have

received the pope's sanction to the transfer. As he was
unable to furnish any written evidence to support his claim,
both the priests and the laity rebelled against him. He
went to Norway to ask the support of the archbishop, but
received none. The confusion in his diocese continued
until he finally obtained the sanction of the Roman Curia
in 1371. Of the bishops of Skálholt, who succeeded one
another in rapid succession at this time, none became noted
for any special achievements. Michael, a Dane, who was
made bishop of the diocese in 1383, sought to impose new
burdens on the people, and was finally driven from the
bishopric. The most confused conditions prevailed. Many
priests had died, some were driven away, and no general
supervision existed for some time, as no new bishop was
chosen till in 1394, when another Dane, Vilchin, abler than
his immediate predecessors, became bishop of Skálholt.

The willingness of the king to grant privileges to the
church hitherto denied reveals a growing indifference of the
Norwegian government to the real welfare of Iceland. An
administration by royal officials had been established as
a result of the union. Two lawmen were appointed by the
king, one for the southern and eastern, and one for the
western and northern quarters; *syslumenn* were appointed
as administrative officials for larger districts, as in Norway,
and *hirðstjórar* were placed as royal governors over the
island. But Iceland was now treated so much like other
dependencies that the chief interest of the government was
to secure from its inhabitants revenues for the royal purse.
Viseyrir, or taxes payable to the king, were levied upon
the whole country, and became a definite income payable
to the king's purse, like the taxes from the Norwegian colonies. This system of taxation gave rise also to a royal
monopoly on trade with the colonies which proved disastrous to their economic well-being, and hindered their
progress. The royal officials usually asserted the authority
of the government with stern harshness, and severe punishments for crimes were introduced. In some instances
criminals were even buried alive; but law and order were
but imperfectly maintained. Even the higher officials

themselves would engage in quarrels which sometimes resembled the bloody feuds of earlier periods. In 1342 it is reported that two *syslumenn*, Jon Hallsson and Arnor Thordsson, engaged in a controversy over a *sysla*, with the result that Jon captured Arnor and had his left foot and right hand cut off.[23] The old spirit of violence was not yet extinct, though some progress had been made toward a new conception of law and public order. Murders and other grave crimes were still of frequent occurrence. Even priests were often attacked and wounded. In the monasteries there was turmoil and violence, and many abbots were deposed. In 1343 the monks of the monastery of Thykvabær attacked Abbot Thorlak, probably because he sought to discipline them. He fled to the monastery of Videy, and two of the monks who had taken part in the attack were put in chains upon the order of Bishop Jon Sigurdsson of Skálholt.[24] Though paganism was dead, the progress toward new ideals was still slow. A reign of law had been substituted for a reign of terror, the most important change effected by the new régime. But throughout the fourteenth century social life in Iceland was characterized by a dull, unprogressive spirit, prone to relapse into the vicious practices of earlier ages. The jealousy and lack of patriotism of the chieftains in the Sturlung period, the selfishness and narrow-mindedness of the royal government after the union, the greed and tyranny of the church had destroyed the people's public spirit and political interest, and had left them to wage their own struggles without the inspiring guidance of true leadership. The lack of inspiration and encouragement in the intense struggle for existence waged in a most unfavorable environment tended to weaken higher aspirations. A spirit of pessimistic unprogressive stoicism was fostered which was strengthened by the frequent recurrence of great calamities, and the sorrows, poverty and hopelessness which followed in their wake.

The Icelandic annals record a series of calamities which in the fourteenth century befell the Icelandic people such

[23] Espolin, *Árbaekur*, part i.
[24] *Ibidem*, ch. lviii.

as are scarcely to be met with elsewhere in history. Cattle diseases, famine and epidemics had sorely tried the people in the closing decades of the previous century; but a series of unparalleled misfortunes began with the outbreak of the great volcano Hekla in 1300, the sixth recorded eruption of this volcano, accompanied by violent earthquakes. For two days a pall of darkness like midnight hung over southern Iceland. Farm-steads were destroyed and meadows were buried under a thick deposit of ashes. The following year an epidemic raged which carried away not less than 500 persons.[25] In 1306 a new epidemic broke out, and the winter was so severe that the northern coast was ice-bound till late in the summer.[26] Earthquakes and volcanic eruptions were very frequent. In 1308 both people and cattle were killed in a new quake in southern Iceland which destroyed a number of farm-steads. Another violent earthquake occurred in 1311, accompanied by volcanic eruptions which scattered ashes over wide areas. In 1339 an earthquake in southern Iceland destroyed many farm-steads and killed many people. This was followed by a new eruption of Hekla in 1341, accompanied by violent explosions and a fall of ashes which destroyed vegetation in large districts, causing the death of large numbers of horses, sheep and cattle.[27] Even the climate seems to have been affected by these violent disturbances, as the winters were often severe with a heavy snow-fall, followed in the spring by excessive rains, which caused destructive floods. These frequent earthquakes and volcanic eruptions had a most disastrous effect on the economic life of the country. The hay crop failed, and a shortage of grazing and fodder was created through the destructive ash deposits. Severe cattle diseases raged, and many people lost all their possessions, so that many cases of famine are recorded in the annals. "From this fall of ashes so many cattle died in the southern districts that many people lost all their live-stock and had

[25] Th. Thoroddsen, *Observations on Volcanic Eruptions and Earthquakes in Iceland*, p. 8.

[26] G. Storm, *Islandske Annaler* (Flatø-annaler, 1306).

[27] Th. Thoroddsen, *Observations on Volcanic Eruptions and Earthquakes in Iceland*, p. 9.

to leave their homes, farm-steads and possessions," says the annalist.[28] "At Skálholt alone eighty head of cattle perished," adds another old writer, and one states that several settlements were destroyed. In 1249 an eruption of the Öræfajökull laid waste a large fertile region.[29] In 1360 the Mydal district was devastated by an eruption of the volcano Trolladyngjur, and the winter following was so severe that the cattle perished in the mountains. In 1389 a violent eruption of Hekla took place, accompanied by explosions so violent that the detonations were heard over the whole island, according to the annalist who gives the following account of the occurrence and subsequent events.

"Fire arose not only from the mountain but from the woods above Skard, the eruption being so violent that two mountains were formed with a chasm between them. In the neighborhood hot springs welled up, forming lakes of boiling water. Seven ships remained in Iceland, which had come there before the outbreak. In the autumn the rainfall was so heavy in northern Iceland that it caused floods after Martinmas, the like of which people had never seen. A number of sheep were killed in Skagafjord and in Desey in Nordrárdal. Avalanches destroyed woods, pastures and meadows. The farm Hjallaland in Vatsdal was destroyed in this way and six persons perished, likewise also the farm Budarnes, where twelve persons lost their lives. In Longuhlid an avalanche took the farm houses and also the church, killing sixteen people. Only two women and a man who were in the stables were saved. The lawman Rafn Botolfsson, his wife and two children and many other people lost their lives. Over a hundred men gathered to search for the dead and their belongings. Some bodies were found, among others that of the lawman's wife, who lies buried at Mödruvellir, but of the goods almost nothing could be saved." [30]

Smallpox and other epidemics harried the country frequently throughout the century. Cattle diseases caused by shortage of fodder and the poisoning of vegetation by volcanic gases also reduced the size and productiveness of the herds, causing widespread distress.

[28] G. Storm, *Islandske Annaler* (Gottskalks Annaler, year 1341).

[29] Th. Thoroddsen, *Observations on Volcanic Eruptions and Earthquakes in Iceland*, p. 9.

[30] G. Storm, *Islandske Annaler* (Flatø-annaler, year 1390).

During years of suffering resulting from these recurring calamities some aid was derived from Norwegian trade with Iceland which was plied quite energetically, especially during the first half of the fourteenth century, since the Hanseatic League had closed all other avenues to Norwegian merchants. It has already been noted that King Haakon Magnusson made trade with Iceland a Norwegian monopoly. The Norwegian kings had been forced by circumstances to increase the privileges of the Hanseatic cities until Norwegian commerce was destroyed. In 1302 King Haakon made the regulation that the Hansa merchants should not trade north of Bergen, or carry on commerce with Iceland or any of the Norwegian dependencies, a stipulation which was repeated in 1306.[31] This trade was retained by the government for the benefit of the crown. Other restrictions on trade were also imposed, probably in the interest of the merchants of Bergen who were soon able to establish a monopoly over commerce with the colonies. In the reign of King Magnus Lagabøter the number of traders was limited by a law stipulating that no one should be allowed to sail on trading expeditions unless he possessed a certain amount of property free from debts. This provision should be in force from Easter till Michaelmas (September 29), but from Michaelmas till the beginning of winter trade should be free to all. This law was repeated in the reigns of Magnus Eiriksson, Haakon Magnusson and Olaf Haakonsson.[32] Foreign merchants were also forbidden to buy cattle in the rural districts, and a law of 1306 forbade foreigners to purchase lumber in Norway, except from the royal castle or the city fathers. Each town received a definite district with which it could carry on trade, and Bergen as the chief commercial city became the

[31] *Norges gamle Love*, vol. iii, no. 53, p. 134. This was a repetition of an older provision of 1294 that the Hanseatic merchants should not trade north of Bergen, Norway, without permission. This restriction was removed in 1343, reimposed in 1348, and again removed in 1361, when the Hanseatic merchants received the privilege to trade everywhere in the kingdom. This privilege was ratified in 1376. *Samlinger til norsk Sprog og Historie*, vol. v, p. 620 ff. Alexander Bugge, *Studier over de norske Byers Selvstyre og Handel før Hanseaternes Tid.*

[32] *Norges gamle Love*, vol. iii, no. 53, no. 119.

center of all trade with the Norwegian colonies. From early times Nidaros had been the center of intercourse with Iceland and Greenland, as trade with these countries had been largely in the hands of rich families in Trøndelagen; but Bergen had now gained such supremacy commercially that even the merchants of Nidaros had to bring their imports to the Bergen market.

One of the chief articles of Norwegian export at this time was dried codfish, a commodity for which the Hanseatic merchants had created such demand that the Norwegian traders began to import it from Iceland in the early part of the fourteenth century. We have already seen that in a memorial to the king in 1320 the Icelanders asked that in periods of famine no more codfish should be exported than the merchants needed for their table. But in 1340 we read in an old Norwegian state document:

"Not long ago little codfish was imported from Iceland, which at that time was called table codfish. Most of the exports from there consisted of *vaðmál*. Now, however, the most and best exports from Iceland consist of codfish and train-oil." [33]

This development of a new important line of export proved a valuable stimulus to commerce, and must have increased also the volume of Icelandic imports, as is shown by the lively intercourse between Norway and Iceland at this time. The annalists state that in 1340 there were eleven ships in Icelandic harbors, and a twelfth foundered at Eyrar in the fall.[34] The following year six ships came to the port of Hvalfjord.[35] How many came to other Icelandic harbors is not stated. In 1342-1344 many shipwrecks are recorded in the annals. In 1345 eleven ships came to Iceland. The next year eleven ships also arrived, besides one which suffered shipwreck. In 1347 thirteen ships came to Iceland. "There came also a ship from Greenland, smaller than the ships which sail to Iceland. It came to Straumfjord inn Ytra. It was without anchor and had

[33] *Diplomatarium Norwegicum*, vol. ii, part i, p. 198.
[34] G. Storm, *Islandske Annaler* (Skálholts-annaler, year 1340).
[35] *Ibidem* (Flatø-annaler, year 1341).

seventeen men on board. They had sailed to Markland
(Labrador) and were driven hither," says the annalist.[36]
"That winter there were twenty-one ships in Iceland,"
adds another writer. But this very encouraging outlook in
commercial affairs was suddenly destroyed by the Black
Death, which in 1349 appeared in Norway and in a short
time carried away one-third of the entire population of the
kingdom. From this stunning blow the country with its
already weakened economic and national life was unable to
rally. All optimism and spirit of enterprise were destroyed,
the expeditions to Greenland ceased almost completely,
and the trade with Iceland and other dependencies was
greatly reduced. In 1349 the Icelandic annals mention only
one ship from Norway, which foundered on the coast of
Scotland. In 1350 it is stated that no ship came from Norway. During the second half of the fourteenth century it
appears from the annals that fewer ships came to Iceland
than formerly. Not till in 1387 is it again recorded that as
many as eleven ships arrived in a single year.

For Iceland, which was suffering from the effects of the
great calamities which had lately befallen the country, this
falling off of commerce was a serious misfortune. But no
less deplorable was the fact that at this critical juncture
the foreign-born and often incompetent rulers who bore the
title of Kings of Norway took little interest in administrative affairs in Iceland beyond what was necessary to secure
the desired revenues for the royal treasury. The old *landaurar* tax on trade and intercourse with Norway was removed by the union agreement of 1262; but these rulers
laid a new tariff on imports from Iceland, the *sekkjagjald,*
contrary to the covenant then made. The first specific
definition of this impost levied for the benefit of the royal
purse is found in laws promulgated by King Olaf Haakonsson in 1382 and 1383.[37] At this time Norwegian trade was
languishing from the effects of the Black Death and the
Hanseatic commercial régime. Under these circumstances
this new encroachment on the rights of the Icelanders also

[36] G. Storm, *Islandske Annaler* (Skálholts-annaler, year 1347).
[37] *Norges gamle Love,* vol. iii, no. 118, no. 119, p. 215 ff.

placed increased obstacles in the way of the dwindling intercourse with the colonies. But considerations for the general welfare of the realm was of little weight with these selfish rulers, who only looked to their own personal advantage. The regulations controlling the collection of this impost were repeated in the reign of Queen Margaret in 1389,[38] and seem to have been made a part of the general revenue system of the government. But nothing was done to encourage ship-building and commerce, which were now falling into complete decay.

In 1397 the three kingdoms Norway, Sweden and Denmark were formally united by the Kalmar "Act of Union." Eirik of Pomerania was placed on the thrones of the united realms, but Queen Margaret, who after the death of her son, King Olaf Haakonsson, had been ruling queen of the three kingdoms, continued to govern until her death in 1412. In Iceland her rule was very unpopular, as she tried to increase the public burdens. In 1392 she attempted to levy a new tax, stipulating that every freeholder should pay her half a *mörk* according to the old standard (*half-mörk forngilda*).[39] This caused great ill-will at first, but later many of the best men gave their consent, says the annalist. It seems, however, that the request was not granted without modifications. When the *hirðstjóri*, Vigfus Ivarsson, the following year presented the request to the Althing, the best men were willing to grant her only eight *alnar vaðmál* from each freeholder, on the condition that it should not be called a tax, and that it should not again be demanded. The men of the Eyjafjord district refused to consent to any grant of any sort. About the elevation of Eirik of Pomerania to the throne the annalist remarks that "a man by the name of Eirik, a child in years, was made king." "About this man it was said that he was the son of Margaret's sister (should be sister's daughter), but his father was a German. All people in Norway disapproved of this act, and especially the people of the dependencies." As the Danish rulers who now sat on the thrones of the

[38] *Diplomatarium Norwegicum*, vol. ii, no. 514.
[39] G. Storm, *Islandske Annaler* (Flatø-annaler, year 1392).

united kingdoms were strangers who regarded the Norwegian colonies only as sources of revenue, no improvement in Icelandic affairs could be expected from the royal government. Trade conditions became so wretched that the Icelanders were again forced to voice complaints and call attention to the union agreement, now wholly ignored. In 1419 they formally pledged their allegiance to Eirik of Pomerania, king of Norway, Denmark and Sweden, at the Althing, but added to this act a specific demand for redress of grievances with regard to commerce. The document says in part:

"But our laws provide that six ships should come hither from Norway every year, which has not happened for a long time, a cause from which Your Grace and our poor country has suffered most grievous harm. Therefore, trusting in God's grace and your help, we have traded with foreigners who have come hither peacefully on legitimate business, but we have punished those fishermen and owners of fishing-smacks who have robbed and caused disturbance on the sea." [40]

Still more offensive than the restrictions on trade was the new method of collecting revenues, introduced by the government. The taxes were farmed out to the *hirðstjórar,* or governors of Iceland, for a certain sum to be paid by them to the royal treasury. Little did the kings care how the people might be oppressed by the tax gatherers, or what sums were collected, so long as they received the stipulated amount. This system was first established in 1354.[41] "Ivar Holm came to Iceland with letters from the king showing that he had leased the whole country with taxes and incomes for a period of three years, and that he had been created *hirðstjóri,"* says the annalist. The same method was often employed later. In 1357 the annals state that one *hirðstjóri* was placed over each quarter, and that these four officials had leased all Iceland for three years with taxes and incomes. "Ecclesiastics on behalf of the church, and these four on behalf of the lay people, traveled through the

[40] *Diplomatarium Norwegicum,* vol. ii, no. 651, p. 485.
[41] G. Storm, *Islandske Annaler* (Lögmanns-annáll, year 1354).

land collecting taxes from learned as well as from laymen whatever they could get. And under the oppression of such burdens the people had to remain," remarks the annalist.[42] In 1361 Smid Andresson was made *hirðstjóri* of all Iceland, and, like his immediate predecessors in the office, he leased the land with taxes and incomes. Church and state officials vied with each other to collect taxes and dues from the impoverished and suffering people. Goaded to the utmost, the *bændur* would sometimes offer so violent a resistance to their oppressors, that scenes of conflict between the tyrannical officials and the angry people became favorite themes with poets and annalists. The following episode may serve to illustrate the nature of these clashes and the conditions prevailing at the time:

"A meeting was held at Hólar at Tiburtiusmas. The men from the district of Eyjafjord in northern Iceland came, both learned and unlearned. Smid and the *officialis* (assistant to the bishop) of Skálholt also came, but no agreement was reached. . . . Smid Andresson arrested Arni Thordsson, and charged him with the Barkadar case. Arni would submit the case to the king, but Smid kept him in prison, and would not grant this request, but caused him to be beheaded at Lambey. Friday before John the Baptistmas, within a month after the execution, Arni's body was brought to Skálholt and interred in the church-yard. After the Althing Smid rode about in the northern districts with a band of seventy men from southern Iceland. The people from Eyjafjord sent out spies, and many men were assembled at Grund in Eyjafjord on Seljumannaday (July 8). Smid and his men had arrived before. The men from Eyjafjord surrounded the house, and a battle followed in which Smid lost his life. Jon Guthormsson, Jarper Hannis, Jon Lang, Bjarni Magnusson, Gudmund Andresson and Thorvald Helgason were slain. Of the men of Eyjafjord Andres Ormsson, Stein Brynjolfsson, Magnus, Björn Thordsson and Gudmund Halldorsson fell. More are not mentioned by name, but there fell fourteen in all." [43]

The resistance to Alf of Krok, and the struggle between the people and the bishops Jon Sigurdsson of Skálholt and

[42] G. Storm, *Islandske Annaler* (Lögmanns-annáll, year 1354).
[43] *Ibidem* (Flatø-annalér, year 1362).

Orm Aslaksson of Hólar have already been mentioned.
These episodes show that the Icelanders had not lost their
old vigor, but were able to resist wanton encroachments on
their rights. In spite of adversity and discouragements the
old spirit of freedom remained to some extent unbroken.
Economically, too, some degree of well-being must have
been maintained, since many rich and influential men were
still found in Iceland. Einar Eiriksson of Vatsfjord, who
was drowned on the Isafjord in 1382, was a powerful and
well-to-do chieftain. His son Björn Einarsson, who became
hirðstjóri over all Iceland in 1413, was so wealthy that he
gave several farms to the St. Olaf church where he wished
to be buried. To eighteen churches he gave in all forty-
three *hundrað*, and to three others other valuable gifts.
To the poor he gave five *hundrað*, to poor relatives fifteen
hundrað, to various churches for masses to be celebrated
for the dead twelve *hundrað*, in all eighty-five *hundrað*,
besides other valuable gifts.[44] Of Lopt Guttormsson, chieftain and poet, it is said that he owned about eighty estates.[45] But such accumulation of wealth by a few powerful individuals in an otherwise poor country could be of
little real benefit to the people in general. Because of the
absence of the law of *odel*, and through the influence of the
church as well as of the government and the chieftain class
landed property had been gathered in the hands of a few.
As the class of smaller freeholders was disappearing, the
people were becoming a struggling and oppressed peasantry
with a limited outlook, few political interests, and less of
public spirit and individual self-assertion than formerly.
The old race of chieftains had disappeared. In this critical
period when they were confronted with so many grave
economic and national problems the Icelandic people lacked
the guidance and inspiration of true leadership. From the
royal government they received little aid, and had to solve
their own difficulties under constant provocation and in-
justices. The irritation caused by wanton encroachments

[44] Finnur Jonsson, *Historia Ecclesiastica Islandiæ*, vol. ii, p. 130.
[45] Finnur Jonsson, *Den oldnorske og oldislandske Literaturs Historie*,
vol. iii, p. 21.

on their rights, and the ceaseless contention about public affairs in church and state could only add increased bitterness to the growing difficulties which helped to produce melancholy, superstition and lack of optimism both in intellectual and social life.

A distinct ebb-tide was beginning to manifest itself in Iceland as everywhere else in the North at this time. But the Icelanders retained their old intellectual life and their national vigor longer than any other branch of the Scandinavian race. To some extent they still kept up the old custom of traveling in foreign countries, and we still hear of Icelanders who occupied positions of trust and honor in Norway. About the Norwegian magnate Erlend Filipsson the annals state that he trusted Icelanders better than Norwegians, and kept them always in his service. Einar Eiriksson was a chieftain of the old type, who often went on expeditions to foreign lands, and was very well-to-do. Still more noted was his son Björn Einarsson Jorsalafari, so-called because of his expedition to Jerusalem. Björn was born in 1350, and became especially well known because of his expeditions to foreign lands. On his first trip abroad in 1379 he visited Rome in company with Bishop Oddgeir of Skálholt. In 1385 he set sail for Norway with four ships, accompanied by his wife, but they were driven to Greenland, where they spent two years. After returning to Iceland he again went to Rome in 1388, also this time accompanied by his wife. When they reached Norway they were arrested by the authorities for going to Greenland and trading with the people there without license, but upon taking an oath before the court that they had been driven thither by storms they were released, and continued their journey to Rome, returning in 1391. In 1405 Björn undertook a trip to the Holy Land, accompanied by his wife, Bishop Vilchin of Skálholt, the lawman Snorri Sveinsson and the monk Jon Halfredsson. They first sailed to Norway, where Bishop Vilchin died in the early part of the winter. The following spring they continued their journey to Rome, Venice and Jerusalem. When they reached Venice on their return from the Holy Land, Björn's wife proceeded

to Norway, but he went to Spain, where he visited the
shrine of Santiago of Compostella. On his way to Norway
he also visited the grave of St. Thomas à Becket at Canter-
bury, England. In 1410 he again sailed for Iceland. Spending the winter in the Shetland Islands he reached home the
following summer. His wife had died on the expedition,
either in Norway, as some sources have it, or in the Orient,
as stated by others.[46] In his life and character Björn
Einarsson bore a striking resemblance to the great chieftains of earlier days. He maintained a *hirð* according to
ancient custom, and kept scalds about him to sing about
his exploits. Upon his return home from one of his expeditions arrangements were made for his son's wedding.
But the bridegroom was shipwrecked on his voyage to
Eyjafjord, where the wedding was to be celebrated, and
lost his life. Björn's sister was then married to Jon Guttormsson, a brother of the wealthy Lopt Guttormsson, with
lavish display of hospitality and a great number of guests
according to ancient usage. Some time afterwards he became involved in a quarrel with Thord Sigmundsson who
had accompanied him on his pilgrimage to Rome. The
two met at Gnup in Dyrafjord, accompanied by large armed
bands, and a battle took place in which two of Björn's men
fell, and he himself with most of his men were wounded.
He was forced to seek refuge in a church, and was not able
to leave till the following day. Attempts to negotiate an
agreement between the two failed. In the winter Björn
traveled about the country to secure support, an effort in
which he was so successful that in June, 1394, he gathered
about him the *hirðstjóri,* the lawman Thorstein Eyjolfsson,
many priests and other prominent persons, and about
ninety armed men. They went to Thord Sigmundsson's
home, and summoned him to appear before the lawman at
Mosfell to answer for the death of the two men killed at
Gnup. Thord appeared on the appointed day, accompanied
by fifty men. He was outlawed together with five others,
but it was left to the king to decide whether he should be

---

[46] G. Storm, *Islandske Annaler* (Flatø-annaler, years 1385 and 1387).
Andvari, vol. xxxviii, p. 142 ff.

allowed to remain in the country. The leading men finally succeeded in arranging a settlement of the affair, according to which Thord was to pay Björn fifty-four *hundrað* in goods or in money, and he should also arrange a suitable feast for Björn and his wife. This rather strange stipulation in the agreement shows that among the chieftains and men of quality the love of feasting was as great as ever. Other instances also show that this feature of early social life was still maintained. The annalist tells that when the newly elected Bishop Vilchin of Skálholt came to Iceland in 1394, he arranged a feast so lavish that no one then living in Iceland had seen anything like it, either in regard to costly arrangement or the number of guests invited.

"Bishop Peter of Hólar was there, and all the prominent people of northern, western and southern Iceland. The feast lasted seven days, and such lavish hospitality was shown that all might drink as much as they wished, both early and late. Three double rows of guests, extending from one end of the room to the other, were seated in the principal room in the bishop's residence, and nothing was drunk but German beer and other costly beverages." [47]

Travels in foreign lands were no longer undertaken, however, as formerly for the sake of study at higher institutions of learning; but were mostly visits to the royal court, where honors and appointments to office might be obtained. Interest in scholarly pursuits was declining, as the foreign-born bishops often showed great lack of interest for the schools of the land. The school at Skálholt continued to flourish till 1236, when the first foreign bishop was placed over the diocese. It was then closed, and was so completely abandoned that it was not again heard of till in 1491, when it was revived by the learned and able Stephan Jonsson, bishop of Skálholt. The Latin school at Hólar, founded by Jon Ögmundsson, was discontinued in the time of Bishop Gudmund Arason (1203-1237), and was not reopened till the days of Jörund Thorsteinsson (1267-1313).

[47] G. Storm, *Islandske Annaler* (Lögmanns-annáll, year 1364).

But although learning was no longer cultivated with the same devoted interest as formerly, it still received considerable attention. During the time of Jörund's successors the school at Hólar continued to flourish, over fifteen pupils receiving instruction every year in Latin, music and other branches. Bishop Laurentius of Hólar (1323-1330) was especially interested in schools, as he had served as teacher in the monasteries of Thverá, Thykkvabær and Thingeyrar. The interest in schools and learning maintained at this time in the Hólar diocese was due chiefly to his efforts. Several of his pupils became teachers, among others his son Arni, Einar Haflidason, Berg Sokkason, and Egill Eyjolfsson, who succeeded him as bishop (1331-1341). After this time the bishops were foreigners without interest in educational activities, and the school at Hólar, like that at Skálholt, fell into complete decay. A school at Hólar is, indeed, mentioned in the Icelandic annals, 1393, but nothing further is known about it. In the monasteries, where literature and learning continued to flourish, schools were yet maintained. Love for reading had steadily increased, especially among the less educated classes. Though the leading schools had disappeared through the culpable neglect and incompetence of foreign-born bishops, love of books had become general in Iceland, and instruction was still so well maintained that the Icelandic clergy was undoubtedly better educated than that of Norway. In northern Iceland the monasteries of Thykkvabær and Helgafell became the chief seats of learning after the disappearance of the schools of Skálholt and Hólar. In Thykkvabær the abbots Brand Jonsson (1247-1263) and Thorlak Loptsson (1314-1351) are known to have taught, and Laurentius Kalfsson served as teacher there until he was elected bishop in 1323. At Helgafell Abbot Thorstein Snorrason Bollott (1322-1351) seems to have devoted himself to teaching, and it is certain that his successor Asgrim (1352-1379) devoted much of his time to this work. About 1362 Einar Thorlaksson sold the estates Botn and Thorisstadir to the Helgafell monastery on the condition that Abbot Asgrim should instruct his son. In 1377 Thorgils Gudlaugsson gave one-half of the estate Kolsvik to the same monastery, on the condition that the abbot should instruct his son so that he could receive consecration as sub-deacon. Similar agreements were also made with the monastery of Videy. In 1380 Valgard Loptsson made a contract transferring to the monastery some lands on Kjalarnes, the consideration being that the abbot should instruct his son for six years. It is also certain that many of the ablest churchmen and parish priests gave private instruction to young men who desired to devote themselves to study. The "Laurentiussaga" states that the priest Thorarin Kaggi at Vellir in Svarfadardal kept a school and had many pupils. This practice was undoubtedly quite common, as it had been in vogue even earlier. Bishop Arni Thorlaksson of Skálholt (1269-1298) received his first instruction from the priest Grim Holmsteinsson at Kirkjubær. Magnus Gizursson, bishop of Skálholt (1216-1236), had been under the tuition of Bishop Thorlak Thorhallsson. At the close of the fourteenth century all schools in Iceland seem to have disappeared, as none are again heard of in the now existing records till about a century later. Such instruction as was given during this period must have been conducted in the homes or by private individuals.[48]

A general retrograde movement is noticeable also in the field of literature during this period. A decay of classical literary style, together with a turning from history writing and more serious prose literature to romantic tales and religious productions of various sorts, occurred already in the thirteenth century. With the beginning of the fourteenth much of the earlier originality and creative imagination had faded out of literary production. From this time forth few original works of real value appeared. The writers devoted their chief attention to translation and copying, or to the compilation of large collections of earlier productions. But love of reading and diligence in literary pursuits were probably never greater than at this time. Iceland continued to be the center of literary life in the

[48] Jon Thorkelsson, *Om Digtningen på Island i det 15de og 16de Aarhundrede*, p. 1 ff.

North. · Her writers were yet able to produce works of
literary merit, the fruit of a scholarly interest which still
remained strong. Of the "Biskupasögur," or stories about
the Icelandic bishops, the most important source of the
church history of Iceland, some continued to appear also in
the fourteenth century. The "Arnasaga Thorlákssonar,"
or story about Bishop Arni Thorlaksson of Skálholt, was
written shortly after 1300, probably by his nephew Bishop
Arni Helgason. The "Laurentiussaga" about Bishop Laurentius Kalfsson, written by Einar Haflidason, appeared
about 1350, and the "Guðmundarsaga,' which Abbot Arngrim of Thingeyrar wrote about Bishop Gudmund Arason
of Hólar, was produced about 1375. To the literary production of the fourteenth century belong especially a number of romantic tales, the "Lygisögur," based on heroic
Germanic tradition and on epic romances of continental
Europe. According to their contents they fall into two
groups, the "Fornsögur Norðrlanda," dealing with traditions
of the North, and the "Fornsögur Suðrlanda," based on the
rhymed romances of the continent. Stories about saints,
and religious rhymes and poems, were also written. This
literary work was done chiefly by clerics whose names are
not known. But now and then also a known writer appears.
One of the most prominent among these is Hauk Erlendsson, the author of the "Hauksbók," a great collection which
contains, besides Hauks own version of the "Landnámabók," the "Kristnisaga," the "Saga of Eirik the Red," the
"Völsungasaga," and many other works. On his mother's
side Hauk sprang from a distinguished family in Iceland.
From 1294 till 1299 he served as lawman. He then went to
Norway, and became lawman in Oslo and later in the Gula-
thingslag. The king showed him great confidence and
esteem. He was knighted, became one of the leading men
of the kingdom, and was repeatedly sent to Iceland on important missions. He died in 1334. Hauk was not an
original author, but worked as a copyist and compiler of
literary works. His critical ability was limited, but he
possessed extensive literary knowledge and great scholarly
interest. Another great collection produced by diligent

copyists is the "Flateyjarbók," compiled in 1387-1395 by
the priests Jon Thordsson and Magnus Thorhallsson from
older sources now partly lost. After the disappearance of
the scaldic *drápur* about 1300 a new kind of narrative
poems, the *rímur*, began to appear in the fourteenth century. Alliteration and scaldic figures of speech were still
used; but the *rímur* were written in rhymed verse, clearly
an imitation of Latin hymns and religious songs. These
poems are really ballads, based for the most part on mythological sagas and romantic foreign traditions, though a few
also deal with persons from Norwegian and Icelandic history. The *rímur* were recited for the entertainment of the
people in the home; but they were also sung, and were then
usually accompanied by dance. As a form of entertainment the *rímur* became very popular and continued to
flourish even into modern times.

The Icelandic language had now assumed its distinctive
traits. Originally it was identical with the Old Norse found
in southwestern Norway in the districts from which the
greater number of Icelandic colonists emigrated. This language has been preserved in Iceland with but little change
even to the present. But in the thirteenth century some
peculiarities developed which distinguished it slightly from
the original mother tongue. The Old Norse *e* and *o* in final
position were changed to *i* and *u,* and the digraphs *œ* and *œ*
were no longer kept distinct, but were both represented by
œ. Words like *bœr* (farm-stead), *bœn* (prayer), *bœli* (den
or dwelling place) were written in Icelandic *bœr, bœn,* and
bœli. This change was completed about 1300. In the fourteenth century the connecting vowel *u* also appears in Icelandic before final syllabic *r,* as *vetur* for *vetr, dagur* for
dagr. After 1350 Norse underwent a new development
similar to that of English and other Germanic tongues,
while Icelandic, by preserving the old inflectional forms
and other peculiarities, henceforth remained a distinct
language.[49]

* M. Hægstad og Alf Torp, *Gamalnorsk Ordbok,* introduction, p. xxiii ff.

12. English Commerce with Iceland. The Icelandic Church. Intercourse of the Hanseatic Cities with Iceland

In 1397 Iceland and all the Norwegian dependencies entered into the union between Norway, Sweden and Denmark established at Kalmar, but no change was made regarding Iceland's relation to the general government. Only gradually did the effects of the union become noticeable in the choice of Danes as bishops and higher officials, and the extension of Danish commercial and administrative policy to the colony. During the fourteenth century the old intellectual life and national vigor were waning, and in the fifteenth literary activity ceased almost completely. Various causes contributed to this growing national exhaustion, but the most conspicuous was the Black Death, which ravaged the island in 1402-1404. The popular estimate that the epidemic carried away two-thirds of the entire population may be an exaggeration,[1] but the loss of life was nevertheless enormous. Many districts were almost depopulated. Whole families died out, farms were lying idle, and all activities suffered a severe setback. Poverty increased, and as the land was now in the hands of the clergy and a few rich proprietors, the people had to live as renters in misery and want.

After the ravages of the Black Death in Norway about the middle of the fourteenth century the trade with Iceland declined. This trade, which now embraced the whole intercourse with the colony, had been gradually monopolized by the merchants of Bergen, with whom the king had entered into a sort of partnership. He owned one-fourth of every merchant vessel licensed to trade with Iceland, without paying any part of ship or cargo. Under more favorable circumstances a lucrative monopolized trade with the colony might have been established. But the prosperity of the Bergen merchants, who were slowly recovering from the depressive effects of the Black Death, was again destroyed

[1] Espolin, *Arbœkur,* part i, ch. xcix.

by the ravages of the Victual Brothers, a powerful organization of pirates who sacked and burned Bergen in 1393
and 1394, and again in 1428 and 1429. Under these circumstances intercourse with Iceland could be only feebly
maintained. But since Icelandic economic life was paralyzed as a result of the ravages of the Black Death, the
need of imports was now more keenly felt than ever before.
In the already mentioned memorial addressed to the king
in 1419 the people stated that they had been obliged to
trade with foreign merchants who visited Iceland in violation of the government decrees. These merchants were
English fishermen and traders who were now beginning to
carry on a clandestine traffic with Iceland.

The intercourse with the British Isles which had existed
during earlier periods of Icelandic history ceased during
the latter part of the thirteenth century. During the fourteenth no trade seems to have been carried on between
Iceland and the British ports. English foreign trade had
hitherto been in the hands of Scandinavian, Venetian,
Genoese, Hanseatic, Flemish and other foreign merchants.
But from the beginning of the fifteenth century the English Merchant Adventurers entered into competition with
these maritime states for the control of their own commerce
and the extension of English trade into new fields. These
bold mariners made their appearance also in Iceland,
tempted by the rich fisheries and prospective lucrative
trade. English merchants in Iceland are first mentioned
in the Icelandic annals in 1412,[2] but they had probably
made voyages to Iceland even in the fourteenth century.
In 1413 "an English trader by the name of Richard came
with a ship to Iceland," says the annalist. He had letters
from the king of Norway granting him permission to sail
unhindered in the realm, and many people bought goods
from him when he came to port in southern Iceland. During this period buccaneering and lawlessness were everywhere prevalent upon the high seas. Even merchants who
were engaged in legitimate trade might turn pirates on
more distant voyages, and seize defenseless merchant ves-

[2] G. Storm, *Islandske Annaler* (Lögmanns-annáll, year 1412).

sels with their cargoes. Along the coasts and in the harbors
little. heed was paid to the rights of private citizens or the
laws of the land by the rude master mariners trained in a
service which knew few principles but daring and prowess.
It is not strange, then, that in so distant and unprotected a
country as Iceland English sailors and sea-captains in an
effort to penetrate into a new field of enterprise should be
guilty of many violent and lawless acts. The first English
vessels which visited Iceland trafficked with the people in
a peaceful way, and sought to establish a friendly intercourse. The later buccaneering activity of English traders,
resulting in outrages, unusual even when measured by the
standards of those times, was due partly to the character
of the English mariners and seamen, but partly also to the
annoying interference of the royal government in a feeble
effort to maintain a monopoly of Icelandic trade.

From the beginning of the fifteenth century the English
engaged extensively in fisheries in Icelandic waters. In
1413 the annals record that thirty English fishing-smacks
came to Iceland.[3] The same year five English merchant
vessels also arrived at Vestmannaeyjar. One of these, a
royal vessel, brought letters from King Henry V to the
government and best men of Iceland, asking their permission to carry on trade in their harbors. But Eirik of Pomerania, king of the united Scandinavian realms, protested
against English traders visiting Iceland without his permission. In 1415 the same protest was renewed, but English trade with Iceland continued to grow. In that same
year six English ships entered the harbor of Hafnarfjord.
One of these was loaded for the return voyage with codfish
and a large sum of money, with which the royal *hirðstjóri*,
Vigfus Ivarsson, himself sailed to England.[4] The protests
of King Eirik finally moved Henry V to issue instructions
to his subjects forbidding all trade with Iceland, and fisheries in Icelandic waters, except in the manner which had
obtained from earlier ages. But the aggressive English
merchants paid little heed to the royal orders, and the

[3] G. Storm, *Islandske Annaler* (Lögmanns-annáll, year 1313).
[4] *Ibidem* (Lögmanns-annáll, year 1415).

number of English vessels in Icelandic waters continued to
grow, so that on April 13, 1419, according to the annals,
twenty-five English ships were wrecked on the coasts of
Iceland in a storm which lasted only three hours.[5]   That
the Icelanders should welcome this trade was quite natural.
The *hirðstjóri* Arnfin Thorsteinsson issued a permit to
English fishermen to carry on fisheries in Icelandic waters,
and at the Althing he joined with the lawmen and the people in a protest to the king against the attempts to exclude
English traders from Iceland.   To this remonstrance they
added a petition requesting the king's permission to trade
with the foreigners who brought them the goods which they
needed, but the king refused to grant them such a privilege.
This interdiction of foreign trade may have provoked many
of the deeds of violence henceforth perpetrated by English
traders in Iceland.   In 1420 they attacked Bessastadir,
arrested the royal official Hannes Pálsson and killed his
assistant Tideke Becker.[6]   In northern Iceland the crews
of three English ships landed in full battle array, killed the
royal official Jon Ibe, ill-treated the overseer of the estates
of the Hólar bishopric in the presence of the bishop and
committed various other outrages.   At Vestmannaeyjar
English ships commanded by John Morris and Rawlins
Terrington seized and carried away large quantities of codfish belonging to the king.   When Thorleif Arnason set sail
for Norway to report these outrages to the government, he
was attacked on the sea by an armed English vessel, and
was able to escape only with great difficulty.   The English
buccaneering traders were emboldened in their aggression
by the knowledge that the government of the united realms
was unable to control affairs in Iceland.   Queen Margaret
had suffered the naval power of her kingdoms to fall into
complete decay, and the weak and worthless Eirik of Pomerania who succeeded her on the throne devoted his attention chiefly to bootless foreign wars which lasted from 1416
till 1435.   Intercourse with Greenland had now ceased

[5] G. Storm, *Islandske Annaler* (Lögmanns-annáll, year 1419).

[6] Finn Magnusson, *Om de engelskes Handel og Færd paa Island i det
15de Aarhundrede* (Nordisk Tidsskrift for Oldkyndighed, vol. 11, p. 137 ff.).

completely, and the Norse colonies on that distant island disappeared. Iceland might have suffered a like fate but for the timely advent of the English traders, who, in spite of their lawlessness, proved of distinct benefit to Iceland. Untrammeled by royal decrees they continued their operations on a growing scale with constantly increasing violence. By lawless terror, directed especially against the helpless government officials, they were able for a time to exercise almost complete control over Icelandic trade. In 1422 two English captains, claiming that they had been denied the privilege of trading with Iceland, attacked Bessastadir and killed some people.[7] The following year English buccaneers ravaged northern Iceland, robbed and burned the churches of Hrisey, Husavik and Grimsey, seized a number of sheep and cattle, and even carried away many people into slavery abroad.[8] In 1424 Bessastadir was again attacked and plundered by bands led by the buccaneering sea-captains John Percy, John Pasdal and Thomas Dale, and several government officials were abducted. Another band under the leadership of John Selby landed at Fljót in northern Iceland, and seized a well-to-do proprietor, Brand Halldorsson, who had to ransom himself with the payment of a large quantity of codfish. The Vestmannaeyjar especially seem to have been a favorite rendezvous for English traders. In a report to the king regarding the aggression of the British merchants the *hirðstjóri* Hannes Pálsson wrote in 1425:

"There is an island near the coast of Iceland called Vestmannaey which belongs entirely to the king of Norway with all rights, so that no one except the king has any authority over it. To this island the English have come every year since this harmful traffic began. . . . On the island they build houses, erect large tents, dig up the ground, carry on fishery and make use of everything as if it were their own property. They have neither sought for nor ever obtained permission from the king's officials, but occupy the place by force, and do not permit the fish belonging to the king or any other persons to be shipped from the

[7] Espolin, *Árbækur*, part ii, ch. xiii.
[8] *Ibidem.*

island before they have loaded their own vessels according to
their pleasure." [9]

In his report he also complains of various outrages committed by British traders on the island. Nicolas Dalstun,
who in 1420 killed Tideke Becker at Bessastadir, and had
carried away large quantities of fish belonging to the king,
continued to be a leader of the English traders, many of
whom were guilty of various crimes. In 1425 the two
hirðstjórar, or royal governors, Hannes Pálsson and Balthasar van Dammin, went to the Vestmannaeyjar to arrest
the intruders and seize their vessels, but this attempt miscarried completely. When they arrived, they were attacked
by the English, who broke their boats so that they could
not even leave the island. They retreated to a favorable
position and sought to defend themselves, but the English
attacked them in battle array with bows and arrows and
other weapons. They were soon forced to surrender, on the
condition that they should be allowed to leave the island.
Captain Dalstun sanctioned this agreement, leaving the
difficulties to be settled by the kings of Denmark and England. But when the officials prepared to depart, they were
again attacked and robbed of all their belongings. Their
followers were finally allowed to leave, with the exception
of one who was treacherously slain, but Hannes Pálsson
and Balthasar van Dammin were brought as prisoners on
board the British ship and carried to England.[10] Hannes
Pálsson's report of the affair was submitted to the English
council and Admiral Duke of Exeter. It was also confirmed as correct by a commission assembled in Bergen to
investigate the affair. Such outrages were frequently repeated along the Icelandic coasts. Officials were intimidated, slain or carried out of the country; .trade and
fisheries not carried on by Englishmen were obstructed, and
boats and fishing-tackle were destroyed. So bold were the
raids on seaports and settlements, and so helpless were the

[9] Finn Magnusson, *Om de engelskes Handel og Færd paa Island i det
15de Aarhundrede*, p. 137 ff.

[10] Espolin, *Árbækur*, part ii, ch. xiv.

government officials that Iceland virtually passed under the complete control of the merchants of Hull, Lynn, York, London, Bristol and other English cities, which could keep large fleets of trading vessels on the sea. Many of these outrages seem to have been committed for the purpose of intimidating the people and the royal officials in order that complete control over Icelandic commerce might be established. In spite of these serious disturbances most of the English trade with Iceland was undoubtedly carried on in a peaceful way, but the annalists, who usually report only special events, paid but little attention to general conditions.

In 1431 King Eirik again made complaint to the king of England of the damage done his subjects through unlawful trade with Iceland and by robberies committed by English traders during a period of twenty years. For these encroachments he asked an indemnity of £40,000. From English state documents it appears that the king of England had tried repeatedly to stop this unlawful trade. In an agreement made by the two sovereigns at Copenhagen in Denmark, December 24, 1432,[11] he promised to punish those of his subjects who had committed robberies or other depredations in Iceland or elsewhere in the Danish-Norwegian realm. All persons who had been abducted should be returned to Iceland, and were to receive a fair compensation for the services which they had been forced to render in England.[12] The royal orders against unlawful trade with Iceland were to be renewed and enforced. On April 28, 1433, King Henry VI issued an order prohibiting trade with Iceland. This proved effective to the extent that no more outrages were committed, but illicit trade was not wholly discontinued. In 1440 King Henry issued licenses to two ships belonging to the bishop of Skálholt to buy goods in England, but since these were Icelandic vessels, this permission would not contravene his previous order.

Christopher of Bavaria was elevated to the throne of the united Northern kingdoms in 1442 and ruled till 1448,

[11] *Diplomatarium Islandicum*, vol. iv, p. 523 ff.

[12] Many of the commercial treaties with England are found in Rymer's *Foedera*, vol. ix, p. 322; vol. xi, pp. 264, 273, 551; vol. xii, pp. 374, 381.

when he was succeeded by Christian I of Oldenburg. In 1449 a new treaty was negotiated between Christian I and Henry VI, prohibiting English trade in Iceland, Haaloga-land and Finmarken without permission from the king of Denmark-Norway, the treaty to remain in force till 1451.[13] That English trade with Iceland continued in spite of these measures appears from the following provision in a law promulgated by King Christian at the time of his coronation in 1450:

"We declare all Englishmen and Irish who trade with Iceland to be outlawed and their property to be confiscated, unless they have our sealed permit, and they may be lawfully seized anywhere."

By new prohibitory orders King Henry VI sought to restrain his subjects from the unlawful trade, but the licenses already granted he permitted to remain in force.[14] Like his predecessors King Christian became involved in useless and expensive foreign wars. Dynastic interests received his attention to such a degree that commercial and colonial affairs were almost completely neglected. In 1453 he appointed the chieftain Björn Thorleifsson governor of Iceland and instructed him to resist the British traders as vigorously as possible. But how such an order was to be carried out seems to have been no part of King Christian's royal forethought, as no effort was ever made to aid the governor. On a voyage to Iceland in 1456 Björn and his wife were seized by the British and carried to England. After a time they were released and were finally able to reach their destination; but in his attempt to carry out the royal instructions Björn was finally slain by the angry British merchants[15] in a clash which led to serious difficulties.

In 1463 King Christian I issued an ordinance forbidding

[13] *Diplomatarium Islandicum,* vol. iv, p. 766.
[14] Finn Magnusson, *Om de engelskes Handel og Færd paa Island i det 15de Aarhundrede,* p. 122. The licenses are found in Rymer's *Foedera,* vol. x, pp. 645, 659, 682, 711, 762.
[15] Arild Huitfeld, *Danmarks Riges Krønike,* tom. ii, p. 904. Björn á Skardsá, *Annálar,* p. 50.

Icelanders to trade with foreign merchants who did not pay the *sekkjagjald*, or duty levied on Icelandic goods imported to Norway.[16] Two years later he concluded a treaty of friendship with Edward IV of England, which should remain in force during the lifetime of both sovereigns. Regarding trade with Iceland this document contains the following provision:

"The king of England shall see to it that unless they ask and receive permission from the king of Norway, his subjects shall not trade with Iceland; nor shall they sail thither, or to Haalogaland or Finnmarken, unless they be driven thither by storm, and they shall not then carry on any trade there." [17]

That these often repeated agreements led to any definite results does not appear. The attempts to prevent trade only aroused the anger of the English merchants, who cared little for treaties which the king of Denmark-Norway was in no position to enforce. In the harbor of Ríf in Snæfelssysla they had established themselves in large numbers, and were carrying on a lively trade. In 1467 they seem to have laid careful plans to attack the governor, Björn Thorleifsson, who was especially hated because he had been very active in collecting the duties imposed on foreign trade. When he arrived at Ríf with a large escort, they fell upon him and slew him together with seven of his men, as already noted. Twenty men made their escape, but his son was taken prisoner. As soon as Ólof, Björn's wife, was able to secure the release of her son by paying a large ransom, she gathered forces and attacked the lawless merchants at Ríf. Three of their ships were seized after a struggle in which many of the sailors were killed. Fifty others who were taken prisoners were released after being

---

[16] Magnús Ketilsson, *Forordninger og aabne Breve,* vol. i, p. 51. The *sekkjagjald* appeared for the first time in 1382 in the reign of Olaf Haakonsson. The king claimed one-fourth interest in every ship which sailed to Iceland, also six out of every 120 fish, and five per cent. of every roll of *vaðmál* and of every barrel of sulphur and train-oil. This tax was collected both from Icelanders and from Norwegian merchants and foreign traders. Dr. Ernst Baasch, *Die Handelsfahrt der Deutschen, Forschungen zur hamburgischen Handelsgeschichte,* vol. i, p. 66.

[17] *Diplomatarium Islandicum,* vol. v, p. 453 ff.

held in custody for a short period.[18]   In 1468 Ólof sailed to
Denmark with her son and reported these events to King
Christian, who is said to have complimented her as a *spec-
tabilis mulier* (i.e., a woman pleasant to behold). A new
governor, Thorleif Arason, was then sent to Iceland. British subjects who sailed to Iceland without the king's permission were outlawed, and four English vessels were seized
in the Sound as compensation for the loss suffered by the
king and Björn Thorleifsson's widow. The English government, thinking that the Hanseatic League had brought
about the seizure of the English merchant-men, arrested
all the Hanseatic merchants in London. War broke out between England and Denmark-Norway in 1469; but it was
not carried on with vigor by either side, and does not seem
to have interfered with English trade with Iceland, which
was still carried on as before.[19] By the peace treaty negotiated in 1474 the old relations between the two realms
were restored. By a new treaty of friendship concluded
between the two kings in 1490 the English received the
privilege of free trade with Iceland for the period of seven
years.[20] The English merchants paid high prices for herring and codfish, Iceland's chief articles of export during
this period. The goods which they brought to the country
were of good quality, consisting of commodities most needed
by the people. Their trade was, therefore, of the greatest
value to the Icelanders, and might have been still more
advantageous if the Danish-Norwegian government had
permitted free and peaceful intercourse, and had limited
its interference to the maintenance of law and order in
the island.

The lack of wisdom and efficiency which characterized
the civil administration in Iceland at this time found its
counterpart in the incompetence and worldly-mindedness
shown in the management of ecclesiastical affairs. During

[18] Espolin, *Árbœkur*, part ii, p. 66 ff. Björn á Skardsá, *Annálar*, vol. I,
p. 25 f; p. 50.

[19] Finn Magnusson, *Om de Engelskes Handel og Fœrd paa Island*. Th.
Thoroddsen, *Landfrœdissaga Islands*, vol. i, p. 113 ff. Arild Huitfeld,
Danmarks Riges Krønike, tom. ii, p. 917.

[20] *Diplomatarium Islandicum*, vol. viii, p. 78.

intervals one or both of the bishoprics might be left vacant because new bishops were not appointed. But this was scarcely as harmful as repeated appointments to the leading positions in the church of uninterested foreigners and incompetent old men, or of unprincipled adventurers who used their high ecclesiastical offices for the most mercenary and selfish ends. From 1403 till 1415 or 1419 the Hólar bishopric remained vacant for reasons not known. Bishop Vilchin of Skálholt went to Norway in 1406, and died there the same year, and as his successor, Jon, did not arrive in Iceland till 1408, the country remained without bishops for a period of two years. Bishop Jon died in 1413 and was succeeded by Arni Olafsson, a native Icelander who seems to have belonged to some monastic order. During his stay in Norway he had been chaplain in the home of the rich nobleman Haakon Sigurdsson of Giske. He had visited Rome, and was consecrated bishop in Lübeck by order of the pope. He is described as athletic, generous and capable in everything which he undertook. He loved display and showed great talent as a flattering courtier and a collector of money. As a royal favorite he succeeded in being appointed *hirðstjóri* over all Iceland, and he was also placed in charge of the vacant bishopric of Hólar. He was thus able upon his arrival in his diocese in 1415 to exercise the highest authority both in church and state. But as he had only his own interest at heart, this extraordinary official authority only gave him the opportunity to display the rapacity and love of power which characterized his whole career. On a journey through the Hólar diocese he collected property of all kinds and had it brought to his residence at Skálholt. He caused expensive improvements to be made in the Skálholt church and bishop's residence, and costly furniture was bought. Because of his liberality he was nicknamed "the generous." Saving was no part of his administrative policy, as he could always secure more goods and money on new journeys through his dioceses. Such government could only be extremely oppressive. But since Bishop Arni conducted himself in all respects as a chieftain, the people condoned his foibles to such an extent that

he even enjoyed some degree of popularity. In 1419 he
went to Norway, probably for the purpose of rendering an
account to the royal government, as he owed the king's
treasury a large sum of money. How this difficulty was
finally adjusted is not known, but he never returned to
Iceland. His successor was the unworthy royal favorite
Jon Gerecksson (John Jerichini), who through the king's
influence had been chosen archbishop of Upsala in Sweden,
but because of his vicious life was tried by order of the
pope and forced to resign from his archdiocese. The king,
who still favored him, caused him to be elected bishop of
Skálholt, though it must have been apparent to all that he
was wholly unfit to hold a higher ecclesiastical office. He
came to Skálholt from England in 1425, accompanied by a
band of followers which he seems to have gathered in the
British Isles, unprincipled adventurers so devoid of moral
character that he could not have controlled them even if
he had desired to do so. With this band of rowdies he
traveled from one district to another, as Bishop Gudmund
Arason had done two centuries earlier. All sorts of deeds
of violence were committed even against the leading men
of the country. Teit Gunnlaugsson, one of the most prominent young men in eastern Iceland, and Thorvard Loptsson, son of the powerful Lopt Guttormsson of Mödruvellir
in the northern districts, were seized without cause and
imprisoned at Skálholt and subjected to all sorts of indig-
nities. After making their escape they laid a plot to
revenge themselves on the bishop and his band. In this
undertaking they were stimulated to redoubled efforts by
new provocations. The bishop's illegitimate son Magnus,
the leader of his unruly band of followers, had been wooing
Margaret Vigfusdottir, one of the most prominent young
ladies in all Iceland. She ignored him, as might be expected, and in order to revenge himself he proceeded to
her residence, Kirkjubol, killed her brother and set fire to
her house. Margaret saved her life only with great difficulty, and vowed that she would marry no one but the man
who possessed sufficient courage to wreak vengeance upon
her assailant. Thorvard Loptsson appeared as her cham-

pion and suitor, and Bishop Jon began to realize that serious trouble was brewing. But when Magnus fled from Iceland, he thought that the storm might blow over without dangerous consequences. In July Thorvard Loptsson and his associate Teit united their forces in the neighborhood of Skálholt, where many people were gathering to celebrate the Thorlaksmas. A number of tents had been erected, and Thorvard and his men were able to approach unobserved. When Teit and his band also arrived, and the bishop learned of their presence, he fled to the church with his priests and associates. Attired in his priestly vestments he began to sing the mass before the church altar, but fifty men led by Arni Magnusson of Dal effected an entrance, dragged him from the church, tied him in a sack and drowned him in the river Bruará. His followers were hunted down and slain.[21] No action seems to have been taken against the slayers of the bishop either by the church or by the royal government. Thorvard Loptsson married Margaret Vigfusdottir, and both he and his associate, Teit Gunnlaugsson, lived long and enjoyed the people's highest esteem.

After Jon Gerecksson's death one Jon, and later Godsvin became bishops of Skálholt. Godsvin died or left Iceland in 1448, and was succeeded by a German ecclesiastic by the name of Marcellus, a royal favorite who was made bishop of Skálholt through the influence of King Christian I, though he was found unworthy by the Roman Curia to become archbishop of Nidaros. Marcellus did not even visit his diocese, but used it as a source of income till his death in 1460. During his incumbency the affairs of the diocese were administered by Gottskalk Gottskalksson of Hólar, who acted as vicarius, and with the consent of the king and the archbishop of Nidaros exercised supreme authority both in ecclesiastical and secular affairs in Iceland. After the death of Jon Stephansson Krabbe, Marcellus' successor, in 1465, three native Icelanders succeeded one another as bishops of Skálholt: Svein Pétursson, 1465-

[21] G. Storm, *Islandske Annaler* (Gottskalks Annaler, 1433, 1467). Finnur Jonsson, *Historia Ecclesiastica Islandiæ*, vol. ii, p. 471 ff.

1475; Magnus Eyjolfsson, 1477-1490; and Stephan Jonsson, 1491-1518. Bishop Stephan Jonsson was a man of high moral character, an active and able administrator, who kept up the cathedral school and created system and order in his diocese. He was succeeded by Ögmund Pálsson, the last Catholic bishop of Skálholt, in 1521.

Olaf Rögnvaldsson, bishop of Hólar, who died in 1495, was a harsh and autocratic man, who was constantly involved in lawsuits, in which he was usually the aggressor. He did not spare his opponents, but forced them to pay heavy fines, and in his efforts to enrich himself he seized their property and estates. His successor Gottskalk Nikolasson was equally harsh and greedy. He lived in concubinage, and it seems to have been his chief care to acquire property for himself and his children. In his relations with the people of his diocese he showed an arrogance and despotic temper which brought him into serious conflicts with the leading men. Clashes had often occurred between the chieftains and the churchmen who sought to establish the supremacy of the Roman hierarchy, but the bishops had usually been moved by a desire to promote the interest of the church by enforcing the principles of ecclesiastical ascendency. No such redeeming features of principles or churchly interest is to be found in the conduct of prelates like Olaf Röngvaldsson or Gottskalk Nikolasson. Entrenched in the power of their high ecclesiastical office they used it ruthlessly only to gain their own mercenary and selfish ends. The noted controversy between Bishop Gottskalk and the lawman Jon Sigmundsson shows how completely they rejected all spirit of fairness and reconciliation in attempting to enforce their own arbitrary dictates.

Claiming that he had found that an unpermissible degree of blood relationship existed between Jon and his wife, who, according to the bishop's contention, were third cousins, he summoned Jon to appear before him at Hólar. When Jon disregarded the summons, he caused heavy fines to be imposed on him. Jon was able to clear himself of most of the charges brought against him by the bishop, but this only increased the relentlessness of the angry prelate. He laid Jon in ban, and summoned his wife to appear at Hólar. She was forced to confess to the bishop, to part from her husband, and to pay a fine of 300 *hundrað*, as she did not have the courage to resist. But even this did not satisfy Bishop Gottskalk. He again cited Jon to appear before him, laid him in the highest ban of the church, and imposed new fines upon him. Jon now went abroad to plead his case to the king and the archbishop. As he was able to show that Bishop Gottskalk had extorted much property from him, had seized many of his estates, and had laid him in ban wrongfully, the archbishop decided that the Skálholt bishop, Stephan Jonsson, should examine his case. The crown prince, who was acting as regent, appointed him lawman in the northern and western districts of Iceland, and ordered that Björn Gudnason, lawman in western Iceland, should decide concerning the estates which the bishop had seized. On Jon's return to Iceland Bishop Stephan Jonsson confirmed the decree of Bishop Gottskalk against him. Björn Gudnason decided that Jon's estates should be returned to him, but this decision was annulled by Bishop Gottskalk. In order to settle the controversy Jon finally agreed to pay the bishop 200 *hundrað* and to swear him an oath that he would obey all rules which he might establish. He was now freed from the ban, but the agreement did not last long. On a visit to Hólar Jon was attacked and wounded with a knife, but the bishop paid no attention to the outrage committed. Instead he summoned Jon to appear before him to receive absolution for his sins. When Jon refused, he was laid in ban by both bishops. He now retired to western Iceland to his friend Björn Gudnason, and the two sought to aid one another in the struggle with Bishop Gottskalk. Jon's son Einar was also accused by the bishop of having aided his father. He was laid in ban and his estates were seized. Jon again went abroad to lay his case before the king. He received a royal letter of protection and the king also issued instructions to the governor of Iceland that Jon's estates should be returned to him. But when the governor arrived in Iceland it is said that the bishop through bribes turned him against Jon. At the Althing it was decided that Jon should not be heard, as it would only tend to disturb the peace. Bishop Gottskalk also tried to kill him by having him shoved from a narrow bridge into the river. Jon fell in, but was rescued. The chieftains had tried to form a confederation to protect themselves against the aggression of the bishops, but this too proved futile, as the church exercised so complete control over the minds and conscience of the people that they did not dare to resist the bishops for fear of ban and excommunication. When Björn Gudnason died, Jon Sigmundsson stood friendless and alone, deprived of his wife and stripped of his property. He died in poverty in 1520. The same year Bishop Gottskalk Nikolasson also died. He was succeeded by John Arason, the last Catholic bishop of Hólar, who was consecrated bishop in 1524.[22] In the struggle for supremacy the bishops had at last won a decisive victory, but it weakened rather than strengthened their position as leaders in the church. Upon the advent of the Reformation they soon discovered that they were waging a losing fight, as they found themselves antagonized by their former influential opponents. Their greed and arrogance deprived them of the support of the best men, and hastened the overthrow of Catholic hierarchic rule.

In the period 1430-1440 the Germans also began to trade with Iceland. This trade is first mentioned in the "Hanserecesse," or official records of the Hanseatic merchants, in the year 1434-1435.[23] The first German merchants who came to Iceland were from Lübeck and Danzig, but in 1476 the Hamburgers also dispatched two vessels to Iceland, and they soon grew strong enough to outstrip their competitors. King Christian I of Denmark-Norway, who was always in difficult financial straits and needed the good-will of the German merchants, granted them the privilege to trade directly with Iceland, without submitting the question to

[22] Finnur Jonsson, *Historia Ecclesiastica Islandiæ*, vol. iv, p. 322 ff.; p. 344 ff.
[23] *Forschungen zur hamburgischen Handelsgeschichte*, vol. i (Die Islandsfahrt der Deutschen von Ernst Baasch). Th. Thoroddsen, *Landfrœdissaga Íslands*, vol. i, p. 128 ff.

the Council of the Realm. According to a royal decree of 1480 they were not allowed to stay in Iceland over winter, but their trade increased so rapidly that in 1482 the Hanseatic merchants in Bergen made complaints to a meeting of Hanseatic representatives in Lübeck of these new competitors in the trade of the North. The Hamburgers replied that the privileges of the merchants in Bergen did not extend to the region north of Bergen; that the king had a right to grant the Hamburg merchants the privilege to trade with Iceland. At that time the Icelandic articles of export were of far more importance to European trade than in later periods when the same goods could be obtained in many other countries. The chief staple was fish, for which there was a great demand throughout continental Europe. Before the discovery of the rich Newfoundland cod-fisheries Iceland and Norway were the chief sources of supply of this important commodity. Sulphur was another product obtained for a long time chiefly in Iceland. Falcons, eiderdown, wool and woolen cloth, mutton, sheepskins, butter, tallow and train-oil were also important articles of export. The goods most needed in Iceland were grain and flour, timber, iron, linen, pitch and tar. Beer, malt, sugar and honey were also general articles of import. As the grain export from Hamburg tended to create shortage and high prices at home, such dissatisfaction resulted that in 1483 the city council was forced to pass an ordinance prohibiting trade with Iceland. The ordinance was formally obeyed, but ships for Iceland were loaded in other places, and the traffic continued. King Hans of Denmark-Norway, who succeeded his father Christian I in 1482, had signed a convention with the Swedish and Norwegian councils that he would forbid the Hanseatic merchants to engage in Icelandic trade.[24] In 1490 he sought to limit their commerce by allowing the English and Hollanders to trade with Iceland,[25] but the Hollanders never engaged extensively in this traffic, and the English intercourse with Iceland was rapidly declining. King Hans' successor, Christian II, was

[24] Ernst Baasch, *Die Islandsfahrt der Deutschen,* p. 16.
[25] *Diplomatarium Islandicum,* vol. vi, p. 689.

an avowed enemy of the Hanseatic merchants. In 1513 he issued an ordinance prohibiting their trade with Iceland.[26] He sought to create a strong Scandinavian trading association which could compete successfully with the Hanseatic merchants. But the plan came to naught, as a revolt drove him from his throne in 1523.

During the reign of Frederick I the German trade with Iceland entered a new phase of development. English and German merchants took part in the deliberations of the Althing, and succeeded in passing a resolution modifying the ordinance which prohibited foreign traders from remaining in Iceland over winter. Young boys and persons who were not engaged in trade were now allowed to remain over winter in the island. This participation of foreigners in the deliberations of the Althing aroused such resentment in Norway that Archbishop Olaf Engelbrektsson of Nidaros in 1531 complained that the Hamburgers held Iceland and the Faroe Islands as fiefs.[27] At this time they seem to have gained the upper hand in Iceland, but they were not yet sole masters of Icelandic trade. The English were vigorously resisting their encroachments. From 1486 till 1532 eight severe clashes are known to have occurred between English and German traders in Iceland. The severest of these took place in 1532, when an English trading vessel, the "Peter Gibson" from London, commanded by John Breye, came to the harbor of Grindavik in Iceland, where it remained for twenty days. The Englishmen carried on fishing and sold the goods which they had brought. But Breye quarreled with the royal *hirðstjóri*, refusing to pay the required toll. Trouble also arose between the English and German traders, the outcome of which was a severe fight. Two hundred and eighty men from eight German vessels attacked the English at two o'clock at night, killed fifteen men, and robbed the ships, so that the English merchants suffered a loss of £1500. King Henry VIII turned to the government of Hamburg and demanded an indemnity. But since King Frederick I of Denmark-Norway

[26] *Diplomatarium Islandicum*, vol. viii, p. 463.
[27] *Ibidem*, vol. ix, p. 683.

supported the Hamburgers, he was unable to secure a satisfactory settlement.[28]

The trade of the Hamburg merchants with Iceland reached its height about 1530, but we possess no statistics regarding the volume of this trade at this time or of the number of ships engaged in it. The laws forbidding foreign merchants to remain in Iceland over winter were now little heeded. The growing influence of the Germans in Iceland can be seen also from the fact that at this time a German church was built at Hafnarfjord. In 1538 the Lübeckers resumed their trade with Iceland, but the Hamburgers, who regarded them as rivals, sought to lay hindrances in their way. In 1540 King Christian III of Denmark-Norway took energetic steps to prevent foreigners from trading with Iceland and from keeping their own fishing-boats in the island. In 1547 he granted Iceland to the mayor of Copenhagen for a certain yearly tax.[29] His policy with regard to Iceland, like that of his predecessors, was wholly dictated by considerations of revenue. The rich sulphur deposits in Iceland were sought by the Hamburg merchants, but the king decided to stop the export of this commodity. The Hamburgers sent a delegation to see the king, but without results. When they attempted to ship sulphur from Iceland contrary to royal orders, he seized their vessels in the Sound and elsewhere, and forced them to pay a fine of 10,000 thaler. This led the king to forbid also the sale of other Icelandic commodities. In 1565 he offered to open to the Hamburgers ten Icelandic harbors if they would loan him 100,000 thaler.[30] But as they feared that ultimately they would have to pay the whole sum, they rejected the offer, though he threatened to stop their entire trade. During the last decades of the sixteenth century the merchants of Bremen also entered into sharp competition with Hamburg to obtain trade privileges in Iceland. They complained that the Hamburgers forced them

[28] Espolin, *Árbœkur*, part iii, ch. lxxvii.

[29] *Diplomatarium Islandicum*, vol. xi, 529, 578. Magnus Ketilsson, *Forordninger og aabne Breve*, vol. i, p. 255 ff.

[30] Baasch, *Die Islandsfahrt der Deutschen*, p. 42.

out of Iceland in an unfriendly and unneighborly way.
Also between Lübeck and Hamburg there was constant
rivalry and contention.

About 1560 Danish merchants began to trade with Iceland, and competing cities obtained from the king the privilege to enter different Icelandic harbors. Since Hamburg
and the king of Denmark-Norway quarreled constantly, the
king found opportunity to thwart the Hamburgers in regard to their traffic with Iceland. In 1572 all Icelandic
harbors were closed to them.[31] Two years later the regulation was made that the fish which had hitherto been sent
to Hamburg should be brought to England. By such measures German trade with Iceland was destroyed in the next
few years. What this interference with commercial intercourse would ultimately mean to the Icelanders the king
does not seem to have seriously considered. But in 1579
former trade relations were finally restored.[32] The volume
of this trade at that time is shown to some extent by the
number of vessels engaged in it, though the size of the vessels is not known. During some years few German vessels
would come to Iceland, but in 1590 seventeen ships arrived.
During the years 1595-1598 the yearly number was fourteen, sixteen, fifteen and seventeen vessels respectively, an
average which was quite well maintained for many years
subsequent.[33]

In the reign of Christian IV German trade with Iceland
ceased. In a letter of July 24, 1601, the king notified the
Hamburg merchants that he wished to reserve the Icelandic
trade for his own subjects. A like notice was also given
the Council of Bremen. In vain the Hamburgers sought to
persuade the king to restore their trading privileges. In
1602 he granted the cities of Copenhagen, Malmø and
Helsingør the Icelandic trade as a monopoly.[34] The Germans could no longer carry on trade with Iceland directly,
but they adapted themselves as far as possible to the altered

[31] *Norske Rigsregistranter,* vol. i, p. 440, vol. ii, p. 4.
[32] Baasch, *Die Islandsfahrt der Deutschen,* p. 47.
[33] *Ibidem,* p. 48.
[34] *Norske Rigsregistranter,* vol. iii, p. 656.

conditions by engaging in the Icelandic trade for the interest and under the control of Danish merchants. Smuggling was also carried on, not only by the Germans, but also by the Hollanders and the English. Toward the close of the reign of Christian IV the Hamburgers again sought to obtain the right to trade with Iceland. In 1645 they offered to lease the island for the sum of 500,000 thaler. But the king seems to have stipulated conditions which they would not accept. Thirty years later the matter was again considered, but without results.

The period 1400-1550 was an era of retrogression and decay in Iceland. The Black Death had sapped the people's strength. At the bishop's seat of Skálholt all learned men died, except Bishop Vilchin himself. In the bishopric of Hólar only six priests, three deacons and a monk remained of all men possessing learning. The monasteries stood empty. The interruption of commercial intercourse with the mother country tended to increase the growing economic distress, and although the traffic of English and German traders brought some relief, the terror and lawlessness usually accompanying it could only tend to disrupt the weakened intellectual and social life. The old literary activity ceased, and religious life struggled under the evil incubus of indifferent foreign and mercenary bishops. For a period even the schools seem to have died out, as nothing is heard of any institution of learning in Iceland from 1393 till 1474.[35] Only in the monasteries could any attention be given to learning, but even here it must have been done only in a feeble and inefficient way. In 1488 Lopt Jonsson sold the estate Hraunhafnarbakki to the abbot of the monastery of Helgafell, on the condition that he should instruct Lopt's son so that he could receive consecration as subdeacon. The next abbot of that monastery, Narfi (1511), is known to have devoted a part of his time to teaching, and the same was done in other monasteries.[36] In 1500 Jon Arason, the later bishop of Skálholt, received instruction from Einar Bendiktsson, abbot of the monastery of

[35] Jon Thorkelsson, *Om Digtningen på Island*, p. 8 ff.
[36] Finnur Jonsson, *Historia Ecclesiastica Islandiæ*, vol. iv, p. 73.

Thverá,[37] and Gisli Jonsson, bishop of Skálholt from 1558 till 1587, received instruction from Alexius Pálsson, abbot of the monastery of Videy. Towards the close of the fifteenth century some efforts were made to revive the schools at the cathedral churches. Stephan Jonsson, bishop of Skálholt, 1491-1518, established a school at his bishop's s at, but it was not continued by his successor, Ögmund Pálsson. School is also said to have been held at Hólar at the time of Bishop Gottskalk Nikolasson (1498-1520), but this work was not continued in the days of Jon Arason, the last Catholic bishop of the diocese. In 1542 Latin schools were to be established at the monasteries of Videy and Helgafell according to royal decree,[38] but little progress was made till 1552, when a permanent Latin school was organized at each bishop's seat. At first these schools were not very efficient, as the leading teachers were foreigners, and the native teachers lacked the necessary education. But interest in learning was reviving. From the latter part of the fifteenth century till the establishing of the Reformation many Icelanders again went abroad to study. Svein Petursson, bishop of Skálholt, 1465-1476, and his brother Odd had received the degree of M.A. and B.A. respectively. In 1472 Stephan Jonsson went to France to study. Ögmund Pálsson traveled in England and the Netherlands, and Olaf Hjaltason is said to have spent six years at the Latin school in Bergen, Norway (1515-1521). Odd Gottskalksson had also studied in Norway. Gizur Einarsson studied in Germany, and Jon Einarsson, together with the two brothers Martein Einarsson and Glerauga-Pétur, traveled and studied in Germany and England. After the Reformation the Icelanders who sought higher education usually studied at the university of Copenhagen or in Germany.[39]

In the field of literature history writing had ceased before 1400. After that time prose production was limited to letters and documents (*máldagar*) and a few annals, im-

---

[37] *Biskupasögur*, vol. ii, p. 326.

[38] Magnus Ketilsson, *Forordninger og aabne Breve*, vol. i, p. 234 ff.

[39] Jon Thorkelsson, *Om Digtningen på Island*, p. 7 ff.

portant only as historical material shedding some light upon an age about which so little information exists. The *rímur,* or ballad poetry, continued to flourish. Professional rhapsodists appeared who traveled from house to house singing *rímur* for pay. So popular became this form of amusement that the clergy felt called upon to inveigh energetically against it as inimical to public morals. "At wakes and other gatherings, and likewise at weddings and parties, there is scarcely any other form of amusement or entertainment than this nonsensical poetry, which God pity!" says Gudbrand Thorlaksson in the introduction to his hymn-book, 1589. Religious songs in scaldic verse were produced in Iceland ever since Christianity became permanently established, but during the period of national decadence also this form of literary activity languished, until shortly before the Reformation. In the fifteenth century a revival of religious interest resulted in the production of a new religious poetry written in rhymed verse, evidently according to the pattern of Latin hymns. As in the case of the *rímur* and other folk poesy, melodies were soon provided also for the religious songs. The singing of hymns as a part of religious worship took its beginning in Iceland already in this century. No Icelandic hymnal exists from the Catholic period, but the number of religious songs about Virgin Mary and other saints was growing rapidly in the period immediately preceding the Reformation. Besides the two national saints of Iceland; Bishop Jon Ögmundsson of Hólar, who died in 1121, and Bishop Thorlak Thorlaksson of Skálholt, who died in 1193, many other saints were venerated. St. Olaf, king of Norway, who fell in the battle of Stiklestad in 1030, was especially popular. Fifty-two churches were dedicated to him in Iceland, and sagas and other literary works were written about him. Virgin Mary was the most generally venerated of all saints in Iceland as elsewhere. About 150 churches were dedicated to her. The great number of songs written to her also testify to the popularity of this cultus. Of the apostles, Peter was the most popular saint. To him sixty churches were dedicated; twenty were dedicated to St. John the Apostle, twenty to

St. John the Baptist, thirteen to St. Andrew, and three to St. Paul. About these and other apostles many songs are found. The cross was generally venerated throughout Iceland in Catholic times. Crosses which were regarded as especially sacred were found in many districts, the most noted being the one at Kaldadarnes, to which pilgrimages were made from all parts of southern Iceland, especially at Krossmas (September 14). All pilgrims brought votive offerings to the cross, unless they were beggars. Sick persons who were unable to walk were glad if they could get far enough to see it, as they thought that this would be sure to bring them relief. In 1518 the pilgrims going to Kaldadarnes met with a great accident. About fifty persons were drowned in the Ölfusá, among others the priest Bödvar Jonsson of Gardar in Alptanes and his daughter. The veneration of the Kaldadarnes cross seems to have culminated shortly before the Reformation. In 1548 the cross was removed by the first Lutheran bishop, Gizur Einarsson, and stored in an obscure place. It was later destroyed by Bishop Gisli Jonsson in 1560.

13. The Reformation in Iceland

The Lutheran Reformation, which was gaining a firm footing everywhere in the North, was brought to Iceland during the period of lowest ebb in Icelandic national life. If it had come as a religious revival in response to a spontaneous public sentiment, it might have produced a new awakening in Iceland, as it had done in many other lands. But the Icelanders had hitherto remained wholly untouched by the movement of religious reform and the intellectual renaissance which accompanied it. They clung faithfully to the established doctrines and the forms of Catholic worship, which had become a system of intellectual and social life as well as of religious belief. The old ways were still dear to them, and since no desire for any change existed, the Reformation was not welcomed as the dawn of a new era. It was thrust upon the people almost as a surprise in the form of royal decrees backed by military force, promoted by methods which remind us of the introduction of Christianity, forced on an apathetic populace under the frowning brows of an angry king. In the establishing of the Reformation similar scenes were enacted. Again the royal government bent itself to the task of forcing upon the Icelanders the king's religion. The first effect of this procedure could only be negative, resulting in the destruction of what still remained of ancient culture. But it can not be denied that the Reformation even in this unattractive form proved so powerful a stimulus to the weakened energies of the Icelandic people that after its introduction traces were soon seen of new intellectual vigor and literary life.

As already noted, the two last Catholic bishops in Iceland were Ögmund Pálsson of Skálholt and Jon Arason of Hólar, both very interesting as types of Icelandic chieftains of this period, rather than as representatives of the Catholic clergy. Bishop Ögmund, the elder of the two, had sought to hinder Jon's election, and a hostile feeling existed between the two prelates. Ögmund, who was an able and energetic administrator, acted no less as ruler than as bishop of his diocese. Though proud and ambitious he was on the whole well-meaning and generous, but withal an arrogant chieftain, violent of temper and wholly unable to brook opposition. Jon Arason was a chieftain to a still higher degree. More gifted than his rival, dignified in appearance, charming in manners, cheerful and spirited in conversation, he was a born leader, highly admired by his adherents, but a firebrand against all opponents. Jon was born at Gryta in Eyjafjord, probably in 1474. At the age of thirty-four he became priest at Helgastadir, and two years later (1510) at Hrafnagil. Upon the death of Bishop Gottskalk Nicolasson he became provost and acting bishop in the Hólar diocese (1520). In 1524 he was consecrated bishop.[1] The statement in the "Biskupasögur" that he knew no Latin

[1] *Biskupasögur*, ii, p. 317 ff; 338 ff. Finnur Jonsson, *Historia Ecclesiastica Islandiœ*, vol. ii, p. 644 ff. *Det danske Videnskabs Selskabs Skrifter*, vol. v, viii. *Safn til Sögu Islands*, vol. i. Jon Egilsson, *Biskupa-annálar*. Björn á Skardsá, *Annálar*, year 1524.

is probably erroneous. As he is said to have received instruction in his youth from the learned Einar Bendiktsson, abbot of the monastery of Thverá, it must be assumed that he also studied Latin, which in those days was the principal subject of instruction in all schools.[2] But he was probably no Latin scholar. From youth up he lived in concubinage with Helga Sigurdsdottir, and reared a family of sons and daughters. But this relation seems to have been tolerated at this time even within the church. "Although priests were not allowed to marry," says the saga writer, "holy and godfearing fathers would permit them (I know indeed not with what authority) to have concubines instead of wedded wives. And as the priestly office was then held in much higher esteem than in these degenerate times, it was easy for the priests to get women, so that they often got the daughters, sisters and relatives of chieftains for their helpmates. Proper and lawful agreement was entered into by both parties, so that nothing was lacking of real marriage but the náme. It was not thought proper for them to enter into holy wedlock, which was otherwise solemnized in church in presence of the congregation, but the binding of the agreement with festivals, documents and formal betrothals was not forbidden."[3]

Though the domains of the two bishops were clearly limited to their respective dioceses, clashes between them were unavoidable whenever they met at the Althing. At their first meeting in 1526 Ögmund was accompanied by an escort of 1300 men. Jon brought 900. Armed conflict between the two hostile groups was averted only through the efforts of the parish priests, who succeeded in maintaining peace on the condition that the controversy should be settled by a fight between two champions selected for the purpose. This duel, contrary even to Icelandic civil law, was fought on an island in the Öxará in the presence of the two bishops and their adherents. Ögmund's representative succeeded in throwing his opponent and was de-

[2] *Biskupasögur*, vol. ii, p. 569.
[3] Jon Espolin, *Árbœkur*, iii, 79, 80. Gudbrand Vigfusson, *Icelandic Prose Reader*, 433 ff.

clared the victor, but Jon and his party were not well satisfied. The following day the cathedral church at Skálholt was destroyed by fire, a calamity which almost overwhelmed Bishop Ögmund. As he considered it a chastisement from heaven, it softened his enmity towards his opponent. He soon set to work with great energy to rebuild the church, and the task was almost completed before his death.

The progress of the Lutheran Reformation in the North, the friendly attitude of King Frederick I of Denmark-Norway to the new movement, and the fact that his son Christian, heir apparent to the throne, and other leading men openly accepted Luther's doctrines, soon made the Icelandic bishops forget their personal rivalries and draw closer together in mutual support against the danger threatening the Catholic hierarchy. Even in Iceland traces of Lutheran influence began to appear. Direct communication with Germany was maintained by the Hanseatic merchants trading in Iceland, who brought Lutheran books from Hamburg.

Jon Einarsson, priest at Skálholt, who had read some of Luther's writings, had been so impressed by them that in a sermon at Candlemas he inveighed against the veneration of saints, which he called idolatry. When Bishop Ögmund reprimanded him, he defended himself and quoted further from the epistles of the Apostle Paul in support of the view that priests had the right to marry. Still more grieved was Bishop Ögmund by the apostasy of Gizur Einarsson from the Catholic faith. For several years Gizur had remained in the bishop's household as a special friend, and had been sent by him to school in Hamburg. After hearing Luther and Melanchthon preach in Wittenberg he had accepted the Lutheran faith. Upon his return home he was repudiated by Ögmund, who had learned what had happened. By still pretending to be a Catholic Gizur succeeded in regaining the favor and confidence of the bishop, who was growing old and was more than ever in need of able assistance under the growing difficulties. Another young man in whom Ögmund had placed great confidence was Odd Gottskalksson, son of Gottskalk Nikolasson, former bishop of Hólar. Odd had been reared in Norway, where he had been trained for the priesthood. Later he had studied in Denmark and Germany, and had become a secret convert to the Lutheran faith. On his arrival in Skálholt he became Bishop Ögmund's private secretary. He was secretly engaged in translating the Bible into Icelandic, but he made the bishop believe that he was busy copying Catholic theological works and church laws. One day Ögmund discovered the nature of his literary work, snatched Luther's translation of the New Testament from his hand and berated him in angry words.

Also in the political field new dangers and difficulties arose at this time. In Denmark-Norway the dethronement of the tyrannical Christian II, and the struggle between the Catholic hierarchy and the adherents of the Reformation, caused the greatest confusion. In 1524 Frederick I had been placed on the throne by the nobility, but upon his death in 1533 the question of the choice of a new king precipitated the bitterest party strife. In Norway the Catholics, led by Archbishop Olaf Engelbrektson, president of the Council of the Realm, favored the choice of Count Frederick of the Palatinate; but they were opposed by the powerful noble Vincence Lunge and his party, who supported the Lutheran Duke Christian, son of King Frederick I. In Denmark the Catholics, who at first favored Prince Hans, a younger son of Frederick I, finally united in an effort to recall the dethroned King Christian II. They allied themselves with the Lübeckers, who, in an effort to maintain their supremacy in the Baltic region, sent an army into Denmark, commanded by Count Christopher of Oldenburg. The people of Jutland rose in rebellion against their feudal lords, and proclaimed Christian II king. Duke Christian was finally elevated to the throne by the Council as Christian III, but war broke out between the two parties, and if Duke Christian wished to reign, he had to win his kingdom with the sword.

During this period of war and turmoil which lasted till 1536 the administration of public affairs in Norway was conducted by the Council of the Realm. On January 30, 1533, the Icelandic Althing passed a decree, "Dómr um landsins nauðsynjar," signed by Bishop Ögmund of Skálholt, Bishop Jon of Hólar, and the best men of Iceland, in which they pledged their allegiance to the king of Norway and the Catholic church.[4] It was evidently the plan of the Icelandic bishops to seek the support of Norway and the archbishop of Nidaros in the struggle against the Reformation. Immediately after the close of the Althing Bishop Ögmund went to Norway to confer personally with the archbishop. He returned to Iceland the following year after the Althing decree had been sanctioned by the Council of the Realm. Bishop Jon Arason also sent his son Sigurd on an important mission to Norway and the continent. What the mission was is not known, but it is likely that an effort was made to determine what support could be obtained from Emperor Charles V and the Norwegian Council. It it said that Bishop Jon also caused a printing press to be brought to Iceland for the purpose of combating the Reformation by printing and distributing Catholic religious literature.[5]

The question which one of the rival claimants to the Danish-Norwegian throne, or whether any of them was to be considered the legitimate king soon caused serious difficulties also in Iceland. Archbishop Olaf Engelbrektson of Nidaros, president of the Council of the Realm, instructed the Icelandic bishops to collect the revenues of the crown in their respective dioceses. Christian III, or Duke Christian as he was still called in Iceland, commanded the royal governor Didrik v. Minden to take charge of the revenues for his account, and Count Christopher of Oldenburg, acting as representative of Christian II, sent letters to the Icelanders announcing that he had appointed Markus Meyer hirðstjóri for all Iceland. These conflicting demands were presented to the Althing by the two lawmen in 1535. A decision was rendered in favor of the claim made by Arch-

[4] Jon Thorkelsson og Einar Arnorsson, *Ríkisréttindi Islands*, p. 37 ff.
[5] *Biskupasögur*, 440. Gudbrand Vigfusson, *Icelandic Prose Reader*, p. 437. Jon Thorkelsson, *Om Digtningen paa Island*, p. 14 f.

bishop Olaf Engelbrektson, "since the Norwegian crown has chosen no king, and we have taken the oath of allegiance to the king and crown of Norway," said the members of the *lögretta* in their decision.[6] In 1536 King Christian III sent Claus v. Mervitz to Iceland as *hirðstjóri,* or royal governor. Bishop Ögmund of Skálholt, who was still seeking to maintain connections with Archbishop Olaf, dispatched Gizur Einarsson as his special representative to Norway. But though he was able to find the archbishop, the position of that prelate in his opposition to the victorious king was now so hopeless that he could give the Icelandic bishops no assistance. With this discouraging news Gizur returned to Iceland, and Bishop Ögmund was forced to make his submission to the king and the royal governors.[7] While his difficulties were thus accumulating, the bishop also had the misfortune to become totally blind. It is said that while on a journey he seemed to notice that darkness was gradually falling. In speaking of this to his companions they said that the sun was still shining brightly. "Then good-by, world," he said, "you have served me long enough!" As the choice of a successor now became urgent, he selected for this position his nephew Sigurd Einarsson, who went to Norway in 1536, and is said to have been consecrated bishop at Nidaros shortly before Archbishop Olaf Engelbrektson was forced to flee from his archdiocese. But Sigurd fell sick and died immediately after his consecration. When this news reached Iceland, Ögmund, who still had confidence in Gizur Einarsson, secured his election as assistant bishop and successor to the diocese. But Gizur hastened to Denmark to have his election sanctioned by the Lutheran Christian III, who was now acknowledged as the rightful king.

In Denmark-Norway many leading nobles supported the Reformation from no higher motive than a desire to despoil the Catholic church of its lands and possessions. The secularization of the monasteries, which had begun

[6] Finnur Jonsson, *Historia Ecclesiastica Islandiæ,* vol. ii, p. 268 ff. Thorkelsson og Arnorsson, *Ríkisréttindi Íslands,* p. 41.

[7] Espolin, *Árbækur,* iii, 79.

already in the time of Christian II and Frederick I, was continued under Christian III. The lands were granted as fiefs to nobles and royal favorites, and by 1555 the total extinction of the monasteries had been accomplished. That the royal officials should pursue a like policy also in Iceland was natural. Didrik v. Minden, the representative of the royal governor, residing at Bessastadir, a German by birth, was a rapacious and tyrannical official, thoroughly hated by the people. In 1539 he proceeded to Videy in the absence of the abbot, drove out the monks, and seized the monastery with all its belongings. At the Althing Bishop Ögmund demanded to know whether he had acted in accordance with royal orders. To this inquiry no answer was given. The bishop appealed the case to the courts, but the defiant official remarked that the pestilence might take the laws.

Shortly after the meeting of the Althing Didrik set out from Bessastadir to seize the monasteries of Thykkvabær and Kirkjubær. On the way it occurred to him that he would visit Bishop Ögmund at Skálholt. He was courteously received, and remained at the bishop's residence over night. The next morning Ögmund again asked him if he intended to seize the monasteries without royal orders. Didrik would not answer this question, but berated the blind old bishop in abusive language. Ögmund ordered him to leave the house. He offered even to supply him with provisions for the journey, but asked him to remember that, blind and helpless as he was, he could not control his people if they were unduly provoked. When Didrik only answered with new insults, the priest Jon Hedinsson, councilor at the bishop's seat, secretly sent word to the people of the district telling them what was taking place at Skálholt. In a short time an armed force of angry *bœndur* assembled. The house was surrounded, and Didrik v. Minden was slain with all his followers, August 10, 1539. Bishop Ögmund claimed that this was done without his will or consent. The case was tried before a jury of twelve men at the Laxaholtthing. The farmers who had taken part in the affair were acquitted, and the decision was rendered that no wergild should be paid for Didrik or his men, as they had fallen as common criminals.[8]   The governor, Claus v. Mervitz, paid no attention to the decision of the court, but reported the affair to the king in a most biased way, laying the blame on Bishop Ögmund, whom he accused of having instigated the attack.[9]

Gizur Einarsson's election as bishop was sanctioned by the king March 15, 1540.   Upon his return to Iceland he was welcomed by the clergy of the diocese of Skálholt, though he was suspected of being a convert to the Lutheran faith.   At the meeting of the Althing he read a declaration stating that he would rule the diocese in accordance with the old church laws, in so far as they did not contravene God's own ordinances.[10]   This he undoubtedly considered necessary, as it became evident that the people would not tolerate a Lutheran bishop or accept the Lutheran doctrine. In 1537 King Christian III had given his sanction to a new code of church laws embracing the Lutheran Reformation. The code was sent to Iceland the following year, but the bishops Ögmund and Jon took no steps to have it introduced.   In a letter of March 12, 1539, to the people of the Skálholt diocese Bishop Ögmund appealed for protection to the pope and the emperor.[11]   He also wrote a letter to the king, saying:

"We will keep the faith and church service which our wisest and most learned men agree to, and which are not contrary to the Norwegian laws.   But if your lordship's officials shall undertake to establish a doctrine contrary to our understanding, then we humbly beseech your royal majesty to grant us permission to leave with our moveable belongings, that we may seek refuge in some land which God may show us."[12]

[8] Björn á Skardsá, *Annálar*, 1539.   Finnur Jonsson, *Historia Ecclesiastica Islandiœ*, vol. ii, p. 552 ff.

[9] Arild Huitfeld, *Danmarks Riges Krønike*, tom. ii, p. 1511.

[10] Espolin, *Árbœkur*, iii, 93.   Thorkelsson og Arnorsson, *Ríkisréttindi Íslands*, p. 55 ff.

[11] Thorkelsson og Arnorsson, *Ríkisréttindi Íslands*, p. 53 ff.

[12] *Safn til Sögu Íslands*, vol. ii, p. 503 ff.   Finnur Jonsson, *Historia Ecclesiastica Islandiœ*, vol. ii, p. 566 ff.   Thorkelsson og Arnorsson, *Ríkisréttindi Íslands*, p. 55.

It was evident that the new church code would not be adopted unless more stern measures were employed. In 1541 the king appointed Christopher Huitfeldt governor, and dispatched him to Iceland with two warships.[13]   The mission of the governor was to secure the adoption of the new church code, to prevail on the people to take the oath of allegiance to Christian III, and to grant him a new tax, the *landshjálp,* as he had been forced to carry on expensive wars to win the throne.   It seems to have been a part of the plan also to break the power of resistance of the Catholic clergy by seizing and deporting the bishops, especially Bishop Ögmund, who was accused of complicity in the attack on Didrik v. Minden.   The Althing of 1541 assembled under the drawn swords of foreign military forces.   The *landshjálp* was granted, and the new church code was adopted for the diocese of Skálholt; but Bishop Jon Arason and the clergy of the diocese of Hólar were not present to give their consent.   Bishop Ögmund of Skálholt was treacherously seized shortly after the arrival of Huitfeldt's expedition.   Upon invitation from the governor Gizur Einarsson is said to have gone to Bessastadir, where the plot for the capture of the bishop seems to have been laid.   But doubt exists as to the complicity of Gizur in the plot.[14]   The people of the neighboring districts were ordered to send horses for the transportation of goods to Skálholt.   When these arrived, a band of armed men were mounted and sent to arrest the bishop.   He had been warned by his friends to retire to the monasteries of Thykkvabær or Kirkjubær while the military forces were in the land, but an apparently friendly letter from Gizur had so far reassured him that on his journey to the monasteries he stopped at Hjalli, near the mouth of the Ölfusá, to visit his sister Ásdis.   Here the armed band sent by Huitfeldt seized the eighty-year-old blind bishop while he was still in bed, and brought him on horseback, thinly clad, to Bessastadir, where he was

---

[13] *Safn til Sögu Íslands,* vol. i, p. 72. Thorkelsson og Arnorsson, *Ríkisréttindi Íslands,* p. 56. Arild Huitfeld, *Danmarks Riges Krønike,* tom. ii, p. 1511.
[14] Jon Helgason, *Islands Kirke fra Reformationen til vore Dage,* p. 28.

placed on board a Danish ship. By holding out the
hope that he might be liberated upon the payment of a
large ransom his captors secured his sister's money, and
persuaded the old prelate to deed them all his property.
The promise was a mere ruse. After gaining possession of
his lands and property they carried him away. According
to some authorities he was brought to Denmark, and placed
in the monastery of Sorø, where he died shortly after.[15]
But it is more probable that he died on the voyage before
reaching Denmark.[16]

The deportation of Bishop Ögmund removed a great
obstacle to the Reformation, but Bishop Jon Arason of
Hólar proved to be a still more formidable opponent. The
capture of Ögmund, which took place shortly before the
meeting of the Althing, did not become known in the northern diocese before Bishop Jon with priests and followers
was on his way to Thingvellir. On June 15, 1541, he had
assembled a church council in his diocese. The priests
promised to pay the king the *landshjálp,* and agreed to assist the royal officials, "if they maintain for us and the
people the Norwegian and Icelandic laws, old liberties and
lawful customs, such as we, our church and the people
should have." [17] When Bishop Jon and his men reached
the Borgarfjord and heard what had happened in the Skálholt diocese, they did not proceed to the Althing, but sent
instead a letter from Kalmanstunga, saying:

"We will honor, swear allegiance to and hold the highborn
Christian Fredericksson as our liege lord and king of Norway,
and pay him all taxes and dues which the thanes owe the rightful
Norwegian king, according to the sworn agreement which we
and our forefathers have agreed to. This summer we received
a letter with our lord the king's seal stating that his officials
would keep the laws and good old Christian customs which have
been observed in our land. Trusting to this we began our
journey to the Althing from the northern quarter to Kalmans-

[15] Espolin, *Árbœkur,* part iii, p. 97 ff. G. Storm, *Islandske Annaler*
(Gottskalks Annaler, year 1542). Björn á Skardsá, *Annálar,* p. 127.

[16] Jon Helgason, *Islands Kirke fra Reformationen til vore Dage,* p. 28.

[17] Thorkelsson og Arnorsson, *Rikisréttindi Islands,* p. 57.

tunga in Borgarfjord. There we received the news that Bishop Ögmund had been made prisoner against his will, and that his property had been taken without judicial proceedings. Therefore it appears to us that the provisions in the royal letter which his lordship this year has sent have not been kept. And this we know for sooth, that the liberty, privileges and sworn agreements have often been disregarded by the king's officials in our land. For this reason the people will in no wise allow that we ride to the Althing at this time. But we will subscribe to the covenants entered into by the best men of the Althing which are not contrary to the Norwegian and Icelandic laws. We will also support and own allegiance to the royal governor appointed for our land in all matters possible, if he will keep for us and the people of the northern quarter the laws and customs of the land, according to the provision contained in the king's letter." [18]

Bishop Jon's son Ari Jonsson, lawman in the northern quarter, also tendered his resignation to the governor, who accepted it and appointed a new lawman. It seems to have been Huitfeldt's hope that Bishop Jon could be persuaded to visit Denmark. He brought royal letters inviting him and Bishop Gizur Einarsson to come to Denmark to consult with the king regarding the Reformation. But Jon would not undertake the voyage, and Gizur did not deem it expedient to leave his diocese under the circumstances. The new tax, the *landshjálp,* was paid for the Skálholt diocese, partly in coin and partly in silver and precious articles taken from the cathedral church. With these treasures Huitfeldt returned to Denmark after the close of the session of the Althing. [19]

Though Gizur Einarsson had embraced the Lutheran faith, and sought to establish the new church laws in his diocese, such friendly relations still existed between him and Bishop Jon that they promised to aid one another. In 1542 Gizur went to Denmark, pursuant to the king's request, while Jon, who was afraid to make the voyage because of his advanced age, sent three personal representatives, who on his behalf took the oath to obey the new church laws. The following summer Gizur returned to Iceland. Jon

[18] *Safn til Sögu Íslands,* vol. ii, p. 207 ff.
[19] Thorkelsson og Arnorsson, *Ríkisréttindi Íslands,* p. 59 f.

still maintained a friendly attitude. He thanked Gizur for the assistance given his representatives in Denmark, but at heart he was as bitterly opposed to the Reformation as ever. In a letter to Gizur he took occasion to revive an old claim to the estate Bjarnanes in the Skálholt diocese, and requested a personal interview in regard to the matter. Gizur sought in a polite way to avoid a clash by promising to give the question his careful consideration. In 1544 he did not go to the Althing, probably in order to avoid trouble with Bishop Jon. The case was submitted to a court of arbitration consisting of six judges, three being chosen by each side; but as no agreement was reached, the matter was finally submitted to the king. Without awaiting the decision Jon seized Bjarnanes, and refused to surrender it, even when it was formally granted Gizur by the king. This terminated the rather hollow friendship which had hitherto existed between the two bishops. Jon did not yet venture to break openly with the king. Evidence exists showing that in 1545 he even paid the royal taxes levied on the bishopric of Hólar.[20] But events were hastening to a final clash between the two parties, which could not long exist side by side in Iceland. Gizur worked diligently for the furtherance of the Reformation. The church service was simplified, priests were encouraged to marry, crosses and images were removed, and old superstitions eradicated. In February, 1548, he rode to the cross at Kaldadarnes, to which pilgrimages had been made from all southern Iceland, and caused it to be removed. But before his return home he fell sick and died in March of the same year after a short illness. As bishop, Gizur had proved himself able and energetic, but in his dealings with his former friend and benefactor, Bishop Ögmund, he had shown a craftiness for which he was justly censured.

Bishop Jon Arason thought that the time had now come for a decisive step. Luther died at Eisleben in 1546; Gizur, the chief supporter of the Reformation in Iceland, had passed away. On the continent war had broken out between Emperor Charles V and the Schmalkaldic

[20] Thorkelsson og Arnorsson, *Ríkisréttindi Íslands*, p. 63.

League of Protestant princes, to which also King Christian III belonged. The overwhelming defeat of the Protestant forces at Mühlberg, and the capture of the leaders Philip of Hesse and John Frederick, elector of Saxony, made many think that the complete overthrow of the Lutheran Reformation was imminent. On the death of Gizur, Jon went to the Borgarfjord district and announced that he would take charge of the Skálholt diocese, but he received little welcome in southern Iceland. He was not well liked by the clergy, and still more unpopular was his son Björn Jonsson, an ambitious and haughty priest, who aspired to become Gizur Einarsson's successor. Even while the Althing was in session the priests and many leading men of the diocese met at Skálholt to elect a new bishop. Those who clung to Catholicism selected as their candidate Abbot Sigurd of Thykkvabær, but the Lutherans, who were in the majority, elected the pious and learned priest Martein Einarsson. The election seems to have taken place without Jon's knowledge, and as he could not annul it, he declared himself in favor of the minority candidate, the Catholic Sigurd of Thykkvabær, whom he persuaded to hasten to Denmark to obtain the king's sanction. He also succeeded in prevailing upon the Althing to pass a resolution by which he himself was put in charge of the diocese until the new bishop could enter upon his duties. But the priests who had been placed in authority by Martein Einarsson refused to heed the decree of the Althing. As Jon could not take Skálholt by force, he returned to Hólar to make more careful preparations. King Christian III seems to have feared that Jon might attempt to make himself master of all Iceland. In the summer of 1548 he summoned him to Denmark, issuing a safe-conduct for him, that he might clear himself of the accusations made against him. Another royal letter was addressed to the clergy and leading men of Iceland in which they were warned not to aid the bishop if he would not obey the king's summons. These letters were read at the Althing in Jon's presence. But neither the royal letters nor the warning of many of his friends, among others of his son Ari, the former lawman, could move him to change his plans. Ari did not favor the course pursued by his father, but he finally yielded to persuasion and joined him. Another son, Sigurd, took no part in the uprising. Jon hoped to be able to seize Skálholt by force. Late in the summer he left Hólar and marched southward with a hundred men. But the priest Jon Bjarnarson, councilor at Skálholt, learned of his approach, and gathered forces from the neighboring districts. The great chieftain Dadi Gudmundsson, who was married to Bishop Martein's sister, was visiting at Skálholt at the time. So was also Pétur Einarsson, the bishop's brother, who on his travels on the continent had learned some of the art of fortification. Under their directions redouts were constructed, guns were mounted, and the works were guarded by many hundred armed men. When Bishop Jon arrived, he summoned the defenders of Skálholt to surrender, under threat of excommunication, but the demand was met with jeers and saucy challenges. The angry bishop attempted to take the redouts by a general assault, but his men were driven back. After studying the situation for some days he left Skálholt. and returned to his bishop's seat.

In order to safeguard himself against sudden attack he is said to have erected a castle at Hólar, surrounded by stone walls, and connected with the church and the bishop's residence by underground passages. On August 27, 1548, he wrote a letter to the pope pledging anew his allegiance to the Church of Rome, and asking what he should do with the church revenues since the archbishop of Nidaros had fled. The pope, who was unable to render him any direct assistance, advised him to give the money to the poor. Jon is also said to have addressed a letter to Emperor Charles V asking him to seize Iceland in order that the Catholic faith might be preserved, but this claim rests on no definite evidence.[21] His chief opponent at this time was the chief-

[21] Björn Jonsson á Skardsá said in 1549: "Bishop Jon had much to do with the English and the Hollanders, and some claim that he wrote to the emperor of Germany asking him to take the land, and to give him aid in maintaining religion in a proper way. This letter a Hollander was to bring, but he met with hindrances in Germany, and the letter was discovered." *Annálar,* year 1549.

tain Dadi Gudmundsson of Snoksdal, a rich and influential
man of shady morals, who had already resisted him in his
attack on Skálholt. In September, 1548, Jon marched into
the western districts, sacked three of Dadi's estates, and
proclaimed him an outlaw under the ban of the church, but
upon his return home this proclamation was annulled by
the lawman Orm Sturlason. The following spring Jon prepared a new expedition against Dadi. But when he learned
that the wary chieftain kept a band of armed men about
him, he abandoned the plan and returned with his followers
to Hólar.

Martein Einarsson, who had been elected bishop by the
Lutheran party, had gone to Denmark where his election
was sanctioned by the king. His rival, Abbot Sigurd of
Thykkvabær, also arrived in Copenhagen. Failing to obtain
confirmation as bishop he joined the Lutheran church and
remained in Denmark, where he died two years later.
Bishop Martein returned to Iceland in 1549. At the
Althing he read letters from the king proclaiming Bishop
Jon Arason an outlaw, forbidding the people to show him
any obedience, and instructing Dadi Gudmundsson to arrest
the bishop and his sons in order that a new military expedition should not be sent to Iceland. Bishop Jon was now
pursuing a course which could only be regarded as open
rebellion against the royal government, but it might still
be a question whether under the circumstances it was not
fully justified. The king had long since ceased to rule
according to the agreements forming the bonds of union
between Iceland and the united kingdoms. Even the most
fundamental rights of freemen were disregarded. The Icelanders were treated as a conquered people. Bishop
Ögmund had been seized and deported without trial, and his
property had been taken on false pretenses, even without
the formality of legal action. The stipulations in the union
agreement that the laws of the land should be preserved,
that no one should be summoned abroad for trial, that only
native citizens should be appointed to office, that no new
taxes should be levied, had been flagrantly violated or totally
ignored. The king had undertaken to force upon Iceland

the Lutheran Reformation and a new code of church laws.
Military forces were sent to Iceland, and new taxes were
levied by the royal governors, aided by foreign troops.
Bishop Jon was summoned to Denmark to answer accusations made against him, was declared an outlaw without
being convicted of any crime, and was ordered to be arrested, not pursuant to the laws of Iceland, but by royal
decree. The king's rule in Iceland was an evident usurpa-
tion of power which transformed government into a despotism wholly foreign to Icelandic laws and institutions.
In resisting such encroachments on their constitutional
liberties the Icelanders were not only within their legal
rights, but they were performing a patriotic duty. The
uprising led by Bishop Jon was not only a religious, but also
a national struggle waged in the defense of what still
remained of Icelandic national liberty. But now as formerly there was a lack of patriotic sentiment and united
action. Not only were the people divided into hostile
groups on the question of the Reformation, but bitter personal hatred among the party leaders often obscured the
real issue and injected into the conflict the characteristic
features of the old feuds.

Bishop Jon did not attend the Althing in 1549, as he had
already heard of the royal letters and their contents. For
some time he remained quietly at Hólar. But when he received a letter from the pope commending his faithfulness
to the Catholic church, and urging him to heroic resistance
against its enemies, he took new courage. Gathering the
priests of the diocese he read to them the papal letter before
the altar of the cathedral church, and took a vow that he
would give his life rather than be in any way unfaithful to
the holy father. On learning that Bishop Martein was traveling in the western districts he sent his sons Ari and Björn
with over a hundred armed men to seize him. The undertaking was successfully carried out. Bishop Martein and
the priest Arni Arnorsson, one of Jon's bitterest opponents,
were captured and brought to Hólar. Dadi Gudmundsson
was in so imminent a danger of being seized that he saved
himself only by mounting a swift horse. The priest Arni

was soon liberated, but Bishop Martein was kept in confinement in the monastery of Mödruvellir and later at Eyjafjord.

Jon was not satisfied with a temporary advantage over his opponents, but pursued energetically the course upon which he had entered. The priest Olaf Hjaltason, who had preached against Catholic customs, was summoned before the bishop and dismissed from his church. In the summer of 1550 Olaf sailed to Denmark to report to the king his own case as well as the imprisonment of Bishop Martein. But even before his arrival the king had taken new steps to suppress the uprising led by Jon. In a letter dated June 27 he instructed Dadi Gudmundsson and Pétur Einarsson to aid the royal commandant Lauritz Mule in arresting the bishop. In a second letter to the people of the Hólar diocese he warned the people that Jon was an outlaw, that a new bishop had to be chosen for the diocese, and that he had selected for this óffice the priest Gisli Jonsson, who was to be sent to Denmark to be consecrated.[22] Bishop Palladius of Seeland also wrote to Bishop Jon warning him of his danger, and urging him to submit to the king, but he refused to yield. When he learned of the order issued for his arrest, he decided to face his opponents boldly. In the summer of 1550 he rode to the Althing with a guard of 200 men, accompanied by his sons Ari and Björn, each with a force of 100 men. The king's commandant, Lauritz Mule, and the chieftains who were to assist him were not prepared to meet so strong a force, and were unable to offer resistance. The lawman Orm Sturlason was forced to resign, and Jon's son Ari was again appointed to the office. From the Althing Jon marched to Skálholt with his whole armed force, bringing with him the captive Bishop Martein. The bishop's residence was surrendered to him, and Martein was left there under guard. From Skálholt he marched to the monastery of Videy, which had been changed into a residence for the royal commandant. Lauritz Mule and the Danes were driven on board their ships, the monastery was rededicated, and the former abbot was again installed.

[22] Krag og Stefanius, *Christian III's Historie,* vol. ii, pp. 430, 459.

Before returning to Hólar he also rode to Helgafell, and reorganized that monastery under its old abbot.

After the success which he had already met with Bishop Jon hoped to be able to cope with Dadi Gudmundsson, his chief remaining opponent. In the fall of 1550 he left Hólar with ninety armed men, accompanied by his sons Ari and Björn. At Saudafell he was also joined by thirty or forty men from the Borgarfjord district. But here he was suddenly attacked by Dadi. His forces were defeated, and he and his two sons were seized in the Saudafell church, where they had sought refuge. Dadi reported what had happened to Bessastadir, the residence of the royal governor. But there was at the time no such official in the country, as Lauritz Mule had already returned to Denmark. The only Danish official present was a clerk, Christian Skriver, who was ordered to keep Bishop Jon and his sons as prisoners in conformity with the royal letters. Bishop Martein at Skálholt was now liberated. Together with Christian Skriver he hastened to Snoksdal, where a court was convened, and Bishop Jon and his two sons were judged to be prisoners according to the king's command.[23] Christian Skriver, assisted by Bishop Martein and the two lawmen, was to retain them in custody. Bishop Martein, Christian Skriver, Dadi Gudmundsson, and many other leading men met at Skálholt to consider what further steps were to be taken. At this meeting Christian Skriver, acting as the king's representative, preferred a series of charges against Jon,[24] stating that he had imprisoned Bishop Martein, that without warrant he had used the royal taxes of the northern districts, that he had disregarded the king's orders regarding the monasteries and beneficiaries, that he had resisted the Word of God, that he had used violence against both learned and lay people, had threatened the Danes, had promised the Hamburgers that by spring there would be no Danes in Iceland, that he had said that Lauritz Mule should not long remain as hirðstjóri or Martein as bishop of Skálholt, etc. Most of these accusations were based on

---

[23] The decision is found in *Biskupasögur* (Jón biskup Arason), p. 458 ff.

[24] *Biskupasögur* (Jón biskup Arason), p. 469 ff.

nothing but prejudice and general rumors; but the assembled leaders were very eager to convict their prisoners, as they feared their revenge if they should regain their liberty. Christian Skriver was afraid also to retain them in his custody at Bessastadir when the men of northern Iceland should come southward to take part in the winter fisheries. After deliberations lasting several days the priest Jon Bjarnason, steward at Skálholt, said one morning at the breakfast table that although he probably was not very wise, he knew a way in which the prisoners could be safely kept. When asked to state his plan he answered that the ax and the earth would keep them best. At first this method of doing away with them without trial met considerable opposition. But Bishop Martein approved of the plan, and when Christian Skriver also gave it ardent support, the opposition was soon overcome. An agreement was made that the prisoners should be put to death, and on November 7, 1550, Bishop Jon and his two sons were beheaded at Skálholt.[25] This lawless act aroused such bitter resentment, especially in the Hólar diocese, that when the men from the northern districts came south to take part in the winter fisheries, a band of Jon's adherents attacked Christian Skriver and slew him, together with his son and several of his Danish followers.

On March 30, 1551, the priest Sigurd Jonsson, a son of Bishop Jon Arason, who had taken no part in the uprising, sent thirty men under the leadership of three priests to bring the bodies of his father and two brothers to Hólar.[26] These men arrived at Skálholt with masked faces, bringing three coffins with them. They demanded of Bishop Martein the permission to exhume the bodies. This demand was granted. The bodies were placed in the coffins, and the return march was immediately undertaken. At Laugarvatn a halt was made; the bodies were washed and dressed with care; bells were fastened under the coffins, and as the funeral escort advanced through the country, the church bells

---

[25] *Biskupasögur* (Jón biskup Arason), p. 450. Espolin, *Árbœkur*, iii, 121 ff. Finnur Jonsson, *Historia Ecclesiastica Islandiœ*, vol. ii, p. 670 ff.
[26] *Biskupasögur* (Jón biskup Arason), p. 337.

were chiming, and the greatest reverence was shown the
dead. On approaching Hólar the procession was met by the
priests of the diocese and a large concourse of people. The
cathedral bells rang out their greeting of peace, and the
bodies were interred in the churchyard with all tokens of
honor and pious veneration. On April 27 the priests of the
diocese assembled and chose Sigurd Jonsson bishop. Danish
rule in Iceland had never been weaker or more unpopular.
It seemed that Christian III might be challenged to maintain his power over the country by force of arms. But the
Icelanders stood divided. The leaders who had dared to
resist the policy of the government were gone. The people
were dependent on Denmark-Norway for their imports, and
no means were at hand for waging a struggle against the
fleets and military forces which the king could send against
them.

When King Christian learned of the imprisonment of
Bishop Martein of Skálholt, he sent four warships to Iceland. Two were dispatched to the southern districts under
Otte Stigssøn. The other two under command of Axel Juul
and the renowned Norwegian sea-captain Christopher
Trondssøn were sent to the northern districts. Upon his
arrival in Iceland Otte Stigssøn as royal governor assembled
the Althing, where he appeared with an escort of 200 soldiers.
The people were ordered to take the oath of allegiance to the
king, a request to which they readily consented, although
the procedure, conducted as an act of coercion with the aid
of military forces, was a flagrant violation of the laws of
Iceland. No attempt was made to alter the union agreement. Otte Stigssøn himself took an oath that he would
maintain law and justice to all people rich and poor, "according to the pledges given by the kings of Norway, and the
agreements made between our gracious king and his thanes
here in Iceland." [27] This new confirmation of the union
agreement must have pleased the Icelanders, although the
proceeding was otherwise offensive and irregular.

In northern Iceland Axel Juul and Christopher Trondssøn
assembled the people to a general *thing* at Oddeyri in Eyja-

[27] *Biskupasögur* (Jón biskup Arason), p. 388 ff.

fjord. The required oath of allegiance to the king was taken, and Olaf Hjaltason was made bishop of Hólar, no attention being paid to the election of Sigurd Jonsson, who had been chosen by the priests of the diocese. Bishop Jon Arason and his sons Ari and Björn were declared traitors, and all their property was confiscated.[28] Severe punishment was also to be meted out to the slayers of Christian Skriver, but they managed to make good their escape. The lawless conduct of that official in executing Bishop Jon and his sons without trial or conviction, even without royal orders, was not condemned or criticized. The treasures belonging to the church of Hólar and the monasteries of Thverá and Mödruvellir were seized, and since no resistance was offered by the people, and no disturbance of any kind occurred, the expedition returned to Denmark before the end of the summer, 1551.

After his death Bishop Jon was venerated almost as a saiht by the people of his diocese. He gradually became a sort of national hero to whom many later bishops, lawmen, and other leading persons were proud to trace their lineage. His opponent Dadi Gudmundsson reaped little satisfaction from his victory. Ten years after Jon's death he became afflicted with cancer of the face, an ailment from which he died after much suffering in 1563. The people gradually adjusted themselves to existing conditions without again attempting open resistance to the government authorities. But silent ill-will against the Reformation, and especially against the arbitrary rule of the Danish government, continued to manifest itself long after Jon's death. Bishop Martein of Skálholt was so aggrieved by the rapacity of the royal officials and the humiliation of his country that he resigned his episcopacy and spent his remaining years in the obscurity of private life. Many priests also chose to resign rather than renounce their Catholic faith and remain in charge of their congregations. The conduct of the royal representatives Didrik v. Minden, Christopher Huitfeldt and Claus v. Mervitz toward Bishop Ögmund; of Christian Skriver and the leaders of the Lutheran party in connection

[28] Thorkelsson og Arnorsson, Ríkisréttindi Íslands, p. 65.

with the execution of Bishop Jon Arason and his sons could
inspire little love and respect for the Reformation. Few
young men would enter the service of the church as pastors.
The people received little religious instruction, and although
they were forced to accept the new church laws, they clung
privately to the Catholic worship. Candles were yet burned
before the sacred images, veneration of saints and pilgrimages to holy places were practiced as before.[29] Many would
not attend the Lutheran churches or contribute anything to
the support of Lutheran pastors.

The Reformation in Iceland was supported by two distinct classes. To the first belonged a few learned men who
had studied abroad and were sincerely attached to the new
doctrines. But many of them showed a spirit of self-interest which often led them to seek their own personal advantage, instead of attempting with true evangelical devotion
to turn the people to the new spiritual light. The second
class consisted of rapacious royal officials and greedy chieftains, who had no real religious interest, but were willing
to destroy the Catholic church in order to despoil it of its
lands and possessions. Under this kind of leadership the
Reformation did not become a work of instruction or conversion, but a series of administrative acts, royal decrees,
assaults upon the Catholic leaders, and encroachments upon
the people's constitutional liberties.[30]

After the death of Bishop Jon Arason, and the overthrow
of the Catholic party, all the monasteries of Iceland were
secularized. At first the king seems to have entertained a
plan to use the income from the lands thus seized to build
schools for the people, but he was persuaded to abandon the
idea, and to retain the revenues for the royal purse. From
1556 one-fourth of the tithes payable to the church, as well
as the fines imposed in suits at law, were also to be considered royal revenues.[31] It does not appear that these im-

[29] Thorkel Bjarnason, *Tímarit hins íslenzka bókmentafélaga*, 1896, p. 38 ff.
Bishop Jon Helgason, *Islands Kirke fra Reformationen til vore Dage*.

[30] *Biskupasögur* (Jón biskup Arason), p. 356. Thorkelsson og Arnorsson,
Ríkisréttindi Íslands, p. 73.

[31] Arngrim Jonsson, *Crymogea sive Rerum Islandicarum*, lib. iii, p. 145 ff.
Eggert Olafsson, *Reise gjennem Island*, p. 231.

portant measures were submitted to the Althing, or that the
people were ever asked to sanction them, though they effected important changes in the country's laws and institutions. The whole spirit of criminal law was also gradually
changed by ordinances imposing severe penalties or capital
punishment for various offenses. In 1563 King Frederick
II, who succeeded his father Christian III on the throne,
ordered that persons guilty of heresy should be executed,
and their property should be forfeited to the crown.[32] Cases
of adultery should be tried and decided according to the
Koldingrecesse of December 13, 1558, given by Christian
III.[33] In 1564 Paul Stigssøn, royal governor in Iceland,
forced the Althing to proclaim an ordinance, the *stóridómr*,
establishing capital punishment for offenses of this kind.
The law was signed by the two lawmen, and received royal
sanction April 13, 1565.[34] A final appeal might be made to
the king and his council, who continued to act as a court of
last resort till 1661, when the *høiesteret* or supreme court of
appeal was established in Denmark. The *stóridómr* remained in force, at least nominally, till 1838. Those who
were convicted under this law were executed, the men being
hung and the women drowned. Half their property was
forfeited to the crown, and the other half was distributed
among needy relatives. In cases of adultery capital punishment should be inflicted only for a third offense, and the
property of the person convicted should be distributed
among the lawful heirs.[35] The harsh features of this
Draconian measure were somewhat softened by royal decrees of 1576, 1578 and 1594 [36] providing for the granting of
absolution to persons convicted under it. Other severe punishments for crimes were also instituted. The old privilege
of sanctuary, according to which criminals could not be

[32] Magnus Ketilsson, *Forordninger og aabne Breve,* vol. ii, p. 16 ff.
[33] This ordinance was not formally accepted as law in Iceland. See
Thorkelsson og Arnorsson, *Ríkisréttindi Íslands,* 171, 176.
[34] *Safn til Sögu Íslands,* vol. ii, p. 368 ff. Magnus Ketilsson, *Forordninger
og aabne Breve,* vol. ii, p. 31 ff.
[35] Magnus Ketilsson, *Forordninger og aabne Breve,* vol. ii, p. 44 ff. *Safn
til Sögu Íslands,* vol. ii, p. 368 ff.
[36] Magnus Ketilsson, *Forordninger og aabne Breve,* vol. ii, p. 80 ff; 85 ff,
191.

seized in churches or holy places, was abolished by an ordinance of 1587,[37] and by a law of 1596 the eating of horseflesh was made an offense punishable by a fine of three marks ($21.60) together with severe flogging. Thieves were to be hung, flogged or branded. Even minor offenses were to be punished by the pillory, flogging or heavy fines.

While such pedantic zeal was manifested for the maintenance of law and order, no steps were taken by the government to protect the people against foreign enemies, though piratic raids on defenseless seacoast settlements had been frequent. In 1579 English pirates came to shore in the Vestfjords, robbed churches, ravished women, and killed people. Eggert Hannesson, a rich proprietor, once lawman and acting governor, was seized, and was set at liberty only upon payment of a large ransom. He was forced to take an oath that he would not make complaint to the king, but this forced promise he disregarded. The affair was reported to the government, and the pirates were finally seized in Holland and executed. As the people had been forbidden to bear arms, and were without military protection, they were helpless even against such bands of robbers who might at any time make raids upon the coast. This finally led to the proposing of the *vápnadómr* in 1581. This measure provided that the people should supply arms for their own protection. All freeholders paying taxes should have a musket, powder and a halberd or spear. Every unmarried man who owned ten *aurar* without debt should own spear and dagger, but these weapons should not be used except against foreign robbers. Those who owned twenty *hundrað* should buy musket, spear and other weapons according to their ability. The royal officials should act as officers, and the men should pay their own expenses while performing military duties. The *hreppstjórar* should keep a list of all men in their district capable of bearing arms, and the *sýslumenn* should see to it that places of safety for women, children, old people and live-stock were provided.[38]

---

[37] Magnus Ketilsson, *Forordninger og aabne Breve,* vol. ii, p. 128 ff.

[38] Espolin, *Árbækur,* part iv, ch. lv, p. 39 f. *Althingisbækur Íslands,* vol. i, p. 438 ff. Jon Thorkelsson, *Saga Magnús Prúða,* p. 76 ff.

The proposal failed to become a law, as it was not submitted to the Althing.

The Althing still sought to maintain its prestige as a representative assembly. Ordinances which had not received its sanction were regarded as having no force in Iceland, and the old principle that the king should rule the people according to their own laws was still adhered to, though henceforth it could only mean the laws to which they had given their consent. In 1588 the lawmen and *lögrétta* made a formal declaration that "we, the inhabitants of the country, should live and be judged according to the old Icelandic laws, and the royal ordinances and letters which our gracious lord the king has sent us for law and protection, and which our country has sanctioned and accepted".[39] It is clear, however, that after the Reformation the power of the crown was growing so rapidly that even the last remnant of legislative power lodged in the Althing, the right to approve or reject laws, was seriously endangered. The king had already forced the Althing to consent to legislation which violated all traditions and principles of Icelandic jurisprudence. At any opportune moment he might sweep away all legislative power of that assembly and allow it to retain only its purely judicial functions. In church affairs he gradually assumed the power formerly exercised by the pope and the archbishop. The bishops were usually elected by the clergy, subject to royal sanction, but in some instances the king placed bishops over the Icelandic dioceses even without consulting the clergy. The Lutheran bishops did not desire to exercise the power of preparing new codes of laws for the church, even when they were asked by the king to do so. In 1607 a new church code for Iceland was prepared by Norwegian churchmen,[40] but only upon formal request of the king, with the result that his will became the highest authority in all ecclesiastical affairs. The bishops no longer exercised authority, as in Catholic times, with regard to fasts or tithes, and many cases which had belonged under the jurisdiction of the church were transferred to the

[39] Thorkelsson og Arnorsson, *Ríkisréttindi Íslands*, p. 88 f.
[40] *Lovsamling for Island*, vol. i, p. 150 ff.

secular courts. The curtailing of the power of the clergy might have proved beneficial, as the Catholic bishops had often used their authority to oppress the people. But politically the Reformation proved unfavorable to Icelandic home rule. Hitherto the clergy had ruled, but it had been a native rule. The laws of the country and the people's fundamental rights had been respected. After the Reformation the king gradually assumed all power, and instituted a rule by royal officials who disregarded the Icelandic laws, acquired large landed estates, and riveted upon the people the tyranny of a selfish foreign bureaucracy.

In social life the low moral standards which had prevailed ever since pagan times continued also in the period following the Reformation. The priests were now allowed to marry, but concubinage and illicit relations continued to be common even among the leading churchmen. Even some of the bishops had illegitimate children, and since such irregularities were tolerated among the leaders, the church could exercise little restraint on the moral laxity prevalent among the laity and common clergy. Among the chieftains even polygamy was not uncommon. Eggert Hannesson married his concubine while his wife was still living, and Benedikt Pjetursson had two wives at the same time. Dadi Gudmundsson had two concubines, both of whom were so closely related to him that according to the church laws the relation was incestuous. The parish priests were often poorly educated, since the schools had been neglected. Complaints were made that they wasted their time in quarrels, lawsuits, horse trading and social frolics, and paid little attention to their pastoral duties. The change of faith which had been forced upon the people tended at first to disrupt their religious life. Many refused to attend church services, or to receive the sacrament in the new form.[41] But the evangelical character of the Lutheran church proved to be a force which gradually affected a religious and moral regeneration of the Icelandic people. It destroyed the images of ceremonial worship, behind which primitive paganism so conveniently hid itself, and turned the people's mind to the

[41] Thorkel Bjarnason, *Timarit hins íslenska bókmentafélags,* 1896, p. 38 ff.

simple truth of the gospel. Positive results of the Reformation were slow in manifesting themselves, but the serious, truth-loving, Biblical spirit of the new faith struck deep roots and imparted a stimulus which launched the nation upon a new intellectual and social development.

Vigorous steps were soon taken by the kings and bishops to suppress Catholic customs and to sharpen church discipline. Priests who offended against the new church ordinances were removed from their parishes. In 1561 the royal governor, Paul Stigssøn, traveled through the northern and western districts to see if the Lutheran church ordinances were duly observed. Four years later he issued orders to all the lay people that they should attend church on all Sundays and holidays, that they should remain quietly seated and listen attentively to the Word of God. If they failed to comply with this order after being thrice reminded by their pastor, they should be excluded from the Lord's Supper, and the *sýslumaðr* should cause them to be flogged. Crosses and images were to be destroyed. It is said that at this time Bishop Gisli Jonsson burned the Kaldadarnes cross which had been removed by Bishop Gizur Einarsson, and that he destroyed the images of saints at Kirkjubær and Thykkvabær. In northern Iceland Bishop Olaf Hjaltason destroyed the images of the Virgin at Hofstadir, and the crosses at Bardi and Stad in Hrutafjord. Persons guilty of grave offenses were expelled from the church, and were restored to the Christian communion only when they repented and publicly confessed their sins. Parents and heads of households were instructed to maintain strict discipline over their children and servants. About Bishop Gisli Jonsson it is said that he ordered the priests of his diocese to visit the homes of their parishioners to see if they had learned the catechism and possessed the necessary Christian knowledge. Other bishops followed the same plan. Especially important was the work of Gudbrand Thorlaksson, who became bishop of Hólar in 1569, and labored with greater earnestness than anyone else in this period to make evangelical Christianity a living force in the hearts of his people. Gudbrand was interested in providing proper reading for his people by translating and printing the Bible, and by collections of hymns and other Christian literature. He sought also to provide religious instruction, especially for children and young people. He asked the priests to require of the children that they learn the catechism, together with such prayers and songs as could be said and sung at the table. No one who did not know the catechism should be allowed to receive the Lord's Supper, except in cases of serious illness. The children were to be catechized in church in presence of the congregation, and should be confirmed before receiving the communion. Gudbrand's younger contemporary, Bishop Odd Einarsson of Skálholt, labored in a similar way to improve religious and moral conditions, and to instruct the people in the Lutheran faith. Due to the efforts of these able and God-fearing men true piety and purity of life soon gave evidence of the growth of a new Christian spirit.

One of the most important results of the Reformation in Iceland was the new interest awakened in education and literary activity. Although the king through the secularization of the monasteries diverted to the royal treasury resources which should have been used in the building of schools, progress was nevertheless made. In 1552 Paul Huitfeldt was sent on a special mission to Iceland. He issued orders that Latin schools should be maintained at both the bishops' seats. The school at Skálholt should have forty pupils, and the one at Hólar twenty-four. The teachers should be paid from incomes derived from estates belonging to the cathedral churches and collected by the bishops, who should also supply the pupils with food, clothes, light, fuel and other necessaries. Students were also encouraged to seek higher education at foreign universities, and many went abroad to study in Copenhagen, Bremen, or Rostock. The Danish government gave free board and later also free lodging to Icelandic students who wished to attend the royal university at Copenhagen; and since graduates of that university were preferred in appointments to positions in the church, all Icelanders who sought higher education were soon attracted to it. The introduction of printing so cheapened books that it became possible also to supply the homes with good literature.

According to tradition the first printing press in Iceland was established at Hólar by Bishop Jon Arason, about 1530. It is quite certain that in that year a printing press was brought to Iceland by Jon Matthiasson, a Swedish priest, who probably brought it from his own country at Bishop Jon's request. The press was first established at Hólar. Here the book "Breviarium Nidrosiense" was printed in 1534, the first book known to have been put into type in Iceland, but no copy of it has been preserved. The press was soon moved to Breidabolstad, where Jon Matthiasson became priest. During the years of turmoil while the Reformation was being established little use was made of the press, which was in the possession of the Catholic party. But in 1572 or 1573 it was moved back to Hólar, and under the direction of the energetic Bishop Gudbrand Thorlaksson it was now put to such diligent use that Hólar since remained the chief seat of printing in Iceland. In 1584 Bishop Gudbrand Thorlaksson printed the first Icelandic Bible, the greater part of which he himself had translated. Of other books printed under his direction may be mentioned his hymn-book, 1589, and the "Graduale," a book of melodies for Lutheran hymns, 1594. In 1685 the press was moved to Skálholt, but it was returned to Hólar in 1703, after being located in various places for a short time.[42] In 1844 it was finally moved to Reykjavik. The first efforts of the Icelandic printers were naturally directed to the printing of religious literature, but in time sagas and other secular works also appeared. The first edition of sagas published in Iceland was that of Bishop Thord Thorlaksson of Skálholt, a great-grandson of Bishop Gudbrand, who served as bishop from 1674 till 1697. He printed the "Landnámabók,"

[42] The writers of the history of printing in Iceland: Gunnar Pálsson, *Typographia Islendica;* and Jon Borgfirdingur, *Sögugrip um prentsmiðjur og prentara a Íslandi,* hold that there were two presses in Iceland at this time. But more acceptable is the view of Prof. Halldor Hermannsson, in his work *Icelandic Books of the Sixteenth Century,* p. 1 ff. After examining carefully all the earliest works printed in Iceland he finds that they must have issued from the same press.

"Kristnisaga," "Íslendingabók" and the "Olafssaga Tryggvasonar." Nothing further was done for the printing of sagas in Iceland till 1756, when new editions issued from the Hólar press. About this time another press was set up in the island of Hrappsey, where the "Egilssaga" was printed. In 1782 the "Annálar Björns á Skarðsá" were also printed here.

The first fruit of the new literary activity aroused by the Reformation were the early Bible translations and the efforts made to provide a collection of hymns for the Lutheran church service. Odd Gottskalksson, Bishop Ögmund's private secretary and later lawman in Iceland, translated the New Testament, which was printed in Roskilde, Denmark, in 1540. The translation of the whole Bible was first made by Bishop Gudbrand Thorlaksson. But part of this work was based on Odd Gottskalksson's translation of the New Testament, and that of some other Biblical books by various translators. Olaf Hjaltason, the first Lutheran bishop of Hólar, was the first translator of Lutheran hymns in Iceland, but his work was poorly done and of little real value. Martein Einarsson, the first Lutheran bishop of Skálholt, was also a translator and writer of hymns. He published the first Icelandic Lutheran hymn-book, which appeared in Copenhagen in 1555. Three years later a new hymn-book was published by Gisli Jonsson, who succeeded Martein as bishop of Skálholt in 1558.[43] But Gisli possessed no poetic talent, and his translations have no real merit. In 1589 Bishop Gudbrand Thorlaksson, translator of the Bible, the Nestor of the early Lutheran church in Iceland, prepared a new hymn-book. Like earlier collections it consisted chiefly of mediocre translations, but it became so popular that it remained in use over two hundred years. Through these works the Lutheran hymns were introduced into the church service, but the writing of original Icelandic hymns did not progress beyond the first frail beginnings prior to 1600. In the period immediately following the Reformation hymns were written by the clergymen Einar Sigurdsson and Jon Thorsteinsson. Jon, also called the martyr, was clergyman

[43] Halldor Hermannsson, *Icelandic Books in the Sixteenth Century.*

on the Vestmannaeyjar, where he was slain in 1627 in an attack made on these islands by Algerian sea-robbers. Especially prominent as scholar was Odd Einarson (1559-1630), bishop of Skálholt. He was the first one after the Reformation who began to record historical events in his own mother tongue; also the first one to collect Icelandic manuscripts and documents, which otherwise might have been lost. The "Grallarinn," a collection of choral melodies for the Lutheran hymns, published in 1594, was also prepared with his assistance. The first great Icelandic hymn-writer was Hallgrim Pjetursson, born of poor parents in 1614. He studied for some time in Copenhagen, and after his return to Iceland he was consecrated parish clergyman by his friend Brynjolf Sveinsson, bishop of Skálholt. He had to struggle with poverty all his life. When he was finally transferred to a better charge so that he could live under more favorable conditions, he became afflicted with leprosy, from which he died in 1674. He was a fine speaker and won great distinction as a poet even in his own lifetime. He is justly regarded as Iceland's greatest hymn-writer, the first one who compares favorably with the great hymn-writers of the Lutheran church in other lands. His hymns reveal a remarkable fertility of thought expressed in striking figures and beautiful language. His greatest work is his "Fimtiu passiusalmar," one of the finest collections of hymns based on the Passion of Christ. In these hymns the afflicted poet follows his Savior from Gethsemane to Golgotha, dwelling with pious reflection upon every word from his lips, every motion of his hand. Pjetursson's hymns have become one of the most coveted literary treasures of the Icelandic people, and have exerted a deep influence on their religious life. In 1914 the whole Icelandic nation celebrated the three-hundredth anniversary of his birth. In speaking on this occasion Professor Haraldur Nielsson said:

"Generation after generation his 'Passiusalmar' have been sung winter after winter in every home in the land, and this is still being done. Generation after generation many have committed them all to memory, and for two hundred and fifty years nearly every person has learned some of them. During all these years scarcely an Icelander has been buried either at home or abroad unless some stanzas of the hymn 'Alt eins og blómstrið eina' have been sung at his bier. Since Hallgrim's time the teachings of Christ have been instilled into the souls of the children through his hymns. The first prayers which our mothers and sisters taught us they had learned from the lips of Hallgrim Pjetursson." [44]

After the Reformation only native-born churchmen were appointed bishops in Iceland. Many of these were men of great ability, who not only guided the people in religious affairs, but distinguished themselves as intellectual leaders, rendering valuable service in promoting enlightenment and general culture. Gizur Einarsson, Martein Einarsson, Olaf Hjaltason, Odd Einarsson and Gudbrand Thorlaksson have already been mentioned. To this group of church leaders belonged also Brynjolf Sveinsson, Jon Thorkelsson Vidalin, and Finnur Jonsson (1704-1789), especially noted as the author of the great work on Icelandic church history "Historia Ecclesiastica Islandiæ." Brynjolf Sveinsson (1605-1675), bishop of Skálholt, known for his majestic appearance and dignified bearing, was well versed in classical languages and cherished a deep interest for the literature of Iceland. He devoted special attention to the collection of old manuscripts of Icelandic literary works, an effort in which he spared neither time nor money until he had created a valuable manuscript collection containing many of the leading works in Old Icelandic. Bishop Jon Vidalin of Skálholt (1667-1720) is reputed to have been the most eloquent of Icelandic ecclesiastics. Chief among his literary works is his "Huspostilla," or "Book of Family Sermons," which has appeared in twelve editions, and is regarded by his countrymen as one of the best works of its kind. Vidalin was an orthodox Lutheran of the great reformer's own type. Adhering to the written Bible word with a sincerity which left no room for peradventure or hesitation, he combined with the intellectualism of orthodoxy an ardent faith and an im-

[44] *Island, Streiflys over Land og Folk,* p. 126 ff. J. C. Poestion, *Isländische Dichter der Neuzeit,* p. 209 ff. C. F. Bricka, *Dansk biografisk Lexikon,* vol. viii.

passioned eloquence which gave him great power over his hearers. He sought to stir the conscience of his people by preaching repentance and conversion rather than the gospel message of salvation through Christ. Raising his mighty voice like one crying in the wilderness he summoned the people to repent, lighting up their secret sins with the burning torch of the Word of God. How submissively and attentively the people listened to his preaching is shown by the number of editions of his sermons, which have remained one of the most popular family books even to the present. Through the work of the Lutheran bishops a spiritual regeneration had been wrought which marks the ultimate triumph of the Reformation. The popularity of Hallgrim Pjeturssson's hymns and of Bishop Jon Vidalin's sermons shows that evangelical Christianity had become a living force in the lives of the Icelandic people. The Icelanders, being strongly individualistics, usually keen, often contentious, and generally given to reflection, have not been stirred by revivals or emotional Christianity. The deepest influence ever exerted upon their religious life is due to the intellectual Lutheran orthodox faith brought them by the Reformation. This influence had now become a regenerating force which stimulated the dormant national powers to a new creative literary activity as well as a new religious life.

Without a university of their own, with only two higher schools, weak and poorly equipped, and at times so neglected that they had to remain closed, higher learning was nowhere more diligently cultivated than in Iceland, and in no land was the number of talented and well educated intellectual leaders relatively so large. Amidst flaming volcanoes and destructive earthquakes which filled the pages of their annals with ghastly tales of woe the Icelanders were experiencing a literary renaissance which kindled new light, not only in their own country, but in foreign lands. Again they wrote works which attracted the attention of all Europe. Invaluable treasures for literary and historical research were made available, and new fields were opened to learned activity. Especially noted are the three scholars Arngrim Jonsson (1568-1648), Thormod Torfason, or Torfæus (1636-1719), and Arni Magnusson (1663-1730), who distinguished themselves in the fields of history writing and antiquarian research. Arngrim Jonsson had studied at the University of Copenhagen, and became rector or master of the Latin school at Hólar. He collected and studied old manuscripts, and wrote several works dealing with the geography and history of Iceland. Chief of these is his "Crymogea sive Rerum Islandicarum Libri III," published in Hamburg in 1609. In 1593 he published "Brevis Commentarius de Islandia," and in 1643 appeared "Specimen Islandiæ Historicum." In recognition of the importance of his work to Icelandic literature and scholarly activity he has been called "the restorer of Icelandic learning." Thormod Torfæus wrote many historical works. In 1697 appeared "De Rebus Gestis Færeyensium," a history of the Faroe Islands; in 1697 "Orcades," a work about the Orkney Islands; in 1706 "Grønlandia Antiqua," and in 1707 "Vinlandia," the story of the Norse discovery of America. His principal work, "Historia Rerum Norwegicarum," a history of Norway till 1387, was published in four large folio volumes in 1711.

For the first time a survey of the history of Norway now appeared in a language which could be read by scholars in all lands. Torfæus showed little scholarly ability in the use of historical material. He accepts fabulous tales as readily as accounts resting on the most trustworthy evidence, but he was acquainted with historical sources, and elaborated them into a connected account, which for a long period continued to be the chief source of information regarding the history of Norway. In 1667 he was appointed royal historiographer. Later he was sent as royal official to Norway, where he resided till his death on the estate Stangeland in Stavanger stift. Arni Magnusson became interested in the old literatures of the North while pursuing his studies at the University of Copenhagen. Receiving appointment as royal antiquary and also as private secretary to the historian Thomas Bartholin, he found opportunity to gather manuscripts and old literary documents in Iceland and elsewhere, a scholarly activity which became his great life-work. In 1701 he was made professor of philosophy in the University of Copenhagen, and the following year he was appointed member of a royal commission sent to take a new census in Iceland. During the subsequent ten years which he spent in Iceland he collected a large number of manuscripts and literary documents. In this collection he succeeded in preserving nearly all of the old manuscripts which were found here and there in private homes in Iceland, often in a decaying condition. In Norway and Denmark he gathered many more, partly as gifts and partly through purchase. A most valuable manuscript library, the "Arnemagnean Collection," had thus been created in Copenhagen, and the old Icelandic literature was saved from destruction. With a few later additions it now numbers 2000 manuscripts and 6000 documents. Many other equally able scholars labored in various fields. Björn Jonsson á Skardsá (1574-1655) interpreted scaldic songs, wrote runes and copied old sagas. His principal work is "Annálar" from 1400-1645. He also wrote a work about the ravages of the Algerian pirates in Iceland, the "Tyrkjaránssaga." Magnus Olafsson wrote the first Icelandic lexicon, "Specimen Luxici Runici," published in Copenhagen 1650. Gudmund Olafsson was called to Sweden, where he became a noted translator of Icelandic sagas. Somewhat later the poet, patriot and scientist Eggert Olafsson became very popular and widely known. His chief scientific work is "Reise gjennem Island," in which he describes economic life and conditions in Iceland. It was largely due to the stimulating influence of the Icelandic scholars that a keen interest in Northern history and antiquities was awakened at this time also in other European countries. In Denmark scholars and historians like Ole Worm, Thomas Bartholin, Jacob Langebeck, Peder Frederick Suhm, and the Norwegian historian Gerhard Schøning turned their attention to Northern antiquities and the Old Icelandic literature. In Sweden Johan P. Peringsköld and his son Johan F. Peringsköld became devoted students in this field, and translated many Icelandic works. Also in England, France and Germany many translations of Icelandic songs and sagas appeared.

The ancient literature of the North began to attract general attention.

A deep shadow was cast upon intellectual and social life in Iceland as in all other lands in the seventeenth century by the witchcraft craze, which, like other plagues, was imported from abroad. Superstition reigned supreme in Iceland as elsewhere in Europe at this time, but it might have been relatively harmless but for this unfortunate delusion, started by clergymen and officials who had been in direct contact with continental culture. In 1625 Jon Rögnvaldsson was burned for witchcraft, the first person who was put to death in Iceland for this imaginary crime.[45] It was then a law in Denmark that persons convicted of witchcraft should be burned, but it does not appear that this law had been introduced in Iceland. The priests and officials engaged in these prosecutions, acting with fanatical zeal, took it upon themselves to sentence the accused according to the provisions in the Danish code, without regard for the right of the Icelanders to be tried under their own laws. Burning or other forms of execution, flogging and other severe punishments for witchcraft grew in frequency. The Icelandic scholar and writer Magnus Stephensen says:

"In the period 1660-1690 sixteen persons were burned in Iceland. . . . Provost P. Björnsson in Selardal, who was a clergyman over fifty years, and until the day of his death was regarded as one of the greatest lights in theology, was a zealous promoter of witchcraft prosecutions. Everywhere he thought that he discovered the influence of the witchcraft evil even upon himself, and this influence he discussed in nearly all his writings. He brought suit against many persons for witchcraft, demanding their death, and the civil authorities aided him diligently." [46]

According to Thorkell Bjarnason twenty persons were burned at the stake for witchcraft in the period 1630-1690.[47]

[45] Espolin, *Árbækur*, part v, ch. xiii, p. 29.
[46] Magnus Stephensen, *Island i det 18de Aarhundrede*, p. 165 ff. Th. Thoroddsen, *Hindurvitni og galdratru* (Landfrædissaga Islands, vol. ii, p. 20 ff.).
[47] Thorkel Bjarnason, *Um siðbótina á Íslandi*, p. 166 f.

According to Bishop Jon Helgason the number was twenty-
two.[48] Many were also flogged or banished for the same
supposed crime. Clemens Bjarnason was sentenced to death
for witchcraft in 1690. He was pardoned, but had to leave
the country. This was the last instance in which the death
penalty was imposed in Iceland for this fancied wrongdoing.
Throughout the seventeenth century capital punishment
was unsparingly inflicted, not only for witchcraft and murder, but for incest, adultery, theft, and other crimes. At
every session of the Althing people flocked together to witness the hangings, burnings, decapitations, drownings, the
floggings and brandings of offenders sentenced under the
harsh laws. All these frequently repeated dramas of suffering only added new measures to human misery, darkened the
outlook on life, and deadened all sympathy with the unfortunate. Toward the close of the century these dark
shadows lifted before the dawn of a more humane and enlightened age. The harsh criminal laws were modified, and
the use of the death penalty was restricted, especially
through the practice of appeal to the king. It is noteworthy that the victims of the witchcraft delusion in Iceland
were men, only one woman being put to death in these
prosecutions.

14. GREAT CALAMITIES IN ICELAND. THE DANISH TRADE MONOPOLY. NEW LITERARY ACTIVITY

THE religious and dynastic wars which rent Europe during the sixteenth and seventeenth centuries did not disturb
the general tranquillity of Iceland, but various misfortunes
occasioned much suffering and awakened serious apprehension for the future of the country. Overseas trade, upon
which the people depended for so many of their necessaries,
was often seriously disturbed and at times completely interrupted by the great wars. Pirates swarmed the ocean, pick-
ing up merchantmen plying between Iceland and continental
ports, and at any moment they might swoop down upon

[48] Jon Helgason, *Islands Kirke fra Reformationen til vore Dage*, 105.

the unprotected shores and sack exposed coast settlements. The lack of adequate protection kept the people in constant fear of piratic raids, which were increasing in frequency and boldness. The annalist Jon Espolin relates that in 1614 Spanish buccaneers carried away sheep and cattle in the district of Vestfjord, and extorted money from the people. English pirates under the leadership of John Gentleman came to the Vestmannaeyjar, where they robbed houses and destroyed property. "They placed muskets before the breasts of the people with laughter and ridicule," says the annalist. "The church bell they seized and fastened to the mast of their ship. But they killed no one, and they sailed then back to England."[1] Trading vessels were also plundered in Djupavog. In 1615 pirates came to Patriksfjord with the intention of ravaging the Vestfjord districts. They had seized some Englishmen whom they brought with them, and after plundering the neighborhood they departed. A little later Spanish buccaneers came to the coast with three ships, and ill-treated and robbed the people. One of their ships was wrecked, so that eighty of them had to seek refuge on shore. These were attacked by the people under the leadership of Ari Magnusson, acting under royal orders. Thirty-one of them were killed in Isafjord, thirteen in Dyrafjord, and eighteen more in Ædey and Sandeyri. The rest operated as robber bands until they were finally exterminated.[2] The buccaneers now became so bold in their operations that in 1616 King Christian IV detailed war vessels to protect the Icelandic trade. In 1618 he sent war-ships under two royal commissioners, Frederick Friis and Jørgen Wind, to drive the pirates from the sea. The commissioners were also given power to deal with all important matters both of church and state in Iceland.[3] They decided many important cases at the Althing, says the annalist. Many persons, both men and women, were sentenced to death and executed for adultery. What success they had in their operations against

[1] Jon Espolin, *Árbœkur*, part v, ch. xiv, p. 133. Björn á Skardsá, *Annálar*, vol. ii, p. 70. *Sögurit*, vol. iv, ch. iii ff. *Tímarit*, vol. xvi, p. 88 ff.
[2] Espolin, *Árbœkur*, part v, ch. xvi, p. 156.
[3] Björn á Skardsá, *Annálar*, vol. ii, p. 92.

the pirates is not recorded, but it soon became evident that
they had not driven them from the ocean. On June 12,
1627, Algerian pirates entered Grindavik and took a Danish
merchant ship with its cargo and several sailors and other
people on board, among others the wife of Jon Gudlaugsson and her sons and brothers.[4] Meeting another vessel outside of the harbor they decoyed it with the flag from the
ship which they had just seized and captured it. The first
one they then sent with their booty to the Barbary States.
Afterwards they sailed to Faxafloi, intending to attack Bessastadir, but the governor, Holger Rosenkrans, had gathered
men and ships in the neighborhood. He constructed breast-
works and mounted some guns. When they saw these preparations for defense they did not venture an assault. One
of their ships ran aground, but they transferred their prisoners and booty to the other ships. As this proved very
difficult the governor was severely criticized because he did
not use this opportunity to attack them. They then sailed
to the Eastfjords, where they seized many cattle, captured
110 persons and killed many others. The greatest outrage
was commited on the Vestmannaeyjar, also in 1627. Arriving there with three ships and 300 men the pirates divided into three bands and overran the whole island with
loud yells, massacring the terror-stricken and helpless inhabitants. After driving the people together in a large store-
house belonging to the Danish merchants they selected the
youngest and strongest and drove them on board their ships.
They then set fire to the building and burned it with those
who remained. The priest in the islands, Jon Thorsteinsson,
the hymn-writer, was struck dead while kneeling in prayer.
His wife and children were driven on board the ships. The
parish church was burned, and those who tried to escape
were mercilessly hunted down and slain. After destroying
what could not be carried away the robbers sailed back
to Africa, where they sold their captives as slaves. Most of
these died soon. Those who survived wrote such touching
letters to their home-folks that money was finally collected
for their ransom both in Denmark and Iceland. In 1632 King

[4] Espolin, *Árbœkur*, part vi, ch. xlix.

Christian IV sent a large sum to the Barbary States to secure their liberation. Thirty-seven persons were thus rescued, besides the priest Olaf Egilsson, who had been liberated after a captivity of two years. Of the people carried away by the pirates only thirteen ever returned to their native land.[5]

Great volcanic eruptions together with cold winters and severe epidemics increased the difficulties under which the people were struggling. In 1695 and 1696 the winters were so severe that not only did the rivers freeze where they were never known to freeze before, but the ocean around all Iceland became ice-bound. Hard winters recurred in 1784 and 1792. In the latter year horses were driven across the southern Hvitá on the ice the twelfth of May, and the frost did not leave the ground all summer.[6] These severe winters were usually accompanied by violent storms, in which large numbers of boats and fishermen were lost.

Still more destructive was the havoc wrought by earthquakes and volcanic eruptions. In 1618-1619 volcanic outbreaks and earthquakes destroyed many farmsteads, causing much suffering and loss of property. A volcanic eruption in eastern Iceland in 1625 lasted for twelve days, and was so violent that ashes fell even in Bergen, Norway.[7] In 1636 the great volcano Hekla became active, this being its fifteenth recorded eruption. Its activity lasted from May 8 until the following winter, and ashes were deposited over large areas. In 1660 an outbreak of the Katla destroyed the presbytery and church at Höfdabrekka, together with many farmsteads.[8] In 1693 occurred a violent eruption of the Hekla, the sixteenth.[9] Ashes were deposited over all Iceland, and were even carried to Scotland and Norway. In the eighteenth century even greater destruction was

[5] Espolin, *Árbækur*, part v, ch. xlix, p. 35. Björn á Skardsá, *Tyrkjaránssaga*. Finnur Jonsson, *Historia Ecclesiastica Islendiæ*, vol. iii, p. 80 ff. Sigfus Blöndal, *De algierske Sørøveres Tog til Island Aar 1627. Søgurit,* vol. iv, *Tyrkjaraniŏ á Íslandi 1627*.

[6] Espolin, *Árbækur*, parts v and vi. Magnus Stephensen, *Island i det 18de Aarhundrede*, p. 37 ff.

[7] Björn á Skardsá, *Annálar*, vol. ii, p. 118.

[8] Th. Thoroddsen, *Observations on Volcanic Eruptions and Earthquakes in Iceland*, p. 11.

[9] Espolin, *Árbækur*, part viii, ch. xxvi.

wrought. In 1727 an eruption of the Öræfajökull began August 3, and lasted till May 25 the following year.[10] Many farms were blotted out, and hundreds of sheep and horses were killed. Through an earthquake at Rangárvellir and Eystrihreppr in September, 1732, eleven or twelve farmsteads were destroyed, and forty were more or less damaged. In 1755 an eruption of the Katla destroyed thirteen farms and covered a large part of Skaftafellssysla with a deposit of ashes so deep that fifty farms had to be abandoned.[11] In 1783 occurred a violent outbreak of the Skaptarjökull, one of the most destructive in the history of Iceland.[12] Nine farms were entirely wiped out, twenty-nine more were ruined, and two parishes were rendered uninhabitable for two years. The meadows were devastated, and a large number of animals died of starvation and disease. According to reliable sources the loss of animals during the years 1783-1784 was: 11,461 head of cattle, 190,448 sheep and 28,013 horses.[13] In 1784 a great earthquake in southern Iceland destroyed sixty-nine farmsteads totally, wrecked sixty-four, and seriously damaged 372. Of houses 1459 were leveled with the ground, 212 were wrecked, and 333 were seriously damaged.[14]

Owing to such calamities which brought about a general dislocation of economic life, famine and disease swept away the stricken people in large numbers. The annalists state that in 1702, 120 persons died of hunger in Thingeyjarsysla alone. The death rate in general was very high, owing to undernourishment and unwholesome food. In 1707 a great smallpox epidemic swept the country, carrying away 18,000 people, or about one-third of the entire population.[15]

[10] Espolin, *Árbœkur*, part ix, ch. lxxx.

[11] *Ibidem*, part x, ch. xxxi.

[12] *Ibidem*, part x, ch. xxxiii.

[13] Magnus Stephensen, *Beskrivelse over den nye Vulkans Ildsprudning—1783*, p. 126. Hans Finsen, *Om Folkemœngdens Formindskelse ved Uaar i Island*, p. 123. Th. Thoroddsen, *Observations on Volcanic Eruptions and Earthquakes in Iceland* (translation by George H. Boehmer), p. 15.

[14] Thorvald Thoroddsen, *Jarðskjálftar á Suðrlandi*, p. 32.

[15] Benedikt Petersen, *Annal.* Eggert Olafsson, *Reise gjennem Island*, p. 348. Hans Finsen, *Om Folkemœngdens Formindskelse ved Uaar i Island*, p. 177 ff.

In 1757, 2500 died of hunger in the Skálholt diocese. The suffering due to these causes became especially great after the eruption of the Skaftafellsjökull, which so seriously depleted the flocks and herds of the country. In a report from the Hólar diocese Bishop Arni Thorarensen states that 2145 persons had died of hunger, and that 315 farms had been abandoned. As a result of this calamity it is estimated that 9238 persons died in Iceland of hunger and attendant diseases.[16] People fell dead from exhaustion in going from one farm to another. Children lost their parents, and in many households not a person survived. "During this century," says Magnus Stephensen,

"Iceland experienced forty-three years of distress due to cold winters, ice-floes, failures of fisheries, shipwrecks, inundations, volcanic eruptions, earthquakes, epidemics and contagious diseases among men and animals, which often came separately, but often in connection with and as a result of one another." [17]

Statistics show how the herds were depleted and how the population of Iceland was decreasing at this time:

Population

1703	50,444
1708	34,000
1769	46,416
1791	40,130
1800	47,086
1850	59,157
1860	66,900 [18]
1877	72,000

Sheep

1703	280,000
1760	357,000
1783	236,000

[16] Hans Finsen, *Om folkemængdens formindskelse ved Uaar i Island*, p. 135. Th. Thoroddsen, *Observations on Volcanic Eruptions and Earthquakes in Iceland*, p. 15.

[17] Magnus Stephensen, *Island i det 18de Aarhundrede*.

[18] *Skýrslur um landshagi á Íslandi (Statistique de L'Islande)*, vol. i, p. 2, 53; vol. iii, p. 347 ff.

1784	49,000
1800	307,000
1870	500,000 [19]

Cattle

1703	35,800
1770	30,100
1784	9,800
1800	23,300
1840	22,300
1872	20,300
1876	20,400

Horses

1703	26,900
1760	32,200
1784	8,600
1800	28,300
1840	32,200
1859	39,800
1876	31,300 [20]

Another cause which tended to deprive the common people of all hope of progress and economic well-being in the eighteenth century was the existing system of landownership.[21] A large part of the soil of Iceland had in course of time been converted into crown estates and church lands, which the people had to till as renters. The crown lands embraced in all 735 farms, the bishop's seat of Skálholt owned 310, that of Hólar 320, the various church estates included 675, and 31 belonged to hospitals and funds for the poor, in all 2071 farms, while 2116 were privately owned. The administration of the royal estates was in the hands of the *landfógeti,* who resided at Bessastadir, later at Videy. He had direct charge of all royal estates in Gullbringusysla, issued leases and collected the rents. At the Althing he met and made public announcements of the estates which were vacant. These were then leased at public auction to the

---

[19] *Skýrslur um landshagi á Íslandi,* 1860. *Tidsskrift for veterinærvidenskab,* 1879.

[20] *Skýrslur um landshagi á Íslandi,* 1861. *Stjórnartíðindi,* 1878.

[21] *Dansk historisk Tidsskrift,* 6te række, vol. iv, p. 563 ff.; Jon Jonsson, *Fæstebondens Kaar paa Island i det 16de Aarhundrede.*

highest bidder. The lands belonging to the bishops' seats were managed by an administrator called *oeconomus*, who leased the lands, hired servants for the bishop's residence and served as steward in the household. The rent was usually fixed at one-twentieth of the taxable value of the farm. But owing to volcanic eruptions, floods and other misfortunes the people were often unable to pay, and would then have to part with their personal belongings to cover the deficit. Magnus Ketilsson wrote in 1770: "The peasants create debts every year, and as they fear these, I must see to my sorrow that they now offer me their own clothes and those of their wives." No changes were made in the rents from generation to generation, or even from century to century, although the farms had often lost much of their original productivity through volcanic eruptions or poor management of impoverished renters. It was stated by many prominent and well informed Icelanders that many farms still renting for the same amount as in the past could not support one-fifth as many cattle as formerly. As a rule the renters also had to agree to keep the houses in repair, a very heavy burden often connected with great expense, as timber was very costly and difficult to procure. But if anything was not in order when the renter left, the manager would demand a considerable sum as indemnity. The royal *landfógeti* would often act in a most unjust and arbitrary way. About Chr. Dresse it is stated in a letter to the *stiftamtmaðr* of 1775 that he was a confirmed drunkard, that he abused the peasants when they were unable to pay their dues, seized all their belongings and drove them from their homes no matter at what season of the year, and that he often failed to give them credit for the property he had taken. He was finally dismissed from office because of his harshness and unseemly conduct. The system of subletting was extensively practised. The royal estates, and likewise also the lands of the bishops' seats, were often rented to priests, officials or other persons of standing, who subleased them to peasants, and lived a life of leisure from incomes pressed from the real tillers of the soil. The sublessees (*hjáleigumenn*) were often reduced to a condition resembling villeinage, as they had

to render service to their landlords in addition to the payment of rent for their small farmsteads, which usually could
keep only a cow or two and a few sheep. The landlord also
furnished a certain number of cattle, called *kúgildi* (Danish
kvilder). The amount of rent for the live-stock was not
fixed by law. As a rule it was very high and had to be paid
in butter, and as the renter was often unable to produce
enough of that commodity to pay his rent, he had to content
himself with a mixture of tallow and train-oil on his own
table. One of the most perplexing features of the relation
between landlord and renter was the question who should
pay the loss when cattle died. It was generally held that if
they died of old age the owner should replace them, that if
they died from the lack of proper care, the renter should
make good the loss. But this rule, fair enough in the ab-
stract, created endless trouble when it was to be practically
applied. In case of cattle and sheep diseases, losses were
often great and the controversy would be accordingly bitter.
When the sheep disease broke out in 1761 and in ten years
reduced the number from 491,934 to 112,054, it would seem
that the renters could not be held responsible for such a
calamity. But many landlords, among others the bishop's
seat of Skálholt, nevertheless demanded that they should
pay the loss.

The service which the renters and poorer classes had to
render the *landfógeti* and the landlords was often very bur-
densome. One duty imposed upon the renters was the
mannslán, which consisted chiefly in rowing the king's fishing
boats during the fishing season. As the *landfógeti* found
fishing very profitable, he often greatly increased the number of boats, and all sorts of threats and intimidations were
used to compel the people to row them. The peasants had
to leave their homes or send their sons to perform this hated
service. Another form of service was the *hrosslán.* At the
Thingeyrar cloister the men had to meet with shod horses
September 30 every year, and make a trip which lasted from
eight to ten days. Horses also had to be furnished to bring
the *stiptamtmaðr,* the *landfógeti,* the bishops and other high
officials to the Althing, together with quantities of food and

drink for the session. Every fall horses and men also had
to be provided to bring the *stiptamtmaðr's* fish to the seaport
towns, and whenever the *stiptamtmaðr* or *landfógeti* needed
horses for home use or travel, the peasants had to stand
ready to render the desired service. The more common form
of service was the *dagsverk,* which consisted in ordinary
work to be performed on the landlord's estates during hay-
ing. The *mannslán* was counted equivalent to twenty *alnar*
(40 fish), the *hrosslán* ten *alnar* (20 fish) and the *dagsverk*
five *alnar.* These three forms of service constituted what
was known as the fixed service. Another kind required on
royal estates and lands belonging to the bishoprics, but
never demanded on private estates, was the undefined service which consisted in help to be given in erection of buildings, in repairing fences, etc. Another burden imposed on
renters was the feeding of a certain number of the landlord's
cattle over winter. During seasons of hay shortage this
burden was very grievous, as the poor peasant often had to
slaughter his own cattle in order to feed those of his
landlord.

The peasant's cheerless hovel, and the lack of most ordinary comforts in his home life, was a striking evidence of the
hopeless poverty to which he had been reduced. As the
merchants brought little timber to the country because it
required much room in their ships, it became so scarce and
expensive that the peasants could not use it even for framework in their cottages, but had to build them of sod and
stone. The *sýslumaðr* Vigfus Thorarinsson gives the following description of a peasant's home: "The living room
(*baðstofa*) is usually eight feet wide and sixteen feet long,
built of sod, with roof of the same material, and without
wooden inside walls. The kitchen and pantry, built of the
same material and in the same way, are about one-half as
large as the living room." The general interior appearance
of these peasants' huts is described by Jon Jonsson as follows:

"The *baðstofa* on the common peasant farmstead was usually
not covered with boards on the inside. One could see between
the rafters to the grass-covered roof, which soon looked like

ordinary sod, and from which mildew and cobwebs were hanging.
The floor was uncovered, consisting only of earth trampled hard.
But during heavy rains when the roof was leaking water dripped
down, and it soon became a pool of mud through which the
people waded. The walls along which the bedsteads were nailed
fast were covered with a grey coat of mildew, and green slime
was constantly trickling down the walls, especially in the winter.
Bed clothes were very few among the poor people. Old hay,
seaweed or twigs did service as mattress, and a few blankets
constituted the covering. In some houses a little loft was built,
the *pallr*, two or three feet from the ground, where the people of
the household stayed. The dark room underneath the *pallr*
was occupied by lambs and young calves which needed special
care. . . . One trouble with all dwellings, though there might be
considerable difference between them, was the want of light. In
a house where there was no heating apparatus, as in the Icelandic
baðstofa, and in a climate as chilly as that of Iceland, it was
necessary to preserve the heat as well as possible. The windows
were, therefore, both few and small, and were usually placed in
the roof above the bed. A window consisted of only one pane,
and this was not of glass, but of a thin membrane (*líknabelgur*)
stretched upon a frame and placed in a hole in the roof. When
the wind was strong, the windows would often break, and the
women would have to mend them. It can readily be understood
that these windows admitted so little light into the room that
the people had to sit in continual darkness even in the middle
of the day." [22]

The effect of this kind of dwellings on the health and well-
being of the people was injurious in the extreme. Magnus
Olafsson, member of a royal commission, writing about conditions in Iceland at this time says:

"One can understand how these miserably constructed houses
of the poor contribute to the spread of all sorts of diseases,
as the houses, especially the dwellings, are very low. There
the people sit on the loft, and the air is so impure that a
stranger who is not accustomed to it can scarcely endure it
for an hour, as it is corrupted by the smoke of the train-oil
lamps, and the respiration and perspiration of the people, of

[22] *Dansk historisk Tidsskrift,* 6te række, vol. iv. Jon Jonsson, *Fæstebondens Kaar paa Island i det 16de Aarhundrede,* p. 601 ff. Eggert Olafsson,
Reise gjennem Island, vol. 1, p. 175.

whom many are affected with scurvy and other diseases. When pregnant women and small children have to breathe this infected air, it is not strange that many even in their youth become affected with tuberculosis and spit blood when they move about rapidly."

"One feature is still overlooked in these reports," says Jon Jonsson, "which did not improve the air in the *baðstofa*, namely, the fact that the men sat all day with their pipes in their mouths smoking, so that the smoke rolled out as from a factory chimney. The merchants had made them believe that if they only smoked a great deal no sickness would attack them."

How wretched and helpless the people must have been in such an environment, when smallpox epidemics and other dangerous diseases broke out, can readily be imagined. The sick and the well were huddled together in their dark hovels without medical aid, and usually even without proper food for the weak and suffering. In the eighteenth century leprosy became a most dreaded scourge, due, no doubt, to unsanitary conditions and unwholesome food. As the lepers could not be isolated, but had to live in the house with the rest, it is not strange that the disease should spread. The four hospitals found in the country could take care of only a small number of patients. How many lepers were found in the country in 1770 is not known, says Jon Jonsson, but in Seltjarnarnes alone, where there were only ten farms, there were twenty lepers. Judging from these figures there must have been at that time a great number in the whole country.

The Icelandic peasants bore their wretched lot with great patience and fortitude. Though complaints were often heard, they scarcely ever resisted their landlords or failed in the performance of the duties imposed upon them. But their hopeless condition destroyed their optimism and spirit of enterprise. Since various calamities had reduced them to abject poverty, and since the system of landownership made it impossible for them to own their houses or the soil they tilled, they lost all hope of accomplishing anything but keeping themselves and their families alive. As the farms were not improved, they lost rather than gained in productivity.

With a stoic mental attitude developed under conditions of extreme adversity the peasants could endure hardships, but their suffering and economic dependence fostered an unprogressive and apathetic spirit unfavorable to social development.

Of the various causes which gradually plunged the Icelandic people into so disheartening economic and social conditions, the most grievous was probably the Danish trade monopoly, which prohibited all foreign intercourse with Iceland. For centuries the Hanseatic League had controlled commerce in northern Europe. After its disintegration great commercial and maritime states had arisen—Spain, Portugal, the Netherlands, France and England—which entered into a sharp contest for trade advantages and colonial dominions in the western hemisphere as well as in the far East. The prevailing economic views governing trade relations at that time were not those of competition and free intercourse, but of trade monopoly and complete exclusion of rivals from markets within a nation's sphere of control. The trade with distant lands was seldom carried on by the governments directly, but was usually granted as a monopoly to commercial companies enjoying the most extensive privileges and powers, and responsible to no one after obtaining their charters and paying the required sum to the royal treasury. The Netherlands, which succeeded Portugal and Spain as the leading commercial state, developed a commercial policy scarcely less tyrannical than that of Spain itself. The colonial trade was carried on by commercial companies which received a monopoly of traffic in certain areas, establishing regulations which often resulted in incompetence and corruption. The Dutch West India Company, founded in 1621, controlled the trade west of the Cape of Good Hope, comprising commerce with the west coast of Africa and the east coast of America. This was virtually a corporation of privateers, who even opposed the termination of the war between Spain and the Netherlands in a remonstrance of 1633, as the cessation of hostilities would lessen their chances to prey on Spanish treasure ships. The Dutch East India Company, chartered in 1602, secured a monopoly of the trade eastward from the Cape of Good Hope. It established numerous trading stations in South Africa, on the coast of Asia, and on the islands in the Malay archipelago, where they broke the power of the Portuguese, and established a monopoly over many of the most valuable articles of commerce. In England trade with France, Spain and Portugal was open to all merchants, but commerce with the rest of the world was carried on by chartered companies exercising a monopoly within their specified territory. The Eastland Company controlled the trade with the Scandinavian countries and the Baltic provinces, the Russian Company with Russia. The Levant Company had exclusive trade privileges in the Mediterranean region, the East India Company in Asia, the Guinea or African Company on the west coast of Africa. The Virginia Company, Plymouth Company and Hudson Bay Company controlled the trade with America, each within its allotted sphere. In Denmark-Norway the enterprising and energetic King Christian IV, 1588-1648, sought to secure for his realms a fair share of the commerce of the world. In his efforts to promote trade he pursued the general policy of the age of establishing trade monopolies and commercial companies. The Danish East India Company was chartered in 1616, the West India Company in 1625, the Greenland Company in 1636. The trade with Iceland was treated in a similar way. Foreign competitors were excluded, and the trade with the island was to remain exclusively in the hands of citizens of the realm. In justice to the Danish government it must be said, then, that this way of dealing with Icelandic commerce did not differ from the general policy pursued by other nations at this time. But the system was so faulty, and the need in Iceland of a well regulated commerce was so great that the corrupt practices and limitation of trade due to the commercial monopoly soon brought serious distress and economic disaster upon the people.

In 1602 the trade with Iceland was granted to a company of Danish merchants of the cities of Copenhagen, Helsingør and Malmø for a period of twelve years, and all foreign trade with the island was forbidden by royal orders.[23] The merchants receiving this trade monopoly should sail to the various Icelandic harbors, and bring thither a sufficient supply of good goods, which were to be sold at the prices which had formerly obtained, and according to weights and measures which had been in use in Iceland. If differences should arise between the merchants and the people, the matter should be decided by the Althing. But these regulations were not obeyed. Things soon took such a turn that after two years the people were forced to bring their complaints to the king.[24] Not only were the goods now brought to Iceland much more costly than before, but necessaries like timber, tar and iron could no longer be had in sufficient quantities. In 1619 the king established a price schedule according to which goods were to be sold in Iceland.[25] But the merchants complained that the prices on their goods were too low, and brought such pressure to bear that a more favorable schedule was granted them in 1631.[26] When this was brought before the Althing, the people made vigorous protest. Bishop Gisli Oddsson was sent to Copenhagen with a remonstrance to the king, which moved him to set aside the new price schedule, and order that the prices of 1619 should remain in force.

King Christian IV died February 28, 1648, and was succeeded by his son Frederick III. Ever since the union of the two realms established at Kalmar in 1397 the king of Denmark-Norway had been placed on the throne through election by the Danish Estates, an arrangement which enabled the privileged classes to exercise a dominant influence upon the government, since the kings had to sign charters restricting their powers and safeguarding the privileges of the nobility. The personal friends of the new king resolved to do away with these restrictions upon his power. Under the leadership of Hans Nansen, mayor of Copen-

---

[23] Magnus Ketilsson, *Forordninger og aabne Breve*, vol. ii, p. 212 ff. *Lovsamling for Island*, vol. i, p. 139 ff. *Althingisbækur Íslands*, vol. iii, p 291 ff.

[24] *Althingisbækur Íslands*, vol. iii, p. 342 ff.

[25] Magnus Ketilsson, *Forordninger og aabne Breve*, vol. ii, p. 289 ff.

[26] *Ibidem*, p. 358 ff.

hagen, and Bishop Svane of Seeland, they overthrew the rule of the aristocracy in a coup d'état in Copenhagen, September 10, 1660, proclaiming Frederick III absolute hereditary monarch. The nobles were forced to give their consent. The charter was returned to the king as a token that the restrictions upon his power were annulled, and on October 18 he was formally hailed as hereditary king of Denmark. In accordance with the principles of absolutism a new constitution, the "Kongelov" (*lex regia*) was prepared in 1665, enumerating in detail the powers which he was to exercise without restrictions of any sort. By an act of 1661 he was formally made hereditary and absolute monarch. The Norwegian Estates, summoned to meet in Christiania, May 27, 1661, also hailed Frederick III as absolute hereditary king. With this accomplished steps were also taken to secure from the Icelanders a pledge of allegiance to the new régime. King Frederick III issued a summons to the leading men, bishops, provosts, priests, lawmen, *sýslumenn, lögrettumenn,* and farmers [27] to assemble at the Althing for this purpose. But as Henrik Bjelke, the *hirðstjóri* (governor-general), did not arrive in Iceland in time to attend the meeting, he asked the men summoned to meet him near Bessastadir on the coast. A meeting was accordingly assembled at Kopavog by the lawman Arni Oddsson, July 28, 1662, where the required oath was taken in the presence of Henrik Bjelke as the king's representative. In order to safeguard their liberty as far as possible the representatives demanded that their laws should be preserved to them, a request which Bjelke seems to have granted.[28] The same summer the assembled Althing declared that the Icelanders would act according to the old Icelandic agreement and the Icelandic laws. Some years before, in 1649, King Frederick III sent a royal letter to the Icelanders with the *hirðstjóri* Henrik Bjelke, saying: "We promise you all separately and collectively to maintain

[27] Magnus Ketilsson, *Forordninger og aabne Breve,* vol. iii, p. 85 ff.

[28] "An oath of allegiance was then sworn to King Frederick and all his offspring both in the male and female line. . . . But the Icelanders asked that the king should preserve to them the old laws of their land, and said that this they expected him to do." Jon Espolin, *Arbækur,* part vii, p. 32.

for you your laws and statutes, and to let you enjoy the
rights and liberties which have been yours hitherto." [29]
The ceremony of yielding formal homage to the king as
hereditary and absolute monarch was celebrated by a festival to which all the representatives at Kopavog were
invited. Salutes were fired, and fireworks illuminated the
sky.[30] The ceremony was staged by the governor chiefly in
glorification of his sovereign, as the Icelanders had not been
consulted. As a matter of form they were asked to ratify
an accomplished act, a request which they were not in
position to refuse. To them the affair at Kopavog was
only a new humiliation, a further encroachment upon their
national liberty and autonomy. How they really felt in
the midst of these festivities, accompanied by the booming
of guns, can be seen from the fact that the aged Magnus
Björnsson, for twenty-three years lawman in northern Iceland, upon hearing of the king's request resigned from his
office, and did not go to the Althing.[31] His son Gisli Magnusson, sýslumaðr a Hlidarendi, was elected to succeed
him, but refused to serve, declaring that he would rather
leave the country and go to Holland than accept the office.
Thorleif Kortsson was then chosen, a man notorious for
his avarice and his zeal in witchcraft prosecutions, a veri-
table scourge of his time. Arni Oddsson, lawman in southern Iceland, was already an old man, but it may have been
due in part to these untoward events that after the meeting
in Kopavog he immediately resigned. In Denmark, where
a haughty nobility had long oppressed the common people,
the introduction of absolutism was welcomed by many, as
the fatherly protection of an absolute king might tend to
shield them against the wanton acts of the feudal lords.
But in Iceland, where no nobility existed, the sudden increase of royal power carried with it no such advantage.
On the contrary, it could only serve to make the royal
officials more despotic and arbitrary, as it would deprive
the people of all control of legislation, destroy the last

[29] Magnus Ketilsson, *Forordninger og aabne Breve*, vol. iii, p. 9 ff.
[30] Espolin, *Árbækur*, part vii, p. 31 ff. *Safn til Sögu Íslands*, ii, p. 748.
[31] Espolin, *Árbækur*, part vii, p. 31 ff.

vestige of power and influence of the Althing, and make
the country wholly subservient to the dictates of a foreign
ruler.

Henrik Bjelke, who was a Norwegian by birth, remained
governor for twenty-three years, but after 1662 he did not
again visit Iceland. He sought to promote many undertakings which might be useful to the people, and strove to
prevent the placing of increased burdens upon them through
the levying of new taxes. But in his absence he was represented by *fógetar* acting as his deputies, many of whom
were cruel and despotic officials who failed to carry out his
plans. The worst of these was Thomas Nikulasson, who
finally drowned in 1665 to the great relief of the people.[32]
For over twenty years after the introduction of absolutism
the government of Iceland remained unchanged, but when
Bjelke died in 1683 many changes were made in the administration. The finances were separated from the other
administrative functions and placed in control of a *landfógeti*,[33] who was to superintend the royal estates, collect
the taxes, and audit the payment of public expenditures.
He was also to watch over the enforcement of the trade
laws. The first incumbent in this office, Christopher Heideman, was an able administrator, jovial and liberal with his
friends, but harsh to those whom he disliked. A new office,
that of *stiptbefalingsmaðr* for Iceland, was created in
1684.[34] This official was to conduct the general administration and exercise judicial authority in cases pertaining to
the church. But as he did not reside in Iceland, a resident
amtmaðr was appointed to act as his deputy.[35] This
arrangement continued till 1770, when the country was
divided into two *amts*,[36] each with its own *amtmaðr*, and
a new superior office, that of *stiptamtmaðr*, was created in
1688. This office was combined with that of *amtmaðr* for
the southern and western districts. The *stiptamtmaðr*
(governor-general) was to live in Iceland. The first *amt-*

[32] Espolin, *Árbœkur*, part vii, p. 41.
[33] *Lovsamling for Island*, vol. i, p. 398 f.
[34] *Ibidem*, vol. i, p. 405.
[35] *Ibidem*, vol. iii, p. 476 ff.
[36] *Ibidem*, vol. iii, p. 654 ff.

maðr in Iceland was the Dane Christian Müller, a man hated by the people for his rashness and blunders in the performance of his official duties. In 1787 Iceland was divided into three *amts*,[37] one for the southern, one for the western, and one for the northern and eastern districts. The highest authority in Icelandic affairs was vested in the *rentekammer* in Copenhagen, which had the supervision of administrative and commercial affairs. Judicial matters were under the control of the *kancelli,* and above all stood the king, who, as absolute monarch, was also lawgiver and source of justice. He also assumed the right to appoint bishops, lawmen and the more important parish priests, who had hitherto as a rule been chosen by the people. The Althing lost the last remnant of its legislative power, and continued to exist only as a judicial tribunal.

In regard to trade the policy inaugurated by Christian IV was continued by Frederick III and his successors. Danish merchants were permitted to send war vessels to Iceland to drive away foreign ships carrying goods to the island. In 1658 a new effort was made by the merchants to increase the prices on their goods, but in 1662 the company was dissolved because they had failed to supply the country with the necessary imports according to agreement.[38] The rule that the Icelanders should trade with no one but Danish merchants was, nevertheless, enforced as strictly as ever. By the ordinance of July 31, 1662, a new company was created, which received a monopoly for the period of twenty years. Iceland was divided into four commercial districts, and it was decreed that the people should not carry on trade with anyone outside their own district.[39] Throughout the seventeenth century English and Dutch fishing smacks often traded secretly with the Icelanders, but the punishments inflicted on those who violated the trade regulations were finally made so severe that no one would attempt to trade with foreigners except in cases of extreme need. In 1678 Páll Torfason, *sýslumaðr* in the Isafjord district,

[37] *Lovsamling for Island,* vol. v, p. 411 ff.
[38] Magnus Ketilsson, *Forordninger og aabne Breve,* vol. iii, p. 83 f.
[39] *Lovsamling for Island,* vol. i, p. 277 ff.

bought a couple of fishing lines from an English trawler in exchange for a few articles of knitted goods which the Danish merchants had refused to buy. For this offense he was brought to trial, and although he showed that without the lines he could not continue his catch, that his boats would have to lie idle, the punishment of the loss of his household articles was inflicted. Jon Vigfusson, *sýslumaðr* in the Borgarfjord district, was accused of trading with foreigners, and was dismissed from his office.[40] Trading outside of one's district was punished with equal severity. In 1684 new price schedules were established, increasing the prices on goods imported and lowering the prices on Icelandic articles of export. At the same time punishments for violating the rules of trade were made more severe. Traffic with foreigners or trading outside of one's district was henceforth to be punished by flogging, loss of property, or incarceration in the fortress of Bremerholm.[41] In 1699 a poor peasant by the name of Holmfast Gudmundsson was flogged in the presence of the *amtmaðr,* Christian Müller, because he had sold a few fish outside of his own district, though the Danish merchants admitted that they had refused to buy the fish.[42] Thomas Konradsson was sentenced to the fortress of Bremerholm for a similar offense.[43] In 1700 three men in the district of Isafjord were sentenced to the loss of their household goods and incarceration in the fortress of Bremerholm because they had bought two ells of kersey from an English fisherman. The *amtmaðr* was secretly in pact with the merchants, and received his share of the profit for their trade. By an ordinance of 1689 the number of districts was increased so that commercially the people were shut up within still smaller areas.[44] It is true that the government seems to have intended to aid the people in this way by compelling the merchants to carry

---

[40] Espolin, *Árbækur,* part vi, ch. xxvi. Thorkelsson og Arnorsson, *Ríkisrétindi Islands,* p. 209 ff. Olaf Stephenson, *Kort Underretning om den islandske Handels Førelse,* p. 4.

[41] *Lovsamling for Island,* vol. i, p. 406 ff.

[42] Espolin, *Árbækur,* part viii, ch. xlii.

[43] *Ibidem,* ch. xlix.

[44] *Lovsamling for Island,* vol. i, p. 481.

goods to all parts of Iceland, as a provision was added that if the merchants did not bring sufficient goods, the people should be allowed to trade outside of their own districts. But the further restriction on free intercourse could only tend to create new hardships. Among the disadvantages of the monopoly trade was not only a shortage of import of necessary commodities, but the fact that no market was created where Icelandic articles of export could be freely sold. The transportation of goods to the designated harbors in the commercial districts was usually connected with great labor and difficulty. When people from far-away districts finally reached the seaport with their wares, the merchants would usually buy only a limited quantity. They could select and reject according to their own notions. Goods of excellent quality were often rated as rejected articles, and when the merchants had loaded their vessels, nothing more could be sold. To bring the goods back home was connected. with so much labor and expense that they were rather abandoned. Hundreds of barrels of train-oil, large quantities of meat and fish, hides and pelts had to be destroyed for want of buyers. Thousands of sheep brought to the seaports had to be driven home again. Even knitted ware would be abandoned, as the transportation home was connected with more labor and difficulty than the goods were worth. Under such circumstances the prices which could be obtained for the goods were often very low, and the futility of producing goods which could not be marketed tended to destroy all spirit of thrift and enterprise. The absence of competition and open markets made the difference in price between Icelandic staple commodities and the imported merchant goods constantly greater and more unfair. A barrel of flour which in 1702 cost two rigsdaler rose to ten rigsdaler in 1800, while the price schedules on Icelandic goods remained practically unchanged. A *skippund* of fish (160 kilograms), which in other markets in 1782 was worth from thirty to forty dollars, was sold in Iceland to the Danish merchants for seven dollars. Often the merchants purchased commodities in Iceland with high-priced brandy, which was in great demand, but only harmed

the people. In 1788, in a period of famine and general
distress, 730 barrels of brandy were imported to Gullbringusysla, and sold for 21,900 rigsdaler.[45] Much harm was
also done because readymade articles were imported, compelling people to pay for work which they themselves might
have performed. Flour was imported, but no grain, muslin
was imported bleached, rope and articles of iron were imported, even tubs and barrels. But the Icelanders could
only export raw materials. The merchants salted the meat,
fish and butter exported from Iceland, cleaned the eiderdown, prepared the codfish and received hides and furs only
in unprepared form.

In 1699 King Frederick IV ascended the throne. Conditions in Iceland were then so deplorable that when the
people assembled at the Althing to take the oath of allegiance to the new sovereign, the general distress of the
country was the chief topic of conversation. A memorial
was drawn up setting forth their sufferings and asking for
redress of grievances. Lauritz Gottorp, a Dane by birth,
lawman in northern Iceland, who was sent to Denmark to
present the memorial to the king,[46] was well received, and
a new and more favorable price schedule was established in
1702 as a result of his mission. The severe punishments for
trafficking with foreign traders were also abolished, a simple
fine being substituted.[47] A commission consisting of Arni
Magnusson and Páll Vidalin was sent to Iceland to examine
conditions and to investigate how the laws governing commerce were observed by the merchants.[48] But trade conditions did not improve. The merchants who had obtained
the privilege to trade with Iceland became more and more
indebted to the government, and were unable to supply
the country with the needed articles of import. The government had gradually increased the sums for which the

[45] Magnus Stephensen, *Island i det 18de Aarhundrede*, p. 306 ff. *þrjár
ritgjörðir kostadar og útgjefnar af 17 íslendingum*, p. 60. Olaf Stephenson,
Kort Underretning om den islandske Handels Førelse, p. 5.
[46] Espolin, *Árbækur*, part viii, ch. lii. *Lovsamling for Island*, vol. i,
p. 577 ff.
[47] *Ibidem*, p. 702.
[48] *Ibidem*, p. 580.

trade privileges were granted, and the merchants spared no efforts to reimburse themselves by preying upon the people, who had become the helpless victims of their greed. In 1602 King Christian IV granted the first monopoly for the modest sum of sixteen rigsdaler a year to be paid by the merchants for every Icelandic harbor in which they carried on trade.[49] In 1619 this was changed to twenty rigsdaler to be paid for every ship sailing to Iceland.[50] The sums charged were constantly increased. In 1690, 13,670 rigsdaler had to be paid.[51] In 1706 the trade with Iceland was granted to a company of merchant houses, especially in Copenhagen, till 1733 for a yearly payment of 20,190 rigsdaler.[52] In that year the same company was given control of Icelandic trade for a period of ten years for the yearly sum of 8000 rigsdaler.[53] When this company was dissolved in 1742, the trade with Iceland was granted to the Hørkræmmer Company of Copenhagen for 16,100 rigsdaler a year.[54] Conditions in Iceland now became worse than ever before, as the managers of this company cared little for the welfare of the people. They managed the trade in such a way that there was always a lack of necessary articles, but a good supply of spirits, tobacco and other articles of luxury. Complaints were constantly made that the goods imported were adulterated, the timber rotten, the flour spoiled, the iron useless; but no reduction was made in the prices of these inferior goods. Not even the rules for good behavior in intercourse with the people were observed. The poor were looked down upon and often ill-treated. The custom of secret bargaining was also introduced by the merchants. The people were called to private conferences behind closed doors, where transactions were concluded to their greatest disadvantage. Neither weight nor measure was properly observed. But among all grievances the chief source of complaint was the shortage of food due to negli-

---

[49] *Lovsamling for Island*, vol. i, p. 139 ff.
[50] *Ibidem*, p. 198.
[51] Jon A. Adils, *Einokunarverzlun Dana á Íslandi* 1602-1787, p. 718 f.
[52] *Lovsamling for Island*, vol. i, p. 637 f.
[53] *Ibidem*, vol. ii, p. 144 ff.
[54] *Ibidem*, p. 391.

gence of the company in supplying the country with the
necessary articles of import. In payment of such goods as
could be obtained the people had to give fish, meat, butter
and other provisions, which were exported even at times
when people were dying of hunger. The often repeated
complaints of unbearable outrages went unheeded by the
government. The merchants asserted that the reports were
exaggerated, that the charges were not true, that nothing
had been proved, that disgruntled persons were creating
trouble and discontent. When volcanic eruptions and other
calamities finally reduced the country to such extremity
that people died of famine and hunger epidemics in large
numbers, the merchants filled the measure of their iniquity
by shipping putrid and wormy flour to Iceland, which the
people were compelled to use because of prevailing famine.

In those days of trouble the Icelanders found an able
leader in Skuli Magnusson (1711-1794), who was appointed
landfogeti in Iceland to succeed the notorious Dresse.
Skuli was the first Icelander appointed to this important
office.[55] In his fight against the merchants he proved himself courageous, energetic and persevering. He towered high
above all the people, possessing a strength of personality
which made him feared and respected, though he was a
haughty and somewhat intemperate man. When he became
acquainted with the general conditions in his country, he
saw the urgent need of reform. He became convinced that
the power of the Hørkræmmer Company had to be broken,
and that a new basis had to be laid for Icelandic economic
life. In 1749 he first voiced these views, claiming that it
was necessary to improve farming and husbandry. The
fisheries were controlled by foreigners to such an extent
that the native population could not profit properly by this
important occupation, as they had no sailboats and had to
fish near shore in shallow water. The merchants complained that the knitted ware which the people brought was
poorly made, and showed that they were deficient in knowledge of treatment of the wool. This Skuli regarded as a
most important matter, as the greater part of the people

[55] Jon Jonsson, *Skuli Magnusson og Island um hans daga.*

made their living by home manufacture of woolen goods. He felt that the only way to solve this problem was through cooperation of the leading men of the country. He urged that a stock company should be formed for this purpose, as he felt sure that the government would be willing to support the undertaking if they saw that the people were determined to do something. He drew up plans, and the company was organized. A woolen mill was built at Reykjavik and German weavers were brought to Iceland. In 1751 Skuli went to Denmark to submit his plans to the government. King Frederick V, who was well disposed to the Icelanders, granted him a money subsidy and several estates in Iceland to further the enterprise. In 1752 a royal rescript was issued sanctioning the plan. The work was now begun in earnest.[56] Besides the woolen mill a fulling mill, a ropery and a tannery were built at Reykjavik; farmers were sent from Denmark and Norway to teach the Icelanders agriculture; trees were imported and planted. Fishing-smacks were purchased abroad. The fishermen were to be aided in constructing larger boats so that they could fish in the open sea, and the people were to learn the best methods of salting meat and fish. Things promised well for a time, but many difficulties were encountered, the chief one being the opposition of the Hørkræmmer Company, which did everything in its power to hinder the new enterprises. The merchants claimed that the law governing the trade with Iceland would be violated if the king supported this new plan. They refused to handle the products of the new industrial establishments, and no agreement could be reached between them and the promoters of the enterprise. Skuli then turned to the government for aid. This was promised, and the important regulation was made that if the merchants would not handle the products of the new Icelandic industries at prices fixed by the *landfogeti*, those who were interested as shareholders in the industries might export their goods directly from Iceland. They might also import in their own ships materials necessary in their

[56] *Lovsamling for Island,* vol. i, p. 107 ff. Jon Jonsson, *Skuli Magnusson landfogeti,* p. 82 ff.

establishments, and might buy wool and hides anywhere in the country. The merchants persisted in their opposition, and Skuli finally brought suit against the company for wrongs which they had committed in Iceland. The legal battle became long and involved. In 1757 the company was dissolved,[57] and the trade with Iceland was carried on by the government for the benefit of the royal treasury till 1763. In that year it was granted to a new company, The General Commercial Company,[58] which also received control of the new industrial enterprises in spite of Skuli's protest. This company pursued the same policy as its predecessor, and Skuli continued his legal fight against it. In order to rid itself of all competition it suffered the Icelandic industrial establishments to fall into complete neglect. In its trade with Iceland the old corrupt practices of the Hørkræmmer Company were continued. In 1768 it was made clear through inspection in Copenhagen that the flour billed for Iceland was so unfit for use that the government was obliged to forbid its shipment. But the company disregarded the government order and shipped the flour. When it arrived there, the *syslumaðr* inspected it, and found it to be unfit for human food. It was so mildewed, putrid and wormy that it could not even be used for feed for cattle. But the merchants had tried to sell it to the people at full price, and many who were poor and starving had no alternative but to buy it. Skuli Magnusson, the *landfogeti*, encouraged the people to seize and destroy the flour, and a thousand barrels were dumped into the sea. He then brought complaint against the company, and forced it to pay a fine of 4400 rigsdaler.

King Frederick V died in 1766 and was succeeded by Christian VII, who ruled till 1808. In 1752 Eggert Olafsson and Bjarni Pálsson had been sent to Iceland to examine conditions. In 1770 a new commission consisting of two Danes and the Icelander Thorkel Jonsson Fjeldsted was sent on a like mission. They traveled through all parts of the country, and many new offices were later created as a result of

[57] *Lovsamling for Island*, vol. i, p. 277 ff.
[58] *Ibidem*, vol. iii, p. 466 ff.

their recommendations. Mills were built so that the people could grind their own flour. The raising of cabbage and potatoes was encouraged, and prizes were offered those who succeeded best in this enterprise. In 1776 a law was passed providing for the improvement of roads, for the carrying of mails, and for granting awards to those who would build homes on devastated farmsteads, of which there were many. Salt works were also erected. These undertakings show at least an earnest desire on the part of the government to improve conditions, but the trade monopoly, famine and epidemics had reduced the people to such a state of misery that no real change could be brought about by belated efforts of this kind. In 1774 the merchant company had to surrender its charter,[59] and the trade was conducted by the government till 1786, when commerce with Iceland was made free to all Danish-Norwegian citizens.[60] But even this step brought no relief. After the outbreak of the volcano Skaptarjökull only 40,000 remained of the whole population, which now seemed to face complete extinction. A committee was appointed by the government to devise means for relief. Large sums of money were collected throughout the realm. Many cargoes of provisions and building material were sent to Iceland. Two ships were set aside to transport necessary articles for the sufferers. The government also provided credit for the people with the merchants in the Icelandic towns. In 1788 the government paid the merchants 57,462 rigsdaler for supplies furnished. During the same year 28,000 barrels of grain were shipped, to which 3499 barrels were added by royal orders. The plan was even considered of removing the entire population from Iceland, and colonizing them on the heaths of Jutland.[61] In this crisis the weakness and inefficiency of the government administration became painfully evident. Of the 40,000 rigsdaler collected throughout the realm as a relief fund not over one-fourth was ever used for the pur-

[59] *Lovsamling for Island*, vol. iv, p. 88 ff.
[60] *Ibidem*, vol. v, p. 301 ff.
[61] Hans Finsen, *Om Folkemængdens Formindskelse ved Uaar i Island*, p. 171.

pose for which it had been contributed. The remainder
was diverted to various uses, such as defraying of the expenses of the coast survey, etc.[62] It was quite evident that
little of real importance could be done to improve conditions until a wiser policy of government should enable the
Icelanders to solve their own economic problems.

Since the earthquake accompanying the volcanic eruption
in 1783 wrecked the buildings at Skálholt, the commission
investigating affairs in Iceland took steps to remove the
bishop's seat and Latin school to Reykjavik, a measure
which was carried into effect in 1785.[63] In 1801 the Hólar
bishopric was discontinued, and one bishopric for all Iceland
was created, with Reykjavik as the bishop's seat. The
schools at Skálholt and Hólar were also united into one
Latin school, located at Reykjavik. When trade with Iceland was finally made free to all citiens of the realm by
ordinances of 1786 and 1787, the harbor towns of Reykjavik,
Isafjord, Eyjafjord, Reydarfjord, Grundarfjord, and Vestmanneyjar received rank and privileges as commercial
cities. Most of these places had no prospects of ever
becoming commercial centers. In 1807 the two last named
were dropped. The others, one in each quarter, retained
in name their classification as commercial towns. But
even Reykjavik had only 300 inhabitants at this time,
though the cathedral church, the Latin school and some
commercial and industrial establishments were located
there. In Eyjafjord and likewise in Isafjord only two
Danish merchants were found; in Reydarfjord only one,
and the prospect of growth of these towns was very
small. The Icelanders had hoped that when the trade
was made free for all citizens of the realm conditions
would rapidly improve, but in this expectation they
were disappointed. As no foreign merchants could trade
with Iceland, there was no competition. The people themselves were too poor to engage in trade, and conditions
remained about as before. The merchants entered into an
agreement to maintain the old prices, and little improve-

[62] Magnus Stephensen, *Island i det 18de Aarhundrede*, p. 290 ff.
[63] Pétur Pétursson, *Historia Ecclesiastica Islendiæ*, p. 149 ff.

ment could be hoped for. The lawman Magnus Stephensen undertook to present to the king a petition, signed at the Althing, asking that foreign merchants should be allowed to trade in Iceland. The petition was signed by all leading officials except the *stiptamtmaðr*, Olaf Stephensen. But such a demand for freedom was viewed with suspicion by the government, and the request was denied. The king expressed his displeasure with the officials who had signed the petition, and reprimanded them, but the *stiptamtmaðr*, who had opposed it, received the thanks of his sovereign. The time for any real change of policy had not yet come. Not till in the nineteenth century, when all restrictions on trade were removed and a more liberal form of government was established, did a new era of development and general prosperity dawn for Ireland.

After the introduction of absolutism the royal officials became more arrogant and arbitrary than before, and aided the merchants in their unjust and selfish operations. Many acted like despots without regard even for the provisions of the law. The *amtmaðr* Christian Müller caused Thord Thorsteinsson to be executed for theft after the lawman had granted the man an appeal to the supreme court. A farmer, Albert Arnfinsson, was flogged in the presence of the *amtmaðr* and the *landfógeti* Heideman because he refused to serve as oarsman on a boat belonging to the merchants. Instances of oppressive tyranny of this sort were many. Arni Magnusson, one of the royal commissioners, offered to prove to the king that Müller was in league with the merchants, and aided them in oppressing the people. The lawmen and *sýslumenn* would decide cases, not in agreement with the law, but according to their own opinion, while higher officials would sell offices to the highest bidder to increase their income. An office bought one day might be sold the next for a still higher price. Whatever the intention and disposition of the rulers, the people became the victims of a lawless and corrupt bureaucracy always fostered by despotism. How these arrogant minions of arbitrary rule flouted all human rights, even the most fundamental, is sufficiently illustrated by the following incident.

A deputy sent word to the farmer Asbjörn Joachimsson ordering that he should row him across a fjord. Asbjörn replied that he did not consider it his duty to do this for nothing; whereupon he was brought to trial before the lawman Sigurd Björnsson, who sentenced him to be flogged twice. This was carried out so effectively that the man fainted each time.[64] Quarrels and cabals between the officials themselves were numerous, one usually trying to ruin the other. Especially bitter was the struggle between the clergy and the officials, in which the latter had the advantage of more direct support of the government. The importance of the Althing dwindled when its legislative power was lost and the number of its members was reduced. The *lögrettumenn* now numbered only twenty, of whom ten should meet yearly at the Althing, but only eight should sit in the *lögrétta*. In 1777 this number was further reduced to five. From that time forth people paid but little attention to the Althing. If they had cases of any importance, they preferred to bring them directly to the king. The men of northern Iceland finally asked to be exempted from the duty of meeting at the Althing. In 1785 the *amtmaðr* Stefan Thorarinsson petitioned the government to grant the people of the northern districts a *thing* of their own. The *stiptamtmaðr* Levetzow proposed that the Althing should meet at Reykjavik, but at this time neither plan was carried out. In 1798 the Althing assembled for the last time at Thingvellir, where it had met for 868 years. Only twelve representatives, eight officials and four *lögrettumenn* came, and all returned home after a short meeting. The next session was held at Reykjavik, which henceforth became the capital of Iceland. On July 11, 1800, the Althing was permanently dissolved by royal orders, and in its place was created a new court, the *landsyfirréttr*,[65] consisting of a chief justice and two associate justices, which should exercise the judicial powers hitherto vested in the Althing. The eclipse of the old Icelandic institutions was thus made complete, a true index to the loss of national autonomy, of

[64] Magnus Stephensen, *Island i det 18de Aarhundrede*, p. 329.
[65] *Lovsamling for Island*, vol. vi, p. 464 ff.

personal liberty and economic well-being, of the spirit of daring and prowess which had been the Icelanders' proud heritage in days of old. Under foreign dominion they had experienced great misfortunes, but none so bitter as the loss of their ancient freedom. But even in these years of adversity their spirit was chastened and made strong for a new era of progress.

Even during the time of greatest social depression and economic distress in the period of absolutism and trade monopoly the Icelanders were able to maintain an active literary life. In the latter part of the eighteenth century rationalism and the cosmopolitan intellectual culture of the "Aufklärung" were transplanted to Iceland through the influence of the University of Copenhagen and the general spirit of the age. The reaction against the superstition and witchcraft delusion which had darkened the post-Reformation period made itself strongly felt. The new movement discarded all belief in the supernatural, maintained that enlightened reason is the only guide for human life and conduct, looked with contempt on national peculiarities as remnants of old plebeian habits, and emphasized the universality of intellectual culture. The chief representative of this movement in Iceland was Magnus Stephensen, who labored with untiring zeal to promote the new enlightenment. Much of value was accomplished. Old superstitions were eradicated, and foreign cultural influence, now freely introduced, helped to refine the tastes and enlarge the outlook of the people. Ancient customs were changing to modern ways. "Up till 1800 the Icelanders, both men and women, dressed according to their native style," says the annalist, "but after that time they gradually adopted Danish styles." [66] The increasing use of imported articles of luxury in spite of prevailing poverty also reveals a growing foreign influence.[67] The value of new cultural stimulus to an isolated and conservative people cannot easily be over-

[66] Espolin, *Árbœkur*, part xi, ch. xcv.

[67] Magnus Stephensen states that in 1772 the sugar import was only 663 pounds. In 1806 it reached 15,500 pounds. In the same period the importation of tobacco rose from 3280 to 32,000 kilograms, though the population was decreasing in number. *Island i det 18de Aarhundrede*, p. 434 f.

rated, but much of Magnus Stephensen's work for the promotion of culture was characterized by an uncritical adherence to European ideas and a disregard for the value of the traditions and institutions of his own country. In his admiration for foreign ways he was ready to give everything a touch of the new cosmopolitan spirit, even when this would lower the intrinsic value of the culture which he sought to promote. He was born in 1762 and belonged to one of the most distinguished families of Iceland. After entering upon his studies in the department of law at the University of Copenhagen in 1781 he received an appointment to the *rentekammer,* an important government department. When the volcanic eruption caused widespread devastation in Iceland in 1783, he was appointed royal commissioner together with another official, Levetzow, to investigate conditions in the stricken region. But the ship on which they took passage was driven by storms to the coast of Norway. Stephensen spent the winter very pleasantly as the guest of his countryman Thorkel Fjeldsted at the estate Holmegaard in southern Norway, where he took a leading part in the gay social festivities, and won the admiration of Fjeldsted's charming wife by his social accomplishments and skill as a dancer. The following year he reached Iceland, and traveled through the devastated districts about which he wrote a book, "Beskrivelse over den nye Vulkans Ildsprudning 1783." After his return to Denmark he was again sent to Iceland to supervise the sale of the lands belonging to the Skálholt bishopric. Finally he found time to complete his university studies in 1788, and was appointed vice-lawman and, in 1789, lawman for the northern and western districts of Iceland. When the Althing was abolished in 1800, he became the chief justice of the new court, the *landsyfirréttr,* which was created in its place, a position which he occupied till his death, March 17, 1833. He married his cousin, Gudrun Scheving, and resided after 1813 on the island of Videy, near Reykjavik, which he had purchased. His intellectual interests were many. Besides his profession as jurist he cultivated theology, singing, dancing and modern languages. By his countrymen he was regarded as a vain and ambitious official, arrogant and intolerant of all opposition, ready to stoop to intrigues in his dealings with the government. He was even accused of playing into the hands of the adventurer Jørgen Jørgensen, who attempted to foment a revolt against Denmark. But he was withal a very diligent man who loved his people and spent his life in devoted service to his countrymen as he understood it. The discontinuance of the Hólar diocese and the creation of one bishopric for all Iceland was largely due to his influence; so also the removal of the Latin schools to Reykjavik, where they were combined in one institution. This arrangement proved to be practical and advantageous, but he was justly criticized for the complete blotting out of Skálholt and Hólar, the two oldest cultural centers in Iceland. The permanent dissolution of the Althing was also done at his suggestion, as he regarded this old assembly as unpractical and out of date. The value of the traditions connected with these institutions dating from the people's earliest history he failed to understand. As it was his aim not only to create a new intellectual life, but also a new literature in his native land, he was an active member of Danish literary societies founded by the friends of the "Aufklärung" for the promotion of culture. In 1794 he founded a new society, the "Landsuppfræðingarfélag," or society for general enlightenment, of which he himself was the head. He also began the publication of the first Icelandic monthly, the "Klausturpósturinn," and other periodicals devoted to the cause of enlightenment. Assisted by Geir Vidalin, later bishop of Iceland, he also undertook to publish a new hymn-book, a work for which he possessed no qualification. In order to bring the hymns into harmony with his own superficial rationalism and conception of poetic art he often destroyed their deeper spiritual meaning, substituting an artificial jingle of rhymes which could not satisfy the demand of devoted Christians. The work appeared in 1801, but met with strong opposition. In order to control the literary production he got possession of the two printing presses in Iceland and combined them into one printing establishment. Under his management the

"Landsuppfræðingarfélag" published many valuable books, both Icelandic works and translations from foreign literatures, for the enlightenment of the people. Of other men of learning and influence at this time may be mentioned Hannes Finsen, who succeeded his father, Finnur Jonsson, as bishop of Skálholt in 1789. Jon Jonsson Espolin, born 1769, was a noted annalist, known especially for his great work "Islands Arbækur i Söguformi," which covers the period 1262-1832, and narrates much of the history of Iceland during this period. Grim Jonsson Thorkelin became noted as a student of Northern antiquities. Magnus Ketilsson, 1731-1803, *sýslumaðr* in Dalasysla and an active disciple of the "Aufklärung," became manager of the printing press at Hrappsey, and published many books. Especially noteworthy is his work "Forordninger og aabne Breve til Island under den oldenborgske Stamme" in three volumes, an important source for the study of Icelandic history. Skuli Thordarson Thorlacius and his son Börge R. Thorlacius distinguished themselves as scholars, the latter becoming rector of the University of Copenhagen, 1813-1814. The most noted Icelandic scholar in this period was probably Finnur Magnusson (Finn Magnusen), 1781-1847, who won general renown, especially through his research in the fields of Old Norse-Icelandic literature and Northern antiquities. He became president of the Royal Northern Text Society, and became associated with the great Danish scholar Rasmus K. Rask in the publication of many important works. But as he possessed a strange love for fantastic combinations and analogies, coupled with strong imagination rather than sound scholarly judgment, his voluminous production does not rank very high.

15. COMMERCE WITH ICELAND DURING THE NAPOLEONIC WARS. THE ADVENTURER JØRGEN JØRGENSEN. IMPROVEMENT OF ECONOMIC CONDITIONS AFTER 1814

THE unfortunate economic conditions in Iceland which had prevailed throughout the greater part of the period of trade monopoly did not improve much during the first decades of the nineteenth century. The Napoleonic wars which gradually paralyzed commerce and all peaceful pursuits brought distress and ruin also upon the maritime neutral nations. One by one the continental powers had been defeated. Finally England alone stood at bay in a determined struggle against the victorious emperor. To crush this implacable enemy by an attack on her commerce now became his aim. In 1806 he issued his noted Berlin Decree declaring the British Isles in a state of blockade, forbidding all trade with England, not only in France, but in all parts of Europe over which he exercised authority, including the Netherlands, western Germany, Prussia and Italy. After the treaty of Tilsit in 1807 he also subjected Russia to this "Continental System." In that year he issued a new decree from Milan threatening to seize all ships which touched a British port. The English retaliated by Orders in Council declaring the ports of France and her allies to be in a state of blockade, but allowing neutral vessels to carry on trade between these ports and Great Britain. For the kingdom of Denmark-Norway the situation became more critical as the billows of war rolled ever closer to the Danish border. It seems to have been the purpose of the Danish king to preserve neutrality as long as possible, but to cast his lot with the English if finally forced into the struggle, for it became evident that a rupture with one or the other of the belligerents could not long be averted even by the most watchful prudence. After the peace of Tilsit Napoleon succeeded in winning to his side Emperor Alexander I of Russia. Alexander promised to attempt to negotiate a peace between France and England, but if the English government should refuse the terms offered by the two emperors, he agreed that Russia should join France. Denmark-Norway, Sweden and Portugal would be requested to close their ports to British commerce, and if they refused, they were to be treated as enemies. By this stroke Napoleon shattered the policy of neutrality, forcing the smaller nations to choose sides in the conflict. The news of the alliance between France and Russia caused the greatest alarm everywhere, not least in England. The English government imagined that Denmark-Norway was a secret partner to the compact, and without even taking the time to investigate the real state of affairs dispatched a large fleet to Copenhagen. An English ambassador submitted to the Danish government an ultimatum that as a guarantee that Denmark would be the ally of England the Danish fleet should be handed over to the British for the period of the war. When this was refused, a battle ensued. Copenhagen was bombarded, and after a severe engagement the Danish fleet had to surrender to the English. This unexpected turn of events forced Denmark-Norway to join France. The blockade of the Danish-Norwegian coasts resulting from the war with England brought upon the whole North a period of intense suffering. Danish trade with Iceland was wholly interrupted, and, as a failure of crops further increased the economic difficulties of the Icelanders, a shortage of the necessaries of life was soon very keenly felt. Often the most important commodities like salt, iron, tar, lumber and staple articles of food could not be obtained. People tried to use sea water instead of salt. They made stirrups and horseshoes of horn, fish-lines from rope, and buried their dead without coffins. Danish and Norwegian vessels were seized by the English. A ship sailing from Iceland with many passengers, among whom was the chief justice, Magnus Stephensen, not knowing that war existed between England and Denmark-Norway, was captured by the British, and the passengers were brought to Scotland. Another vessel, carrying the Icelandic *stiptamtmaðr*, Count Trampe, was seized near the coast of Seeland, but the *stiptamtmaðr* was allowed to proceed to Copenhagen. Magnus Stephensen was also allowed to go to Denmark in the fall. In Scotland he had become acquainted with the English privy councilor, Sir Joseph Banks, with whose assistance he was able to secure the liberation of the other Icelandic captives in England, and also to prevail on the English government to allow free intercourse with Iceland during the war. The British privateers which swarmed everywhere upon the seas also visited the coast of Iceland. In 1808 the vessel "Salamine," commanded by Thomas Gilpin, came to Iceland to seize the royal treasury in keeping of the acting *stiptamtmaðr* Isleif Einarsson. The money, amounting to 35,158 *rigsbank-daler*, was taken by Gilpin and his band. The paper money, which they considered of little value, they compelled the merchants to take in exchange for coin. The house of the former *stiptamtmaðr*, Olaf Stephensen, was plundered, likewise also the shop of the goldsmith Thorgrim Thomasson, and other acts of depredation were committed. Gilpin sailed to England with his booty, but the English authorities did not consider his conduct against an unprotected and defenseless people justified by the existing state of war, and most of the treasures were returned. In the winter 1808-9 Magnus Stephensen went to Bergen, Norway, where he prevailed on some private citizens to send the ship "Providentia" to Iceland with supplies. On February 3, 1809, royal orders were issued that four cargoes of provisions should be sent to Iceland, but it appears that no ship was sent.[1] Stephensen returned to Iceland in the spring of that year. Count Trampe, the *stiptamtmaðr*, had bought the ship "Orion" and dispatched it to Iceland with a cargo, but it was damaged on the coast of Norway, and the cargo was sold. Finally in the spring of 1809 the ship reached Iceland with Trampe on board. Under these circumstances the English merchants found an opportunity to gain control of the Icelandic trade. According to the Danish laws the Icelanders were still forbidden to trade with foreigners, but as the Danish merchants could no longer supply them with the necessaries, they had no alternative but to buy from the English if they were to escape starvation. When English merchantmen attempted to trade with the people, the *stiptamtmaðr* forbade all intercourse with the king's enemies. But when English armed vessels arrived, he was soon forced to desist from his opposition.

It seems to have been the plan of the English merchants to establish complete control over the Icelandic trade, an effort in which they resorted to arbitrary and even violent methods. In 1809 an English armed vessel, the "Clarence,"

[1] *Lovsamling for Island*, vol. vii, p. 241 ff.

owned by Samuel Phelps of London and commanded by Captain George Jackson, entered the harbor of Hafnarfjord to trade with the people. On board was also the Danish adventurer Jørgen Jørgensen, who acted as interpreter. When the government officials refused to grant them permission to trade, the captain threatened to bombard the town of Reykjavik if they persisted in their opposition. As the authorities lacked all means of resisting such an attack, they finally entered into an agreement with the British traders, granting them permission to trade if they abstained from all violent acts. The merchants then sailed to Reykjavik, unloaded their cargo, rented buildings and began trade. On March 22, 1809, the "Clarence" returned to England, but James Savignac remained in Iceland to manage the new commercial enterprise there. In June the *stiptamtmaðr*, Trampe, returned to Iceland with unrestricted power as the governor of the island. He had also bought the houses which the English merchants had rented in Reykjavik. The violent clash between Trampe and the merchants shortly after his return can be explained only by assuming that as representative of the Danish government, with plenary power, he undertook to drive the English from Iceland. Not long after his arrival an English man-of-war, "The Rover," commanded by Captain Nott, came to Reykjavik. Negotiations were entered into with the count, and an agreement was made to establish freedom of trade for all English merchants in Iceland. After the departure of the man-of-war an armed English merchantman, the "Margarete and Anne," commanded by Captain John Liston, arrived, bringing Samuel Phelps himself, the chief promoter of the Icelandic trading enterprise. Phelps was accompanied by Jørgen Jørgensen, who was again serving as interpreter. After a short stay in the harbor Captain Liston and Samuel Phelps, accompanied by James Savignac, Jørgen Jørgensen and a band of armed men, marched to the residence of the *stiptamtmaðr*, Trampe, took him prisoner and brought him on board the ship. They also seized his ship "Orion" and hoisted the English flag on it. On June 26 a proclamation posted in Reykjavik, bearing the signature of Jørgen Jørgensen, stated that all Danish authority in Iceland had ceased; all business men and officials should remain quietly in their homes and not show themselves on the streets. All powder and firearms were to be surrendered, likewise the keys to all storehouses, together with books and accounts. All native-born people would have nothing to fear if they remained quiet, but anyone who failed to obey these instructions would be tried by a court martial and, if guilty, would be shot within two hours. A second proclamation bearing the same date and signature declared that Iceland was now free from Danish rule. Icelandic officials who would behave properly and perform their official duties well would be held in the highest esteem. Pensions would be paid to the widows and orphans of officials. A national Icelandic government was to be established as well as Icelandic laws, such as they had been at the time when Iceland was united with Norway. Trial by jury should also be established. Iceland should have its own flag and should be at peace with the whole world under the protection of Great Britain. The schools and hospitals would be improved; all debts to Denmark or the Danish merchants should be canceled, prices on grain lowered, taxes reduced to one-half, and all intercourse with Denmark was to be prohibited.[2] There can be no doubt that in these affairs Jørgensen acted as the tool and agent of the English merchants. The leading men regarded it as treason to support him. But the people were unarmed and defenseless, and since a state of war existed, and no aid could be expected from Denmark, it was considered prudent to act cautiously and await developments, especially since it was thought that the king of England had sent the usurpers to seize Iceland. Jørgensen surrounded himself with a body of vagrants whom he called "guards," and imprisoned several leading officials. Some resolute men would not watch quietly the treasonable farce enacted by Jørgensen and his followers. Among these are Judge Isleif Einarsson. He made preparations to resist the usurper, but his plan was divulged, and he was thrown into prison. On July 12

[2] Jon Thorkelsson, *Saga Jörundar Hundadagskóngs,* p. 151 ff.

Jørgensen posted a new proclamation in Reykjavik, announcing that he had assumed the management of public affairs as the country's protector, and that the military forces had appointed him commander both on land and sea. The country's flag should be three white codfish on a blue field, and he would defend it with his life and blood. His own seal should be used until the people's representatives could decide regarding a permanent seal for the country. All officials should pledge their obedience to the new government before July 20. Those who would not submit would be treated as traitors. A system of defense for the country was also to be created. Englishmen should have the right to trade and to establish residence in Iceland. As the country's protector on land and sea he assumed the title of "Excellency," but promised to surrender his office July 1 the following year, after a constituent assembly had established a new government.[3] The same day that this proclamation was posted the Icelandic flag was hoisted over the building occupied by the English traders, and was saluted by the "Margarete and Anne" from the harbor. Judge Isleif Einarsson was released from prison and was soon installed in his former office. A new *stiptamtmaðr*, Benedikt Gröndal, was appointed, and work was also begun to construct fortifications at Arnarhol, where guns were to be mounted.

After making these arrangements Jørgensen marched to northern Iceland with a few armed followers to seize the property of the Danish merchants. He met with no serious opposition, but the ill-will of the people was everywhere apparent. On his return to Reykjavik he received a letter from Jon Gudmundsson, *sýslumaðr* in Skaftafelssysla, declaring that he and his followers would be treated as outlaws if they appeared east of the Jökulsá. The redouts at Arnarhol were completed, and a few rusty guns were mounted on the works. A few officials had been forced to yield obedience to the usurper, but it was clear that the people as a whole regarded his operations only as the deeds of a hostile adventurer. When the English man-of-war "Talbot," com-

[3] The proclamation is found in Jon Thorkelsson's work *Saga Jörundar Hundadagskóngs*, p. 169 ff.

manded by Alexander Jones, arrived in the harbor of Reykjavik, August 14, events took a new turn. The sailors of the warship began to destroy the redouts which had been erected, and threw the cannons into the sea. Negotiations were begun between Magnus Stephensen and his brother, the *amtmaðr* Stephan Stephensen, on the one side and Captain Alexander Jones and Samuel Phelps on the other. On August 22, 1809, an agreement was made, according to which all the doings of Jørgensen should be considered null and void. The regular government authority should be re-established and the former officials reinstated in their offices. The English should have the right to trade and to reside in Iceland according to the agreement already entered into with Captain Nott of "The Rover." All Danish property and all valuables which had been seized should be returned to their owners. Magnus Stephensen and his brother Stephan Stephensen should have temporary charge of all public affairs. Magnus was to supervise secular matters and Stephan affairs pertaining to the church. The constructed redouts were razed, and Jørgensen was retained on board the "Margarete and Anne." Count Trampe was not released, but was to be carried to England as prisoner. The following day Magnus Stephensen and the *landfógeti*, Frydensberg, entertained Captain Jones and his men at a public dinner in Reykjavik. The same evening the two vessels "Margarete and Anne" and the captured "Orion" set sail for England with Jørgensen, Count Trampe and a number of imprisoned Danish sailors on board. Phelps also sailed for England. On the voyage the "Margarete and Anne," loaded with train-oil and tallow, was set on fire by some of the imprisoned sailors and burned. The people on board were rescued by the "Orion," which brought them back to Reykjavik. In this calamity Jørgensen rendered the most valuable service and won the admiration of all for his courage. Count Trampe was now released and was told that he could resume his former office, but as he preferred to go to England, where he hoped to get an indemnity from the English government, he was allowed to take passage on the "Talbot." On September 4 both the "Talbot" and the

"Orion" set sail for England with Jørgensen, Count Trampe and Samuel Phelps on board.

Jørgen Jørgensen, the son of highly respected parents, was born in Copenhagen in 1780. At the university he was a classmate of the Danish poet Oehlenschläger, and was known as a gifted but restless and adventurous character. Because of his reckless conduct he had to leave the university. He became a sailor, spending several years partly as whaler and partly as explorer in the Pacific Ocean. In 1806 he returned home and became captain of a Danish privateer in the war with England in 1807. His vessel was captured by an English warship, and he was brought to England as prisoner, but he was given his freedom on the condition that he should not leave the country. He then entered into the service of the English merchants as interpreter and accompanied them to Iceland. When he was brought back to England by Captain Jones, he was thrown into prison because he had broken his word not to leave the country. In prison he became acquainted with criminals and became a confirmed gambler. After many adventures he was finally deported to Tasmania, where he spent the rest of his life as a member of various exploring expeditions and as policeman. He died at Hobartstown in 1844.[4]

Magnus Stephensen attempted to arrange matters in the best way possible after the departure of Jørgensen. He sought to secure an indemnity for the money and valuables taken by the usurper and his assistants, but did not succeed, as Jørgensen had no property, and Samuel Phelps went bankrupt after his return to London. Count Trampe was no more successful in obtaining an indemnity from the English government. He soon returned to Denmark, and was made *stiftsamtmand* of Trondhjems stift in Norway. Between him and Magnus Stephensen a bitter personal controversy arose. That Stephensen in his negotiations with Captain Jones had not acted in a wholly unselfish way seems apparent. It would probably have been in his power to secure the release of Trampe and to have him reinstated

[4] J. F. Hogan, *The Convict King*. Jon Thorkelsson, *Saga Jörundar Hundadagskóngs*, p. 127 ff.

in his office if he had not himself coveted the highest position in Iceland. In 1810 both Magnus Stephensen and his brother Stephan were removed from the temporary management of affairs, and new officials were appointed in their place, among others Judge Isleif Einarsson, who continued to serve till 1814, when a new *stiptamtmaðr*, Castenskjold, was sent to Iceland.

In these years of wars, embargoes, blockades and commercial difficulties American merchants also began to trade with Iceland. In the fall of 1809 an American ship, the "Neptune & Providence," commanded by Captain Samuel Staples, came to Reykjavik with a cargo of rye, oatmeal, barley, indigo, coffee, sugar, rum, brandy, tobacco, etc.[5] In 1810 another American vessel came to Reykjavik, bringing a cargo of wheat, rice, iron, rum and many other kinds of goods except timber, says the annalist Espolin. On a visit to Copenhagen the Danish consul-general, Pedersen, reported that in 1810 he had persuaded an American merchant, Mr. Edward Cruft of Boston, to send a cargo of wheat, flour, rice, tobacco, sugar, hemp and other goods to Iceland, and that Mr. Cruft had sold these goods at prices so low that he lost money on the venture. For a return cargo he had bought at two or three places on the coast such goods as the people had to sell. The following year he sent another ship to Iceland with a cargo still better suited to the wants of the people, but on the return voyage the ship was seized by the English. In 1812 he would have sent still another ship, but was prevented by the American embargo and the war between England and America. In 1815 he wished to resume the traffic, and petitioned the Danish government to grant him a concession to trade with Iceland two or three years with two ships, on the condition that such a concession should not be granted to any other American merchant.[6] In case such a privilege were granted, he promised to bring to the country only goods produced in America. As the *stiptamtmaðr* (governor-general) for

[5] Jon Espolin, *Árbœkur*, part xii, ch. xxv. Jon Thorkelsson, *Saga Jörundar Hundadagskóngs*, pp. 81, 115.
[6] *Lovsamling for Island*, vol. vii, p. 509 ff.

Iceland, Castenskjold, testified that the cargoes shipped to Iceland by Mr. Cruft were the most valuable ever received there, and that he had sold the goods very cheap, the concession was granted. Throughout the Napoleonic wars and even later American merchants seem to have made frequent voyages to Iceland. The annalist Espolin records for the year 1817 that "in the fall a ship came drifting to Skaftafellssysla. There were no people on it. One mast was broken and the other standing. It was laden with American timber, and was much damaged.[7] The same annalist records that in 1821 "a Scotch ship from America came drifting to Eyjafjöll. The men came ashore, and returned home with a mail ship."

Commercial peace and freedom of trade with Iceland was established by England in 1809, but while the war lasted little was imported, and the people suffered severely. In 1809 fourteen ships came to Iceland.[8] Of these, three were owned by the English merchants who had established themselves in Reykjavik, and one was an American vessel, the "Neptune & Providence." Many of the ships were small and the cargoes were not always well selected, as rum and brandy were often brought instead of necessaries. The prices were exceedingly high, and as the financial collapse of Denmark made the Danish paper money so nearly valueless that it became almost impossible for the Icelanders to use it as a medium of exchange, they could obtain the foreign goods only through exchange for home products on most disadvantageous terms. The freedom of trade was but imperfectly observed, as the English merchants sought to discourage all competitors. On July 10, 1809, the Danish ship "Tykkvabær" came to Iceland, sailing under English passport, bringing 10,000 rigsdaler of government funds. The English merchants entered it, seized the money, and then let it proceed to the harbor of Dyrafjord. Other ships were detained for longer or shorter periods before they were allowed to enter the harbors. But such as it was, the free intercourse established by the English was of considerable

[7] Espolin, *Árbækur,* part xii, ch. xc.
[8] Jon Thorkelsson, *Saga Jörundar Hundadagskóngs.*

advantage, as without it Iceland would have been completely isolated. Regarding the trade with Iceland and the cargo brought by the "Clarence" in the winter of 1809 Magnus Stephensen says:

"Though the cargo was ill selected for trade with Iceland, it can not be denied that the English trade at that time and throughout the summer, with their spending of money and all sorts of plans, even the most foolish, gave many people, especially in the winter and spring, great opportunity for labor. Without this the general distress would have been much more keenly felt before the fisheries began."

In 1815 Stephensen made an attempt to improve trade conditions by bringing before the Danish government a proposal to establish free intercourse with Iceland. A commission was appointed to consider the matter, but nothing was farther from the mind of the government than to remove all restrictions on trade. During the long war Danish commerce had been almost destroyed, and now that peace had returned, the government would not willingly surrender the still existing remnant—the trade with Iceland. Sweden had joined the coalition against Napoleon, and Denmark, which had been forced into an alliance with France through the aggression of England, had been defeated. A treaty of peace was signed at Kiel, January 14, 1814, by which Norway was ceded to Sweden, but Iceland, which had been united with Norway since 1262, was not included in the cession, but remained connected with Denmark. After the war the Danish government sought to mend its broken fortunes, and also to improve the conditions of Icelandic trade. In 1816 a so-called agreement was published, providing for increased freedom of commerce. Danish ships sailing to Iceland were allowed to carry Icelandic export articles directly to foreign harbors by paying an export duty. But foreign commerce with the island remained under such restrictions that it could not be carried on. Even the few Englishmen who had established themselves in Reykjavik were ordered to sell what they had and depart. But in spite of the still unchanged government policy some improvement in economic conditions manifested itself after the return of peace. This is evident from the steady growth of the population of the island after 1814, the increase of herds, the development of gardening, fisheries and of import and export trade.

During the eighteenth century the population of Iceland had been reduced 6.4 per cent according to some authorities,[9] and no improvement of conditions is noticeable till the return of peace and the gradual revival of commerce after 1814. From that time the steady growth of population became very marked, amounting to 41.8 per cent in the period 1801-1860. In 1823 Iceland again had 50,000 inhabitants. The census returns after that time show the following figures:

1835	56,035
1840	57,094
1845	58,558
1850	59,157
1855	64,603
1860	66,987 [10]

During the same period a similar progress can be observed also in the various productive occupations. Prior to the beginning of the nineteenth century vegetable gardening remained in a purely experimental stage. In 1800 there were only 283 gardens in Iceland. In 1810 the number had risen to 1194. After that time the census returns give the following numbers:

1821	2768
1831	2977
1841	3657
1851	5400
1861	6749

Progress was also made in the production of hay through construction of drainage ditches, building of fences and the leveling and fertilizing of meadows. Since the people of Iceland derive so great a part of their income from their

[9] *Skýrslur um landshagi á Íslandi,* vol. i, p. 2.
[10] *Ibidem,* pp. 2, 40, 470.

herds, an increased yield of this important agricultural product ·means a general improvement of economic life. Statistics show a steady increase in the numbers of domestic animals after 1800. According to figures already given, Iceland had at that time 307,000 sheep. In 1853 the number had increased to 516,850. But the destructive sheep disease of 1856-1860 caused a sudden decline. By 1860 the number had been reduced to 326,664. In northern Iceland the resolute *amtmaðr* J. P. Hafstein caused the infected animals to be killed. In the southern district the slower and, as it proved, more expensive method of cure was employed. After 1861 conditions improved and new progress was made in this industry. During the same period the cattle herds showed little or no increase. From 1853 till 1865 the number of cattle fell from 23,663 to 20,300.[11] But horses, which became of increasing importance as an article of export, especially after 1850, grew in number even in excess of the increase of population In 1801 there were about 26,000 horses in Iceland, or about fifty-five head to each hundred persons. In 1861 there were 40,823, or about sixty-one head to each hundred people. The fisheries of Iceland, at this time second in importance only to animal husbandry, also showed considerable development, especially during the later decades of the period 1800-1860. The number of fishing boats had increased from 2000 in 1801 to 3186 in 1866. And while the population was growing, and ever larger quantities of fish products were needed for home consumption, the fish export grew from 758 tons in 1801 to 4250 tons in 1855.

After the Althing had been reestablished in 1843, the Icelanders under the guidance of the great political leader Jon Sigurdsson began a new agitation for the abolition of all restrictions on trade. A petition for free commerce was sent to Denmark. The merchants sought to obstruct the movement, but in 1853 a bill was brought before the Danish Rigsdag; and although no Icelander had a seat in that assembly, many supported it and argued that the time had

[11] *Skýrslur um landshagi á Íslandi,* vol. ii, pp. 147, 155, 174, 180; vol. iii, p. 243.

long since come when the fetters on trade, which had oppressed Iceland for 250 years, ought to be removed. The bill became law April 15, 1854.[12] All nations could now trade with Iceland without hindrance, and foreign commerce, especially with England, soon became very profitable to the Icelanders. The year following the passage of the bill 125 ships came to Iceland, of which thirteen came from foreign lands. Icelandic products could now be shipped to ports where open markets and a ready demand could be found; while free competition would lower the prices on imports, and give new stimulus to commercial activity. The rapid increase in the volume of Icelandic trade soon proved the wisdom of the new policy. In 1806 the grain import amounted to only about 50,000 bushels. In 1840 it was over 145,400 bushels, more than twice the amount per capita, even allowing for the increase in population. In 1806 about 8600 lbs. of coffee were imported. In 1855 the import of this commodity reached 88,800 lbs., in 1855 426,980 pounds. The importation of sugar and sirup rose from 23,500 lbs. to 478,000 lbs. during the same period, and other important commodities show a similar increase.

	1806	1855
Iron and steel	65,300 lbs.	152,000 lbs.
Coal	2,181 bu.	22,627 bu.
Salt	1,450 bu.	73,790 bu.
Hemp	14,900 lbs.	37,700 lbs.

A less commendable feature of the growing trade was the importation of distilled liquors, which increased about 200 per cent during this period, owing chiefly to a premium offered by the government for the export of Danish liquor. The cost of this worse than useless article of import was greater than that of all other imported commodities combined.

Of Icelandic exports the products of husbandry represented in 1855 about one half of the total amount. Especially noteworthy is the growth of the export of wool from 260,300 lbs. in 1806 to 1,596,300 lbs. in 1855. This phe-

[12] *Lovsamling for Island*, vol. xv, p. 611 ff.

nomenal increase is explained by the fact that Icelandic knitted ware could no longer be sold to advantage, since the household industries could not compete with the much cheaper machine manufacture of foreign lands. Icelandic knitted articles, such as socks, mittens, jackets, etc., once in great demand, were disappearing from the market, and the Icelandic wool was sold to foreign manufacturers. Other articles of export also show a relatively large percentage of increase.

	1806	1855
Tallow	191,700 lbs.	932,900 lbs.
Meat	2,966 barrels	3,362 barrels
Codfish	695 tons	4,249 tons
Train-oil	2,495 barrels	6,900 barrels
Eiderdown	2,184 lbs.	4,100 lbs.
Feathers	8,500 lbs.	25,100 lbs.

The rapid increase of Icelandic commerce during this period is shown also by the growing number of ships sailing to Icelandic ports. In the period 1800-1809 the average yearly number was forty-eight. In 1850-1854 the number had increased to 128. So notable a progress in all branches of economic life: the increase of production, the development of trade, and the resulting growth of population, show that Iceland was entering upon a new era of social and economic development.

At this time new interest was also awakened for education. The Latin school, which according to provision of 1801 was to be established at Reykjavik, had so little success that it was moved to Bessastadir in 1805, chiefly because no suitable buildings had been provided. In this not very convenient place it had since remained until it had become a difficult problem to solve whether it should again be moved to Reykjavik. In 1832 appeared Thomas Sæmundsson's work about the schools of Iceland, "Island fra den intellektuelle Side betragtet," and Jon Sigurdsson began a vigorous agitation for the improvement of the Icelandic school system. He proposed that common schools for the children should be built wherever they could be accessible, that agricultural schools should be founded in all quarters, that the Latin school should be moved from Bessastadir to Reykjavik, that its courses should be improved, and that a theological school with a three years' course should be established at Reykjavik.[13] With regard to the common schools the conditions of the country with its sparse population even now prevents the maintenance of such schools in many places, but instruction in the homes under the supervision of the clergymen has proved a very efficient substitute. In the early part of the nineteenth century the country was still too weak economically to carry out so extensive an educational program, but the work was undertaken in great earnest. The Latin school was moved to Reykjavik in 1846, and the following year a theological seminary was also established there. Jon Sigurdsson had asked that instruction should also be provided in medicine and jurisprudence. But since the government and many of the Icelanders themselves feared the expenses connected with such a plan, it was postponed, though nowhere was the need of trained physicians greater than in Iceland, where violent epidemics were so frequent. The first doctor sent there in 1760 had to serve both as physician and apothecary for the whole country until he could train some assistants. In 1800 there were still only six physicians in Iceland. In 1850 the number had increased to seven; but in so extensive a country where travel is slow and difficult, it is evident that few sick people could receive any aid from a medical service so inadequate. That students of law had to study in Denmark, where they did not become acquainted with Icelandic jurisprudence, was also a great disadvantage. As a result lawyers and officials often learned to look at all questions from a Danish point of view, and became staunch supporters of the crown in every controversy instead of cherishing a more patriotic sympathy with their own people. The Danish government had long regarded Iceland as a province which was to be connected as closely as possible with the realm. All efforts to provide home training for students of law was therefore opposed, as

[13] *Ný félagsrit*, vol. ii, p. 67 ff.

this would lessen Danish influence over Icelandic officials, and might tend to develop a local patriotic sentiment. The Danish sympathies of the upper social class, consisting of merchants, officials and those who had studied in Denmark, was a safeguard against any separatistic national movement in Iceland. The merchants who were conducting business in Icelandic harbors still had their real homes in Denmark, especially in Copenhagen, where they usually spent the winter months every year. Socially they did not mingle with the Icelandic people, but with the officials and their families, with the *amtmaðr* and other dignitaries in Reykjavik, usually devoted adherents of the crown and strong supporters of its prerogatives. In their fine homes liberal hospitality was shown all Danish friends, and festive entertainments were arranged for those who shared their tastes and belonged to the higher social circles. From the life and sympathics of the Icelandic people they were as a rule isolated and far removed.

16. ROMANTICISM IN ICELAND. STRUGGLE FOR AUTONOMY. THE ICELANDIC CONSTITUTION OF 1874. IMPROVED ECONOMIC CONDITIONS

UNDER the influence of the French Revolution and of great writers, like Voltaire, Rousseau and others, who sponsored it by demanding freedom of thought, press and conscience, the intellectual life as well as the social thought of Europe at this time was undergoing a profound change. In Germany the ideas of the Revolution had made but slight impression, but due to the stimulus of the times a new intellectual movement known as romanticism was started, which brought about a complete literary revolution and created a new national life. Strong feeling and tender emotions were expressed in the new romantic literature. A strong patriotic sentiment tinged with emotionalism swept over the "Fatherland," demanding freedom from the prevalent foreign intellectual influence on the one hand, and from foreign political dominion on the other. Everything national was to be studied and cultivated. The study of Germanic philology began to flourish at the expense of the hitherto predominating interest in classical languages. Folk-songs and fairy-tales were collected, and scholarly knowledge was fostered in everything pertaining to German antiquities. The Germans became conscious of their unity as a people, discovered that they had a common national destiny, and found that their strength lay in building their national political and intellectual life on their own past history and cultural traditions. A new nationalism, destined to win for Germany political unity and independence, and unequaled prosperity and power, was cradled in this new movement. From Germany it soon spread to the North. In 1802 the Danish poet Oehlenschläger began his literary career as leader of the new movement in Denmark, where it soon won the enthusiastic support of the younger writers. In Iceland it won complete ascendency through Bjarni Thorarensen (1786-1841) and Jonas Hallgrimsson (1807-1845), the two greatest poets in modern Icelandic literature. During his stay in Copenhagen as student at the university Thorarensen became a romanticist through the influence of Oehlenschläger and the philosopher Henrik Steffens. In 1805 he wrote the song "Eldgamla Ísafold,' which became so popular that it has since remained the national song of Iceland. In his own country he stood for a time alone as representative of the romantic movement, as the "Aufklärung" under the leadership of Magnus Stephensen was still strong. In contrast to Stephensen he loved all national traditions and institutions. He worked with enthusiasm for the restoration of the Althing, wishing that it should assemble again on the old thingstead of Thingvellir. He also organized a company to improve the overland routes of travel between southern and northern Iceland, a project in which he spent much of his own private means. As a devoted nationalist he was opposed to the whole movement headed by Stephensen—to his rationalism, his corruption of the Icelandic language through the introduction of foreign words, and to his disregard of the ancient traditions of Iceland. Thorarensen was a devout

Christian believer. He desired to restore the purity of the
Icelandic language, and sought to arouse the people's national feeling and love for their own historical traditions.
That two movements so diametrically opposed could not
long exist side by side soon became evident. Sharp clashes
grew frequent, but Thorarensen had the advantage of rare
poetic talent and the support of the reawakened national
sentiment of his countrymen. The people felt that he was
a true Icelander, who loved his country, its history and its
culture. With rare power he conjured up in his poems the
heroic figures of the saga times—Gunnar of Hlidarendi,
Njáll of Bergthorshváll, Skarphedin and others—and encouraged the people to seek the elements of progress, not
in imitation of foreign lands, but in the fortitude and hero-
ism which was theirs in ages past. He sang of the beauty of
Iceland, and pictured its nature and its titanic, mythological
grandeur. Here was a country to be preferred to the level
Denmark. Why should not the Icelanders take heart? He
summons them to fight again as of old, against fire and
frost, against enervating and corrupting foreign influence.
If they fail in this fight, let them sink into the ocean and
perish. Better die with honor than live in shame. Thorarensen did not rhyme with ease or great skill. He was no
master of form, but his poems are like trumpet calls that
awakened his people to strive for new national life and
progress. Jonas Hallgrimsson, his younger contemporary,
loved nature as Thorarensen loved the people of Iceland,
and as he was a great artist in versification, his poems excel those of his contemporary in form and beauty, though
he did not possess his power of imagination. As poets the
two are of equal excellence and supplement each other in
their production, Thorarensen devoting himself principally
to the inner forces and Hallgrimsson to the exterior side of
human life. Hallgrimsson's intimate knowledge of Iceland,
which he acquired while traveling through the country as a
natural scientist, enabled him to write descriptive poems of
unexcelled charm. Among his most noted productions are
"Ísland" and "Gunnarshólmi." When the latter poem
appeared in the periodical "Fjölnir," Thorarensen was so

impressed that he exclaimed: "Now I think it is about time that I quit writing poetry." In the wake of these two leaders followed many poets of less note. Jon Thoroddsen was especially important as novelist. Gisli Brynjulfsson wrote political poems, elegies and love-songs. Grimur Thomsen, a disciple of Thorarensen, devoted himself especially to the writing of ballads in the style of the old folksongs. Sigurd Breidfjord was a productive lyric poet and the last representative of the *rímur* poesy in Iceland. Hjalmar Jonsson, Sveinbjörn Egilsson, rector of the Latin school in Reykjavik, Páll Olafsson and others also distinguished themselves as lyric poets. To this group must also be counted the inspired lyric poet and dramatist Matthias Jochumsson (1835-1920), one of the most influential men in modern Icelandic history. Also in the various fields of scholarly work learned men appeared in this great age of national awakening and intellectual productivity.[1] Jon Arnason collected and published Icelandic folk- and fairy-tales under the title "Íslenzkar þjóðsögur og æfintýri," an excellent work which has been translated wholly or in part into Danish, German and English. In philology the Icelandic scholars won great distinction. Especially noted in this field are Konrad Gislason (1808-1891), professor in the University of Copenhagen, who wrote numerous philological treatises and edited many Old Icelandic works; and Gudbrand Vigfusson (1827-1889), professor in the University of Oxford. He completed and published "Icelandic-English Dictionary," published a complete collection of Old Norse and Old Icelandic poems with English translations, the "Corpus Poeticum Boreale," edited a number of sagas, and wrote numerous treatises dealing with Northern antiquities.

The intellectual awakening in Iceland produced a literary renaissance which gradually broadened into a great national patriotic movement, political as well as literary in character. It had its inception in the romanticism of Germany and Denmark, but it derived its chief strength and impetus

[1] Valtyr Gudmundsson, *Islands Kultur ved Aarhundredskiftet 1900*, p. 54 ff.

from the revolutionary movements which convulsed Europe, challenging the established principles and institutions of the Old Régime. Many events contributed to the growth of liberal ideas, which were remodeling European political thought. The old mercantilistic economic theories had been shattered by Adam Smith, the advocate of free trade and non-interference of government in industrial pursuits, who published his epoch-making work "Inquiry into the Nature and Causes of the Wealth of Nations," 1776. The American Declaration of Independence, the founding of the Republic of the United States and the framing of its constitution, the French Revolution and the constitutions of the French Republic, the Spanish constitution of 1812, the national uprisings against Napoleon, and the Norwegian constitution of 1814, created a liberal sentiment and national spirit in Europe which made the old benevolent despotism antiquated and ultimately impossible. After the downfall of Napoleon reaction triumphed for a while, but the July Revolution in France in 1830 so strengthened the liberal movement that the frightened rulers hastened to make concessions to save their thrones.

In Iceland as elsewhere an intense patriotic sentiment was awakened through the influence of the new national poetry and the stimulus of revolutionary ideas. The people were waking from their apathy to demand freedom from oppression, restoration of their Althing, recognition of their rights and character as a distinct nation, and rehabilitation of their country, which during years of misfortune had been reduced to abject political and economic dependency. In 1835 the young patriotic leader Tomas Sæmundsson, together with the poet Jonas Hallgrimsson, the philologist Konrad Gislason and the jurist Brynjolf Pétursson, founded the periodical "Fjölnir," which became the rallying point and organ of the new patriotic movement. The poet Bjarni Thorarensen also assisted in the undertaking. According to the introduction of the periodical written by Sæmundsson its purpose should be to reform Icelandic literature, purify the Icelandic language, cultivate the people's esthetic sense, and arouse their patriotism and love of liberty by stimulating admiration for the country's ancient greatness, the old Icelandic institutions, language and literature. In a beautiful poem "Ísland," printed in the first number, Hallgrimsson pictures the great national decay by comparing the present state of Iceland with conditions in earlier times. In former days, says the poet, the Icelanders met at the Althing and passed laws. Now there is no longer any Althing, but Snorri Godi's *thing*-booth is used as a sheep pen. Only the country itself remains unchanged, as beautiful as in days of yore.[2] Tomas Sæmundsson, who had studied theology in the University of Copenhagen, had traveled extensively after completing his university studies. On these travels he learned to see more clearly than ever how deep was the national downfall of Iceland, and he became inspired with an ardent desire to create among his countrymen a new national life. When he returned to Iceland he became clergyman in his home parish and later provost. The periodical "Fjölnir" was published in Copenhagen by his associates, but he continued to exercise great influence on the undertaking through his untiring energy. It was his wish that the chief stress should be laid on political and economic questions, the fostering of national patriotism, and the improvement of economic life. These views he could not carry out, as his associates were more directly interested in the reformation of the literature and the purifying of the Icelandic language. Sæmundsson died at a very early age, seven years after his return to Iceland. "How much Iceland and Icelandic literature lost by his death, it is not easy to estimate," says Valtyr Gudmundsson, "but from his writings and letters one gets the impression that he was the greatest personality which Iceland possessed in the nineteenth century."[3]

Denmark had remained an absolute monarchy since 1660, but after the July Revolution in France in 1830 some of the

[2] A Danish translation of the poem is found in Valtyr Gudmundsson's work *Islands Kultur ved Aarhundredskiftet 1900,* p. 130 f. A German translation is found in J. C. Poestion's work *Isländische Dichter der Neuzeit,* p. 343 f. *Fjölnir,* vol. i, p. 21 f.

[3] Valtyr Gudmundsson, *Islands Kultur ved Aarhundredskiftet 1900,* p. 57. *Fjölnir,* 1843, p. 1 ff.

more far-sighted statesmen deemed it prudent to begin to pay some heed to public sentiment. With the support of King Frederick VI they undertook to organize assemblies of estates which were to serve as advisory bodies to the sovereign. By ordinances of May 28, 1831, and May 15, 1834, four such assemblies were created: one for Jutland, two for the duchies of Schleswig and Holstein, and one for Seeland and the islands. In the latter, which numbered seventy members, Iceland was to be represented by two delegates elected by the people. This shadow of representative government in which Iceland was to figure only as one of the smallest and most obscure provinces of the Danish kingdom could in no way satisfy the liberal sentiment and growing national aspirations of the Icelanders. The arrangement was vigorously opposed by the talented Icelandic jurist Baldwin Einarsson, who maintained that Iceland, being so different in character from the rest of the realm, should have its own national assembly, as two or three Icelandic delegates sitting in a large Danish body wholly unacquainted with affairs in so distant a country could exercise but little real influence. Few could speak Danish so well that they could serve as delegates. The voyage to Denmark was long and costly, and the election of delegates was difficult, as they were so few in number that the people had to vote for persons living in distant parts of the country. Neither could the interests of each district be known nor properly furthered by so inadequate a representation. The difficulty connected with being a representative in Denmark was also so great that few would be willing to serve, as a person chosen would have to spend almost two years far away from his family and his business interests to attend one session of the Danish assembly. On the other hand the advantages of a national Icelandic assembly would be many. The people would have the opportunity to take an active part in public affairs, and a center would again be created for Icelandic national life as of old.[4] This reasoning made an impression on the king and the

---

[4] Baldwin Einarsson, *Om de danske Provincialstænder med specielt Hensyn paa Island. Ármann á Alþingi*, 1832, p. 13 ff.

Danish political leaders. In answer to a petition for a separate assembly sent to Copenhagen by the Icelanders, steps were taken to make the Icelandic representation more effective by creating in 1838 a commission of ten royal officials, which was to assemble every other year at Reykjavik under the presidency of the *stiptamtmaðr* to investigate conditions in Iceland and report to the government. But this arrangement was of little practical value and did not satisfy the Icelanders. In 1840 King Christian VIII, who ascended the throne December 3, 1839, instructed the commission to consider the advisability of establishing a national assembly, or Althing, in Iceland with representatives chosen by the people. The commissioners were to express their opinion about the organization of such an assembly, whether it should be called Althing, and whether it should assemble at Thingvellir as formerly. This step on the part of the king caused the greatest rejoicing in Iceland. The poet Jonas Hallgrimsson greeted the news in one of his finest poems, and the patriotic leader Tomas Sæmundsson, who was now a dying man, rose from his sick-bed to write about the organization of the Althing. He urged that it should be organized as nearly as possible like the old Althing, and that it should meet at Thingvellir as in days of old. An assembly differently organized and meeting in a different place he regarded as equivalent to no assembly.[5] In considering the suggestion of the king the commissioners found that it would be advisable to create a separate assembly for Iceland, and that it should be called Althing, but with true bureaucratic spirit they held that since it was to be coordinate with assemblies of Denmark and Schleswig-Holstein, it should resemble them as closely as possible also in organization. They opposed the old thingstead of Thingvellir as a place of meeting for the new assembly, and recommended Reykjavik, the capital of Iceland. The number of representatives was to be small, only twenty to be chosen by the people, and four or six appointed by the king. Only owners of a required amount of land should be eligible or have the right to vote.

[5] *þrjar ritgjörðir kostaðar og útgjefnar af 17 Íslendingum*, p. 73 ff.

The deliberations of the Althing should be conducted in the Icelandic language, but those who could not use it might speak Danish, such speeches to be ordered translated by the presiding officer. The report of the commission was sanctioned by the Danish government. The Althing was reestablished March 8, 1843,[6] but the defects in the fundamental law for Iceland thus outlined were so apparent that a Danish member of the assembly of estates, Balthasar Christensen of Copenhagen, demanded many important changes, such as an increase in the number of representatives, the lowering of the requirements for eligibility and the right of suffrage, exclusive use of the Icelandic language in the deliberations of the Althing, and the selection of the old thingstead of Thingvellir as the place of meeting for the new assembly. But these demands were looked upon by many as radical, and found little real support, since many of the Icelandic representatives themselves stood hesitating and without any definite plan.[7]

A new leader now appeared to guide the Icelanders along the path to self-government. This was Jon Sigurdsson, the greatest figure in modern Icelandic history. This remarkable man was born at Hrafnseyri in northwestern Iceland June 17, 1811. After entering the University of Copenhagen he continued to reside in that city. In his extensive scholarly activity he devoted himself especially to philology, archæology and history, fields in which he showed great talent, and performed a work which attracted wide attention. For the Royal Northern Text Society he published two volumes of the "Íslendingasögur," including the "Íslendingabók," the "Landnámabók" and six other sagas. He also published the "Younger Edda," and wrote a catalogue of the Icelandic manuscripts in Copenhagen, Stockholm and Upsala. In "Annaler for nordisk Oldkyndighed" he published four sagas. He published the first volume of the "Diplomatarium Islandicum," and assisted in the publication of "Scriptores Rerum Danicarum" and "Regesta Diplomatica

[6] *Lovsamling for Island,* vol. xii, p. 454 ff.
[7] Páll Melsted, *Nýar athugasemðir við nokkrar ritgjörðir um alþingismálið.* *Fjölnir,* 1844, p. 110 ff.

Historiæ Danicæ." His articles on themes dealing with history and philology were very numerous, and he was an active member of many learned societies. In 1848 he became secretary of the Arnemagnean Commission, a position which he retained till his death. But, although he distinguished himself as a scholar, it was in the field of practical activity and constructive statesmanship that he was to render his people the greatest service and to win his most lasting renown. He became the peerless leader of his people in their struggle for national liberty and representative government. In all fields of activity his stimulating influence was so strongly felt that the progress made by the Icelanders in the nineteenth century is largely traceable to his guidance and initiative. The Danish writer Kr. Kålund describes him as follows:

"Jon Sigurdsson was a harmonious personality, a healthy soul in a healthy body. He was tall and powerful, and only in his later years was he weakened by sickness. His hair turned white early, but his brown eyes were keen and brilliant. His facial expression was kind but firm, his appearance dignified and attractive. His home in Copenhagen was the meeting place for all his countrymen in the city, who were attracted by his hospitality, though his pecuniary circumstances might often be difficult." [8]

Jon Sigurdsson was a man of deep insight and trustworthy judgment who with singular tenacity of purpose devoted his life and talents to the great cause of championing the rights of Iceland. Together with a few friends he began in 1841 the publication of the periodical "Ný félagsrit," of which he became editor, and which continued to appear till 1873. In this organ all vital questions of the day were discussed: problems of education, finance, trade and politics. Of its thirty volumes Jon Sigurdsson himself has written about two-thirds. In two articles printed in the first vol-

[8] Konrad Maurer, *Zur politischen Geschichte Islands*, supplement, *Jon Sigurdsson*. C. F. Bricka, *Dansk biografisk Lexikon*, vol. 15, p. 575 f. Professor Willard Fiske of Cornell University published a biographical sketch of Jon Sigurdsson in the *New York Times*, January 4, 1879. Valtyr Gudmundsson, *Om Islands Kultur ved Aarhundredskiftet 1900*, p. 30 ff.

umes of this periodical [9] he clearly outlines the issues which gradually became the national program of the Icelanders, demanding an independent national legislature free from all control of the Danish assemblies; greater independence for Icelandic officials, the abolition of the right of the supreme court of Denmark to render decisions in purely Icelandic cases, and finally the greatest possible participation of the people in all political activities. He did not share the romantic ideas of Tomas Sæmundsson and others who wished to reestablish the old Althing at Thingvellir. This form of representation he considered antiquated and unpractical. He wished the new assembly to be a legislative body of popularly chosen representatives, like the national legislatures of other lands. As its place of assembly he favored Reykjavik, the capital of the country, and the growing center of its new national life.

The Icelanders were strongly opposed to the plan proposed by the Danish government on the basis of the report of the royal commission. Petitions were sent to the king and the crown prince, one signed by sixty-three farmers in eastern Iceland, and others signed by the two Icelandic representatives in the Danish assembly and all the Icelanders in Copenhagen, asking for changes in the organization of the proposed Icelandic assembly, but the government paid no attention to these requests. On March 8, 1843, the new Althing was created in accordance with the recommendations submitted by the royal commission. It was to consist of twenty-six representatives, twenty of whom were to be elected by the people, and six to be appointed by the king.[10] It should be an advisory body equal in rank to the assemblies of estates in Denmark and Schleswig-Holstein. Its meeting place was to be Reykjavik, where it assembled for the first time in 1845. The new Althing, though faulty in many respects, represented a most important victory for Icelandic national aspirations. Since the introduction of absolutism in Denmark in 1660 Iceland had been regarded as an integral part of the Danish king-

[9] *Ný félagsrit,* 1841, p. 59 ff; and 1842, p. 1 ff.
[10] *Ibidem,* 1859, p. 6.

dom, governed by royal Danish officials, and often according to Danish laws, though it had retained its old code, the
"Jónsbók," which was still in force. Through the establishing of the new assembly the rights of the Icelanders as
a distinct people were recognized, and Iceland was given
rank with the duchies of Schleswig-Holstein. Reykjavik
became a center of Icelandic political life, a national representation had been created through which the will of the
people could express itself, and the patriotic sentiment was
greatly strengthened.

That the representative government established in 1843
failed to satisfy the popular demand became apparent
even during the first session of the Althing. The rather
stormy and excited debates made it clear that the new
assembly was regarded only as an initial step in the direction of representative self-government. From all parts of
Iceland petitions were submitted, asking for various changes
in the new system of representation. But the royal commissioner read a letter from the king, stating that no further
concessions would be made. With mixed feelings of glad-
ness and disappointment the first session closed without
definite action on the pending problems. When the Althing
again assembled in 1847, the debate on the proposed changes
was renewed. The chief points at issue were: increase of
the number of representatives to the Althing, extension of
the suffrage, public sessions of the Althing, publication of
its deliberations, and the exclusive use of the Icelandic
language in its sessions. Other questions, like that of diet
and traveling expenses of the representatives, were also discussed. For pecuniary reasons the demand for an increase
in the number of representatives was finally dropped; but
the removal of the restrictions on suffrage, the introduction of direct voting in such a way that each five voters
should choose one elector, the publication of the proceedings of the Althing, and the exclusive use of the Icelandic
language in its sessions, were reforms insisted upon. It was
resolved to address a petition to the king, asking for a revision of the fundamental law on these points.[11]

[11] *Tíðingi frá Althingi*, 1847, pp. 25, 36, 739 ff, 832 ff.

While the Althing was taking these initial steps in its work, the political situation was suddenly changed through the death of King Christian VIII, January 20, 1848. The growing national sentiment in the German duchies of Schleswig-Holstein was developing into a strong desire for autonomy, resulting in a bitter antagonism between these duchies and the kingdom of Denmark, where a strong political party demanded unity of the realm with the Eider river as the southern border; an aim which, if accomplished, would result in the absorption of Schleswig in the Danish kingdom. The liberal political ideas had now grown so strong that the new king, Frederick VII, shortly after his accession to the throne issued a rescript January 28, 1848, promising to grant his kingdom a constitution in the hope that this would conciliate the dissatisfied elements throughout the realm. The old absolute régime would give place to a limited monarchy. A general legislative assembly for Denmark and the duchies of Schleswig-Holstein would be created; but the assurance was given that no change would be made in the existing provincial assemblies, the union of Schleswig-Holstein, or the relation of the two duchies of Holstein and Lauenburg to the German Confederation. Iceland was to retain its Althing as before, but how the proposed change would affect the status of their country naturally filled the minds of the Icelanders with nervous apprehension.[12]

In dealing with the demands of the Icelanders for an autonomous home government two aspects of the question had to be considered. The isolated location and natural condition of the country made it advisable, as Baldwin Einarsson had pointed out, to establish a separate Icelandic assembly. The law of 1843 had been framed chiefly on the basis of this policy of expediency. Little attention had been paid to the question whether Iceland had any right to local self-government as a distinct people united with Denmark under a common crown, as the custom had grown up of considering Iceland an integral part of the Danish kingdom. But this question had already been raised by

[12] Ný félagsrit, 1848, p. 3.

Jon Sigurdsson; and with the awakening national sentiment, not only in Iceland but throughout all Europe, it
was clear that no satisfactory settlement of the question
touching Iceland could be made until the relation and
mutual rights of the two countries should be more clearly
defined. Shortly after the appearance of the royal rescript
of 1848 Sigurdsson published in the "Ný félagsrit" an article
entitled, "Hugvekja til Íslendinga," in which he clearly
set forth the views of his people regarding their national
rights and the relation of Iceland to the Danish realm. He
showed that in the study of the history of government in
Iceland three chief features must especially be noted. In
1262 Iceland was united with Norway under the agreement known as the "Gamli Sáttmáli," which defined the
rights and position of the Icelanders. In 1662 they were
persuaded to surrender many of their rights into the hands
of the king by swearing allegiance to King Frederick III
at Kopavog as hereditary monarch. But now that the king
through his own declaration had renounced his absolute
power, and had taken steps to establish constitutional government, the rights which the Icelanders had surrendered
to the king reverted to them. Their relation to the realm
was now the same as under the "Gamli sáttmáli," the only
existing union agreement. According to this covenant
neither the Danes nor any other people had any rightful
power over Iceland, or any show of right to control Icelandic affairs. The Icelanders would deal with the king
alone regarding the constitutional provisions and all questions touching Iceland, for to him alone they pledged their
allegiance of their own free will in 1262. The Icelanders,
he continues, are a distinct people with their own language
and national life, which makes it necessary for them to
have their own government. The chief demands raised by
Sigurdsson on the basis of this interpretation of Iceland's
position were: that the Icelandic Althing should have the
same power in dealing with Icelandic affairs that the Danish Rigsdag had in dealing with Danish affairs; that a viceroy or governor should be appointed for Iceland responsible
to the Althing; that a minister for Icelandic affairs should

have a seat in the king's cabinet, and that the Icelandic finances should be separated from those of Denmark.[13] Jon Sigurdsson had stripped the issue regarding Iceland of all romantic theory, and had given it so definite and practical a form that his compatriots adopted his views as their program in the struggle for national freedom.

Before the plan suggested in the royal rescript of January 28, 1848, could be carried out, the French revolution of February, 1848, further aggravated the political situation in Denmark. The news of the revolution created the greatest unrest throughout Europe. At Kiel in Holstein and Flensburg in Schleswig intense excitement prevailed. The Danish statesmen had adhered with short-sighted tenacity to the policy of a united Danish kingdom with the Eider river as the southern border, a policy which was adopted also by the Danish liberal leaders. In opposition to their effort to unite the whole of Schleswig with Denmark a strong party was organized in the duchies to maintain the union of Schleswig and Holstein. The German population in the duchies in their struggle for autonomy looked for assistance to Prussia and the German Confederation, while the Danes turned for sympathy and support to the Scandinavian kingdoms, Norway and Sweden, and succeeded in developing a strong pan-Scandinavian and anti-German sentiment throughout the North. The uncompromising attitude of the two parties increased the growing tension, rendering a peaceful settlement of the controversy impossible. When news was received of the February revolution in Paris, a meeting of representatives of the two duchies in Flensburg decided to send a deputation to Copenhagen to demand a separate constitution for Schleswig-Holstein and the incorporation of Schleswig in the German Confederation. The Danish leaders, learning of this move, met in the Kasino in Copenhagen, and drafted vehement resolutions demanding a constitution for Denmark, including Schleswig as an integral part of the Danish kingdom. To this pressure the king yielded. In a conference with the delegates from the duchies he stated that

[13] *Hugvekja til Íslendinga, Ný félagsrit,* 1848, p. 1 ff.

he would grant Holstein a constitution, and permit it to remain united with the German Confederation, but with regard to Schleswig he would strengthen its indissoluble union with Denmark. This proposal was rejected and war was precipitated between Denmark and Schleswig-Holstein.

During this conflict the king and his advisers were able to carry out their constitutional program according to their own views. On April 4, 1848, the king revoked the rescript of January 28, and summoned the assemblies of Jutland, Schleswig, Seeland and the islands to consider the calling of a constitutional convention.[14] The Icelandic Althing, although coordinate with these assemblies, was not summoned nor consulted. According to the plan submitted by the government the convention should consist of 145 delegates from Denmark and Schleswig, elected by the people, and forty-eight to be appointed by the king. Among the latter should be five delegates from Iceland and one from the Faroe Islands. The arbitrary and unjust character of this proposal is at once evident. The Althing was ignored, and Iceland should have no popularly chosen representaties, only five delegates appointed by the king.[15] When this news reached Iceland, an assembly of notables was convened at Reykjavik, which demanded that four of the five delegates should be popularly chosen. A petition to this effect was sent to the king.[16] But this rather lame step did not satisfy public opinion in Iceland. The people of Arnessysla and of Borgarfjardarsysla sent petitions to the king, demanding a popularly elected legislative assembly for Iceland. On August 5th, nineteen of the foremost men from the various districts of Iceland met at Thingvellir to consider what measures should be taken to safeguard Icelandic interests.[17] A petition was drawn up and signed, in which they took cognizance of the king's promise to grant a constitution. But they held that the plan of establishing

[14] *Ný félagsrit*, 1849, p. 12.
[15] *Ibidem*, 1849, p. 17 ff.; 1859, p. 22.
[16] *Um hluttöku Íslands í ríkisfundi Dana eptir kónungsbréfi 4 Apr. seinastl. Reykjavíkurpósturinn*, 1848, p. 145 ff. *Ný félagsrit*, 1859, p. 23.
[17] *Ný félagsrit*, 1849, p. 20 ff; 1859, p. 24.

constitutional government could be realized for Iceland only by making the Althing a truly national assembly of popularly chosen representatives. They pointed out that the proposed Icelandic representation in the constitutional convention to be assembled would be wholly inadequate to safeguard Icelandic interests. Finally they demanded that the measures passed by this convention, so far as they had reference to Iceland, should be submitted for ratification to an Icelandic assembly as popularly chosen as that of Denmark, and that a representative national assembly should be established for Iceland with the same powers as that of the Danish assembly which was to be created. The petition drawn up at Thingvellir was repeated in nearly all districts of the country. In all, eighteen like-worded petitions bearing 1940 signatures were sent to the king by the *stiptamtmaðr,* Mathias Hans Rosenørn, who added in a communication to the government his own views on the situation in Iceland. He stated that although the news from Denmark had caused great excitement in Iceland, the people were very loyal to the king. But being imbued with a strong national patriotism they wished to share in the benefits to be derived from a change in the form of government, and would not be satisfied if this change was made without the cooperation of the Althing. They would not object to being represented in a general legislative assembly dealing with the affairs of the whole realm, if matters involving Icelandic interests would be referred to the Althing, and if the interests of Iceland would be properly respected and safeguarded in the reorganization of the government.[18] The petitions together with this communication from the *stiptamtmaðr* made such an impression on the king and government that a very courteous reply was returned September 23, 1848, stating that although the king under the existing circumstances had found it necessary to grant Iceland a representation in the constitutional convention different from that of the Danish provinces, it was not his intention that constitutional provisions touching Iceland should be finally adopted before an Icelandic

[18] *Ný félagsrit,* 1849, p. 41 f.

assembly had been given an opportunity to consider them.[19]
The members of the Danish constitutional convention were
chosen October 12, and it caused general satisfaction in
Iceland that among the five Icelandic delegates appointed
were the two political leaders Jon Sigurdsson and Jon Gudmundsson, the leading advocates of Icelandic autonomy.
At the opening of the convention, October 23, 1848, the
chairman, A. W. Moltke, stated that measures regarding
Iceland would not be definitely resolved upon before an
Icelandic assembly could be consulted.[20] The outline of a
constitution together with a draft of an election law were
submitted to the convention. In the constitution Iceland
was not mentioned, but in the election law it was provided
that Iceland should have seven representatives in the Danish legislative assembly, the Rigsdag, Denmark 153, Schleswig forty-two, and the Faroe Islands two. It is evident
that such an Icelandic representation could exercise so
little influence in a large legislative assembly that the position of Iceland would be that of a province or district in
the Danish kingdom.[21] Through the efforts of the Icelandic delegates the paragraph proposing this representation was stricken from the document, with the understanding that this matter was to be adjusted later. The
same was done also with a similar paragraph regarding the
representation from Schleswig and the Faroe Islands.
With these and a few other minor changes the drafted constitution was adopted and received royal sanction June 5,
1849. As adopted it affected only Denmark, not Iceland,
Schleswig or the Faroe Islands. The election law, which
was also passed, was sanctioned by the king the 16th of the
same month.[22] In Iceland the sentiments and opinions
touching the new constitution were expressed in numerous articles in the leading Icelandic periodicals. Judge
Thordur Jonasson, representing the most conservative view,
urged the importance of preserving the union with Den-

[19] Jon Sigurdsson, *Om Islands statsretlige Forhold*, p. 82.
[20] *Ný félagsrit*, 1848, p. 43.
[21] *Ibidem*, 1849, p. 45 ff.
[22] Thordur Jonasson, *Lítid eitt um islenzk málefni, Reykjavíkurpósturinn*,
1849. *Thjóðólfr*, July 11, 20, 1850.

mark, and the need of an Icelandic representation in the Danish Rigsdag, together with an Icelandic national assembly organized according to an agreement to be made with the Icelanders themselves. In the new liberal newspaper "Thjoðólfr" the priest Sveinbjörn Hallgrimsson, its editor, wrote a series of articles in which he made more radical demands by advocating a national constitution and government for Iceland.[23] In the "Ný félagsrit" it was also urged that an Icelandic representation in the Danish Rigsdag would be useless, that Iceland should have its own constitution defining its relation to the rest of the realm, and that the government officials should reside in the country and should be responsible to the Althing, which should be a properly constituted legislative assembly.[24] Similar opinions were advanced also by other writers, who argued that the relation between Iceland and Denmark was that of a confederation of the two countries under a common king, that the Althing must be an assembly in every way coordinate with the Danish Rigsdag, that an Icelandic executive government responsible to the Althing should be created, which should act together with the king through a minister residing in Copenhagen, and that the Althing should be reorganized on the basis of political equality for all and the most extensive suffrage. Public meetings were held in all districts throughout Iceland to discuss these important questions. Most notable was an assembly of 180 men, representing nearly all the election districts of the country, convened at Thingvellir, June 28-29, under the presidency of Pétur Pétursson, church historian and later bishop of Iceland.[25] Petitions from local meetings were read, and a memorial was drawn up to be presented to the Althing. A new election law was outlined, according to which the restrictions on suffrage should be reduced to the least possible, and the national assembly should consist of forty-eight representatives, forty-two of whom should be chosen by the people in direct elections.

[23] *Thjoðólfr*, 1848, p. 15 ff. 1849.
[24] *Avarp til Islendinga, Ný félagsrit*, 1849, p. 1 ff.
[25] *Thjoðólfr*, July 10, 1849, *Ný félagsrit*, 1859, p. 36.

In conformity with the principle announced by the king September 23, 1848, and sanctioned by the Danish constitutional convention, that provisions touching Iceland could not be adopted before an Icelandic assembly had had the opportunity to consider them, the Icelanders now took steps to deal with their own problems in connection with the new constitution. Since the Althing as a purely advisory assembly did not possess the power to deal with questions of this kind, a constitutional convention would have to be called in Iceland, as had already been done in Denmark. But before delegates could be chosen, the new election law framed by the Danish constitutional convention would have to be submitted to the Althing for ratification. On July 2, 1849, the Althing assembled, but the royal commissioner had not yet arrived from Copenhagen. The assembly was therefore called to order by the *stiptamtmaðr*, Rosenørn. Jon Sigurdsson was chosen president of the assembly, but as he had not yet arrived from Copenhagen, the vice-president, Rev. Hannes Stephensen, presided over its sessions till his arrival. The question of the new election law was brought up; but since the draft prepared by the constitutional convention had not yet come from Denmark, the one proposed by the meeting at Thingvellir was submitted to the assembly and referred to a committee headed by Jon Gudmundsson.[26] After some days Jon Sigurdsson arrived in Iceland, accompanied by the royal commissioner, Páll Melsted, who brought the new election law. This differed from the Thingvellir plan on many important points. Instead of an increased number of representatives to the national assembly, direct elections, and only slight restrictions on suffrage and eligibility to office proposed by the latter, this law provided for a small number of representatives, indirect elections, and unequal representation of the election districts. It was therefore rejected by the Althing. The Thingvellir draft was adopted with but few modifications and sent to the king, together with a petition asking that he would give it his sanction

[26] *Tiðindi frá Althingi*, 1849, p. 118 ff., 559 ff., 709 ff. *Thjóðólfr*, July-August, 1849.

and return it at the earliest possible date, in order that representatives might be chosen to the convention.[27] Some fear was entertained that the king might object to the law, but it was sanctioned September 28, 1849, and returned as requested.[28] In May, 1850, the election of representatives took place, and everything was ready for the meeting of the convention, July 15 of that year.

In the meantime the new reaction which was spreading through Europe was beginning to exert its influence also in Denmark. The wave of liberal sentiment following the revolution of 1848 had spent its force. In France the populace had begun to greet President Napoleon with the shout of "Long live the emperor!" soon to be followed by a coup d'état and the restoration of the empire. In Italy the liberal national movement was crushed in the battle of Novara, March 23, 1849. The Hungarian republic was overthrown in July of the same year. In Austria the liberal movement was completely suppressed, and in Germany the vacillating King Frederick William IV had thrown himself into the arms of the reaction. The Prussian diet was dispersed by troops, and finally formally dissolved December 5, 1848. The war between Denmark and Schleswig-Holstein was renewed after the expiration of an armistice signed at Malmø August 26, 1848. But Prussia, which had hitherto supported the duchies, now took the same attitude as Russia, and the two powers gave the king of Denmark free hands to suppress the uprising in Schleswig-Holstein, which was no longer regarded as a struggle for national self-determination, but as rebellion against their legitimate sovereign. At Isted the Danes won a decisive victory July 25, 1850. Pressed by the great powers and seeing the uselessness of continuing the struggle the Schleswig-Holsteiners dissolved their assembly and disbanded their army. Under these circumstances the attention of the king and the political leaders in Denmark was directed chiefly to the strengthening of the unity and solidarity of the realm. The final determination of the relation between its various

---

[27] *Tíðindi frá Althingi,* 1849, p. 713 ff. *Thjóðólfr,* 1849; July 11, 1850.
[28] *Ný félagsrit,* 1859, p. 40.

parts was to be carried out with a view of uniting all into
a firmly consolidated kingdom. While Iceland was preparing for the meeting of the convention, which according
to royal rescript was to assemble July 15, 1850, orders
were received from Copenhagen postponing the session till
July 4, the following year.[29] The reason for this strange
act was said to be that the provisions regarding the future
relation of Iceland to the realm, which were to be submitted,
had not yet been formulated, and that it would not be
expedient to make final arrangements with regard to Iceland while the question concerning other parts of the realm
was still pending. It is quite evident that the situation in
Iceland was nearly the same as in Schleswig. In both
countries there was a strongly expressed desire for full
autonomy and complete self-government in local affairs,
while the king and government wished to incorporate both
Schleswig and Iceland in the Danish kingdom under a
common constitution. It was undoubtedly feared that any
concession to Iceland at this moment would be cited as a
precedent, and would tend to encourage the national
aspirations in Schleswig-Holstein. The disappointment
and apprehension created by this unexpected action of the
government only increased the people's interest in the constitutional question. The periodicals continued to publish
articles dealing with all phases of the relation to Denmark,
and the features of the new constitution. The "Thjoðólfr,"
which maintained that the only bond of union with Denmark was a common king, advocated a liberal self-government for Iceland, patterned on that of Norway. Local
meetings continued to be held throughout Iceland, the
more representative assemblies being convened at Thingvellir. On August 10, 1850, 200 representatives met at the
old thingstead to consider the question regarding the constitution.[30] Reports and opinions of local meetings were
heard, and a committee was appointed which through its
chairman, Jon Gudmundsson, presented a report demanding
complete autonomy for Iceland, together with a national

[29] *Ný félagsrit*, 1859, p. 40.
[30] *Ibidem*, p. 44 ff.

government consisting of a jarl or governor with an Icelandic cabinet, an Icelandic minister in Copenhagen, full lawmaking power for the Althing, and a return to the old agreement between Norway and Iceland as the basis of union. It was further decided that local committees should be chosen in all election districts with a central committee stationed at Reykjavik, which in conjunction with the local committees should consider all features of the pending questions. On August 23, the central committee in Reykjavik began the publication of a periodical, the "Undirbúningsblað," in which the important features of the proposed constitution were discussed.[31] The government viewed this movement with growing alarm. Among other steps taken to discourage it the *stiptamtmaðr*, Count Trampe, issued a regulation forbidding all "unlawful meetings." When the first impulsive ardor ebbed away, some of the leaders hesitated, and the first vigorous demands were followed by more calm deliberation. One of the members of the central committee stated that to consider the various features of the constitution before the government proposals had been submitted was useless and confusing. But on June 28, 1851, a new meeting of 140 delegates was assembled at Thingvellir. The main features of an Icelandic constitution were outlined. The Althing, according to this plan, was to be a lawmaking body with full legislative power in conjunction with the king, with full power to raise revenues, fix public expenditures, levy taxes, and to deal with all matters which would naturally come within the scope of authority of such an assembly when popularly organized. An executive branch of government consisting of officials responsible to the people should be established within the country itself, and a minister for Icelandic affairs should be stationed in Copenhagen. The demand of the year previous, that a jarl should be placed over Iceland, was dropped. After passing resolutions that this draft should be placed before the convention when it assembled, the meeting adjourned.[32]

[31] *Undirbúningsblað undir þjóðfundinn að sumari 1851. Andvari,* i, p. 31.
[32] *Ný félagsrit,* 1852, p. 110 ff.

After the termination of hostilities in Schleswig-Holstein an assembly of notables was convened at Flensburg, May 14, 1851, to consider plans for the organization of the realm. According to the opinion of the majority of the representatives Holstein should have nothing in common with the rest of the realm but the king, foreign affairs and the navy, but Schleswig should be so closely united with Denmark as to have only a slight degree of local autonomy. The plan of separating the two duchies was opposed by the powers and could not be carried out, but the desire of the Danish leaders to unite all parts of the monarchy into a well consolidated whole had been clearly expressed. That Iceland would be treated like the rest of the realm would naturally be inferred, since no provisions were suggested with regard to it.

On July 4, 1851, the convention assembled at Reykjavik, and after a new delay caused by the failure of the government to forward in time the drafts of the measures to be considered, the law defining Iceland's relation to Denmark was finally submitted. The "Constitution of the Kingdom of Denmark" was attached as a supplement and was to be accepted in Iceland without discussion. It was stated that since the "Kongelov" and the act of 1709 through which it was promulgated in Denmark expressly stated that Iceland was a part of the Danish kingdom, this could no longer be subject to discussion, and since the king by granting a constitution had sanctioned a popular form of government within the limits established by the "Kongelov," only the manner in which the various provisions should apply to Iceland could be submitted for consideration. With regard to the constitution itself the government admitted that many provisions in it could not apply to Iceland, and that others could not be made operative because of the natural conditions of the country; but it was argued that it was not necessary to omit these paragraphs, as it was evident that they could not be enforced. The constitution as applied to Iceland would have to be given an interpretation based on good judgment. The proposed law regarding Iceland's relation to the realm numbered sixty paragraphs, of which the first ten contained the most essential provisions. According to this measure the Danish constitution of June 5, 1849, should apply also to Iceland.[33] In matters affecting the whole realm the king and the Rigsdag should have complete authority, even if Iceland was not represented in the assembly. But an opportunity would be given the Icelanders to elect representatives to the Rigsdag according to the number of their population. In all exclusively Icelandic affairs the king's lawmaking functions should be exercised in conjunction with the Althing and not with the Rigsdag. Also in these matters he should act through his ministers, who should be responsible to the Rigsdag and not to the Althing. The revenues should be divided in such a manner that all indirect taxes should go to the common treasury of the realm, which should pay the government officials, the judges of the superior court, the bishops, the teachers of the higher institutions of learning, and the expenses connected with the mail service between Denmark and Iceland. The direct taxes should go to a local Icelandic treasury, which was to defray the expenses of the Althing and the local government. As an alternative it was suggested that instead of such a division of the revenues Iceland might contribute a fixed sum to the general government, but it was feared that it would prove difficult, if not impossible, to determine what this sum should be. The king promised not to levy new taxes or to increase the burdens on the Icelandic treasury without the consent of the Althing. So far as possible the consent of the Althing should also be obtained to any change in the laws of Iceland proposed in the Rigsdag, and, finally, it was proposed that the Icelanders should send six representatives to the Danish Rigsdag, two to the upper and four to the lower branch. Provisions regarding the election of members to the Althing and the draft of a law governing trade and intercourse with Iceland were also submitted as distinct measures proposed by the government.

In the consideration of the submitted proposals a stern

[33] *Ný félagsrit,* 1859, p. 58 ff.

opposition of the convention to the whole government
plan and the reasoning upon which it was based soon manifested itself. The claim that Iceland was a part of the
Danish kingdom could never appeal with force to the minds
of those who possessed knowledge of Icelandic history,
while the declaration that the Danish constitution, which
had never been promulgated in Iceland, should be the
fundamental law of the land without the sanction of the
convention assembled to consider it, was an evident violation of the royal rescript of September 23, 1848, stating
that no constitutional provisions touching Iceland should
be finally adopted until an Icelandic assembly had been
given the opportunity to consider them. The union of
Iceland with Norway under a common king had been established by mutual agreement, the Icelanders retaining as
before their national assembly, their laws and local administration. No change in this relation was effected either
by the union between Norway, Sweden and Denmark established at Kalmar in 1397, or through the proclamation of
absolute hereditary kingship, sanctioned at Kopavog in
1662. Since the Danish "Kongelov" (*lex regia*) of 1665
was never promulgated in Iceland, even that document
could constitute no basis for the claim set up by the Danish
government.[34] It is true that absolutism was established
in Iceland through the agreement at Kopavog. But the
weakness of the position taken by the Danish leaders in the
union controversy was their claim that thereby Iceland
became a part of the Danish kingdom, that Icelandic nationality was submerged in that of Denmark. The Icelanders claimed that nothing of this sort had happened.
They had done homage to the king as absolute monarch,
as did also the Danes and Norwegians, but this did not
change the relation existing between the two countries.
The Icelanders continued to be a distinct people with their
own national assembly, their local institutions, and system
of jurisprudence. All laws had to be promulgated by the

[34] Jon Sigurdsson, *Om Islands statsretlige Forhold*, p. 86 ff. Konrad
Maurer, *Zur politischen Geschichte Islands*, p. 118 ff. *Ný félagsrit*, 1859,
p. 64 ff.

Althing before they could take effect in Iceland; and although the Althing was finally dissolved in 1800, the *landsyfirréttr* was created in its place, and in 1843 the Althing was reestablished as a recognition of a separate Icelandic nationality. No better evidence could be desired that Iceland was still a separate country with its fundamental right of self-determination than the royal rescript of September 23, 1848. The course now pursued by the government could find no justification in an appeal to the historic past. It could only be interpreted as an arbitrary reaction against the liberal policy inaugurated in 1848.

The committee to which the proposed acts were submitted by the convention returned a minority and a majority report. The minority were willing to accept the measures, at least in principle. Though they could not sanction the method pursued by the government in trying to establish the Danish constitution in Iceland, they would limit their opposition to a demand for amendments to various objectionable provisions. The majority of the committee would not surrender the principle of Iceland's separate nationality and existence as a political entity. They held that the only basis of union with Denmark was a common king, and that Iceland should be mentioned in the king's title, like other parts of the monarchy. They would not accept the proposed constitution as a whole, as this might lead to endless confusion and serious dangers for the future. They proposed instead that a separate constitution should be framed for Iceland, for which they submitted a draft based as far as possible on the Danish constitution. According to this proposal Iceland should remain united with Denmark under a common hereditary king, a joint foreign department, the same flag, currency, university and system of weights and measures. Other common interests could be arranged according to mutual agreement. In purely Icelandic affairs the Althing should take the place of the Danish Rigsdag, the judicial power should remain in the Icelandic courts of law, and the administration of Icelandic affairs should be conducted as far as possible in the country itself.[35] Neither the minority nor the majority would therefore accept the government plan as submitted. The royal commissioner, Count Trampe, *stiptamtmaðr* of Iceland, who represented the government in the deliberations, had gained great popularity through his ability to use the Icelandic language, as well as through the interest he had at first shown in the liberal movement. In 1850 he had served as chairman of the central committee appointed by the patriotic meeting at Thingvellir. But when he discovered the changed attitude of the government, he gradually withdrew from the movement. In March, 1851, the committee announced that its chairman could no longer preside at its meetings because of pressing official duties, and that he had even forbidden the printing at Reykjavik of the reports of the local committees, so that the periodical founded by the central committee had to be published in Copenhagen.[36] His hostility to the patriotic movement in Iceland had become so pronounced that in the summer of 1851 he issued the already mentioned regulation forbidding all "unlawful meetings." In the convention, where he served as royal commissioner, he showed irritation and haughty ill-will when the government proposals encountered opposition. It was also thought that it was in answer to his request that military forces were sent to Iceland, together with secret instructions that he might use them according to his own discretion, a very unusual measure in a country where military uniforms were never seen, and where the people were so peaceful and loyal as to dream of no resistance to government authorities.[37] When it became clear that the government proposals would not be accepted as submitted, the *stiptamtmaðr* grew angry. Proposals of amendments or any real deliberations by which an understanding might be arrived at he would not tolerate. On August 8 it was announced that the convention would meet the following day at 12 o'clock, when the royal commissioner would bring up a very important matter. At the

[35] *Tiðindi frá þjóðfundi Ílendinga,* p. 150 ff.
[36] *Ný félagsrit,* 1859, p. 46.
[37] *Ibidem,* p. 76 ff.

stated hour the delegates were in their seats and deep silence prevailed. Outside the soldiers came marching with fixed bayonets and loaded cartridges, taking their position near the convention hall. The silent anticipation was growing very tense when the royal commissioner stepped forward attired in official uniform. He drew a document from his pocket and began to speak to the delegates in a sharp and upbraiding tone, stating that they had wasted their time, and that the purpose of the convention had miscarried. The session could not be prolonged, and he declared the convention dissolved. Jon Sigurdsson, chairman of the constitutional committee, interrupted him by asking if he would be allowed to explain the action of the committee and the convention; but the presiding officer, a royal officer, answered "no." The count continued, saying: "I believe the delegates have heard that in the name of the king I have dissolved the convention." Jon Sigurdsson responded: "Then I protest in the name of the king and the people against this procedure, and reserve the right of the assembly to complain to the king of this unlawful act"; whereupon the whole assembly arose and cried in chorus: "We all protest!" When the count and the presiding officer had left the hall, someone called out: "Long live King Frederick VII!" a cry which was repeated by all the delegates.[38]

The *stiptamtmaðr* in dismissing the convention probably acted in harmony with the wishes of the government. It was evidently the plan to secure the consent of the convention to the government proposal as quickly as possible without much deliberation, and especially without counter proposals on the part of the assembly. The session had lasted only five weeks, and one week had passed before the proposed acts had been submitted. The statement of the count that the delegates had wasted their time could therefore not be taken seriously, if the assembly, in considering so important measures, should exercise any deliberative functions. After the dissolution of the convention thirty-six of the delegates addressed a remonstrance to the king,

[38] *Ný félagsrit,* 1858, p. 78.

in which they defended the position of the convention, and protested against the procedure of the *stiptamtmaðr* and the presence of troops to intimidate the delegates. They asked that the management of Icelandic affairs be placed in the hands of native Icelanders enjoying the confidence of the people, that the functionary in Copenhagen who had to deal with Icelandic affairs be given seat and voice in the king's cabinet, that a constitution for Iceland be drafted in harmony with the outline submitted by the majority of the constitutional committee, and presented to a new constitutional convention chosen in the same manner as the one just dismissed.[39] This remonstrance was brought to Denmark by Jon Sigurdsson and Jon Gudmundsson. An address was also directed to the Icelandic people, defending the action of the convention. The people on their side showed their approval of the course pursued by the convention in resolutions sent to individual delegates, and by addressing a petition to the king of similar contents as that sent by the constitutional committee, bearing 2200 signatures.[40] But these steps failed to elicit a favorable response from the government. On May 12, 1852, the king issued a manifesto to the Icelandic people, denying the petition of the thirty-six delegates. This document asserted that the views advanced by the delegates and shared by the signers of the petition were in conflict with the laws of the realm, and would lead to the ruin of Iceland and the dissolution of the Danish monarchy, that under the existing confusion of ideas it was not advisable to submit a new constitution. The Althing should continue its sessions until the time arrived when the king should deem it advisable to make new regulations regarding Iceland's position in the realm.[41] In accordance with this provision elections of representatives to the new Althing were ordered, but none of the officials who had signed the petition of August 10 were to be chosen. On January 28 of the

[39] *Thjóðólfr*, 1852, p. 290 ff.
[40] *Ný félagsrit*, 1859, p. 82.
[41] *Forfatnings og Valglove for det danske Monarchie og dets enkelte Landsdele*, Copenhagen, 1856, p. 426 ff. *Tíðindi frá Althingi*, 1853, p. 40 ff.

same year the king had issued a proclamation under pressure of the great powers, announcing that Schleswig would not be incorporated in the Danish kingdom, that the duchies of Schleswig, Holstein and Lauenburg should have their own local assemblies of estates, and that a constitution would be granted for the whole realm, but the proclamation contained no mention of Iceland. Under these circumstances a meeting which was convened at Thingvillir under the leadership of Síra Hannes Stephensen addressed a petition to the Althing of 1853.[42] As soon as the Althing assembled, it sought again to bring the constitutional question to a successful termination by directing a new petition to the king, reminding him of the promises given in the rescript of September 23, 1848, and in the proclamation of January 28, 1852. The petitioners prayed that in presenting new proposals regarding Iceland's relation to the realm the king would grant the Althing lawmaking power in matters in which it already acted as an advisory body, that a local administrative government should be established at Reykjavik, consisting of three officials who should have seats in the Althing, that the number of judges and the jurisdiction of the superior court of Iceland should be increased, that Iceland might get a representation according to its population in the new assembly to be established for the whole realm, and that an Icelandic minister should be appointed. The petition was carefully and courteously worded, and was approved by the royal commissioner, Melsted, but the king again refused to grant the desired reforms in an address directed to the Althing, 1855. The promise given in the royal rescript of September 23, 1848, had already been fulfilled by the assembling of the constitutional convention of 1851, it was stated. But the principal reason for denying the petition was represented to be that such changes in the Icelandic constitution could not be granted because of the burdens which would be placed on the Icelandic people, and that Iceland contributed noth-

Thjóðólfr, July 6, 1853. Ný félagsrit, 1863, p. 14. Tíðindi frá Althingi, 1853, p. 1053 f.

ing to the general treasury of the realm.[43] Shortly after
the adjournment of the Althing the Danish government
published, on October 2, 1855, a constitution for the
whole realm, together with a law governing the election of
members of the Rigsraad, the new assembly of eighty members which was to represent the whole Danish monarchy.
Iceland was not mentioned either in the constitution or
in the election law. The members of the Rigsraad were to
be chosen from Denmark, Schleswig, Holstein and Lauenburg; but even in the division of the realm into election
districts no mention was made of Iceland, which was to be
considered a Danish province. This view was clearly expressed in a work published by the Danish jurist J. E. Larsen, October 6, 1855, entitled "Om Islands hidtilværende
statsretlige Stilling," in which he attacks the position of
the committee majority of 1851 and attempts to prove that
Iceland is an integral part of the Danish kingdom. In reply
Jon Sigurdsson wrote a work, "Om Islands statsretlige
Stilling," in which he refutes with great clearness Larsen's
whole reasoning and the premises on which it is based. But
in spite of Sigurdsson's convincing arguments the policy
of the government with regard to Iceland remained unchanged. The Danish Rigsdag enacted regulations regarding Icelandic trade, and debated the Icelandic budget
without hearing the opinion of the Althing.[44] Some measures were, nevertheless, passed which affected favorably the
situation in Iceland. One cause which Jon Sigurdsson had
earnestly sought to promote was the improvement of Icelandic commercial intercourse, which was still under such
restrictions that only citizens of the realm could engage
in trade with Iceland. In his writings he urged the neces-
sity of making Icelandic trade free to all nations, a view
which at first met with determined opposition in Denmark.

Petitions were sent to the government from many parts of
Iceland, praying for the removal of restrictions on Icelandic
trade. In answer to this growing demand a law was finally

[43] *Tíðindi frá Althingi,* 1855, p. 48 ff.
[44] *Ný félagsrit,* 1852, p. 133 ff; 1856, p. 185 ff.

passed April 15, 1854, making Icelandic trade free to all nations, thus removing the economic yoke under which the people had suffered for centuries. Freedom of the press for Iceland was also established by a law of May 9, 1855, after it had been introduced in Denmark in January, 1851; and in answer to a petition from the Althing a more liberal election law was published January 6, 1857.[45] In response to an Althing petition the king also granted in 1859 that both the Danish and Icelandic texts of all laws for Iceland should be signed by the king. This was a matter of importance, as the people would have officially signed laws in their own language instead of being subject to loose interpretations of laws written in a foreign tongue. The ownership of all wrecks thrown ashore, an old right of which the Icelanders had been deprived by a royal ordinance of 1595, was also restored to them.

The reference to Iceland's economic condition and failure to share in the general burdens of the realm, contained in the king's address to the Althing, 1855, raised new issues which further complicated the controversy which had developed between Denmark and Iceland. It became evident that in order to solve the constitutional conflict it was necessary to make clear the financial relation between the two countries. What Iceland had paid or ought to pay to the general treasury could only be determined by careful analysis of Danish administration of Icelandic affairs. After 1825 repeated complaints had been made by the government that there was a constant deficit in the Icelandic treasury, that the island was unable to pay its own expenses, and had to receive aid from Denmark. But a little inquiry into the true status of affairs revealed that large sums derived from various Icelandic sources had been appropriated by Denmark without returns, depriving Iceland not only of her just belongings but of her sources of revenue. A fair adjustment of accounts would make Denmark the debtor and not the creditor on the financial balance-sheet. Before the Reformation Iceland had been

[45] *Ný félagsrit*, 1854, p. 159 ff; *Tíðindi frá Althingi*, 1855, supplement, p. 69 ff. *Lovsamling for Island*, vol. xv, p. 613 ff. *Andvari*, vol. i, p. 48.

self-supporting. The expenses connected with maintaining her church establishment were paid from incomes derived from church lands and the revenues of the monasteries. For the current expenses of the Althing and the local administration adequate provision had also been made. After the Reformation the king became the head of the church as well as of the state, and the government assumed the management of the church administration. The king issued several rescripts stating that the incomes from the church estates should be used for the establishing and maintaining of schools.[46] He expressly stated that the church lands belonged to the people of Iceland. The same attitude was taken also with regard to the revenues, funds and valuables of the cathedral churches and monasteries. Whenever these passed under government supervision a formal receipt was issued for them.[47] Unfortunately the incomes from the church lands were not devoted to the support of the Icelandic schools as at first suggested, but were swept into the royal treasury. In 1674 the king ordered Henrik Bjelke, governor of Iceland, to sell the lands belonging to the Icelandic monasteries. This order was carried out, and lands were sold for the amount of 24,162 rigsdaler. Other tracts belonging to the various monasteries were sold from time to time until 1866. In a similar way the valuables which had once belonged to the Catholic churches of Iceland, as well as the church lands, were sold and the proceeds turned into the general treasury. When the Skálholt bishop's seat was moved to Reykjavik, the king issued a rescript April 29, 1785, ordering the church lands of the diocese to be sold for the benefit of the royal treasury, with the proviso that the government should pay the bishop's salary and maintain the Latin school. By royal rescript of October 2, 1801, the bishopric and Latin school of Hólar were consolidated with the bishopric and Latin school of Reykjavik, and the church lands of the old bishopric were sold in order to give better financial support

---

[46] Magnus Ketilsson, *Samlinger af Forordninger*, vol. i, p. 234 ff, p. 267.
[47] Thorkelsson og Arnórsson, *Ríkisréttindi Íslands*, p. 59 f. *Danske Magasin*, iii, 1747, p. 351 ff.

to the new school and bishopric. The sale brought the amount of 123,199 rigsdaler. But this sum was not credited to Iceland on the budget. Cash funds of various kinds were also seized. To these sums must further be added the greater share of the relief fund collected for the famine stricken people of Iceland in 1784-1785, not over one-fourth of which had been used for the relief of the sufferers. The rest remained in the general treasury, or was used for purposes of no interest to Iceland. The benefit derived by Danish citizens from the monopolized Icelandic trade, and the economic losses suffered by the Icelanders due to that monopoly would also have to be considered. Even the direct proceeds from appropriated funds and sale of Icelandic property formed a capital which, according to the lowest possible estimates, amounted to 350,000 rigsdaler.[48] Iceland's resources had thus remained in the hands of Denmark for centuries. The income derived from them was entered in the budget as Danish, not as Icelandic revenues, and as the officials connected with the church and civil adminstration drew their pay from the general treasury, it would naturally appear that Iceland did not pay her share in the expenses of the realm. What part of those expenses could be justly regarded as Iceland's share of the public burdens would also need to be determined, and would naturally have to be computed to some extent on the basis of the services rendered the country by the Danish government. These had often been very small, being usually limited to the sending of a governor and a few higher officials to Iceland. No defense had been provided against attacks of pirates and freebooters. The Icelandic coasts were unguarded, the people unarmed and defenseless, without military protection of any sort. In time of war Denmark had been unable to give Iceland any assistance, leaving the country to the mercy of the enemy. Economically the Icelanders had derived even less benefit from Danish rule, as their trade had remained in the hands of

[48] Eirikur Magnusson, *Das staatliche Verhältniss zwischen Island und Dänemark, Unsere Zeit,* 1883, vol. ix, p. 559 ff. Konrad Maurer, *Zur politischen Geschichte Islands,* p. 192 ff.

the merchant companies, who made it impossible to foster
home industries or develop Icelandic resources. It would
therefore seem that Iceland's share of the public burdens
would be limited to the expenses connected with maintaining her schools, her civil administration and her church
establishment, burdens which the people were willing
enough to carry if the government would establish a legislative assembly and local administration, and give them
control of their own affairs. Political liberty was thus found
to be so closely connected with economic independence
that the Icelanders raised the demand for restitution of
the funds and resources appropriated by Denmark, separation of finances, and the organization of an independent
Icelandic budget. In 1861 a joint committee consisting
of three Danes and two Icelanders was appointed to devise
a plan for settling the financial question. Three different
reports were submitted by this committee, Jon Sigurdsson,
who had first started the inquiry into the financial relations of the two countries, and, in articles published in "Ný
félagsrit," had thoroughly discussed the question, was a
member and submitted a report of his own. He held that
Iceland should receive yearly the sum of 119,724 rigsdaler
in lieu of interest due on Icelandic funds in the general
treasury, and that the Icelanders should pay proportion-
ately their share of the royal appanages and of the expenses
connected with the administration of the joint affairs of
the realm. Two other members, the Icelander Oddgeir
Stephensen and the Dane Major Tscherning, proposed a
yearly payment to Iceland of 29,500 rigsdaler and later an
additional 12,500 rigsdaler for a period of ten years, after
which time the payments should be reduced 500 rigsdaler
a year. A third report by the two Danes Bjerring and
Nutzhorn proposed the payment of 12,000 rigsdaler a year,
and in addition yearly payments of 30,000 rigsdaler for a
period of six years, after which time these payments should
be reduced 2000 rigsdaler a year. All members of the committee agreed that the separation of the Icelandic finances
from those of Denmark would be very desirable, but that

this matter could be settled only in conjunction with the constitutional question.[49]

The Althing again petitioned the king that as soon as possible he would order new election of representatives to a convention. To this petition the king answered in an address to the Althing, June 8, 1863, that the question regarding an Icelandic constitution was so closely connected with the question regarding the finances of the country that the former could not be settled except in conjunction with the latter. He stated that a committee had been appointed in 1861, and had closed its labors in 1862, that the ministry of justice and the ministry of finance would now deliberate regarding the financial question.[50] Neither the question of the constitution nor that of finances was submitted to the Althing of 1863.

The attempt of the government to unite the duchies of Schleswig-Holstein more firmly with the rest of the Danish monarchy by granting a constitution for the whole realm met with strong opposition from the European powers. So strong was the pressure brought to bear on Denmark in favor of the German population of the duchies that on November 6, 1858, the government annulled the constitution so far as it applied to Holstein and Lauenburg. The leaders, who desired a strongly consolidated monarchy, now planned to unite Schleswig with Denmark, with the Eider river as the southern border of the realm. This program proved equally unwelcome to the powers, especially to the German states, but the government would make no further concessions. On September 28, 1863, a joint constitution for Denmark and Schleswig was submitted to the Rigsraad. The assembly approved it, but before it could be signed King Frederick VII died, and was succeeded by Christian IX, Nov. 15, 1864. Both Prussia and Russia had protested against the new constitution, but the king signed it under pressure of a strong public sentiment in his kingdom. As a result the united armies of Prussia and Austria entered

<hr>

[49] *Ný félagsrit*, 1863, p. 39 ff; 1870, p. 163 f. *Tíðindi frá Althingi*, 1865, C, p. 33 ff.

[50] *Thjóðólfr*, June 9, 1863.

the duchies. In the war which followed, 1864, Denmark was defeated and had to cede Schleswig, Holstein and Lauenburg, about two-fifths of the area and population of the realm. Thus vanished suddenly the hope of the Danish leaders of a strong centralized monarchy. The problem now confronting them was to save their country from utter collapse. With this in view the settlement of the constitutional question had to be undertaken on the basis of the changed condition in the realm.

The Althing had repeatedly sent petitions to the king and government in an effort to bring about a solution of the constitutional controversy, but these were always denied. The reasons assigned were either that no general settlement of the relation between the various parts of the realm had yet been effected, or that the constitutional question could not be solved so long as the financial problem still remained unsettled, as in the answers returned in 1861 and 1863. But the change in national affairs after 1864 made the government more willing to listen to the supplications of the Icelanders. In 1865 the king submitted to the Althing a law proposing a settlement of the financial question, the promise being given that as soon as this matter was arranged the question of a constitution would be considered. According to this proposal Iceland was to receive 42,000 rigsdaler a year for twelve years. After that time the Danish Rigsdag should fix the amount to be paid.[51] This proposal was rejected, and the Althing demanded that a constitutional convention should be assembled to frame a constitution for Iceland containing provisions for the settlement of the financial question.

On July 28, 1866, a revised Danish constitution, prepared by a committee of the Rigsraad under the direction of the ministry, was signed by the king. Iceland was not mentioned. Her relation to Denmark remained as undefined as before. No constitutional convention was called in Iceland, as requested, but through the efforts of Hilmar Finsen, *stiptamtmaðr* of Iceland, a grandson of Bishop Hannes Finsen, the question of a constitution for Iceland was never-

---

[51] *Tíðindi frá Althingi*, 1865, C, p. 11 ff.

theless brought a step nearer its solution. In 1867 the government submitted to the Althing a draft of a constitution proposing that Iceland should have its own legislative assembly and the management of its local administration. The supervision of Icelandic affairs should be placed in the hands of one of the ministers of the king's cabinet. The Althing should meet once every three years. It should consist of one chamber, and should have the same number of representatives as before. In framing laws regarding the common affairs of the realm, Iceland should have no voice. Such laws should only be published to become effective. The proposal as a whole was favorably received; but amendments to various provisions were submitted, according to which the Althing should meet once every two years, the bicameral system should be established, and the number of representatives increased. Regarding the position of Iceland in the realm the Althing held that instead of making Iceland a part of the kingdom of Denmark, as proposed in the submitted draft, it should be a part of the Danish monarchy with individual rights as a distinct part of the realm. The question as to what amount Iceland should contribute to the general budget should not be decided by the king alone, as proposed in the government draft, but by the king in conjunction with the Althing, and finally it was demanded that the officials in charge of administrative affairs in Iceland should be made responsible to the Althing. Regarding the financial settlement the government proposed to pay Iceland a yearly sum of 37,500 rigsdaler, and 12,500 for a period of twelve years, the latter sum to be diminished by 500 rigsdaler a year. The Althing on the other hand asked a yearly sum of 60,000 rigsdaler.[52]

It is evident that the Althing in suggesting the amendments sought to be as moderate as possible, and it was hoped that they would be accepted by the government. The difference between the proposals regarding the financial settlement was so small that in 1868 a motion was introduced in the Danish Rigsdag to grant Iceland a per-

[52] Tíðindi frá Althingi, 1867, Viðbætir, B, p. 11 ff.

manent yearly sum of 50,000 rigsdaler and a 10,000 annuity for a period of years. If negotiations had been continued in a conciliatory spirit, a final agreement could probably have been reached, but some of the Danish leaders had not yet learned that a union founded on mutual good-will is stronger and more enduring than an artificial compact of constitutional provisions based on distrust and injured national sentiment. The bill proposing a settlement of the Icelandic financial question did not pass. Orla Lehmann, a fiery patriotic Danish leader, more noted for his eloquence than for discretion and political sagacity, said in discussing the measure that it had perhaps never happened before that one had to beg and beseech a people, yes, even promise them money, in order to move them to accept their liberty. And the "Fædrelandet," a leading Danish paper, stated that the honor of adding the picture of a codfish to the Danish coat of arms, and to maintain the union with an old Norwegian colony was dearly paid for.[53] The attitude of the Danish leaders toward Iceland was still that of dictation from above and hostile opposition to its national aspirations. After the opening of the Althing session in 1869 the government commissioner disputed the right of three members to their seats in the assembly, one of these being Jon Sigurdsson, who had constantly been reelected from the same district, and who had repeatedly served as president of the Althing. With the exception of one member who did not vote, the representatives unanimously resolved to seat the three members, and Jon Sigurdsson was again elected president of the assembly.[54] The Danish Rigsdag continued to discuss Icelandic affairs and to propose plans for establishing the relation between the two countries without consulting the Icelanders. In 1869 a new law defining the relation of Iceland to the realm was submitted to the Althing,[55] together with a constitution outlining the administration of Icelandic local affairs, but both proposals were rejected as wholly unacceptable. A bill was then

[53] *Fædrelandet*, October 28, 1868.
[54] *Tíðindi frá Althingi*, 1869, p. 4 ff.
[55] *Ibidem*, 1869, II, *Frumvarp*, p. 10 ff.

passed by the Danish Rigsdag, January 2, 1871, defining Iceland's relation to the realm.[56] It declared that Iceland was an inalienable part of the Danish kingdom, but that it should have its own government in purely domestic affairs. The royal treasury should grant Iceland an annuity of 30,000 rigsdaler and an additional 20,000 rigsdaler for ten years, the latter sum to decrease by 1000 rigsdaler yearly until it ceased to be paid. The Danish *høiesteret* should be the highest judicial tribunal, but in other respects the domestic suits should be separated from those of Denmark.[57] As this law was to become effective April 1, 1871, it was evident that it could not be submitted to the Althing, that the question was to be settled without reference to the wish of the Icelanders, a procedure which would violate even the constitutional right of that assembly to act as an advisory body. When the Althing met in 1871, it received notice of the passage of this law, and the draft of a constitution was also submitted. The committee appointed to consider these measures returned two reports. The majority held that the law of 1871 did not concern the Icelanders, as it was only a Danish proclamation. The constitutional draft was also found to be unsatisfactory, especially the features that the Icelandic minister should reside in Copenhagen, and that the highest official in Iceland should be responsible to him and not to the Althing. Some amendments were therefore proposed, the most important being that the highest executive official should reside in Iceland and should be responsible to the Althing. The minority agreed with the majority on most points, and as they hoped to bring about a settlement of the constitutional controversy, they maintained an attitude of compromise and reconciliation. They would not refuse to accept the law of of 1871, and would be satisfied with a minister residing in Copenhagen. The majority report was adopted by the Althing, but the minority report was also submitted. The

[56] *Lovsamling for Island,* vol. xxi, p. 1 ff.

[57] Konrad Maurer, *Zur politischen Geschichte Islands,* p. 236 ff. Eirikur Magnusson, *Das staatliche Verhältniss zwischen Island und Dänemark, Unsere Zeit,* vol. ix, p. 569 ff.

government would not accept the proposals of the Althing, and decided to let the matter rest for a while.

The arbitrary spirit in which the Danish authorities continued to deal with Icelandic affairs could only increase the bitterness of the struggle and strengthen the Icelandic opposition. Ordinances were passed without paying any attention to the Althing; judges of the Icelandic superior court were appointed without consulting the Icelanders. In 1872 a new office, that of *landshöfðingi*, or governor of Iceland, was created without consulting the Althing or the wishes of the people. Acts of this kind showed that the old bureaucratic despotism, though moved by good intentions and draped in new constitutional forms, had not yet been regenerated by a truly democratic spirit. Before a real settlement of the controversy could be effected, the old bureaucracy would have to learn to bow to the will of the people and do homage to the spirit of a new age. The growing discontent in Iceland found expression in numerous petitions addressed to the king, upholding the Althing and denouncing the law of 1871. Numerous local meetings were also convened to discuss the pending questions and to express the demand for an autonomous local government. A "Society of Friends of the People" was organized [58] to defend the country's rights and to further its interests with all available means. The press of the country was divided into two camps. The two oldest and most widely read papers, the "Thjóðólfr" and the "Norðanfari," as well as the "Ný félagsrit," founded by Jon Sigurdsson, and the "Göngu-Hrólfr," edited by the poet Jon Olafsson, championed the national cause without compromise, while the paper "Tíminn," founded in 1871, was more neutral, and the "Víkverji," founded in 1873, was a government organ edited by Páll Melsted, counselor in the superior court, and Jon Jonsson, secretary of the *landshöfðingi*. The government threatened the editor of the "Thjóðólfr," Jon Gudmundsson, counselor in the superior court, that his lawyer's permit would be revoked. Jón Olafsson, editor of the "Baldur" and later of the Göngu-Hrólfr," was repeatedly

---

[58] *Thjóðólfr,* August 19, 1873.

prosecuted and fined, but the fines were always paid by his patriot friends, until finally he was forced to leave Iceland to avoid new prosecutions, and his paper ceased to appear. The "Norðanfari" advocated that the Icelanders should try to enlist the sympathy of other nations or seek union with some other country. If they failed in this attempt, they should emigrate to America to escape the oppression of Danish overlordship.[59] Brazil and North America were praised as lands of freedom, and a movement of emigration was set on foot which soon carried thousands of Icelanders to the United States and Canada. After 1870 this emigration continued to grow from year to year, but it must be ascribed to economic rather than to political conditions, as most of the emigrants were poor people from impoverished districts where suffering was general. In 1874 a millennial festival was to be celebrated in Iceland in commemoration of the colonization of the country. A farmer suggested that this festival should be made an occasion of national mourning and farewell of an emigrating people. A provost in the church of Iceland wrote, begging the people to wait one more year to see if the king would grant the long expected constitution for this great event, and to leave the country only if this last hope was disappointed. Societies were founded, the members of which pledged themselves not to taste distilled liquors in order that the government might not derive any revenues from these. On New Year's night the students of Reykjavik marched through the streets, singing the "Islendingabragur," a bitter political poem, because its author, the poet Jon Olafsson, had been prosecuted. Demonstrations were also made in front of the home of the *stiptamtmaðr*, Hilmar Finsen. On April 1, 1873, the day on which he was to assume the new office of *landshöfðingi*, a black flag was found fastened to the flag-pole in front of his house, bearing the inscription: "Down with the *landshöfðingi!*" So bitter was the popular feeling that no one ventured to show him any public attention.

On June 26, 1873, a public assembly was convened at Thingvellir, consisting of thirty-five representatives from

[59] *Norðanfari*, August 23, 1872.

the various districts of Iceland. Members of the Althing, and many people from all Iceland came to attend this meeting, among others also Jon Sigurdsson, who arrived from Copenhagen. Jon Gudmundsson was elected chairman of the meeting, and only the chosen representatives should have the right to vote. Nineteen petitions from various districts regarding the constitutional question were submitted. The committee appointed to consider these drafted a complete outline of a constitution, declaring among other things that Iceland was a free and independent country united with Denmark under a common king, and that a bill should become a law when it had been passed three times by the Althing unaltered, even if the king did not sign it. Jon Sigurdsson and Jon Gudmundsson opposed these declarations strongly. They argued that such a plan could not be carried out, that Iceland could be a free country even if it had some things in common with Denmark. To those who understood affairs of government it seemed dangerous to break completely with Denmark. "Danish merchants have indeed oppressed the Icelanders," said the speakers, "but if we had established close relations with other nations, the situation would probably not have been different." The first draft of a petition to be submitted to the king expressed strongly the excited feelings of the people, but the arguments of Sigurdsson and Gudmundsson made such impression that a new draft was prepared in a more modified tone. Even this was so radical that Jon Sigurdsson refused to present it, and Jon Gudmundsson agreed to do so only if it received the sanction of the Althing. It was feared that the strong party feeling which had developed during this period of excitement would bring about violent clashes within the Althing when it again assembled, but instead the men representing different views sought to become reconciled, and an unexpected unanimity prevailed in the assembly. It was agreed to ask the king to grant the country a constitution which would give the Althing full legislative power and control of Icelandic finances. In answer to this petition the king issued a constitution June 5, 1874, granting legislative power to the Althing and establishing self-government for Iceland in domestic affairs. The manner in which this constitution and the law of 1871 were issued did not please the Icelanders, as they were not allowed to participate in the framing of the new fundamental laws, except in so far as they had expressed their wishes in petitions to the king. On many points the measures did not grant what the people desired, but the most important demands had nevertheless been realized. The Icelanders were given control of their own finances, the number of representatives in the Althing was increased, and the bicameral system was established. The Althing was to consist of thirty-six members, six appointed by the king and thirty elected by the people. The upper house, *efri deild*, should have twelve members, six appointed by the king, and six chosen by the elected members from their own number. The remaining twenty-four representatives constituted the lower house, or *neðri deild*. The assembly was to meet on the first work-day in July in Reykjavik every other year for six weeks. Special sessions could be called at the king's pleasure. The king could also dissolve the Althing and order new elections. No bill could become a law without his signature. Bills might be introduced in either branch of the assembly, and the parliamentary procedure was to be the same as in other modern legislative bodies. The executive power in domestic affairs was vested in the *landshöfðingi*, or governor, who was not made responsible to the Althing but to the minister for Icelandic affairs in Copenhagen. Iceland was not represented in the Rigsdag, had no voice in the general affairs of the realm, and paid no part of the national expenditures. The Lutheran church was recognized as the state church, but liberty of conscience was granted to all inhabitants. Titles and privileges of nobility were abolished, sanctity of the home, security of private property, freedom from forced labor, freedom of the press, of association and assembly, and rights of municipal government were guaranteed. The Icelandic government was thus very limited in power. The king's absolute veto in legislation, and the responsibility of the governor to a minister residing in Copenhagen, were

especially objectionable features. Much would depend on
the good will of the *landshöföingi* and the minister, and the
extent to which they would respect the decisions of the
Althing.[60]

The new election law passed September 14, 1877, divided
the country into nineteen election districts, of which eight
elected one representative each, the others two. Suffrage
was granted to all male citizens, not servants, twenty-five
years of age who had lived one year in the election district
and were paying a tax of eight kroner a year as farmers or
citizens of towns, or as peasants were paying a yearly tax
of twelve kroner; further also to all graduates of the University of Copenhagen, and of the Theological Seminary
and Medical School of Reykjavik. Eligible to office were
all voters thirty years of age who had resided in the European part of the Danish realm for a period of five years.[61]

The millennial festival could now be celebrated as an
event of rejoicing over the new era of autonomy and national progress to which the Icelanders could look hopefully
forward. As the constitution should become effective
August 1, 1874, the celebration arranged for this occasion
would have the double purpose of commemorating the
thousandth anniversary of the settlement of the country
and of inaugurating the new national government. This
great event was made memorable also by the visit of the
king of Denmark, Christian IX, who sailed to Iceland to
take part in the festivities and bring the people his personal
greetings. Delegations from many foreign lands, from
Sweden, Norway, France, Germany, the United States, and
England also arrived in Reykjavik. On August 2 com-
memorative services were held in the cathedral, where
Bishop Pétur Pétursson preached. The American poet
Bayard Taylor, who was present on this occasion, writes:
"Lights were burning in the chandeliers on the altar, and
between the gallery pillars; wreaths of heather decorated

⁶⁰ The constitution is found in *Tíðindi um stjórnarmálefni Íslands gefin
ut af hinum íslenzka bókmentafélagi*, vol. iii, p. 698 ff. See also Bayard
Taylor, *Egypt and Iceland*, p. 269 ff. *Stjórnarskrá um hin sjer staklegu
málefni Íslands og lóg um þingsköp handa alþigi Íslendinga.*
⁶¹ Valtyr Gudmundsson, *Islands Kultur ved Aarhundredskiftet 1900*, p. 34.

the walls, choir and galleries, and there was a glow of flowers around Thorvaldsen's baptismal font. The dull red of the walls and dark panels of the wooden ceiling harmonized well with these simple adornments; the building wore an aspect of cheerful solemnity, becoming the occasion. The seats filled rapidly during the chant, men and women sitting together as they could find places. Then the service commenced, after the ancient Lutheran fashion. In fact, it was nearly an exact repetition of that which we have seen in Thorshavn, except that the Icelandic language was used. The hymns were simply and grandly sung; and the "Psalm of Praise" written by Matthias Jochumsson and composed by Sveinbjörnsson—the first musical work by a native Icelander, I am told—produced a powerful effect. In whichever direction I looked I saw eyes filled with tears. The repetition of the refrain: *Íslands þúsund ár* ("Iceland's thousand years") rang through the cathedral in tones which were solemn rather than proud, and gave expression to the earnest religious spirit in which the people had come together." [62] The services were followed by a banquet in the hall of the college, where the king spoke, expressing the hope that the people would be satisfied with the constitution he had granted them, and closing with the toast: "Long live Old Iceland!" The band struck in with the cheers that followed, and the ships thundered their salute from the harbor. In the evening a popular festival was celebrated on the hill of Öskjuhlíð near the city. A rostrum for speakers had been erected, a tent for the king, and 2000 people were assembled. An elaborate program was carried out with singing and speaking. Admiral Lagercrantz spoke for Sweden, the author Nordahl Rolfsen for Norway, and Bayard Taylor for the United States. The formal part of the program, was followed by popular merrymaking, consisting of dancing and fireworks. The king and his party and the foreign representatives also visited the geysers of Iceland and took part in a public festival at Thingvellir, where greetings were read from the universities of Copenhagen, Upsala, Lund, and Christiania, from students' societies in

[62] Bayard Taylor, *Egypt and Iceland*, p. 213 ff.

Denmark and Norway, from Norwegian patriotic societies, and from the Academy of Fine Arts in Copenhagen, which acknowledged the great sculptor Thorvaldsen to be an Icelander. Bayard Taylor brought the greetings of America in a poem written for the occasion. At the door of the pavilion a chorus sang a song, "Minni Konungs á Thingvellir," written by Matthias Jochumsson. A banquet was then served, and the king and his party returned to Reykjavik.

Better days had at last dawned for Iceland. Politically the people had won recognition of their rights as a distinct nation, a new spirit of enterprise and national self-consciousness had been awakened, economic conditions were improving, and export and import trade had increased after the commercial monopoly was abolished. A comparison of the export of leading commodities in 1849 and 1872 shows the following figures:

	1849		1872	
Salted fish	2,783	tons	4,030	tons
Dried codfish	561	"	78	"
Salted roe	308	barrels	1,558	barrels
Salted salmon	2,640	kilograms	18,480	kilograms
Train-oil	3,259	barrels	9,493	barrels
Salted meat	1,235	"	1,985	"
Tallow	646,874	pounds	264,204	pounds
Wool	1,397,148	"	1,295,212	"
Knitted jackets	8,405		118	
Socks	91,145	pairs	54,741	pairs
Seamen's mittens ...	78,962	"	14,347	"
Vaðmál	5,808	ells	759	ells
Sheepskins	9,745		8,382	
Lambskins	13,405		25,481	
Fox skins	396		312	
Swan skins	94		40	
Swan feathers	21,875		21,400	
Eiderdown	3,991	pounds	7.253	pounds
Feathers	19,268	"	26,801	"

This shows that the export of important commodities like fish, train-oil, meat, skins, feathers and eiderdown had increased extensively. The decrease in the export of tallow was due to the fact that people now sold it to the fishermen instead of bringing it to the merchants. In spite of the decrease in the sale of some commodities of less importance the total volume of the export trade was growing.[63] Of still greater benefit to Iceland was the change effected in the relation of prices between imported and exported goods. In 1849 a barrel of rye flour cost 89.6 kilograms of dried codfish. In 1872 it cost only 44 kilograms. In 1849 a barrel of rye flour was exchanged for 39.5 pounds of wool; in 1872 for 15.2 pounds. Because of this favorable change in prices importation increased in volume much faster than exportation, and the people were better able than hitherto to procure the staple commodities. The following table shows the increase in imports of various leading articles in the period 1849 till 1872: [64]

	1849		*1872*	
Rye	23,128	barrels	29,993	barrels
Barley	274	"	439	"
Beans	2,028	"	4,316	"
Peeled Barley	7,635	"	13,710	"
Rye flour	3,849	"	5,711	"
Bread	186,800	pounds	210,310	pounds
Liquor, distilled	64,303	gallons	136,194	gallons
Other liquors	9,948	"	36,971	"
Coffee	293,833	pounds	567,328	pounds
Sugar	272,702	"	608,949	"
Sirup	16,587	"	9,012	"
Tobacco	79,967	"	123,221	"
Salt	17,069	barrels	22,234	barrels
Tar	533	"	584	"
Coal	3,479	"	17,233	"
Iron	108,137	pounds	112,698	pounds
Hemp	38,100	"	26,488	"
Fishing-lines	10,587		24,012	
Timber	4,101	pieces	8,805	pieces
Boards and planks	84,581	"	114,084	"

The increase in the number of ships arriving in Icelandic harbors also shows a considerable growth in trade and intercourse.

[63] *Skýrslur um landshagi á Íslandi gefnar ut af hinum íslenzka bókmentafélagi,* vol. v, p. 816 ff.
[64] *Ibidem,* p. 810.

```
1863 ............................ 148 ships
1864 ............................ 152   "
1865 ............................ 162   "
1866 ............................ 148   "
1867 ............................ 165   "
1868 ............................ 134   "
1869 ............................ 149   "
1870 ............................ 160   "
1871 ............................ 183   "
1872 ............................ 179   "
```

During the period 1865-1872 the trade with Denmark was decreasing, while the traffic with other countries was constantly growing. In 1872 many ships from England and Scotland also began to arrive in Iceland to purchase horses, an article of export which, from this time forth, became of increasing importance. Reykjavik had now be-come the chief trading center in Iceland, with Isafjord as second in rank. Another evidence of the general progress was the steady growth of population. In 1870 Iceland had 70,031 inhabitants, an increase of 3043 since 1860.[65]

17. REALISM IN ICELANDIC LITERATURE. MODERN INTEL-LECTUAL LIFE IN ICELAND

THE year 1874, when Iceland received its constitution and entered upon a new era of national development, coincided very closely with the beginning of a new period of Euro-pean political and intellectual life following the Franco-Prussian War of 1870-1871. That eventful conflict between the two leading European nations dispelled the romanticism which had hitherto remained bound up with the memory of Napoleon's military glory and the resplendent greatness of France. The war shattered the Napoleonic empire and taught the world a new military science; but it also created the bloody conflict in Paris between the old social order and militant communism, and turned the mind of Europe to new political and social problems. New forces also made themselves felt in European life and thought. The woman's

* Skýrslur um landshagi á Íslandi, vol. v, p. 553 ff.

movement raised the demand for women's rights, socialistic ideas were spreading, and international labor unions were organized. The Darwinian theory of evolution, expounded and popularized by able writers like Thomas Huxley and Herbert Spencer, offered a new explanation of man's life and his relation to the universe. In such an age people naturally felt that they were not living in the realms of dreams, but in a practical world with difficult problems which awaited their solution. The inquiring and critical spirit of the age found its expression in a realistic literary movement, and a literary criticism based on the new views which soon rendered archaic the romanticism of the earlier decades of the nineteenth century.

In Iceland the new realistic literary movement began to develop about 1880. The leaders of this movement were the Icelandic students in Copenhagen who had come under the influence of Georg Brandes, the chief representative of this school of thought in Denmark. In 1871 Brandes began a series of lectures at the University of Copenhagen, later published under the title "The Main Currents of the Nineteenth Century Literature." Romanticism and the old views were sharply assailed, and the most radical ideas in politics, religion, philosophy and literature were advanced. Christian faith and national patriotism were considered antiquated remnants of an unscientific age destined to disappear in the broad daylight of modern scientific inquiry. In contradistinction to the nationalists the adherents of the new movement called themselves Europeans, and affected an air of superiority because of their scientific reasoning and cosmopolitan views. All established tenets and institutions; all relations in family, society, and state were subjected to a searing scrutiny. All human problems were discussed in this new literature which aimed to picture life as it really is. Most of the young authors in Denmark, Norway and Sweden were soon found in the ranks of the realists, and it was natural that the Icelandic students in Copenhagen should also join in the new movement. As the periodical "Fjölnir" had been founded as the special organ of the romanticists, a new periodical, "Verðandi," was

founded by the four young authors Berthel E. O. Thorleifsson, Einar Hjörleifsson, Gestur Pálsson and Hannes Hafstein to champion the new realistic views. The first number
contained the poem "Storm" by Hannes Hafstein, the very
fine short story, "Kærleiksheimilið," by Gestur Pálsson, and
another short story, "Upp og niður," by Einar Hjörleifsson,
productions of great excellence. But the "Verðandi" lived
only one year. It was succeeded by two new journals:
"Suðri," published in Reykjavik 1883-1887, and "Heimdal-
lur," published in Copenhagen 1884. But these too died
soon. In the larger European countries realism performed
a useful mission by making literature a weapon in the hands
of social reformers. But in Iceland, where no class distinction, industrial conflicts or social problems existed, it could
be nothing but a new literary style little understood or
appreciated by the people. The cosmopolitan atmosphere
and pessimistic critical attitude which characterized the
realists was little suited to solve the problems which confronted the Icelanders. The reawakening of the old national spirit, the romantic love of their own country, the
pride in their ancient traditions, the confidence in their
ability to make Iceland as prosperous as it is beautiful, fostered by the devoted enthusiasm of the romanticists, had
accomplished great things for Iceland. The critical and
often negative realists could bring no such encouraging
message. In their effort to picture conditions in their
naked reality they could only point to the shady side of
life, the poverty and discouraging economic conditions.
The solace and encouragement found in the Christian faith
they usually discarded, the greatness of past ages they
regarded as idle fancies. The pessimism and discontent
fostered by this attitude could only tend to swell the number of emigrants who at this time were yearly leaving
Iceland, some of the realist leaders themselves setting the
example of emigrating to America. But although realism
could have no direct mission in Iceland as a regenerating
social force, it has been of great importance to modern
Icelandic literature and intellectual life. To the realists
is due in a great measure the development of the modern

Icelandic novel, though it had begun to flourish before their time. Through their discussion of present-day conditions they have fostered among their people a better understanding of the modern world with its complex social life, so necessary to all deeper analysis of human life in our age. By discarding the rather grandiose style of the romanticists they have given literary production a somber and critical spirit, but also a cosmopolitan character which reaches beyond the purely local and national, and makes the Icelandic novel and drama of today distinct contributions to the twentieth century literary art.

The foremost novelists of the new school were Gestur Pálsson, 1852-1891; Jonas Jonasson, 1856-1918, and Einar Hjörleifsson, born December 9, 1859. Gestur Pálsson pursued the study of theology at the University of Copenhagen, but left without taking his final examinations, returning to Iceland in 1882. For some years he published the paper "Suðri." In 1890 he emigrated to America, settling in Winnipeg, Canada. Here he became editor of the Icelandic paper "Heimskringla," but died at an early age in 1891. In his novels and short stories he pictures Icelandic life and social conditions with great force and clearness, dwelling especially on the misery of the poor, and the greed, hypocrisy and egoism of the well-to-do. The leaders in society, who pretend to promote the general welfare when they are only furthering their own interests, are made to feel the sting of his bitter irony. His delineation of character is striking, and his psychological analysis of great mental struggles are true and artistically wrought. His novels have been translated into German, Danish, Norwegian, English and Bohemian. Jonas Jonasson was a very productive novelist, devoting himself chiefly to the picturing of social conditions in ancient and modern times. Einar Hjörleifsson attracted attention as a story writer even while attending the Latin school. In 1885 he emigrated to America, becoming associate editor of the Icelandic paper "Heimskringla," in Winnipeg, Canada. Later he served as editor of the Icelandic weekly the "Lögberg" of the same city from 1888 till 1895, when he returned to Iceland. He

is one of the most noted and influential of Icelandic
writers.[1] Since 1910 he has received a government stipend
for literary work. Among younger Icelandic novelists may
be mentioned Gudmundur Magnusson, better known by
his pseudonym Jon Trausti, 1873-1918, who also received
an author's stipend from the government; Benedikt Björnsson, born 1879, and Gunnar Gunnarsson, born 1889. Hannes
Hafstein, one of the founders of the "Verðandi," is an ideal-
ist and a gifted lyric poet. But as he became one of the
leading statesmen of Iceland, he has accomplished less in
literature than he otherwise might have done, as he has
been chiefly occupied with political questions in a busy
public life. Among the foremost lyric poets of this school
was Thorsteinn Erlingsson, 1858-1914, for a time teacher
in Copenhagen. In religion he was an evolutionist, in
political views a radical. His poems were written to serve
as a vehicle for his radical and evolutionistic political and
social views. Einar Benediktsson, born 1864, is a lyric poet
of great power. In 1903 he organized the political party
known as the *landvarnarflokkur,* or party of national defense, which opposed the amendment to the constitution
proposed by the government. Since 1907 he has lived
abroad, usually in England. The Icelandic dramatic literature has found able representatives in Johann Sigurjonsson, 1880-1919, and Gudmundur Kamban, born in 1888.
Both have written dramas which have been played with
success also in many foreign lands.[2]

In the field of religious literature Valdemar Briem, born
February 1, 1848, has distinguished himself as one of the
great hymn-writers in the North. Since 1909 he has been
vice-bishop of the Skálholt diocese. He was a member of
the committee appointed to prepare a new hymn-book, also
of the committee on ritual for the Icelandic church. Briem
has written many collections of hymns. In 1886 the com-

[1] Valtyr Gudmundsson, *Islands Kultur ved Aarhundredskiftet 1900,* p. 69.
[2] Halldor Hermannsson, *Icelandic Authors of To-day,* p. 48 ff. *American-
Scandinavian Review,* Nov.-Dec., 1916, p. 346 ff. *Modern Icelandic Plays,
Eyvind of the Hills, The Hraun Farm,* by Johann Sigurjonsson, translated
by Henninge Krohn Schanke, American-Scandinavian Foundation, New
York.

mittee of which he was a member gave Iceland a new hymn-book. Of the 650 hymns which it contains, 142 are by him. The hymn-book edited by Magnus Stephensen in 1781 had been in use till 1871, when a revised edition was published. This was superseded in 1886 by the new hymn-book, which is still in use. In 1912 appeared a new Bible translation, the first Icelandic Bible translation from the original texts. The translation of the Old Testament was done by Haraldur Nielsen, professor of theology in the University of Reykjavik. The New Testament was translated by Bishop Thorhallur Bjarnarson, Jon Helgason, professor of theology in the University of Reykjavik, and Eirikur Briem, instructor in the same university. The cost of publishing was defrayed by the English Bible Society.

In the various fields of learning the Icelanders have shown increased productivity during this period. In history, archæology, mathematics and natural science they have able writers. In philology and Northern antiquities they have especially distinguished themselves. A noted scholar in this field was Eirikur Magnusson, born in 1833, and educated at the theological school in Reykjavik. In 1862 he went to England to superintend the publication of an Icelandic Bible translation, was appointed assistant librarian at the University of Cambridge, and became M.A. of Trinity College in 1893. In England he devoted himself especially to the translation and publication of Old Icelandic literature. His chief work of this kind was "The Saga Library," saga translations by Eirikur Magnusson and William Morris, published in London in 1890. He has written articles on Northern mythology and antiquities in various publications; also articles dealing with political and social conditions in his own country. Finnur Jonsson, born at Akureyri in northern Iceland in 1858, became instructor and finally professor of Icelandic language and literature in the University of Copenhagen, and has long been regarded as one of the greatest scholars in this field. Of his numerous works on literature, history and philology may be mentioned "Den oldnorske og oldislandske Literaturs Historie," a compendious and scholarly work in three volumes. He has been knighted, and is a member of many literary and learned societies. Björn M. Olsen, a distinguished scholar, was born in northern Iceland July 14, 1850, died Jan. 16, 1919. After completing his studies at the University of Copenhagen he traveled in Italy and Greece. Upon his return home he became teacher in the Latin School at Reykjavik, and in 1895 he was chosen rector of that institution. From 1911 until 1918 he was professor in the University of Reykjavik, of which institution he became the first rector. He has written many works on literary and philological subjects. Valtyr Gudmundsson, born in 1860, is also a noted philologist. Since 1890 he has been professor in the University of Copenhagen. In 1896 he visited the United States at the invitation of Mrs. Cornelia Horsford to examine ruins in Massachusetts, supposed to be of Norse origin. He has written many works dealing with Northern antiquities.

Of Icelandic historians must be mentioned Bogi Th. Melsted, a grandson of the poet Bjarni Thorarensen, born in 1860. He is the author of many works, among others of "Islendingasaga," a large history of Iceland, of which two volumes have appeared. He resides in Copenhagen, and receives a stipend from the Icelandic government for continuing his historical research. Jon Jonsson, 1869-1920, also received a stipend as historian from the Icelandic government. From 1911 he was professor of history in the University of Reykjavik. His works on the history of Iceland are many. Among others may be mentioned his "Íslandssaga," a short history of Iceland. Jon Thorkelsson the younger, born in 1859, editor of "Diplomatarium Islendicum," is director of the national archives in Reykjavik, and one of the founders of the Icelandic Historical Society. Of his historical works may be mentioned "Om Digtningen paa Island i det 15de og 16de Aarhundrede," 1888, and "Saga Jörundar Hundadagskongs," 1892.

In the field of art little had been accomplished in Iceland till the latter part of the nineteenth century. In earlier times the Icelanders had skilled wood-carvers, tapestry weavers and metal workers, as can be seen from numerous

articles in the Reykjavik museum, in the national museum
in Copenhagen, and in the Nordiska Museet in Stockholm;
but these activities had gradually declined, owing, no doubt,
to the poverty and general misery prevalent in the seventeenth and eighteenth centuries. But the new intellectual
awakening and improved economic conditions revived also
the long neglected artistic talents of the people, and there
is now a prospect of a rich contribution of modern Icelandic
art. Sigurdur Gudmundsson, 1833-1874, was a talented
painter. He founded the Reykjavik National Museum,
and devoted himself to the history of art, especially of his
own country. These activities consumed so much of his
time that he found little opportunity to produce original
works of his own, but he rendered valuable service by re-
kindling the love of art among his countrymen. Thorarinn
Thorlaksson and Åsgrimur Jonsson have shown great talent,
especially as painters of Icelandic landscapes. Einar Jonsson, born in 1874, is Iceland's first sculptor. Many of his
works, as "Dawn," "Evolution," "Ymir og Auðhumla" and
"Monument to Queen Victoria," have attracted wide attention. He has also sculptured monuments of Jonas Hallgrimsson, Jon Sigurdsson, King Christian IX and Ingolf
Arnarson. Probably his greatest production is "The Outlaw," in which he has delineated with powerful realism in
the facial expressions of the central figure, as well as in the
composition of the whole group, the tragedy of hopeless
struggle against the curse of a people pursuing the offender
even into the recesses of an uninhabitable wilderness. With
face set in defiance but furrowed with anxiety the outlaw
carries on his back the body of his dead wife to inter her
remains in consecrated soil. His right hand rests on a
spade. On his left arm he carries his child wrapped in a
sheepskin, clinging to him confidingly in its helplessness,
and his shaggy, half-starved dog follows him with a shy and
wondering look. The agony of suffering and hopeless lone-
liness could scarcely be more pathetically portrayed. The
Icelandic state has brought the sculptor's works to Iceland, where they are preserved as a treasure of national art.[3]

[3] *American Scandinavian Review,* March-April, 1915, p. 91 f.

In music the Icelanders have made great progress since the
middle of the nineteenth century. Before that time little
had been done to cultivate this art. The church hymns
were sung in a primitive way to the earliest old melodies.
Of musical instruments only a few crude string instruments
were in use, especially the *langspil*. Pétur Gudjonsson,
1812-1877, and Jonas Helgason, 1839-1903, both organists
in the cathedral in Reykjavik, did much to create interest
both in vocal and instrumental music. Organs are now
found in nearly all Icelandic churches, played by organists
who have studied music in Reykjavik. In the towns pianos
are found in the homes of the more well-to-do, and the
guitar and violin are in common use. Of late years Icelandic composers have appeared, the most prominent being
Sveinbjörn Sveinbjörnsson, born in 1847, for a long time
a resident of Edinburgh, Scotland. His compositions with
English texts have been published there. Of other Icelandic composers may be mentioned Bjarni Thorsteinsson,
born 1861, Sigfus Einarsson, Arni Thorsteinsson, Jon Frid-
jonsson and Helgi Helgason.

The system of public education has of late years been
brought to a very high state of completeness and efficiency
in Iceland. A school of jurisprudence was established in
1908. In 1911 this school and those of medicine and theology were consolidated into the University of Iceland, and
a department of philosophy was added. On June 17 of that
year this university was dedicated with fitting ceremonies.
Of other institutions of learning there is one Latin school, or
college, located at Reykjavik, two popular high schools,
four agricultural schools and one nautical school. The
facilities for study and research have also been greatly increased. The National Library in Reykjavik, containing
rich stores of the best books of all lands, together with
large manuscript collections, has continued to grow until
it is now the most complete collection of Icelandic books
in the world. The national archives, covering the last two
hundred years of Icelandic history, are also very complete.
The National Antiquarian Museum in Reykjavik contains
a collection of more than 5500 articles, and the Natural

History Museum, founded in 1889, contains nearly all specimens of fishes, plants and birds in Iceland. Also in the field of vocational training able instruction has been provided and great progress has been made. The industrial exposition in Reykjavik in 1911 showed woven tapestries, and hand-carved articles of wood and whalebone, wrought with rare taste and skill of workmanship, showing that these old arts in which the people used to excel in earlier ages are being revived under the stimulus of a new intellectual awakening and social development which has placed Iceland among the most progressive as well as the most enlightened of modern nations.

18. THE STRUGGLE FOR INDEPENDENCE. ICELAND PROCLAIMED A SOVEREIGN STATE. RECENT ECONOMIC DEVELOPMENT

THE constitution granted in 1874 contained many features distasteful to the Icelanders. It was accepted as a first instalment of liberty in the hope that new concessions could be obtained later, but it was evident that the people were not satisfied with an autonomy so imperfectly accomplished. It is said that the first time King Christian IX met Jon Sigurdsson after the millennial festivities, he asked him if the Icelanders were satisfied with the constitution; to which Sigurdsson replied that since the chief wish of the Icelanders had not been granted, His Majesty could not expect them to be satisfied. This answer expressed very pointedly the relation existing between the two countries. No one could doubt that the constitutional struggle would be renewed, though king and government were sure to falter at every step towards a more perfect democracy. The Icelanders wished their administration to be entrusted to native officials residing in Reykjavik, but it was still directed from Copenhagen. No minister for Icelandic affairs had ever been appointed, as provided in the constitution. The management of these matters had been left to the

Danish minister of justice, who had often advised the king
to veto bills passed by the Althing.

When Jon Sigurdsson died in 1879, his able lieutenant
Benedikt Sveinsson, at one time associate justice of the
landsyfirréttr, and later *sýslumaðr* of Thingeyjarsysla, reopened the constitutional conflict by proposing in 1881 a
revision of the constitution. According to the plan submitted both the office of *landshöfðingi* and that of minister
for Iceland were to be abolished, and an Icelandic administrative government was to be created in Reykjavik, consisting of a viceroy with a ministry of not more than three
members appointed by himself but responsible to the Althing. To become law all bills passed by the Althing had
to be signed by the king, or by the viceroy, who should
exercise full royal power. Constitutional amendments
should be signed by the king in person. The ministers, if
accused, should be tried by a special tribunal consisting of
some members of the upper branch of the Althing, and the
justices of the *landsyfirréttr*, or highest Icelandic court. All
members of the Althing, thirty-six in number, should be
popularly chosen, and a supreme court of appeal was to
be created for Iceland.[1] This proposed revision was submitted to every session of the Althing till 1895. It was
always passed by the lower branch, but met determined
opposition in the upper branch. It was at last passed by
two succeeding Althings as provided in the constitution
(i.e., 1885 and 1886, 1893 and 1894), but it was promptly
vetoed by the king.[2] In the reasons for the royal veto submitted November 2, 1885, it was stated that it would be a
violation of the Danish constitution and of Iceland's position as an inseparable part of the Danish kingdom. Furthermore the proposed changes would also entail too big
expenses for so poor a country as Iceland. The more moderate political leaders, in seeking a way out of the difficulty,
began to consider acceptable compromises. In 1889 Sigurdur Stefansson, Jon Jensson, Erikur Briem and Páll
Briem framed such a compromise—the *Miðlun*—patterned

[1] *Thjóðólfr,* July 11, 1885.
[2] *Fjallkonan,* March 21, 1894.

on the government of the Dominion of Canada. But it was not passed by the Althing.[3] In the session of 1895 the majority of the members resolved to drop the old revision plan which was again submitted. In its place a resolution was passed, requesting the government to submit a plan for revision, but this request was also rejected by the government. Among the people great confusion prevailed. Some were in favor of continuing the struggle along the lines hitherto followed. Others thought that this would be useless because of the determined opposition of the government, but all agreed that the existing conditions could no longer be tolerated. In 1897 Valtyr Gudmundsson, professor in the University of Copenhagen, who had been elected member of the Althing, submitted a compromise plan in order to shape an issue which might gain general support. According to this plan nearly all the main provisions in the constitution were to be retained, but a minister for Iceland capable of speaking the Icelandic language should have a seat in the Althing, should take part in its deliberations, and should be responsible to it for all his official acts.[4] This provision, however, if carried through, would bring about a greater change than at first apparent, as it would virtually establish parliamentary government. It is therefore quite noteworthy that the government agreed to accept the plan. The bill was passed in the upper branch of the Althing, but in the lower branch it was defeated by a majority of three votes. In 1899 it was again passed by the upper branch, but failed to pass in the lower. The plan did not provide for an Icelandic administration in Reykjavik, as the Icelandic minister should remain in Copenhagen. In consequence it failed to pass, as it did not solve the constitutional question in a way satisfactory to the majority of the people.

The election of 1900 gave the supporters of Gudmundsson's bill a slight majority. In 1901 it was introduced in the Althing for the third time in a slightly altered form,

[3] *Althingistíðindi,* 1889, C, p. 179.
[4] Valtyr Gudmundsson, *Islands Kultur ved Aarhundredskiftet 1900,* p. 36 ff. *Tíðindi frá Althingi,* 1897, B, p. 20 ff, C.

and was passed by both branches. The bill provided for an increase in the number of popularly chosen representatives to thirty-four, eight of whom should sit in the upper branch, in order that the popularly chosen representatives might be in the majority in both branches of the assembly. Suffrage was extended to all male citizens, not servants, twenty-five years of age who were paying a yearly tax of four kroner. The sessions of the Althing should last for two months.[5]

Even before the measure had been voted upon in the upper branch, word was received that a liberal ministry had been formed in Denmark and that a Dane had been appointed minister for Iceland. A memorial was, therefore, addressed to the king, stating that a fully satisfactory solution of the constitutional question could be reached only when the Icelanders received a government of their own, residing in Reykjavik.[6] To this memorial the king returned a very favorable answer, saying that the desired modifications of the constitution, among others also that a minister for Iceland capable of speaking the Icelandic language and taking part in the deliberations of the Althing, would be granted; that a government proposal would be submitted to the next session of that assembly, containing a plan for establishing an Icelandic ministry in Reykjavik. In the next election the home rule party was victorious. The government proposal providing for an Icelandic minister residing in Reykjavik was submitted to the Althing, and was passed by both branches.[7] New elections were ordered in 1903, the home rule party again receiving a majority. The government amendments to the constitution, passed almost unanimously by the new Althing, received royal sanction October 3, 1903. Iceland had now received home rule. The revised constitution, which was to become effective February 1, 1904, abolished the office of *landshöfðingi*, likewise those of the two *amtmenn*. The Icelandic minister was to reside in Reykjavik. He was to be able to speak and write Icelandic, should take part in the deliberations of the Althing, and

[5] *Isafold*, June 6, August 14, 1901.
[6] *Tíðindi frá Althingi*, C, p. 819. *Isafold*, August 28, 1901.
[7] *Isafold*, August 1, 1903. *Tíðindi frá Althingi*, 1902 (Frumvarp, p. 1 ff.).

should be responsible to it for all his official acts. From time to time he should go to Copenhagen to lay before the king in cabinet meeting bills and other important matters. The Althing should be assembled July 1, every other year, and should remain in session eight weeks. It was to consist of forty members, thirty-four of whom should be elected by the people, and six to be appointed by the king. In organizing itself for legislative work it should divide into two branches, the *efri deild*, or upper branch, to consist of fourteen members, and the *neðri deild*, or lower branch, of twenty-six members. Male citizens not servants and paying a yearly tax of four kroner should have the right to vote.[8] Mayor and *sýslumaðr* Hannes Hafstein was appointed minister for Iceland.[9]

There can be no doubt that the Danish government at this time made an earnest effort to solve the constitutional controversy in a manner satisfactory to the Icelanders, and all hoped that political peace and good understanding would now prevail. But the changing of an old conservative fundamental law to fit a new time-spirit is something like the task of remodeling an old house. One change necessitates another, and many alterations will have to be made which at first were neither foreseen nor contemplated. Together with the provision in the revised constitution that the Icelandic minister should reside in Reykjavik, it was stipulated that he should submit to the king, at meetings of the cabinet, new laws and other important matters for his signature. This had been done, and could easily be done so long as the minister resided in Copenhagen, but no provision in the constitution had existed regarding this matter. Already in the summer of 1902, before the constitutional amendments were passed, anonymous writers began to oppose this provision in the revised constitution and sought to prevent its adoption. A new party was formed, led by Judge Jon Jensson and the political leader Bjarni Jonsson to oppose this feature of the revision program. This new group, calling themselves *landvarnarflokkur*, or party of na-

[8] *Althingistíðindi*, 1903, C, p, 1 ff.
[9] *Fjallkonan*, December 1, 1903. *Ingolfur*, November 29, 1903.

tional defense, soon received the support of the conserva-
tives, now calling themselves the progressive party, *framsóknarflokkur,* who also were opposed to the minister. This opposition to the new administration became as formidable as
it was determined. The cry was raised that through the revised constitution Iceland had been incorporated in the
Danish kingdom, that the law of 1871 regarding Iceland's
relation to the realm had been accepted. Vigorous objec-
tion was also raised because the Danish authorities had
signed the appointment of Hafstein as Icelandic minister, as
this indicated that they still wished to exert influence on
purely Icelandic affairs. With regard to the provision in the
constitution that bills passed by the Althing should be submitted to the king in cabinet meeting, it was demanded
that Icelandic affairs should be separated from those of
Denmark, and should not be laid before the king in the
meeting of the whole cabinet, as this would give his Danish
advisers the right to deliberate and decide on purely Icelandic matters, and would still make the Icelandic government subservient to the Danish authorities.

Up till 1904 the Danes had always taken for granted that
Iceland was an integral part of the Danish kingdom. Even
when important concessions were made to the Icelanders
in their struggle for national autonomy, it had been assumed that no other relation could exist between the two
countries. To this view the Icelanders had never acceded.
As a rule they held the view of their great leader, Jon
Sigurdsson, who had made it clear that after the king had
renounced his absolute power, the "Gamli sáttmáli" was
the sole remaining union agreement. According to this view
the more aggressive leaders claimed that only a confederate
union existed between Denmark and Iceland, as had been established between Norway and Iceland in 1262. We have
seen that according to the "Gamli sáttmáli" the Icelanders
were to retain their own laws and institutions, their national
assembly, and full control of their own affairs; but they
promised to receive a jarl or governor-general appointed by
the king to act as his deputy. It was unfortunate that the
Danish statesmen should have become so attached to the

idea of the unity of the realm as to insist that under all circumstances Iceland must be considered an integral part of the Danish kingdom. They had already made great concessions to the national aspiration of the Icelanders, but their theory gave offense. The struggle was carried into the realm of principle, like the taxation controversy between the American colonies and King George III, rendering practical adjustments difficult. In the light of such a theory the Icelanders could only view all bonds which united them with Denmark as fetters designed to keep them in a state of inferiority and subjugation. Questions were sure to arise about Icelandic commerce, flag and other important matters, as they had done in Norway and Sweden under similar circumstances. Political peace and mutual good-will between the two partners in the union could be established only by recognizing their essential equality. No one could doubt that the struggle would continue until Iceland's complete independence as a sovereign nation should be definitely acknowledged.

When the Althing assembled in 1905, the chief measure under consideration was a proposal submitted by the minister, Hafstein, regarding a projected plan for telegraphic and telephone service in Iceland. The Great Northern Telegraph Company had agreed to lay a telegraphic cable to the Faroe Islands and Iceland if subsidies were granted by the Icelandic government. In the plan submitted it was provided that such a subsidy should be granted, together with funds for the construction of the telegraph and telephone lines between southern and northern Iceland. Since 1891 this project had been discussed, and a strong sentiment had been created in its favor. But the opposition, backed by the paper "Ísafold," began a determined fight against it in an effort to defeat the minister. Securing an offer from the Marconi Company of wireless telegraphic service to Iceland, they held that this would be cheaper, and argued that the subsidies necessary to secure the projected cable would drain the treasury. As thorough investigation finally showed that the cable would be the safest and most advantageous telegraphic connection to be secured, the bill was passed October 20, 1905. The following year a cable was laid to Seydisfjord, and telegraph and telephone lines were soon extended to Akureyri and Reykjavik.

The political events in Norway in 1905, which led to the dissolution of the Swedish-Norwegian union, gave added strength to the demands of the Icelanders for complete independence. When Frederick VIII ascended the throne in 1906, he extended an invitation to the Icelandic Althing to visit Denmark. On the voyage from Iceland the representatives discussed the question of Iceland's position in the union, and agreed on the following points: A joint commission consisting of members of the Danish Rigsdag and the Icelandic Althing should be appointed to draft a new law defining Iceland's position in the realm, to take the place of the law of 1871; the annuity paid by Denmark to Iceland should be converted into a fixed sum to be paid to the Icelandic treasury; the name "Iceland" should be added to the king's title, so that it should henceforth read "King of Denmark and Iceland"; and the appointment of a minister for Iceland should be signed either by that minister himself or by his predecessor in office. On July 29 the Althing representatives were received in the Rigsdag building by a large Danish delegation. During their visit they set forth the plan agreed upon on the voyage. This was courteously received, the king expressing the hope that he would be able to visit Iceland the following summer. On behalf of Iceland the Althing representatives extended a formal invitation to the king and forty members of the Rigsdag, and in the summer of 1907 King Frederick VIII visited Iceland, accompanied by the Rigsdag delegation.[10] Shortly after his arrival a commission was appointed, consisting of thirteen Danes and seven Icelanders, to draft a new law defining Iceland's position in the union.[11] But elections had not been held for some time, and the members of the Althing were no longer in sympathy with the prevailing political sentiment. For this reason the liberal party groups demanded an election before the appointment of the commission, in or-

[10] *Norðri*, August 2, 1907.
[11] *Ibidem*, August 19, 1907.

der that the members, when appointed, might represent the prevailing public opinion. But Minister Hafstein, supported by the *heimastjórnarmenn,* or home rule party, which favored a strong union with Denmark, disregarded this demand, and the Icelandic members were chosen from the old Althing representation. The commission assembled in Copenhagen February 28, 1908. In May of the same year it submitted a draft of a new law defining Iceland's position in the realm.[12] According to its provisions Iceland should be a free and autonomous country united with Denmark under a common king and through such joint matters as should be specified in the proposed law. The name "Iceland" should be inserted in the king's title, as the Icelanders desired. The royal treasury should pay to the treasury of Iceland once for all the sum of 1,500,000 kroner, and thereby the financial question between the two countries should be settled. The joint matters were to be a common king, foreign affairs, and defense on land and sea, together with the same flag, protection of the fisheries, common right of citizenship, and a common supreme court. No treatise should be made regarding affairs in which Iceland was interested, unless the Icelandic government was consulted. The Icelanders should have the right, with the consent of Denmark, to increase their supervision of the fisheries in territorial waters. They might also grant a citizenship which should be in force in Denmark, and they might establish a supreme tribunal for Icelandic cases if the constitutions of both countries were amended to that effect. It was also provided that a judge should be appointed to the Danish supreme court who possessed knowledge of the Icelandic language and government affairs. Danes and Icelanders should enjoy the same right respectively in Denmark and Iceland. They should also have the same right to participate in the fisheries in territorial waters of the two countries, but Denmark should exercise protective control. Icelandic students should be granted stipends by preference, and the Icelanders in Iceland should be exempt from military service. When twenty-five years had elapsed after the

[12] *Norðri,* May 12, 1908.

passage of the law, it should be revised if either the Danish Rigsdag or the Icelandic Althing should demand it. After thirty-seven years either Denmark or Iceland might demand a complete separation in all matters except those of a common king, foreign affairs and defense. All the Icelandic members of the commission, with the exception of Skuli Thoroddsen, signed the draft of the proposed law. Skuli refused to sign, and submitted a report of his own, in which he said: "The Icelanders will not be satisfied except it be clearly stated that Iceland is a sovereign state, that it controls all its affairs, and stands on an equal footing with Denmark, only with a common king temporarily. But this, according to my opinion, is not possible, since certain affairs (foreign affairs and national defense) are exempted from revocation and given into the hands of the Danish government, so that Iceland can have no part in their control, or can assume management of them without asking the consent of the Danish lawmaking assembly." [13] Minister Hafstein had been one of the most active members of the commission, but the opposition to the law which he had helped to frame was very determined. Skuli Thoroddsen's party, the *framsóknarflokkur*, or progressive party, which after 1905 called itself the *þjóðræðisflokkur*, or popular government party, opposed it. So did also the *landvarnarflokkur*, or national defense party, led by Judge Jon Jensson and Bjarni Jonsson. These parties feared that the new law, according to which Iceland should still be a part of the Danish kingdom, would only rivet more firmly the chains which bound them to Denmark. Iceland was not to have her own flag, and the request that Icelandic affairs should not be considered in meetings of the Danish cabinet had not been granted. In their opinion the new law would only be a covenant giving sanction and permanence to existing conditions, only a com-

[13] *Lögberg* (Winnipeg), June 4, 1908. Skuli Thoroddsen was one of the most popular of Icelandic political leaders in recent times. He was born January 6, 1859, at Haga in Bardaströnd. His father was the poet and *sýslumaðr* Jon Thoroddsen. Skuli studied law at the University of Copenhagen, was appointed *sýslumaðr* in Isafjordsysla in 1884. In 1891 he was elected member of the Althing. He became prominent especially as leader of the independence party. *Anðvari*, 1920, p. 1 ff.

promise which would be sure to retard the work for national independence. Together the two parties had called a convention at Thingvellir, June 29, 1907. This assembly passed resolutions demanding that the covenant to be established between Denmark and Iceland regarding the relation of the two countries should expressly acknowledge Iceland to be a free country united with Denmark under a joint king, and possessing full equality with the Danish kingdom, and full sovereign control over its own affairs.[14] It was further to be understood that this covenant could be abrogated by either party to the compact. A proposal was also adopted that Iceland should have its own flag, consisting of a white cross on a blue field. Resolutions were passed protesting against any covenant falling short of these demands, stating that nothing but complete separation of the two countries was possible if such conditions were not granted. After this meeting the popular government party, still led by Skuli Thoroddsen, called itself the *sjálfstæðisflokkur,* or independence party, and its political program became complete separation from Denmark. Jon Jensson, one of the leaders of the *landvarnarflokkur,* or party of national defense, now left his party and gave his support to Minister Hafstein and the *heimastjórnarmenn,* or home rule party, but the *landvarnarflokkur,* led by Bjarni Jonsson, continued to oppose Hafstein. A violent agitation against the proposed law was begun, supported by the paper "Ísafold" and its able editor, Björn Jonsson. In the elections held September 10, 1908, the first in Iceland in which the Australian system of secret ballot was used, the opponents of the proposed measure were victorious. Of the 8146 votes cast, 3475 votes were registered for the measure and 4671 against it. The opposition had elected twenty-four members to the Althing, its supporters only ten. When the new Althing assembled, it passed a vote of lack of confidence in the ministry, and Hafstein resigned in April, 1909.[15] He was succeeded by Björn Jonsson, editor of the "Ísafold," one of the leaders of the opposition, who had been chosen president of the Al-

[14] *Ísafold,* July 3, 1907.
[15] *Althingistíðindi,* 1909. *Ísafold,* Feb. 24, March 27, April 3, 1909.

thing. The new minister promised to work for a better understanding between Iceland and Denmark, and it was agreed that the measure regarding Iceland's position in the realm should not be submitted to the Althing. Instead the Althing majority passed a new measure, declaring Iceland to be a free and sovereign kingdom united with Denmark under a joint king and through such common affairs as might be agreed upon.[16]

While remaining in office Björn Jonsson was especially occupied with the question regarding the management of the Bank of Iceland.[17] Even before his appointment rumors had been abroad that the bank management had been lax with regard to loans on real estate and to the fisheries. Charges were also made against the cashier of the bank, Haldor Jonsson. The new minister appointed a committee to examine the status of the bank. It was found that it had suffered heavy losses, but that these were covered by a reserve fund which would show a credit balance of 250,000 kroner after all losses were paid. As to the officials of the bank the committee found that no blame could attach to them. The minister, however, did not feel wholly reassured. Having lost confidence in the bank officials he removed the cashier, Haldor Jonsson, the two controlling directors, Kr. Jonsson and Eirikur Briem, and the general manager, Tryggvi Gunnarsson, a man of great business ability and member of the Althing for many years. This aroused general resentment, as the people felt that the removed bank officials had been unjustly treated. At a big mass-meeting in Reykjavik, in which 7000 people are said to have participated,[18] the following resolution was drafted: "The people assembled protest against Minister Björn Jonsson's treatment of the bank officials, and regard his action to be an arbitrary use of official power as well as a flagrant disregard of the true interests and honor of Iceland. Since the people assembled find his action to be a positive proof that he can

---

[16] *Ísafold*, May 4, 1909.
[17] *Lögretta*, November 24, 1909. *Thjóðviljinn*, December 3, 1909. *Thjóðólfr*, January 28, February 4, 18, 25, 1910.
[18] *Lögretta*, December 1, 1909.

no longer be tolerated in the high office which he now holds, they demand his immediate resignation." The leading merchants of Reykjavik also addressed to him sharp letters of protest. When he refused to reinstate the bank officials after they had been declared blameless by the investigation committee, his former friend Judge Kr. Jonsson, one of the removed directors, brought suit against him for personal injury and defamation of character, pleading that since he had not been appointed by the government, but had been elected by the Althing, the government had no jurisdiction in the matter and could not remove him. The case was decided in his favor. The minister appealed to the *landsyfirréttr*,[19] but the decision of the lower court was sustained. Even then the minister would not yield. His paper, "Ísafold," announced that a new appeal would be taken to the Danish *høiesteret*, or supreme court, but the case was never brought before that tribunal. Judge Kr. Jonsson was satisfied with his legal victory, and did not resume his office as bank director. The Althing representatives also mixed in the fight, many of them demanding a special session of the Althing in order that the bank question might be considered by the people's chosen representatives. Party feeling ran high both in Iceland and in Denmark. In Copenhagen many leaders assembled to protest against the separation movement, which, it was claimed, was headed by Minister Björn Jonsson himself. Even many Icelanders took part in this meeting to deprecate this movement. A personal union would be equivalent to separation, they claimed, and separation would mean the ruin of Iceland. No one spoke more vehemently than the young Icelandic lawyer Sveinbjörnsson. "I see the danger to the union between Denmark and Iceland," he said, "in the fact that Minister Björn Jonsson stands at the head of a party which openly works for separation of the two countries. When he comes to Denmark, he talks in another tone, but he can not be trusted. This I tell you members of the government who are here present. He is a man who either lacks reason or suffers himself to be controlled by unscrupulous men." A Danish journalist pro-

[19] *Thjóðólfr,* April 29, 1910.

posed to send a warship to Iceland to arrest the leaders of
the independence party. Such hysterical outbursts found
little favor with the people of Denmark. But the secession
movement supported by a radical group in Iceland, which
in 1910 passed a resolution declaring that absolute separation was the only proper solution of the union question,
created genuine alarm. Minister Björn Jonsson was a strong
and upright man, an energetic worker, ever ready to aid
anyone in need or in distress. He always remained faithful
to his purpose of rendering efficient and unselfish public
service in the high office to which he had been appointed.
As leader of the prohibition forces he succeeded in passing
the prohibition law, which received a majority vote in both
branches of the Althing in 1909, and was signed by the king
in June the same year, in spite of the opposition of several
European nations, including Spain. But his stand on the
bank question, and his views regarding Iceland's relation to
Denmark, aroused a strong opposition, which constantly
grew more hostile and determined. In 1911 Skuli Thoroddsen, the leader of the independence party, and others introduced in the Althing a motion of lack of confidence in the
minister. The motion was passed with a small majority, and
Björn Jonsson resigned.[20] While he remained in office, his
paper, "Isafold," was edited by his son Olaf Björnsson.
Through the father's political defeat the paper lost prestige
and support to such an extent that Olaf no longer dared to
accept articles written by him. For this reason Björn
Jonsson founded a new paper, "Magni," in which he defended his position in the bank question as well as on the
very important question touching Iceland's relation to
Denmark.

The *sjálfstæðisflokkur* hoped that the king would now appoint the leader of their party, Skuli Thoroddsen, to succeed
Björn Jonsson as minister, as twenty-one members of the
Althing gave him their enthusiastic support. But the king
selected instead Kr. Jonsson, chief justice of the *landsyfirréttr,* who was a member of Skuli's party. Jonsson accepted
the office, incurring the bitter enmity of all his former po-

[20] *Althingistíðindi,* 1911, vol. ii, p. 674 ff.

litical friends. A large mass-meeting was assembled in Reykjavik to protest against his course of action in accepting the office, as he was not supported by a majority of the popularly chosen representatives in the Althing.[21] So bitter was the feeling that he was formally ousted from the party. The same day a motion for a vote of lack of confidence in the new minister was introduced in the Althing. It was passed in the lower branch, but was not put to a vote in the upper branch. Jonsson, therefore, continued to hold his office, though he was no longer regarded as the leader of any party group. In the press he was violently assailed, the liberal leaders claiming that he had violated the principle of parliamentary government to satisfy his own personal vanity. The new minister was born at Gautlöndum in Thingeyjarsysla in 1852. He had been *sýslumaðr* in Gullbringusysla, later judge in the *landsyfirréttr*, and since 1908 chief justice. For many years he had been controlling director in the Bank of Iceland, and royally appointed representative to the Althing. When he assumed the office of minister, he emphasized in a speech to the Althing that his policy would be to create peace and good understanding, and to secure the passage of a much needed finance law. In April, 1911, the *heimastjornarmenn*, or home rule party, which supported him, introduced a bill for amending the constitution, stipulating that the Althing henceforth should consist of forty members, all of whom should be elected by the people. All men and women twenty-one years of age should have the right to vote for Althing representatives. The executive branch of the government should consist of three ministers responsible to the Althing. Proportional party representation was also provided for.[22] The measure was passed by the Althing, but since it was a constitutional amendment it would have to be passed anew after another general election before it could be submitted to the king for his signature. In the summer of 1911 a bill was also introduced in the Althing providing for a separate flag for Iceland, to consist of

[21] *Fjallkonan,* March 21, 1911. *Norðurland,* March 18, 1911. *Ísafold,* March 15, 1911.
[22] *Althingistíðindi,* 1911, vol. I, p. 400 ff.

a white cross on a blue field.[23]   This raised another important issue, as Denmark regarded it as another step in the direction of complete separation of the two countries. The Icelanders held that without a flag of their own they had no national emblem expressive of their nationality; that the Danish flag flying on their ships and public buildings was only a token of Danish overlordship. The Althing, however, failed to pass the bill. Kr. Jonsson and his supporters did not secure a majority in the next general election. He therefore tendered his resignation, and was again appointed chief justice in the *landsyfirréttr*.[24] In July, 1912, Hannes Hafstein succeeded him as minister. The same year the general prohibition law for Iceland, passed three years before, during the ministry of Björn Jonsson, took effect in so far as it affected importation of liquors. According to this law no liquors containing more than two and one half per cent of alcohol can be imported, except for medical, industrial and chemical use. It is noteworthy that in passing this great social reform Iceland was several years in advance of other nations.

When Hafstein for the second time entered upon his duties as minister, thirty-one members of the Althing declared that they would unite in bringing about a solution of the union question by making such changes in the plan of 1908 as would meet with the approval of the majority of the voters, and would lead to a final agreement with Denmark.[25] In his speech to the Althing Hafstein had called attention to the unfavorable economic condition of the country, saying: "Money is wanting, credit is lacking, Icelandic bonds can not be sold in foreign markets, and sympathy with civilization and desire for progress are decreasing. Why is this? I am convinced that it is no exaggeration to state that one of the chief causes is dissension, quarrels, and party strife at home, together with unsettled disputes abroad. This weakens confidence, creates gloom, and increases all that which is inimical to cultural endeavor, hindering the increase

[23] *Fjallkonan,* April 7, 1911. *Ísafold,* March 18, April 8, 1911.
[24] *Ísafold,* July 24, 1912. *Lögretta,* July 27, 1912.
[25] *Lögretta,* August 7, 1912.

of the true capital of culture which is required in order to turn credit to profitable account. It is my conviction that one of the first steps to be taken in order to remedy this trouble is to bring about a satisfactory settlement of the disputes with our sister nation, the Danes, regarding the union question which so long has diverted the attention from other important matters, and in later years has added fuel to strife and disunion in our own country." In the fall of 1912 Minister Hafstein went to Copenhagen to confer with the Danish government about the resumption of negotiations on the union question.[26] In these preliminary conferences it was pointed out by the Danish leaders that since the plan of 1908 had been rejected by the Althing, the Icelanders would have to submit new proposals before the negotiations could be resumed. Upon his return to Iceland Hafstein sought the advice of a number of Althing representatives. A new plan was outlined which the minister said was neither his own nor one proposed by the Danish government, but which, it was hoped, would gain the sanction of the Danish authorities.[27] When it was published, it met determined opposition. The paper "Ísafold" considered it wholly undesirable, and the whole liberal Icelandic press rejected it.[28] In the fall of 1913 a new revision of the constitution was submitted to the Althing, based on the plan of 1911, but differing from it on many points. This measure was finally passed in both branches of the assembly. It provided for an Icelandic minister, popular election of all representatives to the Althing, proportional party representation, woman's suffrage in general elections and eligibility to all offices.[29] The question of a separate flag for Iceland had also been debated repeatedly in the Althing, but the measure had met with defeat in the upper branch of the assembly. Finally on November 22, 1913, the king sanctioned an Icelandic proposal for a separate flag, with the understanding that it should be so designed as not to resemble too closely the flags of other

[26] *Lögretta*, December 12, 1912.
[27] *Ibidem*, December 11, 1912.
[28] *Ísafold*, December 18, 1912. *Ingólfur*, December 11, 1912. *Norðurland*, December 21, 1912. *Thjóðviljinn*, December 12, 1912.
[29] *Lögretta*, August 20, September 13, 1913.

nations, and that the Danish flag should always be hoisted
with it on government buildings.[30] In the next general elections the opponents of Minister Hafstein secured a majority
of the Althing representatives. He accordingly tendered his
resignation, and was succeeded by Sigurdur Eggerz, who was
appointed minister for Iceland July 5, 1914.[31]

Shortly after Eggerz's appointment followed the outbreak
of the World War, and serious problems confronted the
Icelanders. The Althing took steps to safeguard the country as far as possible. Laws were passed providing that necessaries of life, such as grain, coal, salt, petroleum, machine
oil, fishing gear, and medical supplies, should be bought by
the government; that the ready money in the treasury
should be used for this purpose so far as it could be spared;
that a loan of 500,000 kroner should be negotiated for such
purchases, and that public expenses should be curtailed.[32]
The export of necessaries of life was prohibited, and a commission was appointed to assist the government in taking
the necessary steps to safeguard the country. In an address
to the Althing, August 3, 1914, Minister Eggerz called attention to the problems confronting the government. The
proposed revision of the constitution was still pending, so
also the question of a separate flag for Iceland. He expressed the hope that the king would sanction these measures, and that the people would then turn their minds to
internal affairs. "We ought to devote more attention to our
farming and husbandry than heretofore," he continued.
"The fisheries must be developed, the means of communication on land and sea must be improved. The Icelandic
Steamship Company especially should be encouraged." He
expressed the hope that in those perilous times the government and the legislature would cooperate in every way in
the protection of the country, so that no apprehension of
danger would need to be entertained.

A commission appointed to consider the eventual design

---

[30] *Lögretta,* November 22, 1913, July 8, 1914. *Stjórnartíðindi ýfir Ísland,*
1913, p. 23.
[31] *Lögretta,* May 6, July 22, 1914; *Ísafold,* April 29, July 22, 1914.
[32] *Lögretta,* August 1, September 2, 1914.

of the Icelandic flag found that the one hitherto used, consisting of a white cross on a blue shield, could not be adopted, as it resembled too closely the flags of Sweden and of Greece. A new design would have to be submitted. The revision of the constitution passed in 1913 was again brought before the Althing in 1914 and was passed a second time by both branches of the assembly without change.[33] The king had promised that if the amendments passed in 1913 should again be passed unchanged by a new Althing he would sanction the measure, with the understanding, however, that no change could be made in the practice which had hitherto obtained that all measures should be submitted to the king in cabinet meeting. To this practice, the king stated, he would adhere until he had sanctioned a law regarding the relation between Denmark and Iceland, agreed to by both the Rigsdag and the Althing, which should establish a different regulation.[34] The commission appointed to consider the design of the Icelandic flag submitted a report recommending that the flag should consist of a red cross with white borders on a blue field.[35] It was hoped that Minister Eggerz in going to Copenhagen would secure the king's signature to both measures. But word was soon received that he had failed in his mission. In the negotiations with the minister the king reiterated his promise to sign the measures, but with the proviso that they should be presented in cabinet meeting. This, in the opinion of the minister, raised the issue whether Icelandic measures were to be regarded as joint matters to be considered by the whole cabinet, or as separate Icelandic affairs. He refused to yield on this point, which he regarded as a vital issue, and tendered his resignation,[36] December, 1914.

Early in 1915 the king invited three members of the independence party to Denmark for consultation on the union question.[37] One of these was Einar Arnorsson, who was soon

[33] *Althingistíðindi*, 1914, p. 1 ff. *Lögretta*, August 19, 1914. *Ísafold*, July 4, 1914.

[34] *Lögretta*, October 29, November 19, 1913.

[35] *Íslenzki fáninn, skýrsla frá nefnð*, etc., p. xi ff.

[36] *Morgunblaðið*, December 3, 1914.

[37] *Lögretta*, March 10, 1915.

appointed to succeed Eggerz as minister for Iceland.[38] Arnorsson, born in 1880, was still very young, but he was already a prominent jurist. In 1908 he became instructor in law in the University of Reykjavik. In 1911 he was made professor of jurisprudence. In 1914 he was elected member of the Althing, where he quickly rose into prominence as leader of the independence party. He had written several works dealing with the relation of Iceland to Norway and Denmark. Opposing the views of the Danish professor Knud Berlin he maintained that Danish authorities had no right whatever to meddle with Icelandic affairs. In Iceland a movement was developed in opposition to what was regarded as too supine an attitude on the part of the Althing in the union question. Complaint was made that important decisions on vital Icelandic questions had been left to the king. The supporters of this movement, which finally led to the organization of a new progressive group, were found especially among the adherents of the independence party. They demanded a vigorous national policy and active efforts in promoting Icelandic enterprises. Arnorsson's visit in Copenhagen to carry on private negotiations with the king regarding the union question had aroused suspicion and ill-will among the members of this group. Would he too suffer the king to exert a controlling influence over Icelandic affairs? When Arnorsson entered upon the duties of his office, they convoked large public meetings in Reykjavik, demanding that he should cause the Althing to be dissolved, in order that new elections might be held. But the minister had sufficient support in the Althing to remain in office. The negotiations regarding the Icelandic flag and union question were renewed, and since the new minister did not urge the question regarding the submitting of Icelandic matters in cabinet meetings, as his predecessor had done, the king sanctioned both measures, June 19, 1915.[39] In accordance with the report of the committee appointed to consider the design of the flag, it was to consist of a red cross with white borders on a blue field. It should be used within

[38] *Lögretta,* May 5, 1915.
[39] *Ibidem,* June 23, 28, 1915. *Isafold,* June 23, 1915.

the country and in Icelandic territorial waters, but the Danish flag should be hoisted with it on government buildings.[40] The design of the Icelandic coat of arms was also changed. By royal order of 1903 it was decreed that it should be a silver falcon on a blue field. Still earlier it had consisted of a device in which a split codfish was the principal feature. In 1915 it received its present symbolic and attractive design.[41]

According to the constitutional amendments passed by the Althing in 1913 and 1914 and sanctioned by the king in 1915 there should be an Icelandic ministry in Reykjavik responsible to the Althing and taking part in its deliberations, the number of cabinet members to be fixed by law. The Icelandic prime minister should hold no other office. He should be able to speak and write Icelandic, and should go to Copenhagen to present bills and other important matters to the king for his signature. The Althing has forty members, but this number can be changed by law. It is divided into two branches, the *efri deild,* or upper branch, consisting of fourteen members, and the *neðri deild,* or lower branch, of twenty-six members. The number of members in both branches can be changed by law. Thirty-four of the Althing representatives are elected directly by their constituencies within their respective districts for a period of six years. Six representatives are chosen at large and according to proportional party representation for the period of twelve years. These six members have seats in the upper branch of the assembly. The other eight members constituting it are chosen by the thirty-four representatives elected in the districts from their own number at the assembling of the Althing. Only one-half of the total number of representatives are chosen at each election. Men and women twenty-five years of age, who have resided in the country five years immediately preceding the election, can vote for the district representatives. Men and women thirty-five

---

[40] *Íslenski fáninn, skýrslur frá nefnð,* etc., p. xi. The history of the Icelandic flag is found in *Saga íslenska fánamálsins* by Jon Jonsson, printed in *Íslenski fáninn, skýrslur frá nefnð,* etc., Reykjavik, 1916.

[41] Jon Jonsson, *Saga islenski fánamálsins,* p. 16. Halldor Hermannsson, *Skjaldmerki Íslands, Eimreiðin,* xxii, p. 157 ff.

years of age can vote for the representatives elected at large.
The Althing meets July 1st every other year, but extra
sessions must be called by the king when a majority of both
branches demand it. Such sessions last only four weeks,
unless the time is prolonged by the king.[42] By a law of 1916
the number of members of the Icelandic cabinet was fixed
at three.[43] Minister Einar Arnorsson now resigned, and the
king invited Jon Magnusson to form a cabinet according to
the new provision. The members of this cabinet were Jon
Magnusson, leader of the *heimastjornarmenn,* or home rule
party; Björn Kristiansson, leader of the majority faction of
the *sjalfstæðisflokkur,* or independence party, and Sigurdur
Jonsson of the newly organized *bændaflokkur,* or agrarian
party. This coalition was created at the request of the party
leaders to secure the greatest possible cooperation in view of
the difficult situation caused by the World War. The three
parties represented in the ministry controlled thirty-six out
of the total forty votes in the Althing. In 1917 Björn
Kristiansson, minister of finance in the new ministry, resigned, and former minister for Iceland, Sigurdur Eggerz,
was appointed to succeed him.

Through their constitution as finally amended the Icelanders had established complete democracy in their political institutions: parliamentary government, unrestricted
suffrage for men and women, and a legislative assembly
elected by the people. They had gained control of their
finances, and the executive branch of their government had
been located in Reykjavik. But difficult problems still remained unsolved. The all important controversy regarding
Iceland's relation to Denmark had not been settled, and the
question of a separate Icelandic flag had so far found only
a preliminary solution. The flag already granted was little
more than a decoration restricted to local use in connection
with the flag of Denmark. As Icelandic commerce was ex-
panding, the flag question was revived. It was evident that
this was no longer a matter only of national sentiment, but of
growing practical importance. In 1914 the Icelandic Steam-

---

[42] *Althingistíðindi,* 1914, p. 1 ff.
[43] *Lögretta,* January 1, 3, 1917.

ship Company was organized with a capital stock of 1,200,-
000 kroner, the Icelanders in the United States and Canada
subscribing a large part of the stock, and the Icelandic government contributing 400,000 kroner. Four steamers were
to be built. The first of these, the "Gullfoss," was launched
at Copenhagen in 1915.[44] The question would naturally arise
whether Icelandic ships in foreign waters should continue
to sail under the Danish flag. In August, 1917, a measure
was introduced in the Althing requesting the assembly to
demand an Icelandic merchant flag.[45] The proposal was
adopted, and the Icelandic prime minister Jon Magnusson
went to Copenhagen to lay it before the king. In a meeting
of his cabinet November 22, 1917, the king refused to sanction the measure. In stating the reasons for his refusal he
said: "I can not sanction the proposal submitted by the Icelandic minister, but I wish to add that when Danish and
Icelandic views do not coincide, negotiations, no matter how
they may be inaugurated, will do more than direct action
on a single question to create that good understanding which
ought to form the basis for the relations between the two
countries." [46] After considering carefully the king's words
all political parties in Iceland agreed to try negotiations.
The Danish Rigsdag appointed a commission to meet a
similar body of Icelandic representatives in Reykjavik. The
Danish members arrived in Iceland June 29, 1918.[47] The
negotiations were begun at once, and on July 19 the Icelandic telegraphic bureau wired a message that full agreement had been reached regarding the flag question and the
relations between Iceland and Denmark. An act of union
defining Iceland's position was signed by all the delegates,
and submitted to the Danish Rigsdag and the Icelandic Althing.[48] After these assemblies had approved the measure,
it was finally ratified in Iceland by a general plebicite.[49] In
the Althing the measure was carried by thirty-eight against

[44] *Ísafold*, January 24, November 4, 1914.
[45] *Lögretta*, December 8, 12, 1917.
[46] *Ibidem*, December, 1917.
[47] *Frón*, June 24-July 20, 1918.
[48] *Ibidem*, September 14, 1918.
[49] *Ibidem*, September 14, 1918.

two votes. In the plebiscite 12,040 votes were cast in its favor, and only 897 against it. On November 30, 1918, it was signed by the king.[50] The following day, Sunday, December 1, Iceland was proclaimed a sovereign kingdom in union with Denmark according to provisions in the act of union. The Danish flag, "Danebrog," was lowered, and the new national flag was hoisted over Iceland. The city of Reykjavik was decorated for the occasion. Shortly before twelve o'clock the orchestra opened the program for the occasion by playing the Icelandic national anthem "Eldgamla Ísafold." Minister Eggerz then spoke, saying in closing: "By sanctioning the act of union the king has carried out the thoughts of Frederick VIII, who possessed the most intimate understanding of our affairs. Today the king has decided to grant Iceland its own flag, which is now raised over the Icelandic state. Our sovereign has won the sympathy of every Icelander. The flag is the symbol of our sovereignty, of the most resplendent thoughts of our nation. The honor of our flag is our national honor. We pray God the Almighty to preserve our state and our king. We pray God to help us to carry our flag to honor. May the good fortune of king and people follow it. So let us hoist the flag!" As the flag rose to the top of the staff the orchestra played the Icelandic flag song, and the Danish man-of-war, "Islands Falk," lying in the harbor, fired a salute of twenty-one shots. Captain Lorck of the "Islands Falk" spoke for Denmark. The orchestra played the Danish national song, "King Christian," and a "Long live the king!" echoed through the city. A speech by City Judge Johannesson, president of the Althing, was followed by three times three cheers for the king. From Copenhagen the following telegram was received from King Christian X: "After signing in meeting of my cabinet the 'Danish-Icelandic Act of Union,' which upon preliminary negotiations between Danish and Icelandic delegates has been passed by the legislative assemblies of the two countries, and ratified in Iceland by a general vote; and after having determined the appearance and use of the Icelandic flag, I wish to express the hope

[50] *Stjornartíðindi fyrir Ísland*, 1918, p. 81.

that this new arrangement may form the basis for a happy national development and cordial relations between the two peoples. I also send my dear and faithful Icelanders my royal greetings and best wishes for Iceland's future success and happiness."

"Danish-Icelandic Act of Union" [51]

Denmark and Iceland are free and sovereign states united by a common king.

Danish citizens in Iceland are to enjoy equal rights and privileges with the citizens of Iceland, and vice versa.

The citizens of each country are exempt from military service in the other country.

Access to fishing within the maritime jurisdiction of both countries is equally free to Danish and Icelandic citizens, regardless of residence.

Danish ships in Icelandic harbors have the same rights as Icelandic ships, and vice versa.

Denmark will act in Iceland's behalf in foreign affairs. In the ministry of foreign affairs there will be a representative appointed in consultation with the government of Iceland and familiar with Icelandic conditions. Attachés who are well informed on Icelandic affairs shall be appointed to the already existing consulates and legations. All agreements entered into by Denmark with foreign countries and already published shall, in so far as they concern Iceland, be in force for that country also. Agreements ratified by Denmark after the proposed Law of Confederation has gone into effect shall not be binding upon Iceland without the express consent of the Icelandic authorities concerned.

Until such time as Iceland shall decide to take charge of the inspection of fisheries in whole or in part, this duty will be performed by Denmark under the Danish flag. The monetary system shall continue to be the same for both countries as at present, so long as the Scandinavian monetary system exists. Should Iceland desire to establish her own coinage, the question of acknowledgment by Sweden

[51] *Althingistíðindi*, 1918, A. *The Nation*, December 14, 1918, p. 749 ff.

and Norway of the coins and notes stamped in Iceland will have to be settled by negotiation with those countries.

Denmark's supreme court has jurisdiction in Icelandic cases until Iceland shall decide to institute a supreme tribunal of her own. Until then one member of the supreme court shall be an Icelander.

Matters of importance to both countries, such as coinage, trade, customs, navigation, mails, telegraphs and radio telegraphs, administration of justice, weights and measures, as well as financial arrangements, shall be regulated by agreements of the authorities of both countries.

The sum of 60,000 kroner contributed annually by Denmark to Iceland shall be discontinued, and instead Denmark shall establish two funds of 1,000,000 kroner each, one at the University of Copenhagen and one at the University of Reykjavik, for the promotion of intellectual intercourse between the two countries.

There shall be established an advisory body of at least six members, one-half from Iceland and the other half from Denmark, to be appointed by the Althing and the Rigsdag respectively, to deal with any bills brought forward in the parliament of one country which also touch the interests of the other.

If differences of opinion should arise concerning the provisions of this Law of Confederation which can not be adjusted by the governments, they shall be laid before a court of arbitration consisting of four members, two to be appointed by each country. This court of arbitration shall settle differences by a plurality of votes, and in case of a tie the matter shall be submitted to an arbitrator appointed alternately by the Swedish and the Norwegian governments.

This Law of Confederation may be revised until the year 1940 upon the request of either the Rigsdag or the Althing. The agreement may be abrogated only by a two-thirds vote of each parliament, which must afterwards be confirmed by a plebiscite.

Denmark will communicate to foreign powers its acknowledgment of Iceland as a sovereign power in accordance with the provisions of this Law of Confederation. At the same time Denmark will announce that Iceland declares itself to be perpetually neutral, and has no naval flag of its own.

In accordance with the provisions in the act of union a Danish minister is stationed in Reykjavik as Denmark's official representative in Iceland. The Icelanders are similarly represented in Denmark through their own minister.

In the summer of 1921 elaborate preparations were made in Reykjavik to receive the royal family, who were to visit Iceland. For the first time in their history the Icelanders were to greet a king and queen of their own. "During the last two weeks Reykjavik has been the busiest city in the world," says a report from Iceland of June 27, 1921. "Houses have been painted, streets repaired, and many hundred people have been busy decorating the city. For months the committee on arrangements has labored to make the reception an honor to Iceland." In the forenoon of June 26 the Danish man-of-war "Valkyrie," carrying the royal visitors, entered the harbor of Reykjavik. A triumphal arch had been erected, where the king and queen were received by the city authorities, and greeted by the huzzas of the populace. At twelve o'clock the bishop of Iceland conducted religious services in the cathedral church. Then followed a royal reception in the Althing building, where the king spoke in Icelandic to the assembled people in response to an address of welcome by the Althing president. Gifts from the people of Iceland were presented to all the members of the royal family, the queen receiving a beautiful national costume. In describing the festival Editor Svenn Paulsen wrote in the "Berlingske Tidende": "At seven o'clock in the evening the streets of Reykjavik resounded with huzzas and orchestral music. The royal pair were coming. The king wore a general's uniform. The queen was attired in Icelandic festival costume, wearing a golden diadem, with white veil flowing over a black silk dress ornamented with gold embroidery, and fastened about the waist with a belt of pure gold. The costume, a present from the women of Iceland to their first queen, cost 70,000 kroner. Queen Alex-

andra looked very beautiful in it, and the people were highly
elated. At the royal dinner Icelandic girls in national costume waited on the guests." The royal family also visited
Thingvellir, where they were received by a large number of
people in national attire, many of whom had come from a
great distance to greet the king and queen of Iceland. When
the king ascended the Mount of Laws, a body of Icelandic
trumpeters struck up their solemn measures as a welcome
to the distinguished guests from this old center of Icelandic
national life. On July 1 the royal family visited the great
waterfall Gullfoss, stopping on the way in a typical Icelandic farmhouse, which the king examined thoroughly with
great interest. After a trip to Geysir they proceeded to
Ölfusá to view the great suspension-bridge spanning that
stream. On Saturday, July 2, the royal visitors were brought
in automobiles to the waterfall Irafoss, whence they returned to Reykjavik. On Sunday the royal family attended
religious services in the cathedral church. At one o'clock
the king gave a luncheon at the royal residence for the Icelandic officials and the officers of the men-of-war "Valkyrie,"
"Heimdal," "Fylla," and "Beskytteren," forming the royal
escort squadron. The afternoon was spent in viewing men's
and women's gymnastic exhibitions and national sports.
Monday, July 4, the royal family left Reykjavik on the man-
of-war "Valkyrie," sailing to Hafnarfjord, where they embarked on the steamer "Island" for a trip to Greenland before returning to Denmark.[52]

Before departing King Christian X created an Icelandic
order of knighthood, the Order of the Falcon, with the three
classes, grand cross, commanders and knights. The insignia
of the order is a white enameled star-shaped cross with gilt
edges. In the center of the cross is a blue oval bearing the
Icelandic symbol, a silver falcon ready for flight. On the
reverse side is the name of the founder of the order in gold
on white enamel, surrounded by a blue border with the inscription: "Fyrsti December 1918." The ribbon of the order
is blue with white borders containing a red stripe, the same
colors as the Icelandic flag. The knights of the grand cross

<hr />

[52] *Morgunblaðið*, May-July, 1921.

carry also an eight-pointed star bearing the device of the order. The head of the order is King Christian X.

During the last decades political freedom and economic progress have transformed Iceland into a prosperous and progressive modern state. The old pursuits have become more productive than past generations would have considered possible. Great natural resources are being made available which were wholly unknown in the past, and new pursuits are developing which give promise of still greater progress in the future. Of special importance are the fisheries, which of recent years have grown to be the most paying pursuit and chief source of income in the country. In 1895 Iceland had only seventy fishing vessels. In 1902 the number had increased to 144. Iceland has now over twenty steam trawlers, over a hundred sail and motor cutters, 600 motor deck boats, and about 1000 fishing boats, a fishing fleet which gives employment to nearly 11,000 people, or about one-eighth of the population of the country. In 1913 the export of fish products brought a total income of 13,327,000 kroner, or more than twice the amount derived from animal husbandry, which gave a return of 5,195,000 kroner. And yet the rich fisheries in Icelandic waters have been only partially utilized by the Icelanders themselves. In 1913, 1413 fishing steamers and sailships entered Icelandic harbors, and there is no sign of any decrease in the vast schools of fish and herring in these waters.

Also in animal husbandry and farming considerable progress has been made, though not in the same proportion. In 1918 Iceland had 24,311 cattle, 644,971 sheep and 53,218 horses.[53] Especially important is the development of dairying, a pursuit which has been taught the people by the Danes, just as the valuable herring fishery has been taught them by the Norwegians. The first Icelandic creamery was built in 1900. In 1906 the number had risen to thirty-four. During the last few years the annual export of butter is valued at 500,000 kroner. It is thought that dairying in the rich lowlands of southern

---

[53] *Hagskýrslur Íslands* (Statistique de L'Islande), No. 27, p. 8 ff. *Bunadarskýrslur, Árið* 1919.

Iceland, if properly developed, could support the entire
present population of the country. But because of lack
of proper means of transportation dairying can yet be
pursued with profit only during the summer months. For
this reason the project has been set on foot to build a railway about seventy miles in length (112 kilometers) from
Reykjavik to Thingvellir, Selfoss and Thjorsá, with a short
side line to Eyrarbakki. This road will open this important
district to new economic development. Dairying is now
pursued also in northern Iceland. But lack of transportation facilities makes further progress difficult. During the
winter the ice-bound harbors are closed to traffic. Not till
the northern districts are connected with Reykjavik and
southern Iceland by railways can their economic possibilities be fully developed. In all Iceland there are 6558
farms. One-half of these are owned by the farmers who till
them, the other half of the farming population are renters.
About one-tenth of the soil is owned by the state, but the
government estates are now being sold as rapidly as possible at low prices and on easy terms. Relatively the farming population is decreasing in number. For some time the
number of farms has remained stationary, though large
areas could yet be cultivated. The work of developing new
farmsteads can not be done, as the growth of the fisheries
and the increase in trade and traffic have attracted the young
people to the seacoast districts. In 1900 Iceland had a
population of 79,000, of which only 9000 lived in the towns.
In 1915 the population was 89,059, of which 20,705 lived in
the towns. The growth of population in the decade 1910-
1920 was 9513, from 85,183 in 1910 to 94,696 in 1920. During the same decade the rural population fell from 65,987
in 1910 to 65,032 in 1920. But great progress is being made
towards better conditions in rural life.[54] The old primitive
farmhouses built of sod and stone are disappearing, and fine
modern homes are built of lumber or concrete, usually two
stories high, with large windows and jutting chimneys. "The
new houses are built according to American far-west mod-

[54] *Hagskýrslur Íslands*, No. 24, p. 11. *Mannafjölðaskýrslur, Árinn 1911-
1915*. Reykjavik, 1921.

els," says a recent writer.[55] A similar transformation is being wrought in the means of communication and travel. Fifty years ago there was not a bridge across a single river, nor was there a wagon in use in all Iceland. Now two-fifths of the revenues of the country are used for building roads and improving the means of communication. Fine roads are being built in all parts of the country, so that the old horse-back caravans will soon be replaced by wagons and automobiles. From Reykjavik a fine road has already been built to Thingvellir, and another almost to Hekla. All great rivers have been spanned by costly bridges, and fine highways are already in use along the valleys and streams in all parts of the country. Fifteen times a year the mail caravans go to all parts of the island, so that every home receives its mail regularly. Houses have been built and equipped at regular intervals along the mail routes as places of refuge for the mail carriers in stormy weather. In 1906 a telegraphic cable was laid to Iceland, and the first telephone lines were constructed in the island. In 1914 the Icelandic Steamship Company was organized. Regular steamship service is now maintained with Denmark and around the whole coast of Iceland, sixty places being entered by the steamers on their trip around the island. Motor boats are also plying the navigable rivers. Before many more years the tourists may be able to travel on electric railway trains from one place to the other in the saga island.

Industry is still of little importance in Iceland, but possibilities exist of great future development in this field. Lignite coal is found in several places, and beds of bituminous coal have also been discovered. These coal deposits will probably be of value only as fuel for private homes, but Iceland possesses a great supply of water power which can be made available as motor power in industries and on electric railways. Of the countries of Europe, France has the greatest amount of water power, amounting to 10,000,000 horse power. Norway has about 7,500,000, Sweden about 6,000,000, Austria 6,000,000, Italy 6,000,000, Germany 1,500,000, Spain 1,500,000, England 333,000, and Switzer-

[55] *Island, Streiflys over Land og Folk*, p. 40 ff.

land 167,000. The amount of water power in Iceland is not definitely known, but it has been estimated to be not less than 2,500,000 horse power, or as much as that of Germany, Switzerland, Spain and England combined. Foreign companies have already purchased great Icelandic waterfalls, and the building of railways and factories already planned will undoubtedly be begun in the near future. A fair index to the growth of prosperity in Iceland in late years is the rapidly increasing volume of trade. In the period 1880-1890 the yearly export and import together amounted to 10,000,000 kroner. In 1910 this total had mounted to 30,000,000 kroner, in 1913, before the outbreak of the World War, 36,000,000 kroner, the export being 16,717,734 kroner, the import 19,128,143 kroner. In recent years this rapid growth of commerce has continued. The official statistics show the following figures:

	Export	Import
1914	18,111,351	20,830,465
1915	26,260,067	39,633,155
1916	39,183,647	40,107,310
1917	43,465,501	29,715,225
1918	41,027,701	36,920,200

The greater share of this trade is carried on with Denmark, Great Britain, Norway, Sweden, United States, Spain and Germany. In the period 1886-1890 the average number of ships which came to Iceland from foreign lands every year was 264. Since that time that average has increased as follows:

1891-1895	331
1896-1900	368
1900-1905	385
1906-1910	384
1911-1915	413
1915	514
1916	450
1917	178 [56]

In 1920 the population of Iceland numbered 94,696. The leading cities are:

[56] *Hagskýrslur Íslands*, 1921.

Reykjavik   with a population in 1920 of 17,976
Akureyri   "   "   in 1915 of   2,099
Isafjord   "   "   "   1,778
Hafnarfjord   "   "   "   1,766
Seydisfjord   "   "   "   902

A correspondent from Reykjavik to the Danish paper "Berlingske Tidende" wrote in 1921:

"There is scarcely another Scandinavian city which in the last fifty years has experienced such a development as the capital of Iceland. When Christian IX in 1874 landed in Reykjavik, it consisted of a cluster of houses around a small church at the upper end of Faxi bay. Many of the houses were built of sod and stone. The town gave the general impression of a primitive village or a group of fishermen's homes. When Frederick VIII and members of the Danish government and Rigsdag landed in Iceland in 1907, Reykjavik had become a city of about 10,000 people, but the king and members of the Rigsdag had to land on a small pier on the open shore, and the town with its unpaved streets and low houses irregularly placed gave the impression of a large country town. Now at the time of the visit of Christian X and Queen Alexandra the town has nearly 20,000 people, and is not only a real city, but it deserves to be called the capital of Iceland. When the royal squadron entered the harbor, a beautiful seacoast town lay stretched before it with an elegantly constructed harbor. Ready to receive the king and queen stood the population of a well built capital, a city with government buildings, churches, colleges, public library, museums, hospitals, in short the whole complex equipment belonging to a European capital. The age of the small tripping horses is past. Automobiles and motor trucks speed through the streets of Reykjavik. The old general stores with their collections of all sorts of wares, from ship anchors, oil-coats and empty herring barrels to candy and millinery, have been replaced by stores of the latest model, carrying only special lines of goods, some so large and well equipped that they compare favorably with the stores in any Scandinavian city. Down by the harbor, the only great commercial harbor in the North Atlantic, great steamers are loading and unloading at the wharves, instead of as formerly when the goods had to be brought from the ships to the shore and from the shore to the ships in barges. Reykjavik has also a fleet of modern trawlers and large motor fishing boats not equaled in any Danish city, not even in Esbjerg. . . . The city is a real capital, where nearly all of what Iceland possesses of political, administrative and academic talent and ability is gathered."

An evidence of the high moral character of the Icelandic people is the almost total absence of crime in their country. In 1904 sixteen persons were convicted of crimes or minor offenses, one being a woman. In 1905 and 1906 the number of cases were twenty-two men and two women, and twenty-eight men and five women respectively. But only two-thirds of the accused received a prison sentence. The prisons in Iceland usually stand almost empty. When we consider that more than one-fifth of the whole population live in seacoast towns, and are engaged in trade and fisheries, this is so unique a record that we must give the Icelanders the credit of being the most orderly and law-abiding people in the world.

19. ICELANDIC IMMIGRATION. THE ICELANDERS IN AMERICA

A feature of singular interest and importance in the modern history of Iceland as of other European countries is the emigration to America, a movement in which also the Icelanders have participated. The economic development which during the last few decades has wrought such improvement in social conditions everywhere in the North had not made itself felt at the time when the real emigration from Iceland began. Some progress had been made, but the condition of the peasantry and the poorer classes was so little improved that emigration to America from all Scandinavian countries was increasing rapidly under the stimulus of improved facilities for ocean travel. This migratory movement of the ventursome and oppressed of Europe to the new world with its hopes and opportunities exerted its influence also on Iceland. The economic conditions there were still very unfavorable, and the bitter and hitherto fruitless struggle for political liberty had led leading newspapers to advocate emigration as the only solution of the pending national questions. Emigration from Iceland to the United States and Canada may be said to have begun in 1870, but even long before that time a few Icelanders who had been converted to Mormonism had sought new homes in America. In 1851 two Icelandic Mormons from Copenhagen came as missionaries to the Vestmanneyjar. In 1855 a few persons who had accepted that faith, among others Samuel Bjarnason and his wife, emigrated to the United States, founding a settlement at Spanish Fork in the state of Utah. Other converts followed later. In 1857 thirteen persons from Iceland arrived in the colony. Of late years many of the Icelandic Mormons have returned to the Lutheran faith, and the colony at Spanish Fork is neither large nor prosperous.[1]

In 1863 the first emigrants to Brazil departed from Iceland under the leadership of Magnus Eiriksson. A few left later at different times, going by way of Copenhagen to Germany, where they joined German emigrants going to South America. But this emigration was never of great importance, and no Icelandic settlement was founded there. In 1873 many persons signified their desire to go to Brazil, but as Magnus Eiriksson, who had hitherto acted as guide, declared that he would no longer act as leader of emigrants going to that country, they joined another group going to the United States and Canada.

The immigration to the United States, begun in 1855, was continued in 1870 when four young Icelanders from Eyrarbakki came to Milwaukee. They settled on Washington Island, Wisconsin, thus founding the second Icelandic settlement in America. A few more immigrants arrived the following year, but although the colony still exists, it has never grown beyond a small group of families.[2] In 1872

---

[1] *Árný gefid ut af félagið Íslenzka studenta i Kaupmannahöfn*, p. 33. *Tímarit þjóðrœknisfélags Íslendinga*, Winnipeg, 1919, p. 98 ff. E. H. Johnson, *Saga Íslendinga i Utah, Almanak*, 1915.

[2] *Tímarit þjóðrœknisfélgs Íslendinga*, 1919, Rögnvald Pétursson, *þjóðrœknissamtök meðal Íslendinga i Vesturheimi*, p. 100. Arni Gudmundsson, *Landnám Íslendinga a Washington-ey, Almanak*, 1900. American-Scandinavian Review, March-April, 1915. Björn B. Jonsson, *Following Leif*

almost 300 Icelanders came to America. Among these were the leaders Sigtryggur Jonasson, one of the founders of the large Icelandic colony New Iceland; Páll Thorlaksson, who founded the Icelandic settlements in North Dakota, and Hans B. Thorgrimsen, who took the lead in founding the Icelandic Lutheran Synod in America. In 1873 a ship carrying 153 emigrants sailed from Akureyri in northern Iceland to Canada. Thirty more emigrants who found no room on the ship followed later in the fall. All agreed to settle in the same place, but when they arrived at their destination, some went to Nova Scotia, and a few to Milwaukee, Wisconsin, but the greater number founded a colony on the Rousseau river near Muskoka, Ontario, where the post office Hekla was built. Many men who later became prominent among the Icelanders in America were in this group of immigrants, among others the poet Stephan G. Stephansson, Baldwin L. Baldwinsson, and Jon Jonsson Bardal. In that year came also Rev. Jon Bjarnason, who later became so prominent a leader in the Icelandic church in America. He had been moved to come to America with his wife through letters from his friend Páll Thorlaksson, who had entered the theological seminary of the German Lutheran Missouri Synod at St. Louis. Bjarnason and his wife came to Milwaukee, and after a few days proceeded to St. Louis, where they met Páll Thorlaksson. Rev. Bjarnason did not enter the theological seminary in St. Louis, but went instead to Decorah, Iowa, where he became assistant to Rev. V. Koren, one of the leading ministers of the Norwegian Lutheran Synod. In January, 1874, he was appointed teacher in Luther College, Decorah, Iowa, but in the spring of that year he resigned and returned to Milwaukee, Wisconsin.[3] When news was brought that Iceland had received a constitution, the Icelanders in Milwaukee arranged a celebration in which all the Icelanders in the city took part. Speeches were made by Rev. Jon Bjarnason, by the editor Jon Olafsson, who had accompanied him from Reykjavik, and others.

Ericson. Hjalmar Ruud Holand, *Norske Pioner Setlementer, Decorah Posten,* January 16, 1920.

[3] *Minningarit um Síra Jón Bjarnason,* 1915.

At this time an Icelandic society, "Islendingafélag," was founded for the purpose of promoting intellectual interest among the Icelanders in America. A movement was also set on foot to find a suitable place for an Icelandic colony, where the immigrants might dwell together. As Wisconsin did not seem to offer the desired opportunity, committees were appointed to investigate where a suitable location might be found. Sigfus Magnusson and Jon Halldorsson were sent to Nebraska. As a result of their visit a few Icelanders settled in that state, but it was not selected as a site for the new colony. Another committee, led by Olafur Olafsson and Jon Olafsson, was sent to Alaska. About their expedition Jon Olafsson later published a book ("Alaska. Lysing á landi og landskostum, etc.," Washington, D. C., 1875), probably the first Icelandic book printed in America. But Alaska was not found to be a suitable place for a colony.

The Canadian government carried on active work and sent paid agents to Iceland to encourage immigration to Canada. In September, 1874, the steamer "St. Patrick" brought 365 Icelandic immigrants directly to Quebec. At the entrance to the harbor a government officer, accompanied by Johann Arngrimsson, who had come to America in 1872, met them, and sought to persuade them to settle in Canada. Many of the immigrants said that they intended to go to the United States, but after some negotiations they entered into an agreement with the government representatives, promising to settle in Canada on the following conditions: They were to enjoy full liberty and right of citizenship at once on the same terms as native-born citizens. A sufficiently large and suitable tract of land for a colony was to be granted them. They were to preserve unhindered their personal rights, their language and their nationality for themselves and for their descendants forever. The reason for this agreement was that the immigrants believed that there was more freedom in the United States than in Canada. Journeying westward from Quebec to Ontario, they founded a settlement at Kinmount, about sixty miles north of Toronto. But the land here proved to

be so poor that the settlers grew discontented and wished
to find a better location. In the fall of 1874 Johann Arngrimsson, representative of the Canadian government, came
to Kinmount and urged the discontented settlers to move
to Nova Scotia, where a suitable tract for a settlement
would be granted them. About eighty families promised to
go. They moved early in the spring of 1875, and others
followed later in the summer. About thirty miles from the
coast, at a place which they called "Elgshæðir," they founded
the settlement Markland.[4] But as the land was stony and
covered with timber, it was little suited for cultivation.
The following year more people from Iceland came to the
settlement. It is thought that it numbered at one time
about 200 people. Brynjolfur Brynjolfsson was the leader
in the settlement in all things pertaining to religious and
educational work. He was a gifted man, and worked with
untiring zeal to promote the welfare of his people. But the
settlement did not prosper. In 1881-1882 most of the
settlers moved away to join their countrymen in other
localities.

In 1875 Gunnlaugur Pétursson and his wife, who had
settled in Wisconsin in 1873, moved to Lyon County,
Minnesota. More settlers from Wisconsin joined them the
following year, and in 1877 many immigrants from Iceland
arrived. People of other nationalities also settled there,
but the Icelanders are very numerous around Minneota
and Marshall, Minnesota.[5] In 1878 the Icelanders in this
settlement organized a society for the purpose of printing
books and papers, for establishing a common burial ground,
and for gathering together for the reading of the Scriptures
on Sundays. The first clergyman who visited the settlement and helped to organize congregations was the pioneer
leader Rev. Páll Thorlaksson, who visited the settlement
in 1877 and 1878. Four congregations were organized, all
of which were served by the same minister. In 1897 an

[4] Tímarit, Winnipeg, 1919, Guðbradur Erlendsson, *Markland.*
[5] *American-Scandinavian Review,* March-April, 1915; Björn B. Jonsson,
Following Leif Ericson, Almanak, 1900; *Landnám Islendinga i Minnesota,*
p. 55 f. *Framfari,* Feb. 15 and 22, 1879.

Icelandic quarterly, the "Kennarinn," was founded, edited by B. B. Jonsson and Rev. Jonas A. Sigurdsson of Akra, N. Dakota. This periodical continued to appear till 1905. In 1902 the Icelanders in Minnesota began the publication of a monthly edited by Thordur Thordarson, M.D., and Rev. Björn B. Jonsson. The periodical ceased to appear in 1908. Among the prominent men reared in this settlement is Hon. G. B. Björnsson, editor of the "Minneota Mascot," for years a leader in the Minnesota state legislature.

As the Icelanders in eastern Canada were dissatisfied with conditions in the localities where they had settled, Lord Dufferin, governor-general of Canada, who was very friendly to them, moved the Canadian government to grant them financial aid to move their colony to a new site. John Taylor, who had become acquainted with the Icelandic settlers at Kinmount, offered to serve as guide in searching for a better location. In 1875 a committee headed by Sigtryggur Jónasson was sent from Muskoka under the guidance of Taylor to find a suitable place for a colony. They selected a strip of land along the west shore of Lake Winnipeg, calling it New Iceland. In the fall of that year a few settlers from Ontario arrived in the new colony.[6] The following year about 1200 immigrants arrived from Iceland. The colony grew so fast that it already numbered about 1400 people, the largest Icelandic settlement in America. On January 4, 1876, a general meeting was held, and a council of five was chosen to act as temporary government for the colony. Shortly after New Iceland had been founded the two most influential church leaders among the Icelanders in America, Rev. Páll Thorlaksson and Rev. Jon Bjarnason, arrived in the colony. Páll Thorlaksson, who had served some Norwegian congregations and an Icelandic congregation which he had organized in Wisconsin, and had served as missionary preacher in other Icelandic settlements, was called as minister by settlers in New Iceland in 1876. He arrived in the colony October 9, 1877, and organized the first congregation there. Jon

[6] Gudlögur Magnusson, *Landnám Íslendinga í Nýja Íslandi, Almanak,* 1899, p. 28 ff. *Tímarit,* Winnipeg, 1919, p. 106 ff.

Bjarnason, who, after leaving Luther College, had worked for a time as assistant on the Norwegian newspapers "Skandinaven" and "Budstikken," was also called as minister by some settlers in New Iceland in 1876. In the summer of that year he visited the colony, and on November 8 the following year he arrived there with his wife, and entered upon his work as pastor and church organizer. Between these two leaders a church controversy soon arose which divided the Icelanders in America into two parties. Páll Thorlaksson adhered to the conservative Lutheran views of the German Lutheran Missouri Synod and the Norwegian Lutheran Synod. He sought to prevail on his countrymen to associate themselves in church work with the Norwegians of the Norwegian Lutheran Synod, but Jon Bjarnason opposed the plan. He considered the Synod too conservative, as he rejected the doctrine of the verbal inspiration of the Bible, and differed with Rev. Thorlaksson also on other doctrinal questions. The meetings held between the two leaders and their adherents March 25-26, 1878, and March 17-18, 1879, to discuss these questions only widened the breach between the two parties.[7] During the first years in the colony the settlers suffered much, as they were poorly equipped to live in the severe climate of Canada. An epidemic also broke out which carried away hundreds of people. In these trying days the Canadian government granted them a loan to aid them, and Rev. Páll Thorlaksson solicited aid among the Norwegians in the United States, who contributed $1300 to the relief fund. In 1880 Jon Bjarnason had to go to Iceland to visit his dying father. He bid farewell to his congregations, and did not return to New Iceland.[8]

In 1877 steps were taken to organize a more permanent government for the colony. Two meetings were assembled, each choosing five men to act as a committee in drafting laws for the people. These laws were later submitted to a general meeting assembled at the town of Gimli, February

---

[7] *Minningarit Síra Jón Bjarnason*, p. 37 ff.
[8] Gudlögur Magnusson, *Landnám Íslendinga í Nýja Íslandi, Almanak*, 1899, p. 46 ff. *Tímarit*, Winnipeg, 1919, p. 106 ff.

5, 1877. The colony was divided into four settlements: the Viðinesbygð, Árnesbygð, Fljótsbygð and the Mikleyjarbygð. At an election held February 14 each settlement chose five men to act as a local council. Each council chose one of its members as president (*bygðarstjóri*). The four presidents formed a general council for the whole colony, the *nýlenduráð*, with a president and vice-president. This council had charge of all matters common to the four settlements. A constitution for the colony was framed at a meeting held January 11, 1878. This fundamental law, the only one of its kind among the Icelanders in America, remained in force till 1887. New Iceland was a state with its own constitution, laws and government, even its own language and distinct nationality. No other people than the Icelanders were allowed to settle within its borders. But in all except local affairs it remained under the authority of the Canadian government. In 1877 a company was organized in the colony to print and publish books and papers, the "Prentfélag Nýja Íslands." A printing press was bought in Minneapolis, and on September 10 of that year the first Icelandic paper in America, the "Framfari," began to appear, its editor being Halldor Briem. In 1880 the paper ceased to be published. But although it lived only a short time, it is of great importance as a source for the early history of the colony. Other papers were published later: "Dagsbrún," 1893-1896; the periodical "Svava," 1895-1904; "Bergmálið," 1897-1901; "Baldur," 1903-1910; "Ný Dagsbrún," 1904-1906; and "Gimlungur," 1910-1911. The colony of New Iceland is still prosperous, and remains the most exclusively Icelandic settlement in America. It has been represented in the Manitoba legislature by several able men born in Iceland, first by Captain Sigtryggur Jonasson, and later by B. L. Balwinsson and S. Thorvaldsson.[9]

The religious controversy between the adherents of Páll Thorlaksson and Jon Bjarnason, together with the hardships caused by poverty and epidemics, led to an emigration from New Iceland, which resulted in the founding of new

[9] *American-Scandinavian Review*, March-April, 1915, p. 103 ff. *Tímarit*, Winnipeg, 1919, p. 106 ff.

Icelandic settlements in other localities. In the spring of 1879 Rev. Páll Thorlaksson, accompanied by several leading men of the colony, set out to search for a suitable location for a new settlement. A tract in Pembina County in the northeastern corner of North Dakota was selected. Some settlers from New Iceland arrived there that same summer, and many people came the following year from New Iceland, Nova Scotia, and from Icelandic settlements in Wisconsin and Minnesota. Before the new settlement in Pembina County was ten years old, it was one of the largest Icelandic colonies in America. In 1880 the first congregations were founded there by Rev. Páll Thorlaksson, the father of this new and flourishing settlement. On March 12 this gifted and faithful worker died, deeply mourned by all his countrymen. Brave, gentle and resourceful, a true and devoted leader, he had worn himself out in untiring effort to aid his people in their various needs. In that year Rev. Hans B. Thorgrimsen graduated from the theological seminary of the Missouri Synod in St. Louis. He was called as pastor by the newly organized congregations in Pembina County, arriving there in the fall of 1883. At this time a congregation was also organized in the town of Pembina, the real center of the Icelandic settlement. In 1884 Thorgrimsen organized new congregations farther west in the settlement, and also at Grafton in Marshall County, North Dakota, where some Icelanders had settled. That same year he proposed that the Icelandic congregations in America should unite and organize an Icelandic Lutheran Synod. At a meeting of delegates from various places, assembled at Mountain in Pembina County, January 23-25, 1885, this proposal was discussed. A constitution for a general church organization was drafted and submitted to the various congregations for their approval. On June 24, 1885, a new meeting was assembled at Winnipeg, where the proposed synod was organized by the thirteen congregations which had already signed the constitution. Rev. Jon Bjarnason, who had returned from Iceland in 1884, and had become pastor of Icelandic congregations in Winnipeg, was elected president of the synod. He was also chosen editor of the church paper "Sameininginn," which began to appear in December of that year. In 1905 the Icelandic Synod had thirty-seven congregations. In 1919 the number had increased to fifty-eight. In 1886 Rev. Hans B. Thorgrimsen moved to South Dakota, where he took charge of some Norwegian congregations. He returned in 1900, and continued to serve the congregations in Pembina County till 1912. Many Icelanders in the Pembina settlement have become prominent in the public affairs of their state. Among these men may be mentioned Hon. D. J. Laxdal, land commissioner of North Dakota, deceased; Hon. M. B. Brynjolfsson, a brilliant lawyer and political leader, also deceased. In both houses of the state legislature Pembina County has been repeatedly represented by men born in Iceland.

While New Iceland was being settled many Icelanders came to Winnipeg, the chief point of communication in that part of Canada. Many remained in the city, forming a colony which dates its origin from the same years as that of New Iceland. This flourishing city in time attracted so many Icelanders that it became the center of the Icelandic settlements and of Icelandic intellectual life in America. Already in 1877 an Icelandic society, the "Íslendingafélag," was organized there for the purpose of guiding Icelandic immigrants in finding homes in settlements founded by their own countrymen, so that they should not become scattered everywhere. Another aim of the society was to provide instruction for children and young people both in the English language and in their own mother tongue, to cultivate among their people love of reading and intellectual pursuits, and to aid the sick and needy. A Sunday school was organized, in which children received instruction in religion and in the Icelandic language. In 1877 teachers were hired, and a general public school was maintained throughout the winter. Instruction was given in writing, arithmetic, English and Icelandic, forty pupils being in regular attendance. In 1881 the "Íslendingafélag" was reorganized under the name of "Framfarafélag." The aim of the society should be to further everything which might be of benefit to the Icelandic people in America. A school committee was chosen, and money was collected to support the school, which had hitherto been maintained through the efforts of private individuals. The same year the Society of Icelandic Women was organized in the city, the aim being to aid Icelandic immigrants, who were arriving every year in large numbers. The society also labored and contributed money to the support of the Icelandic school. For this purpose one of the members, a young girl, Gudrun Jonsdottir, gave one-half of her yearly earnings of $15 a month, a striking illustration of the devoted self-sacrifice which characterized the brave Icelandic immigrants. In 1883, two years after the society was organized, the treasurer reported that about $500 had been contributed to various charitable purposes, and that a cash balance of $150 remained in the treasury. The society continued to exist till 1890.[10]

Both Páll Thorlaksson and Jon Bjarnason had visited Winnipeg on their journeys to New Iceland, but no Icelandic congregation was organized in the city till 1878, when Rev. Jon Bjarnason organized the Trinity congregation. The real growth of this congregation began in 1884, when Rev. Bjarnason returned from Iceland to become its pastor. It was then reorganized under the name of the First Luthern Church of Winnipeg. A church was erected in 1887. In 1904 it was destroyed by fire, and a new church was built the same year, finer than any Icelandic church which had hitherto been built. There are now four Icelandic churches in the city, and several societies. Rev. Jon Bjarnason made the church service as simple as possible, discarding cassock and chanting, the most characteristic features of the Lutheran ritual. He was not only a learned man and an able speaker, but an inspiring leader, more highly beloved and honored by his people than any other Icelander in America. When he died in 1914, Rev. Björn B. Jonsson was elected president of the Icelandic Lutheran Synod. A small Unitarian synod has also been founded by the Icelanders in Winnipeg. Many Icelandic papers and

[10] S. Högnason, *Islendingar i Winnipeg, Framfari*, February 22, 1879.

periodicals have been published in Winnipeg: "Leifur," 1883-1886; "Heimskringla," which began to appear in 1886; "Lögberg," which has been published since 1888, and many periodicals. About 6000 Icelanders are now living in that city. Most of them are prosperous, not a few being wealthy merchants and men of prominence in civic life. Hon. Thomas H. Johnson, who has represented central Winnipeg in the legislature, is one of the leading men in western Canada. One of the leading surgeons in this part of Canada is Dr. B. J. Brandson, F.A.C.S., professor in the Winnipeg Medical Institute.

From the mother colony on Lake Winnipeg sprang other Icelandic settlements in Canada. One of the most prosperous of these is the one at Argyle in southwestern Manitoba, founded in 1880 by Sigurdur Kristofersson and other settlers from New Iceland. Many Icelanders have settled in Saskatchewan, Alberta and British Columbia. In the Saskatchewan legislature one of their leading men, Hon. W. H. Paulson, has served as representative. Groups of Icelanders are also found in various cities in the United States and Canada. In Chicago and Minneapolis they have settled in considerable numbers. Many also live in Seattle, Bellingham, Victoria, Marietta, Blaine, Point Roberts and other places on the Pacific coast. The Icelanders in America now number about twenty thousand. About one-third of them belong to the Icelandic Lutheran Synod.[11]

One of the most notable traits of the Icelanders in America as well as in their own country is their love of learning, poetry and intellectual pursuits. Even as immigrants in a new environment and living under difficult circumstances they did everything possible to educate their children and to foster intellectual life among their people in the newly established settlements. Literary societies were founded, congregations were organized, schools and reading circles were established, papers and periodicals were published as soon as the settlers had thatched their first cottages. While

[11] *Árny*, p. 34 ff. *American-Scandinavian Review*, March-April, 1915, p. 105.

they were yet few in numbers they began to consider the possibility of founding a higher school, preferably a college, for their own young people. In 1884 a young Icelander, Frimann B. Anderson, from Toronto, came to Winnipeg. He urged that a higher school should be established for the Icelandic young people. Much interest was awakened, and a committee was appointed to promote the plan. But the difficulties to be overcome were found to be so great that the plan was abandoned. It was revived at the yearly meeting of the Icelandic Synod in 1887 by Rev. Fridrik J. Bergmann and Fridjon Fridriksson. The president of the synod, Rev. Jon Bjarnason, had received $100 as pay for his service as editor of the church paper. This sum he donated as the beginning of a fund to be raised for establishing an Icelandic college under the auspices of the synod. Since that time the college question was brought up at every yearly meeting of the church, and money was gradually collected for the college fund. In 1900 the question of a higher Icelandic institution of learning took a new turn. It was then decided to create chairs in Icelandic in Wesley College, Winnipeg, belonging to the Methodist church, and in Gustavus Adolphus College of the Swedish Augustana Synod at St. Peter, Minnesota. In 1901 Rev. Fridrik J. Bergmann was appointed teacher in Icelandic in Wesley College under the auspices of the Icelandic Lutheran Synod, which also paid his salary. He continued to serve till 1909, when he was succeeded by Runolfur Marteinsson, who served till 1913. In 1905 another chair in Icelandic was established at Gustavus Adolphus College, St. Peter, Minn. Magnus Magnusson of Cambridge, England, a nephew of Eirikur Magnusson, was appointed professor, serving till 1909, when the chair was discontinued. The desire of the Icelanders to establish a higher educational institution of their own was finally realized in 1913, when a resolution was passed at the yearly convention of the Icelandic Lutheran Synod assembled at Mountain, North Dakota, to establish an Icelandic institution of learning in Winnipeg, Canada. Before the next yearly meeting of the church Rev. Jon Bjarnason died, and the school founded according to the resolution of the previous year was given the name of Jon Bjarnason Academy. Rev. Runolfur Marteinsson was elected president of the institution. During the first year it had thirty students and a faculty of three teachers. The aim of the school is to bring the young people who attend it under Christian influence, to preserve for them as far as possible their Icelandic heritage, and to prepare them for useful service in church and state. In 1914 efforts were made to raise an endowment for the school, the Jon Bjarnason Memorial Fund. This fund now yields a yearly income of about $1400. The other necessary means for the operation of the school are derived from tuition fees and private contributions. Unexpected difficulties were created by the outbreak of the World War. Collection of funds and the erection of suitable buildings had to be postponed until peace and normal conditions should again invite a distraught generation to constructive efforts.

What the Icelanders in America themselves have been unable to accomplish for the promotion of scholarly interest in their literature and culture has at times been done by American higher institutions of learning which have created extensive collections of Icelandic books, and are offering courses of instruction in older Icelandic language and literature. The largest collection of this kind has been created at Cornell University, Ithaca, New York, through the initiative of Professor Willard Fiske, formerly librarian of the university. The collection, which is now in the charge of a special custodian, Professor Halldor Hermannsson, is considered to be the largest Icelandic library outside of Iceland.

INDEX

INDEX

Icelandic personal names in this index are arranged according to the given name, not according to the surname.